# *The Diary of a Lifetime*

Edited and selected by Peter Whiteley

Trafford
PUBLISHING

*The photograph of Mabel on the front cover comes from her personal album. It was taken in Canterbury, probably in the autumn of 1899, when she would have been thirty-three.*

Order this book online at www.trafford.com/07-1891
or email orders@trafford.com

Most Trafford titles are also available at major online book retailers.

© Copyright 2008 Angela Whiteley
All rights reserved. No part of this publication may be reproduced, stored in a retrieval system, or transmitted, in any form or by any means, electronic, mechanical, photocopying, recording, or otherwise, without the written prior permission of the author.

Note for Librarians: A cataloguing record for this book is available from Library and Archives Canada at www.collectionscanada.ca/amicus/index-e.html

Printed in Victoria, BC, Canada.

ISBN: 978-1-4251-4477-7

*We at Trafford believe that it is the responsibility of us all, as both individuals and corporations, to make choices that are environmentally and socially sound. You, in turn, are supporting this responsible conduct each time you purchase a Trafford book, or make use of our publishing services. To find out how you are helping, please visit www.trafford.com/responsiblepublishing.html*

*Our mission is to efficiently provide the world's finest, most comprehensive book publishing service, enabling every author to experience success. To find out how to publish your book, your way, and have it available worldwide, visit us online at www.trafford.com/10510*

 www.trafford.com

North America & international
toll-free: 1 888 232 4444 (USA & Canada)
phone: 250 383 6864 ♦ fax: 250 383 6804 ♦ email: info@trafford.com

The United Kingdom & Europe
phone: +44 (0)1865 722 113 ♦ local rate: 0845 230 9601
facsimile: +44 (0)1865 722 868 ♦ email: info.uk@trafford.com

10 9 8 7 6 5

*Acknowledgements*
I would like to thank both my wife Angela and Anthea Secker for the help and encouragement they have given me in preparing this book.

*Introduction*
Mabel Eden began her diary on 3 October 1878, when she was twelve; she closed it for the last time in November 1949. By then she had filled seventy-six notebooks with over two million words. Apart from occasional breaks (usually due to illness) she wrote up her diary two or three times each week.

I have reduced Mabel's text by around two-thirds; I have not indicated the omissions as that seemed unnecessarily pedantic in what is essentially a personal record rather then an historic document. I have tidied up her wayward punctuation and her erratic use of initial capitals, but otherwise my text is her text, unaltered. Where I have wanted to include a short explanatory note I have put it in square brackets; longer notes are placed between entries in italics..

Mabel was an upper-class lady and in many ways reflected all that that meant in late victorian times. She was a 'woman of the world', but unsurprisingly the word 'sex' never appears in her diaries. She was perfectly capable of falling in love and of attracting it, but the two never seemed to coincide and she remained single all her life. She was musical, well-read and a regular theatre-goer, and she had a fluctuating interest in religion. Above all she enjoyed people, and she comments freely on her family, her friends and her acquaintances, usually with sympathy but occasionally with an acerbic sharpness

These diaries came into my wife's possession nearly fifty years ago by direct inheritance from Mabel, who was Angela's first cousin four times removed. But only recently have we found the leisure to study them, and to discover the spell they cast on the unsuspecting reader.

PW

# The Descendants of Sir Robert Eden, 3$^{rd}$ Baronet (d1755)

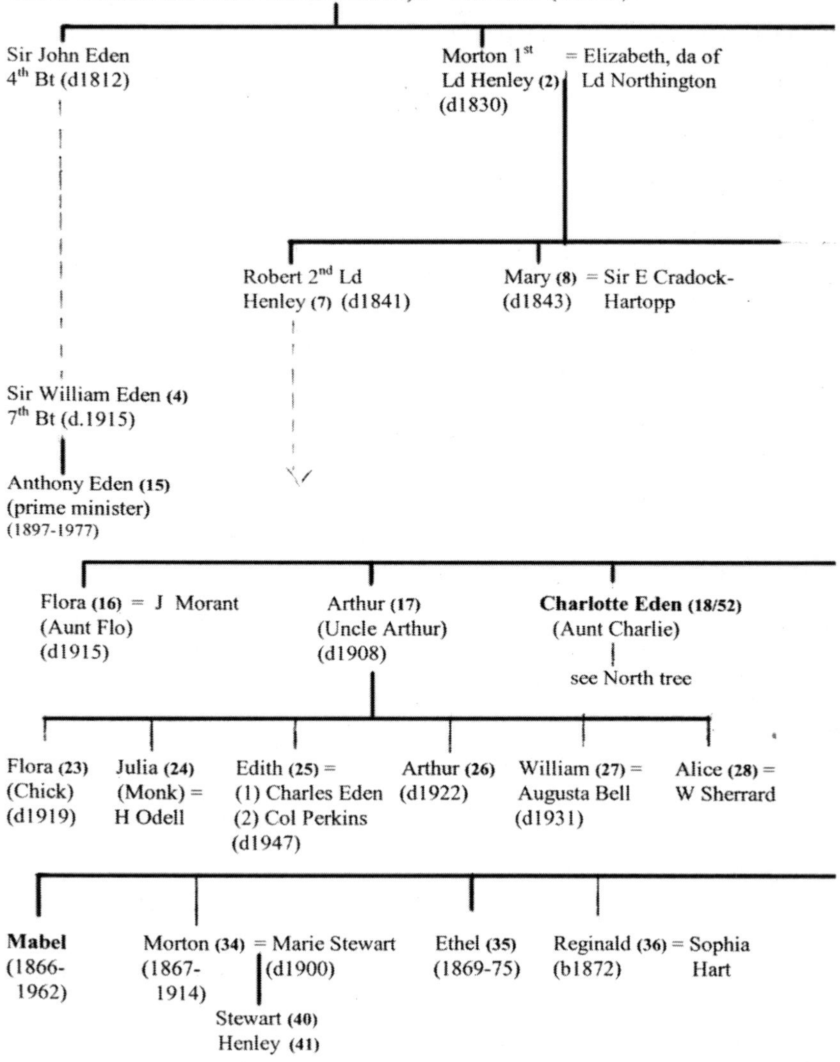

Sir John Eden
4$^{th}$ Bt (d1812)

Morton 1$^{st}$      = Elizabeth, da of
Ld Henley **(2)**    Ld Northington
(d1830)

Robert 2$^{nd}$ Ld          Mary **(8)** = Sir E Cradock-
Henley **(7)** (d1841)        (d1843)    Hartopp

Sir William Eden **(4)**
7$^{th}$ Bt (d.1915)

Anthony Eden **(15)**
(prime minister)
(1897-1977)

Flora **(16)** = J Morant        Arthur **(17)**              **Charlotte Eden (18/52)**
(Aunt Flo)                (Uncle Arthur)              (Aunt Charlie)
(d1915)                  (d1908)
                                          see North tree

Flora **(23)**   Julia **(24)**   Edith **(25)** =        Arthur **(26)**   William **(27)** =   Alice **(28)** =
(Chick)    (Monk) =    (1) Charles Eden  (d1922)     Augusta Bell    W Sherrard
(d1919)    H Odell     (2) Col Perkins                (d1931)
                       (d1947)

**Mabel**       Morton **(34)** = Marie Stewart   Ethel **(35)**     Reginald **(36)** = Sophia
(1866-      (1867-      (d1900)           (1869-75)      (b1872)       Hart
1962)       1914)

                    Stewart **(40)**
                    Henley **(41)**

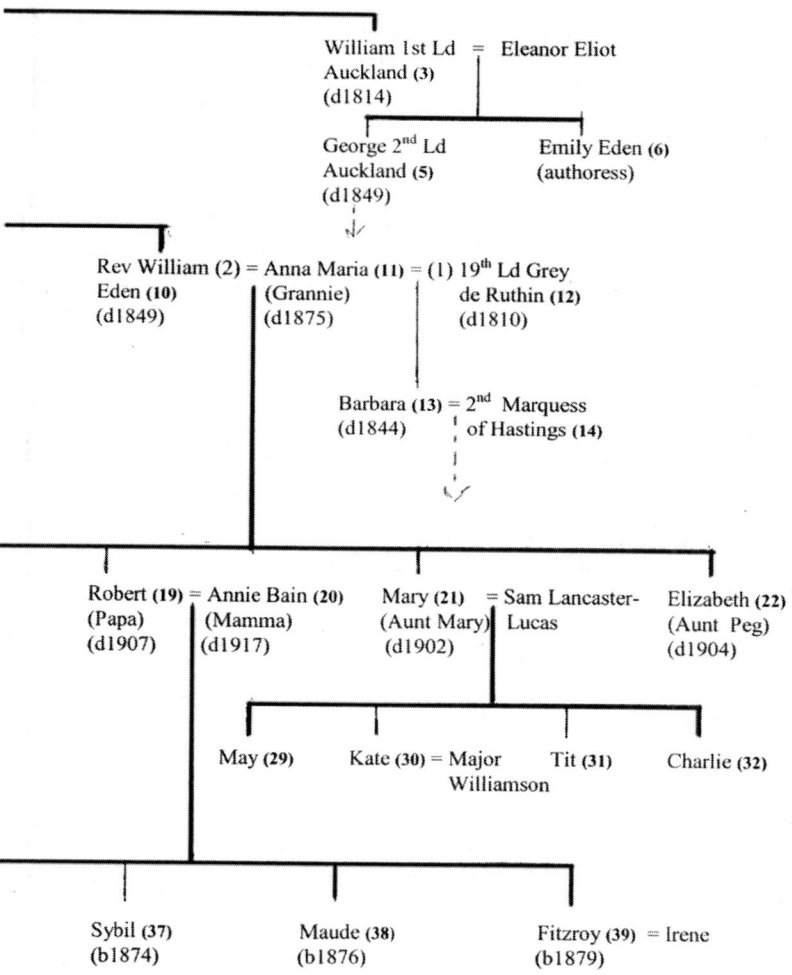

*The numbers in bold are repeated after the first appearance of the character in the diaries*

William 1st Ld Auckland **(3)** (d1814) = Eleanor Eliot

George 2nd Ld Auckland **(5)** (d1849)

Emily Eden **(6)** (authoress)

Rev William Eden **(2)** **(10)** (d1849) = Anna Maria **(11)** (Grannie) (d1875) = (1) 19th Ld Grey de Ruthin **(12)** (d1810)

Barbara **(13)** (d1844) = 2nd Marquess of Hastings **(14)**

Robert **(19)** (Papa) (d1907) = Annie Bain **(20)** (Mamma) (d1917)

Mary **(21)** (Aunt Mary) (d1902) = Sam Lancaster-Lucas

Elizabeth **(22)** (Aunt Peg) (d1904)

May **(29)**

Kate **(30)** = Major Williamson

Tit **(31)**

Charlie **(32)**

Sybil **(37)** (b1874)

Maude **(38)** (b1876)

Fitzroy **(39)** = Irene (b1879)

# The Descendants of Francis North, 6<sup>th</sup> Earl of Guilford (d1861)

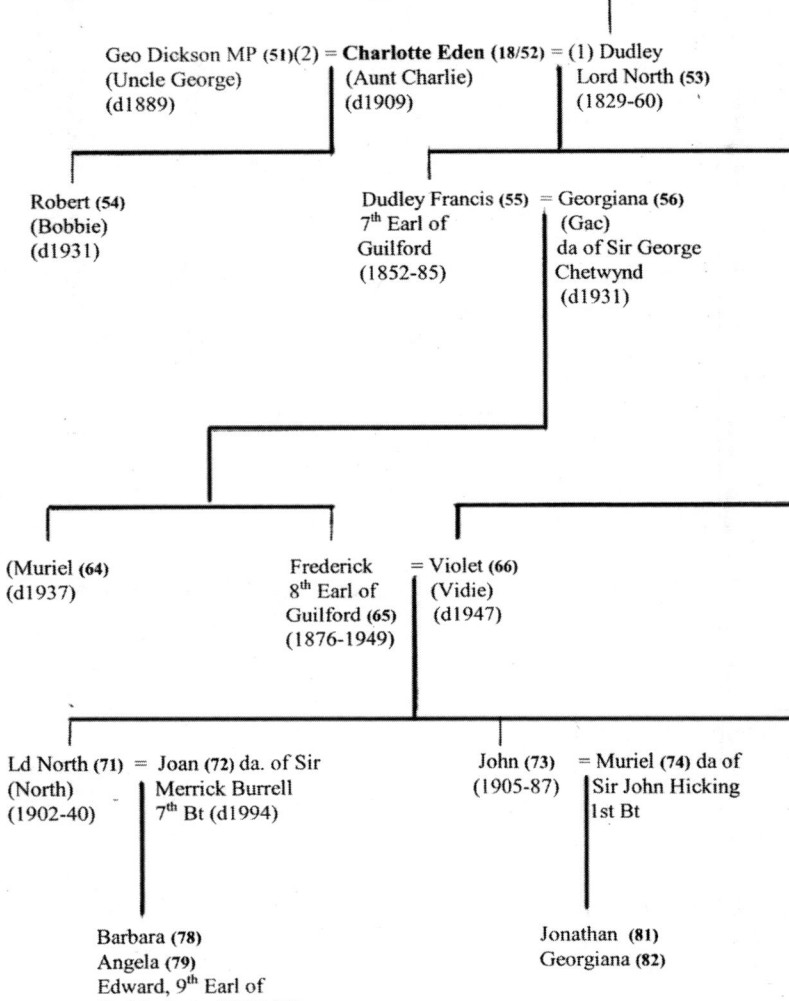

Geo Dickson MP (51)(2) = **Charlotte Eden (18/52)** = (1) Dudley
(Uncle George)        (Aunt Charlie)       Lord North (53)
(d1889)              (d1909)            (1829-60)

Robert (54)               Dudley Francis (55) = Georgiana (56)
(Bobbie)                7<sup>th</sup> Earl of        (Gac)
(d1931)                Guilford          da of Sir George
                         (1852-85)         Chetwynd
                                      (d1931)

(Muriel (64)            Frederick    = Violet (66)
(d1937)               8<sup>th</sup> Earl of     (Vidie)
                     Guilford (65)    (d1947)
                     (1876-1949)

Ld North (71)    = Joan (72) da. of Sir          John (73)    = Muriel (74) da of
(North)            Merrick Burrell            (1905-87)      Sir John Hicking
(1902-40)        7<sup>th</sup> Bt (d1994)                              1st Bt

Barbara (78)                               Jonathan (81)
Angela (79)                                Georgiana (82)
Edward, 9<sup>th</sup> Earl of
Guilford (80) (1933-99)

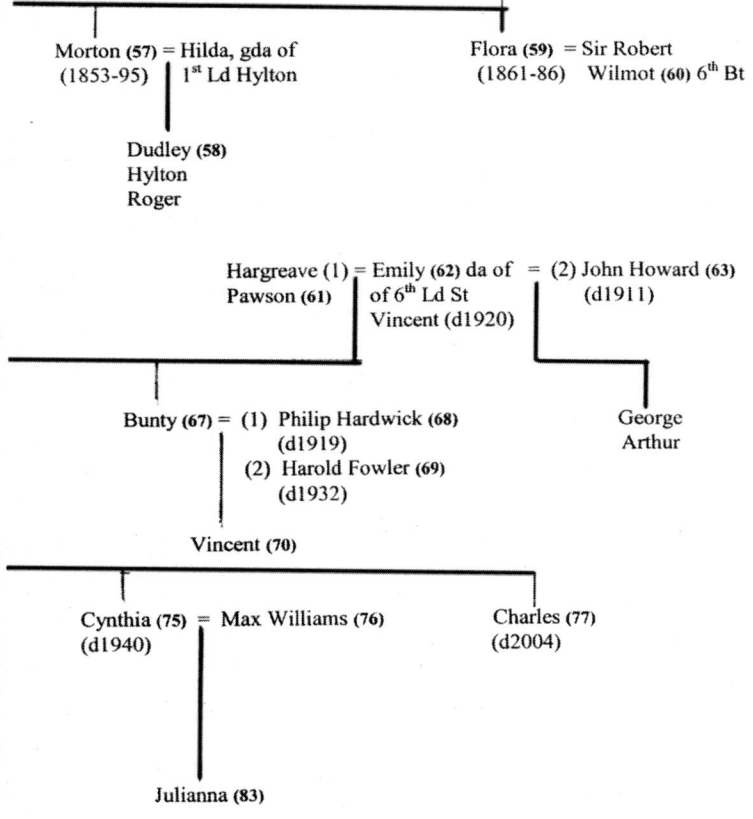

Morton **(57)** = Hilda, gda of
(1853-95) | 1st Ld Hylton

Flora **(59)** = Sir Robert
(1861-86)   Wilmot **(60)** 6th Bt

Dudley **(58)**
Hylton
Roger

Hargreave (1) = Emily **(62)** da of
Pawson **(61)** | of 6th Ld St
Vincent (d1920)

= (2) John Howard **(63)**
(d1911)

Bunty **(67)** = (1) Philip Hardwick **(68)**
(d1919)
(2) Harold Fowler **(69)**
(d1932)

George
Arthur

Vincent **(70)**

Cynthia **(75)** = Max Williams **(76)**
(d1940)

Charles **(77)**
(d2004)

Julianna **(83)**

# THE DIARY OF A LIFETIME
## Volume one 1878 to 1903

### 1878
*The Eden family were living in a house on The Parade, Dover.*

*Friday 18 October* I went back to school this morning. It is a good deal changed; there are a lot of new girls. There is a very pretty one named Adelaide Donnit. She is very dark with lovely blue eyes and very clever. I am sure we shall be great friends.

*Friday 8 November* Mr Moens, a yacht owner, dined with us. He was taken prisoner by the brigands near Paestum some years ago, and he looks as if he had never got over it.

*Saturday 23 November* The Waterhouses came again. We had a lot of people for dinner, and Mortie (34) and I made a dreadful noise in the hall which made Papa (19) angry, and then Mortie fell and cut his head while we were fighting.

*Friday 13 December* I went with Mrs Donnit and Adelaide to the Citadel to see the Colonel of the 84ᵗʰ. He gave us tea in his rooms. His name is Brownrigg and he was very nice. I dined with the Donnits.

*Friday 20 December* I went with Adelaide to a school feast given by the officers of the 30ᵗʰ to the soldiers' children. They had tea, then lots of sweets and toys were given to them. We had tea in the ante-room afterwards with Captain Clarke and Captain Prendergast. They showed me the regimental photographs. I dined with the Donnits.

*Wednesday 25 December, Christmas Day* Mamma (20) gave me a dressing case and I got a lot of cards and other things.

*Saturday 28 December* Mamma had a lot of people to tea, who played and sang. Adelaide came too and we sat in the small drawing-room eating all the cakes we could steal. It was great fun. There was an awful girl who sang an Italian song. Adelaide and I nearly got turned out of the room because we laughed.

## 1879

*Friday 31 January* I went with the Donnits to see Major Buxton of the 29th, who has been thrown from his horse.

*Friday 14 February* I bought a copy of Byron for a valentine for Papa (19).

*There are no entries for March and April and only one short one for May.*

*Monday 2 June, Dover* I have got a very bad throat and the doctor says I am to stay indoors for a long time. What a nuisance throats and lungs are.

*Wednesday 18 June* Mrs Lister gave a garden party today and had six girls, myself among them, to pour out tea etc. We were all in a sort of fancy dress. The gardens were lovely, all the roses in blossom, and the party was very nice. Aunt Geana and Adele van Ari came by the afternoon boat. Mamma met them and brought them on to Mrs Lister's. Adele is very pretty, fair and quiet. I hope we shall be good friends. She is to go to school with me until the holidays.

*Tuesday 1 July* We had a holiday as it was the Sunday school centenary. All the Sunday schools met in Pencester Street and marched in procession to the North Foreland meadow where they had tea. Before starting they sang the Old Hundredth and God Save the Queen.

*Saturday 5 July* Adele and I went for a walk along the shore and were caught by the tide; we had to climb up the cliff to get home. The path is very steep in places, where it was broken it was very difficult to get along. Adele was awfully frightened and I was afraid she would lose her head and fall, but we got home quite safely.

*Saturday 23 September* I went to the Cornhill coastguard station with Papa to signal to the Citadel with the officers. We had a heliograph and they had flags; we understood each other perfectly although we were about six miles apart.

*There is a gap of two years before the next entry.*

## 1881

*Saturday 14 September* I walked to Guston with the two Kirbys after some blackberries, we only got a few, and when we were about a mile from Guston it began to rain. We took shelter under a hedge and got drenched.

We got awfully miserable, we were tired out and hungry with five miles between us and home and we had to walk every inch in pouring rain.

*Monday 31 October* We went to a hunt breakfast at Waldershare. All the Dover and county people from miles around were there. The Pitts were with us and General Newdigate sat next to me at breakfast. Mr and Mrs Tattersall and their eldest daughter Emma were there too, she seems a very nice girl. It was very cold and the ground was white with snow. Guilford (55) did not come into the house for long and Gac (56) looked cold. The house is such a chilly one no fire can warm it.

*Waldershare Park is the country seat of the Earls of Guilford. It is in Kent, roughly half way between Canterbury and Dover.*

*There are no entries for the first half of 1882.*

### 1882
*Thursday 13 July, Crabble, Whitfield, near Dover* We went back to Crabble. Mamma went to stay a night with the Tattersalls at Charlton near Canterbury. Their house is a large white one, rather ugly but very pretty inside. Papa lived in it when he was a little boy. Only two of the Tattersalls besides the mother and father were at home. Betty who is older than I and Bob who is at Oxford. I do not like Betty much. She is very clever but I think she is rather conceited. There are lots more of the Tattersalls; the eldest son is a soldier but I have not seen him.

*Robert Eden's father the Revd William Eden (10) held various livings in east Kent, and it was during one of them that his family had lived at Charlton.*

*Saturday 22 July* Mamma is going to send me away to a school in Kilburn. It will be horrid going to school. I know I shall fight with the girls.

*Thursday 3 August* I had a tremendous ducking today. I tried to paddle in a big tub in the river but the horrid thing wouldn't go and at last it upset altogether. I went right over my head into the water.

*Thursday 10 August* We have built a little house of logs in the meadow and tonight we made a fire and roasted potatoes in it. The only drawback to the house is that we have to get in through the roof as we forgot to make a door. But it is awfully jolly and I wish Mamma would let us sleep in it.

*Monday 14 August* There is to be a bazaar in Dover and Mrs Hay has asked me to help sell fruit.

*Tuesday 15 August* Lady Ely sent me two bushels of flowers and fruit and I am to have a stall of my own. I started for Dover early and went straight to the hall to arrange my stall. I did it all myself. I had a lot of boys, Howard Douglas-Williams and Reggie Hay among them, to help me sell my things, and my stall was soon quite cleared. It was great fun.

*Wednesday 16 August* This was the second day of the bazaar and it was much nicer than yesterday. Mr Oakley gave me a fan and Mr Harris, an officer in the 83$^{rd}$, a most lovely doll. I won an enormous loaf in a raffle and gave it to Major Firebrace who is going to give it to his company for breakfast tomorrow. It was about five feet in diameter, a soldier came and took it away.

 Howard Douglas-Williams and I had a grand time at his mother's stall. It was the refreshment one, and we got under the counter and ate ices out of the ice pails and stole all the sweets and cakes we could see.

*Monday 4 September* Mamma had a letter from Papa; he is to be home on Friday. I had lunch with Mrs Chambers in Dover, and she drove me back to Crabble after tea. Mamma dined with Miss Roe and I went into dessert.

*Thursday 7 September* Mamma went up to London today to meet Papa and he will be here tomorrow. I am so glad, it will be simply delicious to see him again.

*Friday 8 September* Mamma wrote to say that she found Papa very ill at the hotel with malarial fever. He did not know her and is very bad indeed, and he will not be home for a long time. How dreadfully disappointing, and we thought we were going to see him today.

*Saturday 16 September* Papa is ever so much better and will come home as soon as he can be moved. We leave Crabble on Wednesday and go back to Dover. I shall be sorry to leave the country.

*Thursday 21 September, Dover* Papa came back today and we were so glad to see him, but he looks dreadfully ill and so much older, not like Papa a bit.

*Thursday 28 September* I am going to school in London on Saturday, it is like a dreadful nightmare. I am sure I shall be miserable.

*Friday 29 September* Mr Campbell came to see me as I am going to this awful school tomorrow, and he is horrid enough to say it will do me a lot of good. I am sure it *won't*. I hate girls and there are forty where I am going, and I expect I shall quarrel with every one of them.

*Saturday 30 September, at school in Kilburn, NW London* We went up to London by the early train and spent the morning in shopping. After lunch Mamma took me to the school. We were shown into an awfully prim tidy drawing-room which I should have liked to disarrange.

My school-mistress, Miss Smith, is very nice and I am sure I shall like her, but the girls are something too horrible. They are all ugly but three, and I should like to know where they get their dresses made. They do nothing but giggle and make idiotic jokes. I felt so angry I could have thrown the plates at the girls' heads they are such idiots. They all go about with their arms round each other's waists in the most ridiculously gushing fashion.

*Sunday 1 October* I awoke very early and could not at first imagine where I was. We had prayers and went to church for two hours. The church is a very dull one and the sermons are never shorter than thirty minutes. After church we went for a long walk, two-and-two, with four governesses all watching us, it was too dreadful. After dinner we had a long scripture lesson and then sang hymns till tea-time, and then we all went to church again. This is the most awful Sunday I have ever passed.

*Monday 2 October* I began lessons today and liked them very much. We got up at seven and had breakfast at eight and then went for a walk until nine, when lessons commenced and went on until 12.20 when we had another horrible walk. I had a music lesson from Sydney Smith which I liked very much, he is very good-tempered and patient.

*Wednesday 19 October* Once a month we have to all go into the drawing-room to play all the music we have learnt to Miss Smith. We all put on our best dresses and sit round the room, and each girl sings and plays her pieces. It is awfully nervous work as the girls all quiz each other most unmercifully. It took nearly seven hours to hear it all, and we were not allowed to speak a word but had to listen to that dreadful music. Only three of the girls can play at all well, all the others were too frightened, and the singing was something awful.

*Wednesday 26 October* Mamma sent me a hamper of cakes etc and said Papa is much better and will soon be coming up to town, when he will come and see me. I have made friends with three girls, their names are Frances Kent, Sara Owen and Maude Kennedy. They are quite the nicest girls in the school.

*Wednesday 1 November* We had a very jolly walk today. There was a tremendously high wind and all our hats got blown off and of course we had to break the ranks to get them back again, and we behaved so badly that the governess was nearly mad with anger.

*Sunday 19 November* Papa came for me early in the afternoon and took me to see Aunt Mary (21) who lives in South Kensington. The three girls, May (29), Kate (30) and Tit (31) were there. I have not seen them for ten years and they do not seem a bit changed. I dined with them and got back to school about eleven.

*Sunday 3 December* Papa took me to lunch with Colonel and Mrs Atkinson. They live in Queens Gate and he won the Victoria Cross in the Mutiny, and when I told the girls about it at school, they asked what the VC was. I can't imagine how girls *can* be so ignorant.

*Sunday 10 December* Papa came for me at ten and took me to Aunt Mary's. There was such a thick fog that we could not see a yard in front of us. Dear Aunt Peg (22) was at the Lucas's which made it very nice. It was so foggy at night that I could not go back to school, and so I remained at Aunt Mary's which was simply heavenly.

*Monday 11 December* I spent the morning shopping with the two aunts, and they put me in a cab and sent me back to school after lunch. It was horrid going back and the girls were all so curious to know what I had been doing. It was so amusing: my hair smelt of tobacco as I had been sitting on Papa's lap while he smoked, and those idiot girls were quite shocked, as if they did not like the smell of tobacco. I am sure they do, only think it unladylike to say so.

*Thursday 14 December* Everything is in a tremendous state of excitement for the party comes off this evening. We all were turned out of the big schoolroom early in the morning and six of the girls decorated it with evergreens and pink paper roses, and all the paintings and drawings we have done during the term were stuck up on the wall. After dinner we all went up to our rooms to prepare our dresses. I am going to wear black and red.

The guests began to arrive at eight and until ten the girls had to perform, singing or playing. They were all dreadfully nervous and it was altogether awful. At ten we girls had supper in our own dining room while the guests had a very grand one in Miss Smith's rooms. Maude Kennedy and I pretended to two boys that we were guests and made them take us down to supper with the others. So we had a better one and much more fun than the other girls, and luckily none of the governesses saw us. After supper we danced until three. We were awfully tired but we had a very good time.

*Friday 15 December, Dover* Papa came at eleven and took me off to the station and put me in the train for Dover. The holidays do not commence until tomorrow but I have got away a day earlier. It was so nice to get home and the children seem to have grown a great deal.

### 1883
*Thursday 18 January* We dined with Mr Hammond and he asked a curate and a doctor to meet us. His nephew did the honours, and he took me down to dinner *before* Mamma.

*Thursday 25 January, Kilburn* I went to horrid old school today. It is dreadful leaving Dover to come to such a place as this. Very few of the girls are back but there are a lot of new ones expected.

*Sunday 28 January* Papa is in town and he came for me today. We dined with Aunt Mary; she had a lot of people there. Arthur Gibson was there. I have not seen him since he was a little boy at Wateringbury and now he is twenty. He is very good-looking and seems a nice boy.

*Tuesday 30 January* I had a music lesson from a new master today, Carl Weber. I got tired of Sydney Smith, he did not teach me anything. I do not know if Herr Weber will be able to either; I am so awfully careless that I shall never be able to play well.

*Sunday 25 February* Papa came for me and we went to church at a church in Southwark, a very nice one with beautiful music. We dined with Aunt Mary as usual. I am getting rather tired of dining with her. Papa told me that Mamma and the children are coming to live up in town, so I shall not go back to dear old Dover again.

*Friday 9 March* Miss Smith gave a party this evening and Papa came; only nine of the girls were allowed to go into the drawing room as it was a grown-up party. It was very amusing, the girls had to sing but I got out of it as my cough was so bad. We sat up till very late and enjoyed ourselves immensely.

*Tuesday 20 March* This was my seventeenth birthday. I had lots of letters and presents. Mamma wrote to me from the Tattersalls where she is staying. I spent the whole day with Papa. He took me to the South Kensington Museum where we had lunch. I had a very nice birthday.

*Monday 26 March* I went out with Mamma this morning. We went to look at a house in Kensington which we are going to take. I am sorry we are leaving Dover. The children come up on the 17$^{th}$. I went back to school after tea. It is so delightful to think I have only a few more weeks of it. I like my lessons and music, but I do hate the girls and the horrid strict rules. We are not allowed to do anything we want to.

*Thursday 29 March* I had a very good time today. Papa came for me and we dined with Major Atkinson at the Salisbury Club. It was very nice and the girls were awfully envious when I told them I had dined at a real man's club. I believe they thought it was very fast.

*Tuesday 10 April, Kensington* Today I had a holiday and went to our new house in Kensington to wait for Mamma and the children who come up from Dover today. They all arrived with an enormous load of luggage, a governess, a maid, a pug-dog and a bird.

*Tuesday 17 April* I came home today and now I am no longer a school girl. I am not coming out for a year or two which I am very glad of.

*Wednesday 9 May* We went to a concert at the Albert Hall and heard Christine Nilsson sing the Jewel Song from Faust and Connais tu le Pays. She has a lovely voice, so sweet and clear, and she sings so simply.

*Christine Nilsson (1843-1921) was a famous Swedish soprano..*

*Saturday 9 June, East Winch Hall, near Kings Lynn, Norfolk* I went down to Norfolk today to stay with Frances Kent. Her home is a lovely one called East Winch Hall; it is about two miles from Kings Lynn. Her people are very nice and she has an elder sister named Muriel who is very pretty.

*Wednesday 13 June* We drove into Kings Lynn today. It is a very funny town, dull and dusty with some quaint buildings in it and a funny old gateway. I would think it is a most uninteresting place to live.

*Monday 18 June, Kensington* I left East Winch today. Francis and Muriel saw me off and I was very sorry to go. It is such lovely weather and London is so hot and dusty. Mamma met me at St Pancras with Kate Bain who has come to stay with us for some months. She is very pretty, but I do not think I shall like her very much.

*Monday 30 July* Miss Smith gave a breaking-up party and we went to it. I went early in the day to help with the decorations. It was a very nice party. I sang and Sydney Smith played my accompaniment most beautifully. It seemed so funny being a guest because I felt just like a schoolgirl.

*Saturday 25 August* We went to see dear Peg. She is staying with the Lucas's. She does not seem at all well; she has never got over the fever she had in Malta last summer. She is going to Madeira next month with Mary Cobbold, who is supposed to be dying of consumption, poor thing.

*Monday 3 September* Mamma is going to Turkey for three months to stay with some people she knows there. I wish I was going too.

*Thursday 27 September* Everything was in a state of bustle and confusion as Mamma left for Turkey by the boat train from Victoria. We went to see her off and I would have given anything to have gone too.

*Tuesday 9 October* I practised very well today and had a singing lesson, and for a wonder I pleased Dr Gilbert. I so seldom satisfy him. Miss Stevenson, a new friend, dined with me. She is a very nice girl and plays beautifully. She won a medal at the Royal Academy for her music.

*Friday 19 October* Maude Kennedy came to say goodbye as she starts tomorrow for a convent in Belgium. She is to be there for some time and I do hope she will not end up as a nun.

*Monday 22 October* We had a letter from Mamma today. She is having a very good time and Lady Dufferin called on her the other day.

*Saturday 17 November* Papa and I dined with the Atkinsons; Alec Barton took me in to dinner. We heard from Mamma and she will be at home in three weeks. She is in Athens now, she is going to Venice and home by Paris.

*Monday 26 November* I had my music lesson and Herr Weber asked me to play at a concert he is giving on the fifteenth. I am to play Greig's sonata in A flat.

*Saturday 1 December* Mortie and I went to Victoria to meet Mamma. She came by the twelve o'clock train from Newhaven. She is looking very well and has seen a tremendous lot. I am so glad to have her back.

*Tuesday 25 December, Christmas Day* I went to church in the morning. Papa and I came out before the sermon and went to see Aunt Mary. When I got home I found ten letters waiting for me and innumerable cards and a silver spider from the Pitts. Mrs Preston and her dear baby dined with us and afterwards we danced and played with the children.

### 1884
*Friday 4 January* I am going to Dover tomorrow to stay with the Kirbys so I was very busy all day getting ready. I went to a children's party with Sybil (37) and Maude (38) at the Whiphams. It was great fun. I danced with two Rugby boys who pulled me about and jumped on my feet. They could not dance a bit but they were very jolly and not at all offended when I scolded them for their clumsiness.

*Thursday 10 January, Dover, staying with the Kirbys* I went for a walk with the girls and met Mrs Dorehill. I had tea with Mrs Hay and met some nice girls named Lord who know Aunt North (18/52) very well.

*Sunday 13 January* We went to Old St James's church this morning and after lunch called on Mrs Winter who is lodging on the Parade, but it was a dismal visit as she only talked of her son who has just died.

*Monday 21 January* I lunched with Mr Hammond. He was very nice and kind and gave me loads of good advice, but it was rather dull and I did not stay very long. Maude [Kirby] was too ill to go out and had the doctor, who says she has outgrown her strength.

*Thursday 31 January* We went to see a pantomime called Aladdin. It was great fun it was so awfully badly done, and the actors were such sticks. There were a lot of political hits which were tremendously cheered.

*Friday 1st February* I went and paid some farewell calls as I leave Dover tomorrow; I shall be sorry to leave Dover. Our photographs came today and they are too dreadful, perfect caricatures, we all look simply hideous, ten times worse than we really are.

*Monday 4 February, Kensington* I took Sybil and Maude down to May Lucas's studio; she is going to paint them. I helped Aunt Mary to dress some dolls for a bazaar she is going to have.

*Tuesday 12 February* The little ones [Sybil and Maude] went to May's studio as usual today but they fidget so dreadfully that she cannot paint them, and so they are not going any more. She wants me to sit to her instead. I went out with Mamma after lunch and paid some calls. We had tea with Mrs Whipham and then went to see Mrs Macgregor who is ill.

*Thursday 14 February* I went down to the studio again this morning and spent three weary hours in sitting to May. I got so dreadfully tired. After lunch we went to the Peasant Fair at the Albert Hall. It was the Royal Day so the place was crammed with people. The arena was lined with stalls and all the stall-holders were in fancy dress. Kate Lucas was at Lady Tarbat's stall and she looked very pretty in a Swiss dress. Lady Tarbat herself was lovely. Lady Lonsdale was at the refreshment stall but I did not admire her at all. Lady Randolph Churchill was at one of the stalls. She is very pretty and animated with very large black eyes. The things that were for sale were not worth buying and they were atrociously dear.

*Friday 15 February* We are going to leave this house in March and have taken one in Trebovir Road near Earls Court Station. It is a very much larger house than this one we are in now.

*Saturday 16 February* Today we went down to our new house to look over it; I had not seen it before as I was away. It is a very nice house and there is a dear little room on the second floor that I am to have for a den; it is about eight feet by ten and opens on to a balcony with a window that takes the whole of one side. It is certainly very tiny but I shall do it up and make it look quite lovely.

*Friday 22 February* We spent the whole morning shopping, a horrid business that I hate. We went to a musical At Home at Herr Weber's, and got there so late that they were playing the last piece and we missed a lot of very good music, and Herr Weber was vexed with us for being so late.

*Saturday 23 February* Mamma and I went to a silly little bazaar in Warwick Road got up by the Macgregors and Edwards in aid of some church in the East End. The rooms were very small and there was a great crush of people. We saw Captain Skinner for a minute or two. He was looking very persecuted; I wonder how many dolls etc he had been obliged to buy.

*Monday 25 February* We are to have our new house by 10ʰ March. Major Macgregor says we won't get in to it until May there is so much to be done to it. We went to a bazaar at St Mathias Schools, and on our way down we resolved to answer everyone who asked us to buy things in French. To our disgust the first person we attacked answered us back in capital French, and we were obliged to buy a lot of things we did not want.

*Tuesday 4 March* Dear Peg is staying with Aunt Mary so I went and sat a long time with her; she was as sweet and kind as ever. She has just got back from Madeira and she does not seem at all well. She was with Mary Cobbold at the time of her death, which tired her dreadfully.

*Thursday 6 March* I spent the whole day at the studio and May dressed me in an orange silk gown that belonged to an old friend. The waist is directly under the arms, and it is cut very low with immense sleeves that are like wings, very uncomfortable and *awfully* unbecoming.

*Friday 7 March* The Kirbys came to see me today; they came up to town yesterday and have taken rooms quite close. Maude has been ill and does not look well but Mabel is looking charming. We went to a musical at-home at Herr Weber's but they did not enjoy it at all: the music was too classical. I played in a duet for piano and violin and got on very well. Mabel and Maude came back with me to tea and we had a long talk about Dover people. D'Arcy [Kirby] is going to be married to Ada Braddell in May. They have been engaged on and off for years.

*Thursday 20 March* This was my eighteenth birthday and I have had lots of presents. Mamma gave me a brass lamp for my room in the new house, Papa a pair of brass frames for ditto. All the others gave me things, and I had lots of cards and letters.

I shall come out now in six months, when I am eighteen and a half, but I do not look forward to it at all.

*Saturday 22 March* We were very busy all day packing to go into our new house. We are in a wretched state of confusion and I am sure it will be months before we are all settled down. There is nothing I hate worse than moving into new houses, and we have had so much of it lately.

*Tuesday 1 April* Everyone is wearing black for the Duke of Albany [Queen Victoria's youngest son] and all the shops have their shutters up; it makes things look very dismal. We spent the day as usual in packing. We get into deeper confusion every day, and there is scarcely a corner in the house that is fit to use.

*Monday 7 April, Trebovir Road, Earls Court* The boat race was rowed today and that wretched Cambridge won. The Oxford men were over-trained and had no chance from the beginning. I slept in our new house with two of the servants and Mademoiselle. The others come tomorrow.

*Trebovir Road is between the Brompton Road and the West Cromwell Road, almost opposite the present Earls Court Exhibition Building.*

*Saturday 26 April* I dined with the Atkinsons and she chaperoned me. I enjoyed myself immensely. Dr Pollock took me down to dinner. Captain Tattersall, the Atkinson's nephew, was there, and he talked to me all the time after dinner. He is very nice, the nicest man I have ever met. He is very tall and slight with beautiful dark eyes. He has rather a peculiar manner, very quiet and stiff to most people, but he was altogether charming to me. I heard someone say he was prig, and if he is I like prigs very much. He is very gentlemanly and I am sure that he is not priggish. He is in the Queen's Bays.

*Saturday 18 May* I dined with the Atkinson's and Captain Tattersall took me down to dinner. He was nicer than ever. He did not pay me idiotic compliments like other people, but talked as if I was a sensible being instead of a mere doll. He played very well on the banjo.

*Wednesday 3 June* We went to a party at Mrs Woodrow's in honour of a bride and bridegroom. The bride was attired in her wedding-gown, and very unbecoming it was. She gave herself tremendous airs, and had a *brown* fan with a *white* gown.

*Saturday 28 June* We lunched at Ealing today. There were a lot of people there and it was a lovely day, but I did not enjoy it a bit. Captain Tattersall was to have been there, but the Queen kept her birthday today and he had to stay at Aldershot for some idiotic review. Why can't the Queen keep her birthday on the proper day like other people? I talked to a little man named Moser, but he was very stupid and I nearly went to sleep instead of talking to him prettily. Major Atkinson drove me back to town in his mail-phaeton, and I dined at Cleveland Square. Captain Tattersall was there; the review was over at four and he came up to town directly. After dinner we sat out in the Square garden under the trees until nearly eleven talking about all sorts of things. It was very nice and I was very happy, only the time passed so quickly.

*Saturday 5 July* We went to a garden party at Ealing that I enjoyed very much indeed. Captain Tattersall was there and he talked to me the whole time and rowed me about on the lake. It was a lovely day, very hot and sunny. There were a lot of people at Ealing, it was an unusually big party.

*Wednesday 16 July* We made a lot of calls today on different people and they were all out, which was rather a bore as it was intensely hot and I was longing to get into some cool dark drawing room.

*Monday 28 July* I dined with the Atkinsons. It was very dull as no one was there but Colonel Karslake and Major Atkinson, who took me down to dinner. We went to a concert at the theatre in the South Kensington Museum afterwards. Miss Casabianca sang twice but I don't like her voice.

*Thursday 31 July* Jack Burne came to see me today and brought one of his school-friends, a boy named de Bentham. They spent the afternoon with us and it was rather dull for they did not talk much, but sat playing and fidgeting with their hats and gloves, and looking almost as much bored as we were. I cannot imagine why they stayed so long.

*Tuesday 12 August* Sybil has diptheria. The doctor came twice; he is rather anxious about it as it is such a dreadfully infectious thing.

*Wednesday 20 August* I got up this morning but had to go back to bed as I broke a small blood vessel and got very seedy: they think I have diphtheria. It is a horrid bore at this time of year.

*Sunday 24 August* I got up for a little while today; it was such a blessing to get out of bed again. I feel as if I should never care to get back to it. Of course I was very weak and had to lie on the sofa. Sybil is getting all right but Maude has diphtheria now and is worse than either Sybil or I were. It is a great nuisance for Mamma.

*Monday 25 August* If I am well enough I am going down to Hampshire on Wednesday to stay with the Goldies. They have taken a place near Aldershot called Winchfield.

*Thursday 28 August, Winchfield, near Aldershot, staying with the Goldies* I went down to Winchfield by the 5.00pm train and got there in time for dinner; Millie and Kate Wadworth met me. Winchfield is a lovely place, and from my window there is an eight-mile view to Aldershot.

*Sunday 31 August* We all went to church in the little Winchfield church and sat in the Manor pew. It has a high carved oak screen all round which prevents the other people from seeing us; it is rather like a cage. The church is pretty and very old with a queer little chancel. We had a capital sermon and the singing was very good.

*Tuesday 2 September* The men were shooting all day and we had lunch with them again, in a different part of the woods. We stayed with them for some time and then went for a long drive through Hartley Row towards Reading. It was a lovely day and we had a very jolly drive, only we behaved very badly and made such a noise that it was a wonder the horse did not bolt.

*Friday 5 September, Trebovir Road* We were in the woods all the morning and after lunch I went back to town. It was horrid to go back to London and leave the lovely country at the very nicest time of the year.

*Thursday 18 September* The Goldies came up to town and want me to go back to Winchfield for a week or two. Of course I shall be only too glad to go.

*Monday 22 September, Winchfield, near Aldershot, staying with the Goldies* I left town about three and got to Winchfield in time for tea. Millie came to meet me. It was very nice going back and seeing them all again. The country was looking quite lovely, and the view to Aldershot is clearer than ever.

*Tuesday 23 September* I was up at seven and played tennis until breakfast with Millie. We spent the morning in walking, and after lunch we drove into Aldershot in the big landau. We did not take a footman and we took it by turns to sit on the box beside the coachman and drive, but the horses were very fresh and soon tired us, and besides, Victor shied at everything he saw, he is such a brute. We drove about Aldershot and twice through the cavalry barracks. We bought a lot of chocolate at one of the shops. Aldershot is a horrid place, dirty and with nothing to look at.

*Sunday 28 September* This was harvest thanksgiving so the church was beautifully decorated with quantities of fruit and flowers and sheaves of corn. The service was very nice and the singing was beautiful. I think there is nothing like a country service for sincerity.

On our way back we saw hundreds of pheasants; Major Goldie is longing for the shooting to begin.

*Thursday 2 October, Trebovir Road* I took the twelve o'clock train back to town; Millie saw me off and I was very sorry to go. It was a very fine day and the country looked lovely, which made it all the harder to leave it and go back to smoky, dirty London.

*Wednesday 8 October* Mr Lester took us over St Thomas's Hospital today. It is said to be a very good hospital but I saw nothing fine in it. It was most depressing, the people looked so dreadfully ill and the smell of drugs and chloroform was overpowering. We saw everything including the museum, which is a perfect chamber of horrors, I know I shall dream of it.

*Wednesday 22 October* We went to a very dull party at Miss Nisfield's. A dreadfully aesthetic young man took me in to supper and talked the most awful rubbish imaginable; he had long black hair and glared at me through a pair of gold pince-nez.

*Wednesday 5 November* Peg came to tea to see us to say goodbye as she goes to Venice for the winter on the twenty-seventh. I met a very nice Spaniard; he came to call; his name is Emilio Noati.

*Thursday 6 November* I went to Woolwich with Mrs MacMahon today to hear a concert that was given by one of the officers. The music was severely classical. We were met by Captain Macintosh; he showed us all over the mess, even the smoking rooms as no one was in them

*Tuesday 18 November* We went to a dance at Miss Smith's and took the two Noati boys with us. I danced a little and talked to the girls most of the time, but very few of my old schoolfellows are left. We did not get home till four o'clock, it is such a long way from Kilburn to South Kensington.

*Friday 28 November* Kate and the two Noatis came to tea. They are very nice boys. I like Emilio the best; he is the eldest. The youngest is named Cesar; it reminds me of a Newfoundland dog.

*Monday 29 December* I went to my first grown-up dance tonight so now I am 'out'. Tibbie and Emilio Noati went with us and I danced a good deal. At first I did not enjoy myself at all, I felt horribly shy and could not dance a bit I was so nervous, but after a while I liked it awfully. I did not sit out any dances but Mamma made me go home early. I danced twice with a very nice man named Rose. I wore a very pale pink dress almost covered with white lace.

*Wednesday 31 December* Captain Tattersall sent me a letter to wish me a happy new year; I wonder if wishes do much good. We went to the midnight service at St Mary Abbotts. It was a glorious night, with a bright full moon.

### 1885
*Monday 26 January* We went to a very good ball at the Kensington Town Hall, the floor and the music were perfect. I had some very good partners and danced thirty-one dances. We did not get home until past five and I nearly fainted with fatigue, but it was a very nice ball and I enjoyed it immensely.

*Monday 2 February* I went to Victoria at eleven to meet Mabel Kirby who has come to spend a week with us. She is looking so well and handsome. I am so glad to have her to stay with us.

*Thursday 5 February* Mabel and I went to call on D'Arcy's wife Ada. I do not like her: she seems so frigid and deceitful.

*Friday 13 February* Mabel and I were photographed today; it was an awful ordeal. The man pulled us about so much, especially Mabel. It seemed impossible for her to get a good expression, and when he told her to smile sweetly the grin she assumed was absolutely satanic. Mab was taken in two positions, I was contented with one.

After lunch we went to Charbonels in Bond St to drink chocolate. The shop was as usual full of foreigners, among others the secretary to the Spanish Ambassador.

*Saturday 21 February* I played tennis all the afternoon. I saw Emilio Noati who has been very ill for some days; I am afraid England does not agree with him. He goes back to Buenos Aires in April to study, and hopes to return to England in three years as secretary to some legation.

*Wednesday 4 March* Indoors all day and so dull. My bird died; he has been ill for some time and now he is dead. I am so sorry. I buried him in the flower box on the balcony and Cesar came and made a monument for his grave.

*Friday 20 March* This is my nineteenth birthday. I had lots of presents. Mabel sent me a silver smelling bottle; Emilio gave me a plain gold bracelet; Cesar a cut steel chatelaine with any number of appendages; Mrs MacMahon a mirror framed in crimson plush for my den, and Papa and Mamma gave me a Japanese cabinet.

*Saturday 24 March* 'Varsity boat race! Oxford won by four lengths and made me richer by a pair of gloves from Cesar.

*Monday 6 April* The Macgregors dined with us to meet the Noatis. We were not a very jovial party; we were too depressed at the idea of the parting that is to take place on Thursday. What *shall* I do when they are gone? London will be a desert without them.

*Thursday 9 April* We were at Waterloo by nine to see those two dear boys off. It was bitterly cold and dull. It was an awful ordeal to say goodbye, and it was only for the sake of appearances that I managed to keep from crying. Emilio looked as white as a sheet and poor Cesar had hard work to keep back his tears. They are going so far away that it made the parting worse.

*Friday 10 April* Such a dull miserable day. I miss Cesar so much, I can scarcely realise that he is gone.

*Thursday 16 April* Cesar wrote today from Lisbon and asked me to marry him.

*Friday 17 April* I wrote and accepted Cesar today. I do not like him half well enough to marry him, and yet I am half afraid to refuse him.

*Monday 4 May* We went to see the opening of the Inventions Exhibition; we went at four and remained until past ten. We could not see many of the exhibits as there was such a crowd of people. The gardens were illuminated at night by small incandescent lamps instead of the usual oil. The effect is not so good as the light is not concentrated enough; I believe it is the first time the electric light has been used in that way.

*Wednesday 3 June* I spent the afternoon with Mamma shopping. We saw Mr Rose, and he wants me to join the Primrose League.

*Tuesday 9 June* I had a notice to attend a meeting of the Primrose League on Monday. Captain MacMahon and his actor brother and his wife, who is an actress, dined with us. After dinner the actor recited in a highly dramatic manner. It was impossible not to laugh as his brother was in convulsions all the time, and I think a dramatic recitation in a drawing room before one or two people is always rather absurd.

*Thursday 11 June* Today we went out to Norwood to see some amateur theatricals. It was an awful experience. How can amateurs have the impertinence to drag people out from town to listen to such awful rubbish? They did not know their parts and were conceited to a degree. It will be a long time before I again go to an amateur performance anywhere.

*Thursday 18 June* Mamma and I with Mr Pra and Arthur went to the Exhibition to hear Strauss's orchestra. They played several waltzes and their time and expression is perfect; it would be impossible to dance badly to such music. Strauss conducts with a violin bow and has his violin ready to play upon. The band of the Pomeranian Hussars was also playing: they gave Rule Britannia as a compliment to us, and Der Wacht am Rhin as a compliment to themselves.

*Monday 22 June* Today I joined the Primrose League and went to the inaugural meeting. There were about thirty ladies present and a few men, Mr Rose among them.

*Saturday 25 July* I went to hear Patti in Trovatore. Her singing is most beautiful. It was the twenty-fifth anniversary of her first appearance in London, and after the opera Colonel Mapleton presented her with a diamond bracelet. She had a perfect stack of bouquets and a wreath of laurels tied with the Italian colours. After the presentation she sang God Save the Queen.

*Adelina Patti (1834-1919), was, according to The Oxford Companion to Music (ninth ed), 'the most celebrated soprano vocalist for the long period 1860 to 1906, in which latter year she retired'.*

*Tuesday 4 August, Sutton, Surrey, in a rented holiday house* We went to Sutton today. We have a dear little house in the corner of a large garden which belongs to the house of our landlord. The country is lovely, so well-wooded, and we are on the top of a high hill.

*Thursday 13 August* This life here is dull to distraction. I have studied Italian and worked point-lace until I am tired, and there is nothing else to do. It has rained every day since we came, and we cannot get further than the garden. I do wish it was time to get back to town.

*Sunday 18 August* Today Reggie and I walked over to Morden for church under a blazing hot sun, but we were well rewarded for our trouble. The church is about 200 years old, a long narrow building with white walls covered with escutcheons, and huge black beams. The pulpit and reading desk are in one, standing in the centre of the church and made of the same black oak, the pulpit with an enormous sounding board over it. The chancel is also oak, most perfectly carved, and over the altar is a curious old stained glass window.

The service was quite in keeping with the church. There was a choir of village children in a gallery led by a man with a terrible cracked voice that made itself heard over all. The church doors were open all the time and the farmyard sounds came floating in. The churchyard is a queer old place, with some very old monuments in it. The village itself is a sleepy old place, and it is almost impossible to believe that one is barely twelve miles from London.

*Thursday 3 September, Surbiton, staying with the Kirbys* I left town for Surbiton at five. Mabel and Maude were both looking very well; their figures are almost perfect, and Maude is very pretty. She has become engaged to an Irishman named Cockman. The Kirbys have lodgings near the river, with two boats.

*Sunday 6 September* D'Arcy and Ada Nassau came to see us, and rowed us up to Hampton Court. We spent some time in the Palace, and then went on to Moulsey lock and watched the boats. There were crowds of people, and lots of pretty well-dressed girls. I wore a red and white gown that made quite a sensation: I heard two or three people admire it.

*D'Arcy Nasssau was born a Kirby, brother to Mabel and Maude. He had for some reason evidently changed his name, possibly because of an inheritance.*

*Sunday 8 September* We rowed up to Hampton and had a series of adventures on the way. First of all we were attacked by two swans while we were having tea in the boat. Maude was pale with fright but Mabel and I armed ourselves with the oars and drove them off. All the time a man was grinning at us from the banks and never offering to rescue us. Coming back we were accosted by a drunken man who nearly swamped us, and before we had recovered from that shock we were almost run down by two racing outriggers.

*Tuesday 13 September, Trebovir Road* I went today to see two men received into the convent; the ceremony was very impressive. The two novices were covered with a pall and a requiem chanted over them. Benediction followed and during the offertory an Alsatian sang a hymn with such passion and feeling it might have been a love song.

*Sunday 4 October* Dr Barry, Capt MacMahon and Mr Lester dined with us. A very nice Spaniard came after dinner named Perez y Ventoso. He is very good-looking but has a bad-tempered expression that rather alarms one.

*Friday 16 October* I spent the whole day at a home in Seven Dials for poor girls. I read and sang to them, and tried to amuse them, but it was not easy, they were so utterly callous and indifferent. The poverty is dreadful; I pitied the children most, they did look so miserable.

*Wednesday 22 October* Mamma and I were escorted over the school of mines by Mr Perez. It is very interesting to those who understand mining etc, but I don't, so I was rather bored.

*Tuesday 10 November* Mabel Kirby spent the afternoon with me but could not stay for dinner. She was as sweet as ever and looking so well. She is not exactly pretty but she has the nicest face imaginable, which is much better, and her figure is *sans reproche*.

*Saturday 14 November* I had 270 envelopes sent by the Secretary of the Primrose League to be addressed to the electors of South Kensington on behalf of Sir Algernon Borthwick, the Conservative candidate. The elections begin on Monday. I do hope the Conservatives will get in, but we are not very sanguine.

*Tuesday 24 November* Mabel Kirby spent the day with us and after lunch we did a little canvassing. I was very successful on the whole, and got a lot of promises to attend the meeting tonight. The feeling seems to be distinctly Conservative.

*Wednesday 25 November* I spent the whole day at home as it was very wet. Uncle George [Dickson] (51) was returned for Dover yesterday with a majority of 648. So far the Conservatives have the majority.

*Thursday 26 November* Mabel goes back to Dover on Saturday, so I shall not see her again until Xmas, when she is coming up to town. Cecil Tattersall sailed for India with his regiment last week. I had a Spanish lesson today and got on very well.

*Friday 27 November* Sir Algernon has got in with a majority of 2,436. I am so very glad.

Mr Perez brought me some lovely tea roses. I am so sorry to say it has got about Kensington that we are engaged; it does seem too bad that such things should be said. People think it impossible to have a platonic friendship unless one is about sixty.

*Saturday 28 November* The Liberals have seven more seats than the Conservatives, but the county elections have not yet come off, and it is then that we hope to make a sweeping majority. It will be too dreadful if the Liberals get into office.

*The Conservatives under Lord Salisbury failed to get a clear majority as in the country constituencies the newly enfranchised labourers voted for the Liberals, who had recently given them the vote.*

*Thursday 3 December, Bognor, staying with Mr and Mrs Donnit* I went out with Mrs Donnit this morning and explored Bognor, it is quite a small place. There is a long straggling high street and a few score houses scattered promiscuously about over a mile or two of land. There is an iron pier and a long parade but there seems to be no one to use them but a few idle boatmen.

We went to a concert, got up for the local RC schools and supported by local talent (?). It was a very awful performance and the audience were nearly as bad: such hats and general toilettes I never saw. They all stared very hard at me, and I was introduced to several of the people.

*Saturday 5 December* I begin to think that there is no place like London in the winter, and no place like home at any time. It was very dull here today, nothing but rain and wind and a grey monotonous sea. We got out for a little shopping before lunch. I had a letter from Mamma today telling me that Lady Borthwick has invited me to a tea on Tuesday.

*Monday 7 December* A lot of women came to tea and two novices from the monastery; they were very nice and quite gay and amusing. One of them actually talked slang. I was rather surprised as I always thought monks were serious and glum. I lent one of them some music. He talked about opera, theatres and even actresses, just like a man of the world. I am afraid he must be rather a frivolous monk.

*Thursday 17 December, Trebovir Road* We went to a dance at Miss Ashleigh Smith's and took Mr Perez and Libbie with us. Mr Perez gave me a lovely bouquet to match my gown, which was black and scarlet. I did not enjoy myself much as I got so dreadfully tired and could not dance. I had to sit out nearly all the dances. The were a lot of people and two or three pretty girls. Everyone said Mr Perez was the best dancer in the room.

*Saturday 19 December* We saw in the papers today that Guilford [the Earl of] had a bad accident yesterday while hunting. His horse slipped at a fence and fell on him. We had a telegram from Gac saying that he was in great pain.

*Monday 21 December* Poor Guilford is dead. He had severe internal injuries and died on Saturday, conscious to the last.

*Tuesday 22 December* We were very busy all day getting black clothes. It seems such a pity to go into mourning just at Xmas time, and I shall have to give up so many dances.

*Wednesday 23 December* Mamma and Papa went off to Dover for Guilford's funeral, which takes place tomorrow, and I am left in command. Mr Perez brought me a bouquet of yellow roses.

*Friday 25 December, Christmas Day* I went to church with Papa. The church was rather well decorated and there were any number of holly berries, which are remarkably plentiful this year. I got cards from Mr Franchy, Mr Chavers, Mr Lewis, Libbie and the Lucas's. We dined at six o'clock, all together. Mr Lester and Captain MacMahon and the children were our guests.

I am going to the ball on the fifteenth after all. I only saw Guilford a very few times and it seems rather hard that I should have to give up my ball on account of his death. Mrs MacMahon will chaperone me as Mamma won't go.

## 1886

*Sunday 3 January* I heard today that Cecil Tattersall has gone to India for two years only, so it will not be long before I see him again.

Mamma and Papa spent the day with William Eden (27) and his wife; dear Peg was there and Artie, who sails for China on Tuesday but comes back again in May. He was in the Soudan when Wolseley was there and he says the proceedings were shameful. Wolseley wrote home to say that the times were so bad that he had even to groom his own horse and he had scarcely anything to eat, and Artie saw with his own eyes a train of every luxury imaginable going up to Wolseley's camp. He says the amount of humbug that went on was appalling and that Wolseley is unlikely to have another important command.

*General Lord (Garnet) Wolseley's force had failed by three days to rescue Gordon in Khartoom, a failure that was - largely unfairly - blamed on Wolseley and ill-received at home. The real culprits were Gladstone and his government which had dithered for too long before authorising the expedition.*

*Tuesday 12 January* This was a filthy day. There was a rapid thaw and the streets were simply awful. The three children went to a ball at Major Musgrave's; Sybil and Maude were in pink and looked very pretty. They came back at 12.30. Sybil put on tremendous airs and exhibited her programme, just like a girl of eighteen. She really is awfully precocious.

Mr Perez gave me some preserved peaches that came from the Canarys.

*Friday 15 January* We went to the Mining School Ball tonight. My gown was lovely and I started in the very best spirits but - the ball was a complete failure as far as I was concerned. I lost my temper over a mistake that Mr Perez made. I was abominably rude, and altogether made a perfect exhibition of myself. I think I must have been mad. I cannot realise how horribly ill-bred I was, and now I am so sorry when it is too late.

Mr Perez is furious with me, as he may well be, and the ball I looked forward to so much for more than three months has been a terrible fiasco. The worst of it is that it was all my own fault. I cannot imagine how I was so rude. I would give everything I have to recall what passed, but now it is too late and by my own temper and jealousy I have lost the good opinion of one of my best friends. I have such a dreadful temper and lately it seems to have got worse instead of better.

*Sunday 17 January* I made up my quarrel with Mr Perez. I saw him in the morning and we had a grand explanation. I am very glad. I do hate fighting more than anything. I went to evening church and heard a capital sermon, that really made an immense impression upon me.

*Tuesday 19 January* Mamma had a very sad letter from poor Gac giving us particulars of Guilford's death. She says she scarcely yet realises her loss, but feels stunned and benumbed.

*Wednesday 20 January* Today the Queen came to town to open Parliament tomorrow. We went to Victoria at 1.30pm and saw her very well; I had never seen her before. She is very fat and short but has a dignified appearance. Her face had a very sad expression and she bowed constantly without smiling at all. Princess Beatrice, who was with her, was looking very disagreeable and haughty as usual. She is very handsome and would be pretty but for her unpleasant expression.

*Friday 22 January* Mr Perez has asked me to marry him and I do not know what answer to give him. I hate to say no - and I cannot say yes. He is very charming but one requires more than that for a husband, and I do not care enough for him to marry him. I do wish he had not been so foolish as to fall in love with me. I never gave him any encouragement. In fact he says himself that I have been atrociously rude to him at times, and yet he is absurd enough to like me. I need not give my final answer until June when he returns from Teneriffe, but I know so well what it will be that I might just as well settle the matter now. I am so afraid of hurting him. What a nuisance it is.

*Tuesday 26 January* I heard today that Captain Tattersall is coming back from India in two years from last December. I wonder if I shall see him; it seems such ages since we last met. This was the twenty-first anniversary of Mamma and Papa's wedding and next March I shall be twenty. It is positively appalling to think I am growing so old.

*Tuesday 2 February* I heard today that Umballa is a frightfully unhealthy place, and Capt Tattersall is there with his regiment. I hope it will not upset his health as Egypt did. Mr Perez told me a lot about his home today, in Teneriffe. He says it is one of the loveliest places in the world.

*Thursday 4 February* We went to a party at Mrs Wheeler's, Mamma, Mortie, Mr Perez and myself. We had a little music first, but began to dance later on. I sang and had a lot of pretty speeches about my voice. I wonder if people think I do not know I have a good voice that they consider it necessary to tell me so every time I sing. All the same it is very nice hearing these compliments and I enjoy it immensely.

I had some good partners and one very bad one, who confessed that he had no ear for music and danced quite mechanically. I danced once with Mr Perez and sat the rest out with him. He proposed to me again and I accepted him, so now I suppose I must consider myself engaged. Mamma won't hear of it, but I think if we persevere we may soften her heart. Mr Perez cannot marry for two years, and I do not care to tie myself down before then -besides, the chances are it will come to nothing. I do not believe in long engagements nor in my own constancy. I think he is also a rather fickle young man. He may be very much in love with me, but when he goes back to Teneriffe in July will be the time to test him. Absence does not *always* make the heart grow fonder; sometimes quite the reverse. I wish I were a little girl again. I do hate being engaged and growing up and all that sort of thing.

*Saturday 6 February* Papa and Mamma won't hear of any engagement between Mr Perez and myself, so I must give up all idea of it. There are a great many objections: first he is a Roman Catholic; second he is Spanish, and Papa hates foreigners, while I like them; third he is too young; and fourth not well enough off. I do not in the least object to his religion, in fact I like it better than my own, but there is no use in trying to go against everyone, and I know there would be a tremendous outcry if I persisted in marrying him. As for my feelings, I leave them quite out of the question. I do not believe I have a heart or if I have it is asleep.

*Sunday 14 February* The Borthwick girls gave me a piece of Lorne's wedding cake, and last night I passed it through a wedding ring and slept with it under my pillow, but it was a swindle: I did not dream of anything in particular, and most certainly not of my future lord and master.

*Thursday 18 February* After dinner I went to one of the nicest dances I have ever had; Mamma did not go but Mrs Rose chaperoned me. I filled my card two deep and had the best dancers in the room for my partners. The Roses gave the dance and I had seven dances with him. We sat most of them out, talking and enjoying ourselves immensely. I had great fun with a man named Spiers; I had five dances with him and some extras. The dancing was very good and six of my partners said I was the best dancer in the room. I had lots of compliments and pretty speeches which nearly turned my head. I am afraid I am getting rather conceited, but really I cannot help it. There is to be another ball at the same place next month and I have already engaged all my dances for it.

*Saturday 20 February* Victor and I have had a great quarrel. I told him about a man who kissed my hair at the dance on Thursday and Victor is so angry he told me to consider our engagement at an end, but after he had gone I wrote him asking him to make it up, so I hope it will be all right.

*Sunday 16 February* Victor and I have made up our quarrel which was only caused by his jealous Spanish temper. My acquaintance with him has been one long tissue of quarrels. He is so intensely jealous that the very slightest act on my part makes him furious. If I marry him I shall be miserable unless he learns to be a little more reasonable.

*Wednesday 24 February* Kate Borthwick came to tea. It was a very cold day and my cough is worse. It makes me feel so bad that I cannot help being sharp and irritable, and then everyone says how bad-tempered I am, when in reality I am one of the most amiable of mortals.

*Saturday 27 February* I wish this weather would go. Lent begins on Wednesday, then Easter and then the season. I did used to look forward to it so much for I always met Cecil Tattersall, but now he is in India and there is nothing to care about. I do wish I could forget him, but it is impossible; he seems to be mixed up in my life and I think of him every day.

*Monday 1 March* I dreamt last night that Victor and I were married and that I was utterly miserable. I wonder if that dream is a warning.

*Tuesday 2 March* Today we received news of the death of Aunt Flo Wilmot (59) which occurred yesterday. She died from an overdose of chloroform. Poor Flo, how awfully sad it is. Guilford has not been dead three months and now his only sister is gone. I wonder how Aunt Charlie will stand it; I am afraid it will break her heart. Flo was only twenty-six.

*Thursday 4 March* Bobbie Dickson (54) wrote this morning about Flo. He calls her 'his darling bird' and seems quite distracted with grief. He was so devoted to her that I am afraid he will feel her loss more than anyone.

This was a very cold day; I do not think we are ever going to have warm weather again. My hands are covered with chilblains, and are so red and swollen that a scullery maid would be ashamed to own them.

*Saturday 6 March* Poor Flora was buried today at Glemham in a spot she once chose herself. Snow fell all the time of the funeral. Her grave was buried with ivy and flowers and the coffin quite hidden by them. It seems incredible that she is lying in her grave. Last week she was well and happy and now - poor Bobbie was terribly cut-up, more so than anyone. Her husband was very calm; he does not shew his feelings much. Aunt Charlie, who is in the Riviera, has never written or telegraphed and they do not even know if she has received the news. It does seem so strange, and I cannot help feeling anxious about it.

*Saturday 13 March* I had a long talk with Victor today and he accused me of flirting with everyone, which is a vile slander.

*Wednesday 17 March* We went to a crowded meeting of the Irish Land Defence Association, held at the Town Hall with Sir A Borthwick in the Chair. The proceedings were rather disorderly but the resolution was carried by a huge majority. It was 'That the English people should strenuously oppose the policy of Home Rule in Ireland', and the consequent separation of the British Empire. Lord de Vesci, a Liberal, Lord Castletown, Conservative, and a host of others of both parties spoke. Also Arnold Foster and W.E.H.Lecky. The last made a magnificent speech. Lord Castletown spoke well too, but was constantly interrupted. We women were in the gallery, from where we could see and hear everything and at the same time be out of the reach of the mob. Lecky is writing a history of the time, but as he is a Liberal it will most likely make a hero of the Grand Old Man [William Gladstone].

*Thursday 18 Marsh* A few days ago Victor came and apologised for his behaviour to me but I did not forgive him. Since then I have not seen him, and now I can consider that at last my engagement is broken off. I am so glad: it is such a relief to think I am free and accountable to no one for all I do or say. His jealousy was appalling. I pity Spanish women if all their countrymen are like Mr Perez y Ventoso.

*Saturday 20 March* This was my twentieth birthday. It is dreadful to think I have left my teens behind me and I do begin to feel so old, I wish I was seventeen again. The last three years of my life have been such wasted ones, I have learnt nothing, and now at twenty I am more ignorant than Sybil or Maude. I have changed most dreadfully since I was seventeen, and I wonder of it is as apparent to other people as it is to me.

I believe I am very fast and I am sure I do not mean to be, but everything I do seems different from others, and I am afraid I often shock and offend people without knowing it. If I could only live my life over again I would act *so* differently, and then perhaps I would not have so much to regret as I have now, so many lost opportunities and chances that I shall never have again. I have become so suspicious and distrustful too. I do not believe in anyone and feel that the world is trying to deceive me.

*Wednesday 31 March* After dinner we went to a meeting of the Primrose League held at Captain Thackeray's. Mr Rose was not there so I found it very dull. A lot of business was done but I cannot remember it all. I was told I looked very pretty, which was the most interesting thing I heard in the whole evening.

*Tuesday 6 April* Maude [Kirby] and Victor Perez dined with us and we had a very jolly evening. Mamma told our fortunes: mine was a good one, and so was Victor's. I enjoyed myself immensely today; it was such fun having Mr Rose and Mr Perez together to tea. Victor was furiously jealous, but for once he did not scold me for flirting.

*Wednesday 7 April* This was an awful day, nothing but wind and rain and general depression. My life is made up of intensely happy days and frightfully dreary ones, there is no medium. I am either perfectly happy or perfectly miserable; it is a most unpleasant sort of nature. I begin to think it is rather a bad plan to keep a journal as it is utterly impossible to avoid being egotistical in writing it. I get almost tired of writing about myself and my doings, and yet I cannot very well write about anyone else.

*Tuesday 13 April* We went today to call upon Mrs Whipham in Grosvenor Street and found her at home. We met a lot of people in her house, most of them uninteresting as five o'clock-tea people usually are. It was a lovely day, very warm and bright. I never saw Bond Street more crowded or more women with painted faces. It really is horrid, every second woman one meets is painted and dyed like a doll, it is such a pity. We saw Lady Burdett-Coutts, with a delicate mauve bonnet over her wrinkled old face. Why *will* people with parchment-coloured complexions wear those pale, trying tints? She did look such a terrible old scarecrow.

*Baroness (Angela) Burdett-Coutts (1814-1906) a noted philanthropist and a partner in Coutts Bank; she had been created a baroness in her own right. King Edward V11 is reputed to have said of her, 'after my mother the most remarkable woman in the country'. At the age of sixty-six, however, she deeply shocked Queen Victoria by marrying a man of twenty-nine.*

*Wednesday 21 April* Victor came to see us today. He has not been for nearly a fortnight and I was simply furious with him, and gave him a tremendously long, severe lecture. He has been awfully busy and has not been able to go anywhere. He has almost decided to go to Colorado in June and wants me to go out and marry him in a year's time, but I cannot, I do not care enough for him.

*Sunday 25 April, Easter Day* I went to early service at eight o'clock to St Phillips and again at ten-thirty to St Matthias, where I was perfectly disgusted at the ritual: it was nearly impossible to believe one was in a Protestant church. I do hate that high church business, it is nothing more nor less than a tawdry imitation of the Roman Catholic service.

*Monday 3 May* We went today to see Sarah Bernhardt in Adrienne Lecourveur at Her Majesty's. It was a most wonderful performance and the death scene was painfully real. Sarah is not pretty but extremely graceful and dressed so perfectly that it is a pleasure to look at her. She was very indifferently supported. Her voice is beautiful, very rich in quality and as clear as a bell. At first I thought her stagy and affected, but afterwards she lost all that and was simply superb. Her articulation is perfect and her voice is so well modulated that one could listen to it for ever without tiring. She looks quite young and girlish, although she must be nearly fifty. She is very tall and slight and graceful to a degree. It is a picture to watch her move across the stage. Her hands are good too, and in every way she is charming. No wonder Paris goes mad over her.

_According to the Dictionary of National Biography, Sarah Bernhardt (1844-1923) 'was not simply the most famous actress the world has seen; she was among the most gifted'. Adrienne Lecouveur was written by Victorien Sardou (1831-1908). He was noted for lavish melodramas in which the 'Divine Sarah' often appeared._

_Friday 7 May_ I went to the Exhibition with the Glynnes and had tea there. Their son is very nice, a perfect specimen of an Englishman: he hates foreigners and got perfectly rabid on the subject. I wonder why Englishmen have such a dislike of foreigners; it is horribly narrow-minded and illiberal.

_Sunday 16 May_ This was such a dull day. Mamma was ill and I could not go out either to church or to tea with the Nassaus as I had promised. I was wondering today why it was I liked Mr Rose so much, and I came to the conclusion that it must be because he is such a sympathetic listener. He never appears to be bored at anything one says, but listens with the greatest attention to whatever he hears. I think the art of listening well is one of the best social qualities one can possess, but it is so rare.

_Friday 28 May_ I went to the Army and Navy stores today with Mamma. On our way back she suddenly noticed that I was covered with a rash. I got home and to bed immediately, and to my disgust I have got measles. Mortie has got it too; what a nuisance it is. I do feel so furious. I shall have to stay in bed for a week; it is simply awful. I do not feel a bit ill and yet I am not allowed to eat anything and every time I sit up a huge fur mantle is put round me until I am nearly roasted.

_Saturday 29 May_ This was an awful day. I am beginning to feel weak and seedy but Mortie is simply outrageous, making an awful noise and utterly refusing to remain in bed. He is hungrier than ever, and when the dinner bell rang and the smell of food came floating upstairs he got perfectly desperate.

_Monday 7 June_ We had a letter from Nellie Fitzgerald to say that they left America on the first and would be with us today or tomorrow. I do feel so excited at seeing my godmother; it is ten years since she was last in England.

_Thursday 10 June_ Miss Atkinson wrote today and asked us to a garden party at Ealing on Monday. I have not been there since 5th July 1884 when I saw Captain Tattersall for the last time, and that is nearly two years ago.

At night we had a telegram from the Fitzgeralds. They landed in Liverpool this morning and will be here tomorrow afternoon.

*Friday 11 June* The Fitzgeralds have come at last. We went to Euston at three-thirty to meet them. Nellie is very charming, a real American girl. She is a most amusing talker and makes the most daring americanisms. I think we will get on very well together. My godmother is a quiet, gentle woman.

*Saturday 12 June* Papa has been away since the Fitzgeralds came, but he returned tonight and saw them for the first time for ten years. Mrs Fitzgerald was in love with him before he married Mamma and she is still devoted to him, so the meeting was very sentimental. She never knew he was engaged and not till after they were married did she know of Mamma's existence. It must have been a great shock to her, and she is just the romantic sort of person to feel such a thing deeply.

*Monday 14 June* This was Whit Monday, so to avoid the holiday-makers we spent the day at Ealing. I did not enjoy it very much. I could not help thinking of the last occasion on which I was there, and I missed Captain Tattersall very much. I am sorry to hear he has quarrelled with Major Atkinson and they never hear anything of him.

*Saturday 19 June* I went to Dr Whipham this morning to have my throat examined. He looked rather grave when he saw it and said I must not talk or exert myself at all. Unless I take great care I shall never sing again.

*Tuesday 22 June* Fred Eden and his wife came after dinner and we had a very jolly evening. Nellie, Mr Lewis, Mr Fournie, Mortie and I commenced to play nap at eleven-thirty and played for some time. It was great fun, we were all in the wildest spirits and made noise enough to arouse the dead. Fred Eden brought a chart of our pedigree with him. It was made by old General Eden and traces us back to Wodin, the Scandinavian god of war. It includes Hengist and Horsa, the Vikings, and any number of royalty and distinguished people. I suppose it is quite true, as we have all the quarterings in our coat of arms.

*Saturday 26 June* I went to Cleveland Square and drove down to Ealing with the Atkinsons and a large party. It was a glorious day, too hot to do anything, so I spent the day on the water under a tree talking to Captain Alexander. There was a very large party and I rather enjoyed it. There is only one drawback to going to Ealing: I get too sentimental in thinking of two years ago, which is stupid, for it can do no good but only makes me feel miserable

I drove back to the Square with Mrs Atkinson and dined there. Papa and Miss Ramsbottom were the only guests. I was awfully tired and did not enjoy it very much. We sat in the Square garden after dinner which reminded me of an evening ages ago. It seems like several hundred years.

*Monday 28 June* We went to see Irving and Ellen Terry in Faust after dinner. It is the most exciting piece I have ever seen. Irving is perfect in it and Ellen Terry quite lovely. Margaret was very touching in the last act; I nearly cried, not for her but for Faust. It seems rather hard that he should be torn away to endless torment in spite of all her prayers.

*Sir Henry Irving (1838-1905) was for many years both manager of the Lyceum Theatre in London, and a famous interpreter of the great Shakspearian roles. His female lead was often played by Dame Ellen Terry (1847-1928). Opinion was divided on whether she was his mistress.*

*Tuesday 29 June* This was a lovely day, hot, but with a delicious cool breeze which the others grumbled at and called a nor'east wind, when I am sure it was nothing of the sort. I never saw such people as the English, they are never satisfied with the weather, always finding something to complain of. After dinner Mortie, Nellie and I went out for a walk and behaved so badly that I wonder we were not taken up. As it was we positively trembled every time we saw a policeman. We threw stones at windows, rang bells and frightened cats, and had a grand time all round. It is such a relief to be natural once in a way. I get so tired of trying to be well-behaved and ladylike.

*Friday 9 July* Tibbie tells me I am looking very ill and old; I am so sorry: it is rather hard to begin to look old at twenty. If my health was only better I might look younger, but I am always so seedy that in a few years I shall have quite lost my youth, and be a horrid fussy old maid.

*Monday 12 July* It rained hard all day. We were to have gone to tea with the Lawsons but Nellie was afraid of the weather so we remained at home. After dinner we danced as it is Tibbie's last night. He goes away tomorrow and by the time he returns I shall probably be gone, so it may be a very long time before I spend another evening with the dear old boy. He expects to go to Ceylon in October but I half hope he won't. I shall miss him so much; he is like an elder brother to me; Mortie is too young to fill that part.

*Tibbie spent some time staying with the Edens, so he may have been a relation, perhaps from Mrs Eden's side of the family.*

*Tuesday 13 July* Nellie and I went to a sort of party at Mrs Wheeler's after dinner; it was rather dull. There was a dreadful old man, a General Tulloch, who recited and sang an Italian song which he did not know very well. He rather floundered in the middle but recovered and ended with a triumphant yell on the wrong note. His wife and daughter were there and I pitied them.

*Saturday 17 July* I went to the doctor today and had my lungs sounded. They are all right, which is satisfactory: *now* I am not afraid of going into consumption.

*Sunday 18 July* This was a very dull day. Mr Glynne came to see us after dinner. His son came home on leave yesterday. I had a talk with him over the garden wall and he gave me a piece of music written by a girl in Dublin. It is a waltz, very silly and with a sentimental title, My Lost Love!! Fancy giving a *waltz* such a name.

*Tuesday 20 July* Alice Eden came to see me, and Mr Furlong after dinner. I asked him to write me some verses and he wrote the most awfully sentimental rubbish I have ever had the misfortune to read. After he had gone Morton went into fits over it and made a capital parody.

    Sir William Eden (4) was married today to Sybil Grey, a very lovely girl only nineteen years old and he is thirty-seven.

*Friday 23 July* I had a letter from Emily Chetwynd and one from Mr Bose, whom I have not seen for weeks. I seem to be drifting apart from all my old friends and making new ones, which is hateful. Morton had an invitation from Aunt Mary to spend next month with her at Oxford; it will be very jolly for him. I should like to go too but she is not likely to ask me, she dislikes me too much.

*Saturday 24 July* I went to see the doctor today and he said my cough was serious, which is a bore. I do not believe I shall ever get entirely rid of it. It is a great nuisance to myself and to other people too. I think a horrid loud cough is so vulgar, and mine is like a bark.

*Saturday 31 July* I went to see Dr Whipham this morning. My cough is not much better. It is a great nuisance but rather amusing in one way, as everyone tells me how careful I ought to be and they all advise different remedies, but I begin to think mine is incurable and that I shall have it to the day of my death.

*Friday 6 August, Ripley, near Woking, Surrey, in a rented holiday house* At 4.00pm I took the train for Woking and got there about 6.00. The children met me at the station. It is a lovely place, very hilly and covered with pine trees and heather.

*Saturday 7 August* All day we have been out walking everywhere. I wish I could give some idea of the beauty of this place but it is beyond me. It is very hilly and covered with magnificent trees, and every here and there a little cottage buried among the greenery. In the morning we walked to Old Woking; the church must have been lovely a hundred years ago, but some wretch has tried to restore it and succeeded in utterly ruining its beauty.

We have a very nice little house, and behind it there is a large convent where we shall go to church. We are at the top of a hill and can see stretches of pine woods for miles around. It is so peaceful and quiet that I think I could be good if I always lived in the country. Here God seems to be near one, while in town it is sometimes difficult to believe that he exists at all. I suppose I should get tired of this life after a while, but just now it seems heaven itself. All day I have nothing to vex or hurt or tempt me, and as a consequence have been more amiable than I can ever remember myself to have been before. I wonder what sort of person I should have been if I had always lived this placid uneventful life.

*Monday 9 August* We walked to a little village called Byfleet, such a pretty place buried in trees. After tea we went by a new way to Old Woking through one of the loveliest, leafiest lanes imaginable. For a mile or more it was like an avenue with deep hedges, and then suddenly turned into a high road with ghastly new red-brick villas in the very worst taste. It was an awful surprise, but the builder seems to have penetrated everywhere.

On our way home we met one of the drawbacks of the country in the shape of a large herd of cows, and I believe we were all rather frightened, although we would not have owned it for the world. An old man met us and said to me, 'It's a fine 'ot day, young woman'. I do not believe I have ever been called a 'young woman' before, certainly not to my face.

*Wednesday 11 August* We went for a long walk round Ripley, through lovely cornfields all ripe and yellow, in many of them reaping was going on. We found ourselves at a little village called Wisley. If it had not been for a friendly tramp whom we met, I do not think we would have got home again: he walked with us for nearly three miles and put us in the right way. He was very nice to talk to, told us all his history and picked me two bunches of cornflowers.

*Wednesday 18 August* This was Sybil's twelfth birthday and we spent the whole day out of doors. We took our lunch with us and had it on the banks of the Basingstoke canal, along which we walked for two or three miles. We came home by a different way, across country. The harvest is being cut everywhere, by men and women with the old-fashioned scythe; there seem to be no horrid, ugly reaping machines in this part of the world.

*Friday 20 August* This was a glorious day. We started early on a long walk and took our lunch with us, not returning until teatime. For the first time we were spoken to impertinently by some of the natives. Hitherto they have been very civil but today I had on rather a bizarre hat of coarse plaited grass, turned up with some real scarlet berries and leaves. I thought it very pretty but they evidently resented it.

At Woking a very nice coach and four with a party of good-looking young men passed us, which was quite an adventure as they were the first people of our own class that we have seen since we came down. This place is singularly deficient in 'gentry', which is perhaps rather a good thing. It is a fortnight today since I left town and it seems like a month.

*Wednesday 25 August* After lunch we went blackberrying again and got even more torn about than yesterday. My hands are aching from all the scratches I got and we spent some time in picking the thorns off our arms and legs. We got a splendid lot of blackberries only I do wish my hands were not so awful; they are never beautiful at the best of times and now they are simply disgusting.

*Monday 30 August, Trebovir Road* We left Woking today by the 2.15pm train. I was sorry to leave the country but it was delightful to get home. Our dear old house did look so nice and large after the poky little lodgings we had. All the flowers on my balcony are dead as no one watered them, they were growing so well when I left home. London is very empty; everyone seems away.

We went to the Exhibition after dinner but it was not nice: there was such an awful crowd of very horrid people, excursionists, all hot and disagreeable. The noise and crowding seems dreadful after the quiet of the country.

*Tuesday 31 August* I did not go out until after tea, when I went for a walk with Mortie, and he bought me two photograph frames as a peace offering, because when I was away he went to my room and stole Nellie Fitzgerald's photograph, and of course I was very angry. He is very devoted to Nellie, which is quite ridiculous as she is about eight years older than he is.

Today is Papa's birthday. He is fifty and he looks ever so much younger and is wonderfully well and strong. I wish he was not quite so old though; fifty does seem such an awful age, but I suppose it is not so much after all.

*Wednesday 1 September* Dear Peg is coming to stay with us on the 13th September, and is going to bring Geana and Adele van Ari with her. I have not seen them since '79 and I used to hate Adele. She was very pretty and perhaps I was jealous of her. I hope I shall get on better with her this time, I do so hate quarrelling.

*Thursday 9 September* At home all day. Mr Furlong came to dinner and Mortie and Arthur behaved so badly I was really ashamed of them. After dinner we had table turning in which those two wretched boys joined, and they tipped the table right over, so of course it was impossible to do any serious spiritualism, although I do not believe in it a bit.

Mr Furlong sang a great deal as usual and brought me a lot of music to try over, and also his book of poems. He wrote me a piece on the spur of the moment, the most horrible sentimental rubbish I have ever read. It is a pity he cannot write sense; I do hate that silly sickly sort of trash, and I very nearly told him so.

*Monday 13 September* I spent the whole day with Arthur at Lords watching the Australians v MCC. W.G.Grace was playing and was caught for seventy-four. It was a three-day match and when we left the MCC had made 297 for eight wickets. The bowling was splendid and Grace was in very good form. It was a glorious day.

Dear Peg and Geana and Adele arrived at five minutes to eight, just in time for dinner. Adele is very much changed, she has lost all her beauty and appears dull and uninteresting. Peg is if possible sweeter than ever.

*Tuesday 14 September* I spent the whole morning in shopping with Peg and Aunt Geana. It was an awful experience, it took about half-an-hour to decide on a yard of ribbon, and other things in the same proportion. We spent nearly three hours buying a ball dress for Adele, a few ornaments and one or two other trifles, such an awful waste of time.

Adele was ever so much brighter today and seems more like her old self, but she is painfully quiet and evidently finds it impossible to talk.

*Thursday 16 September* We went down to see the fireworks at the Crystal Palace with a party whom we met at Victoria. It consisted of Peg, Aunt Geana, Adele, Aunt North, Bobbie [Dickson], Lady Edward Clinton, a sculptor Story with his wife, and the Spanish ambassadress to Bucharest, such an artificial idiot of a woman, all paint and dye, and with an excruciating waist of about sixteen inches. Uncle George [Dickson] took us down in a special train and we had the directors' saloon, which was very comfortable. He is the chairman of the Palace now, so we were received by the chief officials and had the best places. The fireworks were splendid and there was a good wind to carry off the smoke, but it was intensely cold and I shivered in my light summer gown. Aunt Charlie was very sweet, she is looking wonderfully well, and does not seem to feel Flo's loss at all. The ambassadress, the Marchese de las Moralles, interested me more than anything, she was so intensely conceited, and so fearfully and wonderfully dressed. Peg likes her, but I took a violent dislike to her from the first.

*Saturday 18 September* In the evening I went to see Faust at the Lyceum with Aunt Geana and Adele. It is a beautiful piece and I never tire of it. Irving acted splendidly and looked the Devil to perfection. Ellen Terry was simply thrilling; her very voice is worth alone the trouble of going miles to hear, and she seems to grow more graceful every time I see her.

Adele is so funny, she is never interested in anything, and even in the great scene on the Brocken she showed no signs of pleasure, she seems to care for nothing. I have done my best to induce her to show some slight interest for *something* but it is impossible; she is utterly apathetic and un-satisfactory, and a girl who refuses to be moved by Ellen Terry or excited by Irving is past all hope.

*Sunday 19 September* I took Adele to church this morning; until within a few months ago she was a Roman Catholic but has become a convert to the Protestant Church, which I consider a pity.

Major Macgregor, Captain MacMahon and Mr Lester came to dinner. They had a long argument about religion which shocked me dreadfully.

Major Macgregor believes in nothing and holds the most startling views, and I am sorry to say dear Peg is a Unitarian. It is such a pity, she is almost perfect, the most generous faithful woman that ever lived, and in everything but religion most Christian. She is so clever too, that I wonder she has not more faith, and it grieves me more than I can say, but she is so good in her life that perhaps at the end God will forgive her, and then she will see what a mistaken idea she had.

*Monday 20 September, Dover, staying with the Kirbys* I went down to Dover by the 2.05pm train. On the way down I passed Bishopsbourne and saw the graveyard where Grandmamma is buried, and further on dear old Crabble where I passed such a jolly summer three years ago. I got to Dover at 5.00 and was met by Mabel and Maude, both looking very pretty and well.

We went to a concert after dinner in the Town Hall at which I saw many of my old Dover friends. The music was very good, Mrs Hutchinson sang, and a man who reminded me strangely of Cecil Tattersall.

*Thursday 23 September* By the evening post I had an invitation for a ball on the 29th from the Munster Fusiliers. I am looking forward to it very much, it will be my first military ball and I shall be sure to enjoy it. I really am awfully lucky to get invited.

*Wednesday 29 September* We spent nearly the whole day in walking about which tired me rather for the dance. Mrs Hay chaperoned me and we got there in very good time; my card was very soon filled. I danced every dance and enjoyed myself immensely, only the people here dance very badly, they are so rough and dance so quickly that one gets quite hot and tired. I had some very nice partners, especially a man named Dunstable, and another, a Mr Ainley, with whom I danced a good deal, both in the Surrey regiment.

I have never been to a military ball before and it certainly is ever so much prettier than an ordinary one, the men's uniforms are so picturesque and nearly every girl was dressed in white. The music was capital and the floor too, and I believe there was a very good supper but I did not have time for any. I always used to think that officers danced so well and it was a dreadful disillusion to find that it was rather difficult to get once round the room, and they guided so badly. I have never been so woefully banged about before.

*Tuesday 5 October* After tea we made ourselves smart and walked on the Parade, We saw lots of people but spoke to no one but the Gooches, who asked me to tea on Friday. Hitherto they have cut me, but Mrs Gooch explained that she did not know me because I was 'so much improved', not exactly complimentary!

*Sunday 10 October* I dined with Aunt North which was just a wee bit dull. She was very kind and Bobbie was rather amusing. Aunt Geana and Adele were both there. They start for Guernsey tomorrow night. I had to sing to them which was a great bore, as my throat was queer; it always is when I am particularly anxious to do well. It was a lovely night and Bobbie walked home with me. He is very much changed since Flo's death: he has grown thin and his manner is much quieter and graver. He is said to be like me in appearance, and I really think he is the very image of me.

*Wednesday 13 October* After dinner we had a very stormy game of whist, Mabel and Maude against Mr Braddell and I. The girls completely lost their tempers and were so rude to Mr Braddell I wonder he did not box their ears. He kept his temper admirably for they really were most awfully irritating. I have never seen Mabel in that sort of temper before, and I never thought she could be so insolent.

*Thursday 14 October* At eight we began to dress for the ball. Mabel and Maude were in a great state of excitement over it; their dresses were pure white, very pretty and simple, and they looked wonderfully well. The ball was at the Shaft Barracks and was given by the Surrey regiment. I did not enjoy it very much; I am sure I do not know why, as I had plenty of partners, but there was no one I cared very much about.

*Monday 18 October, Trebovir Road* Mabel and I left Dover this morning by the 12.08pm train and had a very long, tiresome journey up to town. I was more sorry than I can say to leave Dover. Fitzroy had got a very bad cold and Sybil and Maude are not as well as they might be. London is dirty and horrid as ever.

*Tuesday 26 October* We went to call upon Ada Nassau and found her looking very thin and wretchedly ill; she looks as if she were dying. We saw the baby but it howled all the time so we did not see it to the best advantage

*Thursday 4 November* Mamma had a letter from Mrs Kirby saying that

Mabel must go back to Dover on Thursday, which is all nonsense, she must stay for much longer. I shall be so horribly lonely without her.

*Friday 5 November* This was a dreadfully wet day; we meant to have gone out but it rained so hard we could not. I spent the morning in washing some point-lace that was nearly black with London smoke and dirt.

*Tuesday 9 November* This was Lord Mayor's Day and as the Socialists had threatened to make a row we were not allowed to leave the house all day. It rained hard so it was no privation staying at home.

*Tuesday 23 November* The fog was thicker than ever. We took the Levis and Mr Gresswell to the St James Theatre to see the Kendals. Mrs Kendal is a charming actress, very natural and refined and with a beautiful voice.

*The actor/manager William Kendal (1848-1817) and his wife Dame Madge (1848-1935) were a famous stage pair in both Shakespearian and lighter roles; after her marriage she refused to play opposite any other man than her husband. A contemporary periodical commented in 1885, 'Mrs Kendall, one of the best artists of her sex on the London stage, is in private life the epitome of all domestic virtues and graces'.*

*Monday 6 December* I went to a very stormy meeting of the Primrose League: the question was whether we should admit associates or not. I was in favour of admission but we lost by one vote. Several people lost their tempers; I love to see people squabble. I had a talk with Captain Thackeray who said he had heard of me at Dover. I wonder what he heard.

*Tuesday 14 December* I went to tea with Mrs Glynne and had a good long talk with her and her sister. I like Mrs Glynne very much now, better than I used to. I saw her son for a minute or two, but he had not much to say. What idiots men are: they are not fit to speak to until they are over thirty.

*Tuesday 21 December* I dined with the Borthwicks and went to a ball in Cavendish Square. I did not know anyone and thought I should not enjoy it, but it was very amusing and my card was soon full. My partners were not very nice; there were only three I really cared about, and their names were Leslie, Gardiner and Medlicott. Mr Gardiner knows a lot of our people and Mr Medlicott is an RE quartered at Chatham. I danced about five dances with him. I got very tired but we did not leave till nearly 3.00am.

*Wednesday 22 December* I was dead tired this morning and slept until twelve, when Kate Borthwick paid me a visit and woke me up. I was mad with her for she insisted on pulling up the blinds and waking me thoroughly.

*Saturday 25 December, Christmas Day* I could not go to church this morning because I got up so late, but I went to the Carmelite church after lunch, and heard a service with beautiful singing that lasted for nearly three hours. The church was well decorated and the music was perfect.

We had dinner at seven with all the children and three of Reggie'schoolfellows. They were all very well behaved during the first part of the meal, but when the pudding appeared their shyness wore off and they were riotous for the rest of the evening. Captain MacMahon dined with us too; after dinner we all danced and had games until the boys grew so rough that they had to be sent to bed. We all sang God Save the Queen and dispersed the children.

*Thursday 30 December* I spent the whole morning shopping with Mamma and lunched with Alice Eden, who is all alone. I remained some little time with her, and then came back to find dear Mabel waiting for me. She is going to stay in the Nassau's house for a month while Ada is in Dover.

*Friday 31 December* Mr Braddell came to tea with us and took us all to the Avenue Theatre to see a pantomime. Arthur Roberts acted in it, he is very amusing but rather vulgar. I rather wanted to go to church at twelve o'clock, but we were not back from the theatre until past midnight. The Kirbys came back to our house, and we sat until one talking and laughing and commenced the New Year in a very riotous fashion.

### 1887

*Saturday 1 January* Captain Romero dined with us and brought me a lovely bouquet of roses, and promised me some more books of Spanish poetry. We played nap after dinner and had a very jolly evening, only I do not like Captain Romero very much, he pays one such compliments and I hate that.

*Monday 3 January* I went to a very nice dance at the Whiphams. I was very lucky for during the whole evening I had only one bad partner. I danced a good deal with Philip Macgregor. This was his first grown-up dance and he put on airs accordingly, but was very amiable when I called him a 'boy'.

*Wednesday 12 January* After lunch Reggie and Fitzroy went with me to see a Rugby football match at Battersea Park. Mr Lewis was playing but I did not like it, the game is horribly rough and there does not seem to be any play in it.

*Saturday 15 January* I spent the afternoon at the Museum with Fitz who insisted on examining all the engines and machinery while I was longing to get to the pictures. I wish I understood machinery etc. Mortie and Papa and all their friends talk of nothing but, and it makes me feel so ignorant not to know even a piston from a gauge.

A friend of Mortie's named Hawkins dined with us. He was rather interesting and talked down to my level about books and pictures, but he did not care for music, so there must be something very wrong or deficient in his organisation.

*Sunday 23 January* Major Macgregor came to tea and stayed until past seven. He has promised me two books on Buddhism, and *The Light of Asia* by Edwin Arnold.

*Monday 24 January* Major Macgregor sent me the book on Buddhism, *Isis Unveiled*, but it is such rank blasphemy that I am not going to read it. I am very disappointed as I expected something quite different.

*Isis Unveiled was written by Madame Blavatski, founder of the Theosophical Society. It offers an interpretation of ancient religion partly based on Edward Bulwer-Lytton's novel The Last Days of Pompei.*

*Tuesday 25 January* I spent the evening with Miss Faulkner who is staying in Cromwell Road; it was very amusing. There was an embryo actor there, who asked me to do the Juliet to his Romeo. I read it from the book while he raved round the room, gesticulating and shouting out his love for me (Juliet).

*Saturday 29 January* I went to tea with Mrs Glynne and heard a long tirade against servants. Everywhere it is the same cry, that servants are so bad, but I think the mistresses must also be to blame.

*Sunday 6 February* After lunch, when Mamma had gone into the drawing room, we were playing football with an old hat and smashed a big porcelain lamp globe. Every day since the boys came home something has been broken. Yesterday it was one of the biggest windows in the hall.

*Sunday 13 February* I went to Westminster this afternoon to hear Canon Farrer. He preached a most stirring sermon, warning us all of the sin that is among us. He says we are sinful, selfish and luxurious, and shutting our eyes to the revolution that is brewing. His sermon was a very depressing one, but so eloquent that it must have roused some of the congregation, only people seem to be so utterly callous that if St Paul himself came they would not practice what he preached. Canon Farrer is wonderfully clever; he preached ex tempore for forty minutes, and every word was to the point.

*Tuesday 15 February* This was a most awfully dull day. I do not think I have ever felt more restless or wretched. I had nothing to do and no one to talk to. It is such hard lines not being able to sing; I miss it more than I can say, and it seems my throat is getting worse every day, and soon I shall not be able to talk, much less sing.

*Tuesday 22 February* I went for a long walk in the Park and saw Captain Henriques riding and spoke to him twice. Captain Romero sent me three volumes of Spanish tales and verses bound in red with my name in gilt letters on the cover. Such lovely books to look at, I hope they will be as nice to read.

*Saturday 26 February* This was a lovely day, warm and sunny. I went for a long walk in the Park. Mrs Fred Eden came to see us bringing her awful child with her, a spoilt brat of about seven that cries for everything it sees. I made faces at it when the mother was not looking and succeeded in making it thoroughly unhappy.

*Tuesday 1 March* Papa has been away for a month today. Mamma had a letter to say he would be back in a week. It is dreadfully dull without him.

*Wednesday 2 March* I went for a walk in the Park this morning and saw the Queen, who is on one of her rare visits to London. Princess Beatrice was with her, and her outriders were in scarlet instead of the usual black. The Queen is in a very melancholy state and appears unhappy. It was a lovely day and the Row was full of people who all galloped after the Queen to stare at her.

*Monday 3 March* Mrs Glynne came to see us today and told us the latest news of her son Tommy in Ireland. Colonel and Mrs Tremlett also came. They all talked about the badness of their servants; it really seems there is not a good servant left in England. They are getting worse every day.

*Wednesday 9 March* The music that Mr de Shelminski promised me arrived today from Poland, where he is now living. It consists of three volumes, the entire works of Chopin. The printing is excellent, and it is one of the nicest, most welcome presents I have ever had. Mamma and Sybil went to a concert, and I practised my beloved Chopin all the evening.

*Sunday 13 March* This is Emilio Noati's twenty-third birthday. I wonder where he is. We have not heard from him for ages.

*Wednesday 16 March* It was awfully cold and utterly miserable today; the streets are knee-deep in horrible slush and everything is dripping with thaw. Mortie is going away to Manchester for some months to do some electric lighting; we shall miss him dreadfully.

*Friday 18 March* Papa came home today after his long absence. He is looking wonderfully well and younger than ever. It is such a comfort to have him back again.

*Saturday 19 March* It was colder than ever today. No fresh snow fell and I am tired of looking out on a dirty white world.

I had a very sad letter from Mabel. Ada Nassau is dying of consumption, and Mabel herself is suffering from her heart and is not allowed to exert herself at all.

*Sunday 20 March* This was my twenty-first birthday, my coming of age. Mr Lewis gave me a very pretty scent bottle; it was good of him to remember me.

I wrote a long letter to dear Mabel begging her to take the greatest care of herself. I do wish she was here or I was with her; it worries me to think that she is so ill.

*Wednesday 23 March* I heard from Mabel this morning and she is much better.

I went with Mamma to hear Bach's Passion Music at St Anne's, Soho, and did not like it much. It was not very well sung and I do not care for oratorio at the best of times.

*Saturday 26 March* This was a glorious day, very warm and sunny. The 'varsity race was run and Cambridge won, greatly to my disgust. Everyone was wearing the colours and we saw an engine with large bands of dark blue paper round its chimney and valves. Piccadilly was full of all sorts of conveyances coming back from the race, and all profusely decorated with dark or light blue. I am sorry Cambridge has won. The Cantabs put on so much side when they win anything, they really fancy themselves superior to Oxford.

*Sunday 27 March* Ronald Beaumont came to see us and we met again for the first time for sixteen years. I last saw him in Scotland where we were inseparable, and I can only remember him as a small boy in kilts, very naughty and always getting into scrapes with everybody. He left Scotland before we did in 1871, and I have not seen him since. It seems hardly possible that the tall young man who appeared today can be Ronnie.

*Monday 4 April* I had a letter from Maude Kirby telling me that Mabel is very ill and that Ada Nassau is dying fast. It is very sad and I am sorry for poor D'Arcy.

*Tuesday 5 April* Spring cleaning began yesterday and there is not a room fit to sit in; everything is upside down. I spent the afternoon in washing the china, and in mending all the broken china that has been accumulating all the winter. We went to tea with Mrs MacMahon and she accused me of tight-lacing which is *not* one of my vices.

Papa went to a big dinner at the Holborn last night given in his honour by the British Light staff. They also gave him a lovely clock in bronze and brass with an inscription upon it.

*Wednesday 6 April* I had a letter from Maude Kirby this morning telling me that Mabel was better but that poor Ada Nassau died yesterday morning. D'Arcy is dreadfully cut up about it; she leaves a baby of only six months old.

*Thursday 7 April* Papa and I dined with Major Atkinson at an Italian hotel, Previtalli in Arundel Street, such a nice foreign place. We afterwards went to see Gilbert and Sullivan's Ruddigore at the Savoy. I liked it immensely. The music is lovely and the acting very good. Grossmith is capital.

*George Grossmith (1847-1912) premiered the comedy parts in the Gilbert and Sullivan operettas. With his brother Weedon, he also wrote* The Diary of a Nobody.

*Monday 18 April* Papa dined with Major Atkinson last night and he told Papa that he had struck Captain Tattersall out of his will because he made such a fool of himself two years ago. I wonder what he did; I should like very much to know.

*Tuesday 19 April* After lunch I went with Mamma to call upon Ronnie's mother, Mrs Beaumont, who is the most lymphatic person I have ever seen. I believe that if one bit or pinched her she would never take any notice.

This was Primrose Day, the sixth anniversary of Beaconsfield's death. A great many people wore bunches of primroses and many horses and shops were decorated with them.

*The Earl of Beaconsfield, formerly Benjamin Disraeli, the Tory leader.*

*Thursday 21 April* I went to a very nice dinner party at the Montefiores, which I enjoyed immensely. Captain Henriques was there and took me down to dinner and talked to me all the time afterwards. He is very sleepy and rather absent, but really very nice.

*Monday 25 April* I dined with Papa and Major Atkinson at the hotel Previtalli, and then went to see Lady Clancarty at the St James theatre. Mrs Kendal as Lady Clancarty was better than I have ever seen her before, and looked wonderfully young and handsome in some very lovely gowns. We afterwards went to Wiltons and had some oysters and did not get home till very late.

*Saturday 30 April* Sybil, who has been very seedy all the week, has got measles. It is very provoking as it puts us all in quarantine.

*Sunday 1 May* Fitz has measles now and I expect Maude will be the next. It is really most annoying, the house will be like a hospital.

*Wednesday 4 May* Mamma went to see Miss Faulkner after dinner and heard that Mr Ray, who was studying for the stage, has suddenly resolved to become a Carmelite monk. He has fitted up an oratory in his bedroom and prays there nearly all night, and is all day in church. Last time I saw him we arranged to do Romeo and Juliet together. He had rather a fancy for me and is now doing penance for it, as he considered it a sin to care for any girl.

*Monday 9 May* The Kirbys dined with us and we had great fun in the garden afterwards. When it got quite dark we walked about on the wall and tried who could jump the highest etc, and we also sang songs with choruses that must have deafened the whole neighbourhood. We were in the wildest spirits and it only wanted Mortie to be here to complete it.

*Wednesday 11 May* As I was walking in Cromwell Road I met the Queen on her way back from the American Exhibition. Princess Beatrice was with her, looking very pretty and amiable, and Prince Henry of Battenberg, who is wonderfully good-looking. The Queen was very closely veiled. She had a hearty reception, all the people waving their handkerchiefs.

*Wednesday 18 May* I spent the afternoon with Maude Kirby. She is going to live with D'Arcy and keep house for him. She came to tea with us and remained for dinner, and we had a very jolly evening. Mamma went to some dull card party and left us to our own devices. Maude was in capital spirits, and if Mortie had only been here it would have been perfect. As it was we had Reggie and Mr Lewis. We sang songs with tremendous choruses, and danced and laughed until we were weak.

*Friday 20 May* We went to a splendid ball tonight given at Westminster Town Hall by the Poles in London. I was rather afraid I should get no dancing, but Captain Beaumont and Count Dudley Gurowski, who were both stewards, got me more partners than I knew what to do with.
    The Prince Ladislas Czartoryski, who would be King of Poland if that country were free, was present and Count Gurowski, who was in attendance, presented me to him. He is a charming old man, and I talked to him in French for a long time. He asked if I was devoted to Poland and, of course, I said I was, and then he said he was glad, 'for he wanted pretty faces and true hearts to help him regain his kingdom'.

*Monday 23 May* I went to a very awful party at the Mockfords tonight. It was a musical affair and was something awful. A *very* young man was the first to sing and he sang a most difficult and lovely song, but he murdered it. He was introduced to me afterwards and fished for compliments outrageously, and of course I snubbed him as much as I could. A lot of women sang soprano, and each tried who could yell the loudest.

*Tuesday 31 May* This was a lovely day; it was such a treat to see the sun after so long and it was very warm. I had a letter from Captain Henriques telling me he would not be at the Macgregor's dance tomorrow as he is going away. I am sorry and disappointed.

*Wednesday 1 June* Maude Kirby dined with us and helped to dress me for the Macgregor's ball, which I did not enjoy at all. It would have been so different if Captain Henriques had turned up. I danced with Mr Cresswell and Philip Macgregor and my cousin William Eden the actor, who is very nice and dances beautifully, but my other partners were men I had never seen before and they were profoundly uninteresting. There was a tremendous crowd and I got dreadfully knocked about, and altogether the dance I had been looking forward to so much was an utter failure.

*Saturday 4 June* I had a splendid drive with Major Atkinson this morning on the box seat of his brake. We drove through the Park. It was crammed full; it was hardly possible to get along and we had to pull up several times. The Princess of Wales was there with her three daughters. She looked prettier than ever, and was constantly bowing and smiling. The three princesses are very pretty, and they were all so quietly dressed in brown, such a contrast to all the other women, who were in the brightest of colours.

*Monday 6 June* Alice Eden **(28)** came for me at five and we went to see a cousin of Alice's, Marian Granville, who lives with her grandmother Lady Cook in Bolton Street. She seems a fairly nice girl, but she is rather ill now so it is not easy to judge what she is like.

We finished the day by having an ice at Gunter's, which spoilt my dinner, and then strolled slowly home. The streets were crowded, London has never been so full before, and although it is the Jubilee season, the Queen has gone to Scotland and only intends to pass two days in London. It is bad of her, and people are furious after all the pains they have taken to celebrate the Jubilee. Many of the houses are already covered with gas piping for the illuminations on the twentieth.

*Tuesday 7 June* Mamma and I went to a party in the Cromwell Road which was rather amusing. There were some extraordinary people present; an old woman of nearly eighty with £12,000 a year who is going to marry a man of about thirty, who was with her; also the young man's mother, who is also going to marry again, and a whole galaxy of old maids, one of them raving mad. The rich old lady was dreadful: she was painted and dyed and covered with magnificent diamonds, and so old and feeble that she could hardly keep awake.

*Tuesday 14 June* I went with Major Atkinson in the brake today but there was another woman, a Miss Clarke, so I did not get the box seat, which was horrid. I lunched with the Atkinsons. Miss Casabianca was there; I like her less every time I see her. We afterwards went to a concert at Grosvenor House. It was a very good one, and Grossmith gave a capital musical recitation. We walked in the Park for about an hour after the concert, it was fuller than ever; I think London has never been so full.

*Saturday 18 June* I was at home all day. A very nice new piano came and I spent a long time trying it. After dinner I went over to the Glynnes to see their arrangements for illumination on the Jubilee. They say there are seven million people now in London, and there has never has been such a brilliant season before. The Park is so full that it is impossible to get along, and Piccadilly is almost impassable.

*Monday 20 June* This morning I hung a lot of Japanese lanterns on the balcony for the illumination tomorrow night. Nearly every house in London is adorned in some way with flags or drapery of all colours and materials, and thousands of little glass lamps or lanterns. After lunch we drove down to Piccadilly but could go no further in the cab as there was a complete block, the carriages were five or six deep, and it took three-quarters of an hour to get from St James's Street to Piccadilly Circus.

We walked through Trafalgar Square, down Whitehall and past the Abbey. Huge stands have been erected on every possible space to accommodate thousands of people. The crowd was appalling and it is impossible to realise what it will be like tomorrow. Excursion trains are being run from Scotland and the north at four shillings the return journey, and so about half the population of England will be in London tomorrow for the Queen's Jubilee. Ambulances have been placed in all the side streets to carry off those who will be sunstruck or trodden down by the crowd.

*Tuesday 21 June* The Queen celebrated her Jubilee today, but I did not go to see it. It was a glorious day and everything passed off without accident. Ronnie Beaumont came to see me after it was all over and told me all about it: the Queen looked very serious, and the Prince of Wales was more cheered than she was. After dark we went out to see some of the illuminations. Every house was covered with flags and all sorts of Japanese lanterns and oil lamps, the effect was superb. Some houses were done up with electric light, which far outshone the others. The streets were crowded but the people behaved very well.

*Saturday 25 June* I went to a big garden party given by the Atkinsons at Ealing, and enjoyed it more than usual. I talked to Mr Cridland, whom I like, and a Mr Graham, who would be nice only he is rather fast, and I hate that more than anything. Evie Sangster was there, looking very fresh and pretty, such a contrast to all the other women, who were painted up to the eyes. Some of them were like masks, and in the strong country air their faces looked blue with the powder and filthy cosmetics they had smeared themselves with. The effect is bad enough in town, and in the country here everything is so pure and fresh it is simply ghastly.

*Thursday 30 June* I went to the American Exhibition with the Lewis's after dinner and saw the Buffalo Bill show, which is very amusing. He has a herd of buffalos and more than a hundred red indians and cowboys who ride races and do all sorts of wonderful things on horseback. It is all lighted by electric light which is very well managed.

After the show was over we went and looked at the Exhibition and tried the switchback railway, which is an awful invention. The track was up and down in such steep ascents and descents that it took our breath away and nearly jerked us off our seats.

*Sunday 3 July* No one came to see us in the afternoon except Tibbie, who arrived from Chatham where he has been playing cricket. He and I sat out in the garden for a long time talking over the dear old times when he and Mortie and Harry Lewis used to turn the house upside down, and almost drive us wild with noise. I would give anything to have those days again.

*Monday 4 July* This was a very hot day, late in the afternoon it was eighty-six in the shade. I drove in the brake with Captain Atkinson all the morning. I had the box seat and he was trying a new pair of leaders, so it was very nice.

I lunched alone with Captain Atkinson and afterwards he showed me a lot of photographs, and talked a good deal about Captain Tattersall, and was altogether very kind and amiable.

*Tuesday 5 July* We spent a very jolly day at Lords; it was the second day of the 'varsity cricket match, and so it was crowded with very smart people. The cricket was very good. Oxford were playing splendidly and winning, of course.

*Sunday 10 July* I did not go to church and I am sorry I did not go with Papa, for perhaps it is his last Sunday in England. He thinks he has got an appointment in New York, and if it is all settled he may sail next Saturday.

It is too dreadful to think how we shall miss him. If he goes we shall most probably join him next spring, but I hate to think of leaving dear old England and all our friends.

*Tuesday 19 July* We dined very early and went to see Sarah Bernhardt in Theodora at the Lyceum. It is a horrible piece by Sardou: Theodora kills two men on stage and then is strangled herself by an executioner, and the whole thing from beginning to end is tragedy and woe, but she is a marvellous actress. After the great fourth act she was recalled three times. Her expression is extraordinary. After she killed the first man she looked a perfect fiend, and in a minute seemed to grow years older. She was beautifully dressed in eastern costume that showed off her figure to perfection. She is very tall and graceful, like a tiger in her movements. Her voice is perhaps her greatest charm: she modulates it so well and is always distinct. At first she seems affected and self-conscious but that soon wears off, and then she is peerless. I do not wonder that the French call her the Divine Sarah.

*Thursday 21 July* At home all day. I spent the morning with Peg in my room and we had a long talk, and she begged me to marry as soon as I could. It was of no use to tell her I did not want to just yet. She insists that I should accept the first good offer I get, as it is my duty. It is very hard that such a thing as marriage should be made a duty, but Peg knows best; she is one of the wisest and dearest of women, and I should always do what she told me.

*Wednesday 27 July, Baglan Lodge, Neath, south Wales, staying with the Flowers* I spent nearly the whole day in travelling down to Neath. I met Edith and Lewis Richards at Paddington and went down with them, so the journey was not so bad. We got to Neath at 4.30. Mrs Flower, Edith's aunt, met us; we are going to stay with her until Saturday. She has a dear old house and lovely gardens. The sea comes quite close and there is a lovely view of it from my windows.

*Thursday 28 July* I woke up very early this morning and watched the tide come in. This house is right on the slope of a very high hill, and the garden is made in terraces up the side. After lunch we drove over to a flower show about six miles away. We met Harold Flower there and Harry Lewis, who came back to Baglan Lodge with us to stay for a few days. We had a very jolly meal, half-supper and half-dinner, and went into the garden afterwards to look at the lighthouses on Mumble Head and Swansea pier. This is one of the nicest places I have ever been to.

*Neath is a few miles east of Swansea, on the road to Cardiff. It is not easy to sort out the various people Mabel stayed with or met on her Welsh trip, but at Baglan she was the guest of Mr and Mrs Flower and their son Harold, and at West Cross her hosts were Mrs Richards and her son and daughter, Lewis and Edith. The third house that Mabel visited (on a day trip) was Cepn Glas, the home of Mrs Lewis and her sons Harry and Will.*

*Friday 29 July* Harold and Mr Earle dined with us which was great fun as we were all very excited and jolly and after we danced, quietly at first, but after a while we simply raced up and down the long corridor while Harry played a gallop. It was a very jolly evening and I enjoyed it immensely.

*Saturday 30 July, West Cross, near the Mumbles, a headland south-west of Swansea, staying with Mrs Richards* After lunch we went to a cricket match at Aberavon in which Harry and Willie Lewis and Harold Flower were playing. The cricket was poor but it was great fun talking to the boys and Mrs Flower is such a good chaperone, she lets us do what we like.

We had tea on the ground and stayed there till seven when Mrs Flower went back to Baglan and Edith and I went with Harry and Harold to Swansea by train, and then drove to her home at the Mumbles. Swansea seems to be a horrid place, all smoke and bad smells from the factories. We had only time to eat some food and get to bed and I was awfully tired, and those wretched boys had a pillow fight, in and out of my room.

*Monday 1 August* We had lunch early and drove to the Swansea races which are held on the new racecourse on the top of a big hill. The course is rather uneven but there is a capital grandstand, with a wonderful view across the bay. We were a large party and had tickets for the County Stand where I was introduced to a lot of people, and a man I took a particular fancy to I was told to avoid because he is very fast. I was so sorry because he was very nice and did not seems a bit fast to me.

We did not get home until late. After dinner we sat on the veranda in the moonlight and then went into the house and danced until we were dead tired. It was a very amusing day. Harold is great fun and keeps us in constant roars of laughter, and I think that that tires us more than anything.

*Tuesday 2 August* Harold went away this morning and left us very dull. He is so light and amusing that we miss him dreadfully.

We sat out on the veranda after dinner in the bright moonlight and watched the different lights at sea. I am enjoying myself so much that it seems dreadful to think I have to go back to that awful London.

*Wednesday 3 August* This morning we four, Mrs Richards, Edith, Harry and myself, drove into Swansea and looked about the town a little. It is a very dirty old-fashioned place with no good houses in it. It was the Assizes, and at twelve we went into the Court House to hear some of the cases. I had never been in a court before and it was rather interesting, only I felt sorry for the prisoners and would have liked to let them off. There were a lot of barristers, Lewis Richards among them. Justice Field was on the bench and he was horrid, turning everything into ridicule; even when he was sentencing a man he made a joke, which was very undignified.

*Friday 5 August* In the afternoon we had a big tennis party that I liked very much. Harold came with Mr Byass; they are both going to stay until Monday. Lewis brought three barristers and they all stayed to supper. Harold took me in and I had a barrister, Mr Fox on my other side. He was not very nice, much too sentimental and paid me too many compliments.

*Saturday 6 August* It was rather a dull day on the whole but the evening was very nice. Lewis came and Mr Byass, and we had a very jolly dinner party. After dinner I sang, and then we went into the garden and stayed there until past twelve. There was a glorious moon in a perfectly cloudless sky and, I think, it bewitched us all. Harold Flower asked me to marry him but of course I said 'no'. It is rather absurd, he is a year younger than I am, and in a week he will have forgotten all about me, but he is very nice and I like him a good deal better than most people. He is so very good-looking and always amiable, even when we are awfully rude to him.

*Sunday 7 August* Edith and I went to church, all the others were too done-up by their late night. Harold and Harry met us at the church door after service and we walked very slowly home. Three of Lewis's barrister friends came to lunch. They were all nice and one of them was a QC, and very clever and charming. We were a very jolly party, eight men and only three women.

Edith and I with Harold, Harry and Mr Byass went off on our own account for a long walk along the coast from Langdon Bay to the Mumbles Head. When we got back to West Cross we found Mr Bartlet and three other men had called. Mr Bartlett remained for dinner and amused us immensely. He sings most beautifully, all sorts of songs from operas and some of the prettiest ballads I have ever heard. We sat in the garden as usual after dinner in the bright moonlight.

*Wednesday 10 August* Mamma wrote to tell me that Papa sails for America in three weeks, and that I must curtail my visit to see him before he goes. I suppose it is a very good thing but it is awful to think of leaving dear old England. We will have to go out in March. I feel rather bewildered; it will be such a tremendous change.

*Thursday 11 August* We had an early lunch and drove over to Neath to a flower and dog show; it was a very long drive through the worst part of Swansea, all the dreadful smoky, dirty black country. The show was a grand success. All our particular friends were there, and Mr Earle bought us each some lovely clove carnations.

After the show we all went to tea with Mr Bartlett. There was a great crowd, the Lewis's, Flowers, ourselves and all the nice people from miles around. It was very amusing and I ought to have enjoyed it immensely, but I feel very low at the idea of leaving all these dear people. I have never been happier in all my life or had more attention showed me. I am getting awfully spoilt.

I drove Mr Flower, Edith, Harold and Harry up to tea from the show and ruined a pair of new gloves, whereupon everyone insisted on getting me a new pair. It was a *very* happy day, and during the long drive home we talked it well over.

*Friday 12 August, Baglan Lodge, Neath* I spent the best part of the morning packing. I am sorry to leave West Cross; I have had such a happy time here. After lunch Mrs Richards drove us to Swansea station and saw Edith and I off to Baglan, where we are going for a week. Harold met us at Briton Ferry station and looked very pleased to see us again. He brought the phaeton and I drove back. The Flowers were delighted to see us. It is really extraordinary how kind everyone is to me; they behave as if I were the only person in the world.

We got to Baglan only in time to dress for dinner. We were a very jolly party: Harry who is staying here, Harold, Mr Earle, Mr Bartlett and Major Hill, with only me, two girls and Mr and Mrs Flower. After dinner we danced and Harold dances better than any of the others. It was a very nice evening.

*Saturday 13 August,* Harry drove the pair in the big wagonette over to Bridgend this morning. We all went and started early. Half way we picked up Harold and Mr Earle, who brought me some more beautiful carnations. It was a very jolly drive, the horses went splendidly, and the road was through the loveliest part of the county. It is fifteen miles, and we got to the Lewis's house, Cepn Glas, in time for an early lunch.

After lunch we all drove down to the cricket ground and saw a match between Bridgend and Aberavon. Wickets were drawn at six, and we all went back to Cepn Glas for a nondescript sort of meal, and at seven-thirty we all started for Baglan, two wagonettes full, all the Lewis's and Mr Byass, Harold and Mr Earle, beside our own party. Coming over in the morning I had the box-seat beside Harry, but at night I went with Will, who drove the other conveyance. We were a very long time, not reaching Baglan until past ten, and it was intensely cold.

I had a letter from Papa telling me I was on no account to go back to town, but I must see him before he sails. It would be dreadful if he went away without saying goodbye to me, and he will not tell me the date of his sailing.

*Sunday 14 August* On Thursday night I spoilt a pair of gloves driving with Mr Flower, and this morning I found under my plate two lovely pairs that he sent to London for.

After lunch we all lay on rugs on the lawn and amused ourselves very well. I had Harry and Will to talk to, and Edith had Harold. About five we had a perfect influx of visitors, Mr Byass, Mr Earle, Mr Bartlett, Major Hill, and a very nice man named Scrivenor. We all sat on the lawn eating peaches, and then went for a walk into the woods at the back of the house. Everybody stayed for the sort of nondescript meal we have on Sundays and we had a very amusing time.

*Monday 15 August* After lunch we all went over to Coed Park, the Nash's place, to lawn tennis. Edith and Mrs Flower in the brougham and I drove Mrs Lewis, Harry, Will and Mr Flower in the wagonette, and just as we were turning a sharp corner the mare shied and went into a public house window, breaking the glass and cutting her nose. It frightened me awfully for I thought she would kick or bolt, but she behaved splendidly.

We all dined at the Nash's, and then there was a very nice dance that I enjoyed immensely. Will gave me a lovely bouquet of blush roses which I wore with a black dress, and Harold brought me a bouquet of carnations, but I could not take them as Will's had come first. I danced a good deal with Will, and with Harold too; he is the best dancer I have ever met.

*Tuesday 16 August* We all drove over to lunch with Mr Byas today. He has a beautiful old house right on the hill behind Cwn Cwon. He gave us a very good lunch and we were a capital party. At five we all went to a tennis party at Mrs Stanley's. All the Nash party were there, with two awful girls who are staying with them. We sat rather apart and every man in the field surrounded us, not one of the other girls was noticed, and we had a perfect court. It was a tremendous triumph but there was a great fuss about it, as Mrs Nash was so angry: it was not our faults a bit.

At eight we put on our ball dresses in Mrs Stanley's house and had a sort of a meal, after which we danced. The meal was great fun. Edith and I had seven men round us, who danced with us the whole evening. I had a most lovely programme, specially made for me; no one else had one like it.

*Wednesday 17 August* We were all rather feeble this morning after our dissipation last night, and to make matters worse, Edith and I had a long lecture from Mrs Flower and Mrs Lewis on our behaviour yesterday. It was not our fault that everyone spoke to us and neglected the other girls.

Lewis Richards came to stay for a day or two, and we had a small and rather dull dinner party. Mr and Mrs Nash came with one of their guests, a girl whom I detest, and Harold took her in to dinner, much to his disgust and mine. I went in with Lewis and Edith had Mr Byass. I hate dinner parties, they are so long and ceremonious, but there was a band in the garden that played during dinner, which was rather nice.

After dinner I went for a walk in the garden with Harold and got a scolding from Mrs Flower because I stayed out too long. He is a very nice boy and I like him very much.

*Thursday 18 August* I had crushing bad news this morning and was wretched all day in consequence. Papa sails on the twenty-seventh for New York, and I must go back to town at once and miss a picnic that was to be given entirely in my honour by Mr Bartlett, Harold and Mr Byass on the twenty-fourth. It is dreadfully hard luck.

After lunch we went to a flower show at Melyn, and Edith and I had to judge one of the exhibits. Mr Flower is the chief man in these parts, and anyone who is with him plays a conspicuous part. Harold was at the show; he was awfully cut-up to hear I was going away. He seems miserable.

*Friday 19 August, West Cross, near Swansea* This was a wretched day. We left Baglan and went back to West Cross. We have spent such a happy week there and it has gone so quickly.

After lunch we went to a tennis tournament given by the Gwynns at

Duffryn. I drove Mr Flower and Will in the phaeton, and the others came in the wagonette and picked Harold up on the way. Everybody was very kind to me and I had lots of attention. It is too dreadful to think I am to leave all this on Tuesday and that these are the last days of the happiest month I have ever had. Poor Harold looks very seedy and says he is wretched. He is such a dear boy, much too good to trifle with.

*Saturday 20 August* We dined at six and then roamed about a bit until eight, when we had tea and sat round a big fire for it was getting dark and chilly. I did not enjoy it very much for Harold and the others were so troublesome. If I looked at one the others frowned and looked sulky, and Will would not speak to me the whole evening because I went for a walk with Mr Scrivenor. Harry told me that last night at Baglan Mr Flower would let no one sit in my place at the dinner table, and this morning a bunch of flowers was brought and put in my empty chair. It was very sweet of the dear old man.

*Sunday 21 August* I had a letter from Mamma telling me that I can wait for the pic-nic on Wednesday, so I shall not go back until Thursday.

We had a great crowd to tea. All our own party and all the people who were at the pic-nic yesterday. It was a very nice day. I like having lots of people to talk to, and they all seem to be very glad that I can stay for the picnic.

I engaged most of my dances for Wednesday evening and gave Mr Scrivenor an IOU for them.

*Wednesday 24 August* Mrs Richards, Harry and I drove over to Neath this morning to join the Baglan party, and we all went together to the picnic that was given by Mr Bartlett, Mr Earle, Mr Byass and Harold entirely in honour of Edith and I. It was given at a half-ruined tower on the top of a very high hill that nearly killed our horses. We all met at two and had a very good lunch. Edith and I sat together with her friend Miss Bishop, who arrived here yesterday. We had great fun and more attention than anyone else. After lunch I walked off with Harold and we had a last long talk, for I go away tomorrow. I think he is very sorry I am going and I hate to grieve him, for he is such a dear boy, and he likes me a good deal better than I deserve. We talked until teatime, when we had to join the others.

I had a lot of flowers given to me, Mr Scrivenor brought me roses, Mr Flower roses too, Will some lovely white asters, and I had two other bouquets of different flowers. We dawdled after tea, and about seven we commenced to dance. There was a very good room in the tower and it was beautifully decorated. The music was good and there was not a flaw or hitch from beginning to end. It was one of the nicest parties I have ever been to. I had more partners than I knew what to do with, and Mrs Lewis told me that I was thought the prettiest girl in the room, and that pleased me more than anything. I had loads of compliments, and my head is completely turned.

When it got dark the scene was lovely for the room was lighted by Japanese lanterns that shed a very soft light. The tower is in the midst of wild woods, far from any house, and it felt very isolated and strange. There was a bright moon, and between the dances we walked about on the mountain and watched the lights of Neath far below. I enjoyed it more than I can say, but it came to an end too soon. I said goodbye to Harold and all the others, because I go home tomorrow and I may not see them again. I hate going away. I have been so happy down here, and now it has all come to an end.

*Thursday 25 August, Trebovir Road,* I got up very early this a.m. and ate a hearty breakfast and caught the early train to town. They all got up to see me off, and Will went as far as Bridgend with me. It was so dreadfully sad saying goodbye and I did hate going away. Dear old Mr Flower was very kind, and packed a large basket with all sorts of eatables and a big box of bon-bons, and it was impossible to say who was the kindest.

At Bridgend Will left me and I felt very dull and lonely. The journey was a very long hot one, it was four o'clock before I got to Paddington, and for the first time in my life I was sorry to get home. I feel dreadfully unhappy, the whole conversation is about our journey to New York, and I hate the idea of leaving this country. Papa is very glad to go, but I do not think Mamma cares about it.

I wrote to Mrs Flower to announce my safe arrival. London is dustier and dirtier than ever. The children are all looking well, and Papa looks ten years younger he is so delighted to get back to America.

*Saturday 27 August* I spent the whole morning trying to settle down but I feel very restless and fidgety, and will not calm down till after Papa goes.

I had a letter from Harold and a prayer book and hymn book in a case as a souvenir of him. It was very sweet of him to send it, and I shall value it immensely.

*Sunday 28 August* Mortie arrived very early this morning. At 6.30am I was aroused to find him by my bedside. He is looking very well and he is in very good spirits and funnier than ever. It is like old times having him back again.

*Monday 29 August* This was a very unsettled day. We lunched early and then went down to the Albert Dock to see Papa safely into his ship. We got there about 2.00pm and the steamer did not leave the dock until past 7.00. Papa had a very good cabin and I think he will be quite comfortable. We said goodbye to Papa at 7.00 and left him standing in the stern watching us out of sight. It was very sad letting him go all alone, even though we are going to meet him again so soon, for I think we shall very probably go out in March.

*Wednesday 31 August* I had a telegram from Harry telling me that Mr Byass and Edith are engaged, but I hardly believe it and I will not write to her until I hear a little more.

*Thursday 1 September* I had a long letter from Harry with a lot of news, and telling me that Edith is really engaged to Mr Byass. I am very glad; she is very fond of him and has been worrying herself ill about him. He is very lucky and I do hope they will be very happy. Mr Byass is very nice and good-looking, he paid Edith a lot of attention and now I am very glad to hear it is all settled.

*Saturday 3 September* I had a long letter from Edith this morning telling me all about her engagement. She is not very happy because Mr Byass has to gain his father's consent, and she is afraid there will be some trouble.

*Sunday 4 September* I commenced a letter to Harold in answer to one I got from him last night. He still thinks about me. I wish he would forget for nothing can come of it, and he is much too good and honest to trifle with.

*Saturday 10 September* I had a long letter from Edith this morning. She told me a lot of news, and she seems very happy with Mr Byass, who is staying at West Cross now.

*Sunday 11 September* Major Macgregor came to see us and was very sorry to hear that Papa has gone to America without seeing him first He talks of going out to America next summer to see us, and it will be very nice seeing an old friend among all those strangers whom I am sure I shall hate. I do wish we were not going; every day I hate the idea more.

Mamma went to hear Mr Spurgeon preach but did not like him very much; she says he is illiterate.

*The Revd Charles Haddon Spurgeon (1834-1892) was a well-known Baptist minister and preacher. Virulently anti-Roman Catholic and considered by some to lack academic or theological rigour, yet for the last thirty years of his life he regularly attracted congregations of 5 - 6,000 to the Metropolitan Tabernacle.*

*Wednesday 14 September* Maude and I walked down to Gunnersbury to lunch with the Veals. I was very glad to see them again and spent all the afternoon in telling Mrs Veal all about our doings in Wales. They are all very pleased with Edith's engagement as Mr Byass is one of the richest men in that part of the county. Mr Veal had a lot to say about Harold Flower. He thinks him the handsomest man he ever saw and one of the nicest. It is extraordinary how popular he is with everyone.

*Saturday 17 September* This was an awful day. It rained incessantly and was very dark and gloomy, it was impossible to go out, so I sulked at home.

We heard this morning that Papa's ship arrived at New York after a passage of eighteen days.

An American professor named Cromwell dined with us. He is rather nice. He has travelled a good deal and is not so arrogant and ignorant as most Americans. All the Americans I have met in London I hate, they are so horribly ill-bred, and I dread going out to live among them.

*Tuesday 20 September* Mr Conant had a farewell dinner with us as he leaves London tomorrow on his way back to America. All the children dined with us by special request and Fitz, who drank two glasses of champagne, grew perfectly outrageous. They were all very excited and made a lot of noise, and Sybil looked very pretty and animated. She grows prettier every day and I long to see her when she grows up.

*Wednesday 21 September* I had a letter from Mabel this morning and a long one from Harold telling me that Mr Flower is very ill, and that they are all anxious about him. He is a sort of king among the people down there and they will be lost if anything happens to him. Baglan was such a paradise that I used to wonder if it were not too perfect, and that something must happen to spoil it, and it was Mr Flower that made it so nice.

*Thursday 22 September* I had a letter from Harry this morning giving me a very bad account of Mr Flower: he has paralysis, and the left side is entirely powerless. It is very sad to think of such a calamity at dear old Baglan.

*Thursday 29 September* I had a long letter from Edith Richards this morning, and one from Harry, and they both gave a bad account of Mr Flower: he is a little stronger but his brain is failing, and he is dreadfully difficult to manage. Harry sent me some lovely roses off a tree at Baglan that used to be a special favourite of mine.

I had a very long and interesting letter from Papa. He had only been in Newark two days when he wrote it, so could give no account of Newark, but he says it seems to be a pretty place. New York he thinks very ugly. He does not write in the best of spirits; I am afraid he is lonely without us.

*Tuesday 11 October* I went to a party at Captain Beaumont's. It was rather a nice party and Captain Beaumont's rooms are lovely and much too luxurious for a bachelor. There were a lot of people, Captain Shaw the fireman among them. He was introduced to me but I did not care much for him, he has a very blasé air and fancies himself a good deal. He is very good-looking, but more like a fashionable man about town than a brave fireman, as he really is. I am afraid I was rather disappointed in him

*Thursday 13 October* We went this afternoon to see the fire brigade drill at the head office in Southwark. It was very interesting. We went over the stables and saw an engine that was completely wrecked at Whiteley's fire, and some dead bodies were found round it. We also saw helmets belonging to firemen who had been killed on duty. The helmets were all bruised and battered and one was nearly burnt away. The engines were turned out twice for us, and it was marvellous how quickly the horses were put to, and the whole affair clear away. We went all through the workshops and saw everything.

Captain Shaw was very much nicer today, and took a lot of trouble to show us everything. His two daughters were there, very nice girls, and one of them took me all over the house they live in and showed me her father's study. It is a very business-like room, with any number of testimonials from all sorts of people, and photographs of firemen who have lost their lives on duty. In the dining room there is a clock given to Captain Shaw by the Queen, and pictures of all the great fires. He has a silver helmet, but I did not see it as he was at a fire this morning where it got dirty and it was being cleaned.

*Monday 17 October* I went to see Mrs Glynne and found her son from Ireland there. He has two months' leave and does not join his regiment until Xmas. He had some hard work in Belfast, picket duty etc., and sleeping in tents during the hot weather. His regiment was ordered to Belfast to suppress the riots, and they had all the difficulties and dangers of a campaign without any of the glory.

*Sunday 29 October* I went to see Mrs Glynne and found her rather seedy with neuralgia. From there I went to the Edens and had a talk with Fan, who was more disagreeable than ever. Alice came back from Scotland this morning, I met her on my way home; she is looking very well. I am glad she has come back as she will be a companion for me, and I have been so dreadfully dull and lonely. Mabel had never written to say if she can come and stay with us, so today I wrote to ask her father if anything was wrong, and why she had not answered my letters.

*Monday 31 October* This was Mamma's birthday, and Harry's too, his coming of age. He got loads of presents, some of them very nice. I had a letter from Harold, and one from Mabel to say she may come tomorrow. I am rejoiced at the idea of seeing her again.

After lunch Mamma and I went to the City to see the American consul about getting our things into New York duty free. In Bishopsgate we met a band of the Socialists, carrying a red flag and whistling the Marseillaise. They were very well behaved, and were accompanied by nearly a hundred policemen, mounted and on foot.

*Wednesday 2 November* Mabel wrote to say she could not come to stay with us and asked me to go to Dover instead, so I shall go on Saturday.

*Saturday 5 November, Dover, staying with the Kirbys* I went down to Dover today by the boat train, which got down in a little under two hours. It was a glorious day and Kent looked lovely. Mabel and Maude met me, and after a lunch we went for a walk. Dear old Dover is as nice as ever but the people I knew have nearly all gone, and everyone says the society has changed for the worse.

*Friday 11 November* Gac Guilford came to see me and paid a long visit; she had a lot of news about everyone. Guilford (65) is very happy at school and Muriel (64) is learning to play very nicely with her governess. Gac looked very well and younger than ever. She has left off her widow's weeds although Guilford has not been two years dead.

*Sunday 13 November* Cecil Hoseason came to tea. He has tried to pass into the army but could not do the examinations, so he enlisted in the East Surrey regiment. He came in his uniform and looked very nice. I think he is getting on well and hopes to get his commission some day. He is rather shy of walking about Dover in his uniform as so many of his old friends do not care to recognise a private soldier. I think it is awfully snobby and very hurting to his feelings.

*Wednesday 16 November* It was very fine today and the sun was almost warm. We went for a walk in the morning, up and down the Parade. I am rather sorry I came to Dover, I have been so completely disillusioned. I always used to think of it as being such a nice place, but it has changed so awfully in this short time that I begin to almost hate it and will be very glad to get back to town.

*Saturday 19 November, Trebovir Road* Mabel, Maude and I all came up to town today by the twelve o'clock train. Mr Kirby saw us off and Colonel Chatfield came to the station to see me. He did not recognise me and I had to rush up to him and introduce myself. I was not altogether sorry to leave Dover, although I am not likely to see it again for ages. We got to London at three and put Maude into a hansom for West Kensington, and Mabel and I went home.

*Sunday 20 November* There was to be a great meeting of the Socialists in Hyde Park, so we went to see if there was any row, but it was all very quiet, there was no meeting. After lunch Harry went off to Trafalgar Square to see if there was anything going on there. There were hundreds of policemen and the mob were marching down Piccadilly singing the Marseillaise, but he did not see if there was any collision with the police.

*Saturday 3 December* After dinner we went to a card party at Mrs Wheeler's, which was a truly awful entertainment. Mabel and I did not play but sat on a sofa criticising all the other people. Mr Wheeler sang and we nearly laughed aloud, it was such a painful exhibition. We certainly behaved very badly. It was so dull and monotonous that after a while we got quite hysterical and simply shook with laughter. This went on till past twelve when we were released and went home.

*Wednesday 7 December* After lunch I walked across the Park to Welbeck Street to see the Flowers who are lodging there. They were all out but Mr Flower. He has come up to town to consult a doctor but I am afraid no one can do him much good. It is too sad to see the change in him and to remember what he was like when I last saw him in Wales. He is entirely helpless and his mind seems very weak.

*Sunday 11 December* Mabel lunched with D'Arcy and Maude. I could not go as I have been away so much on Sundays lately and Mamma does not like it. Captain Beaumont came to see us and brought me some chocolate, my favourite sweet. As usual he had a score of anecdotes, many that I had heard before, and it was awfully hard work pretending they were quite new to me.

*Tuesday 13 December* Mabel went back to Dover today and I feel very lonely without her. I went with her to D'Arcy's house where we met Mr Kirby and Maude, and they all went down to Dover together. I miss Mabel very much; we have been over five weeks together, and I do not know when we shall be together again.

*Sunday 18 December* Alice and Fred Eden called for me and took me to morning service at St Augustine's, Queens Gate, where we heard a sermon by the celebrated Father Stanton. He is a great ritualist, and like all the high church preachers he affects great simplicity of language, which is apt to be rather childish at times. He has a very theatrical delivery and an exceedingly disagreeable nasal twang in his voice, and his sermon was very namby-pamby.

*The Revd A.H.Stanton (1839-1913), high churchman and Gladstonian Liberal, spent much of his ministry in the poor parish of St Alban the Martyr, Holborn.*

*Tuesday 20 December* Mamma went to Dover today to stay with the Kirbys and I am left in charge. I went out after breakfast and did the household shopping, with Fitzroy to carry my parcels.

*Friday 23 December* Harry went off to Wales early and left us very lonely. He gave me a large screen to hold cabinet photographs, a very nice one.

*Saturday 24 December* I went out shopping with Mamma this morning and bought my dress for the fancy-dress ball on the 29th. I am going as a snow flake, rather an ordinary character but it is pretty. Mamma bought me a lovely white ostrich feather fan for a Xmas present.

*Tuesday 27 December* Alice and Maude Macgregor came to see me this morning. Alice looks very well, much improved since this time last year when she was supposed to be in consumption. I did not go out all day but worked hard at my fancy dress.

*Thursday 29 December* Will Lewis came in time for dinner, and we sat talking afterwards until past ten when we dressed for the fancy dress ball. Mamma was in a Spanish dress and looked very nice; Will went in plain evening dress and I as snow, in a pure white net gown covered with down to represent snow, and silver dust that dropped off and covered everybody. I had a crown and veil, and my hair thickly sprinkled with silver dust; it shone like diamonds.

The ball was a very pretty one; it was given by the Lanes in Earls Court Square. There was not too great a crowd and some pretty gowns, but nothing very original. I danced nearly every dance with Will, which was very wrong I know, but it was very nice, and infinitely better than dancing with strangers I had never seen before.

## 1888

*Sunday 1 January* After lunch Sybil and I went down to Gunnersbury to the Veals. Will Lewis met us half-way, and we went for a walk to Kew Gardens and then round the Green, which has some beautiful old houses and a church on it. We had tea with the Veals; it was very jolly, they are such nice people.

We got home about seven and I dressed and went off to a party at the Duncombe-Shafto's, which was simply charming; there were a lot of very nice people. I sang twice and got a lot of pretty speeches.

*Tuesday 3 January* Harry came back from Wales and brought very bad news of poor Edith: her engagement is broken off because Sidney Byass's father will not give him a large enough income. It is a great pity, and I am afraid Edith must feel it dreadfully; she was so fond of him, and she is not the sort of girl to console herself easily.

*Wednesday 11 January, Mill Hill, Middlesex, staying with the Bishops* At four I took the train at St Pancras and went down to the Bishops at Mill Hill. All the Bishops were at home, twelve of them, and we had a very jolly dinner party. At eight we started for a dance at Hendon, Edith, Harry and I in a small brougham, and the others in the big carriage. The fog was so bad that we could not see the horses' heads; three times we were nearly upset by driving up the bank, and once we were all but in the ditch.

However we did arrive safely and the dance was very successful. I did not know a soul in the room but I danced every dance. I wore white tulle with garlands of scarlet poppies.

The drive home was a very eventful one. We had eight miles to go and the fog was worse than ever. We had to walk the horses all the way, and part of the way they had to be led; we took a good deal more than an hour to do it. Edith and I sat up until very late talking and she told me Fred Flower asked her to marry him, and it is to be decided in May. I hope it will be all right.

*Saturday 14 January, Trebovir Road, Earls Court* I went to lunch with the Montefiores and found her looking much better and the children grown a good deal. I walked home across the Park and went to tea with Alice Eden. She has just come back from staying with the Rokebys in Northamptonshire where she met Bay Middleton, whom she considers very fast.

*Bay Middleton acted as 'pilot' for the Empress Elizabeth of Austria across the Pytchley hunting country.*

I had a letter from Edith Richards. She seems very wretched and and says there is no hope at all, and that she can never marry Mr Byass. I am so sorry. It is such a sad ending, and I am sure she will never marry anyone else.

*Wednesday 18 January* I went out this morning to do some shopping. It was bitterly cold and I made my cough ever so much worse. I had a very busy day doing the housekeeping etc; everything went quite smoothly.

*Sunday 22 January* After lunch Sybil, Maude and I went down to Gunnersbury with Harry to the Veals, where we remained for tea and dinner. We got back to Trebovir Road at about ten and found that Jack Burne and Lewis Richards had called; I was sorry to miss them both.

*Monday 23 January* Mamma came back about five and brought us the latest news of Mortie: he is engaged to Nellie Fitzgerald and will marry her as soon as he gets a good appointment. It is very absurd to think of Mortie's being engaged; he is a mere boy, only twenty, and Nellie is twenty-nine; I cannot understand it at all. He is happy and well, and sent us all presents.

*Wednesday 25 January* We were busy all day packing and arranging things for our departure. I do wish we were safely landed in America and that all this trouble and worry were over. I dread the next few weeks. We cannot decide which line to go by, but I hope it will be from London, and save the long tiresome journey to Liverpool.

*Tuesday 31 January* At night we all went to the Covent Garden panto-mime, seven of us including Harry. We had capital seats, the front row, and saw splendidly. I was rather disappointed with the children: they took it all so calmly and hardly smiled although it was very funny. It was the best pantomime I have ever seen, and although it lasted over four hours I was not a bit tired of it.

*Wednesday 1 February, Mill Hill, staying with the Bishops* Colonel Chat-field sent me a lovely bouquet of white hyacinths and lilies for the ball tonight. I took the train down to Mill Hill; Harry Bishop came for me and we met Mr Richards at St Pancras and went down together.

Harold's sister Maude Flower is staying at Highwood. I was rather disappointed in her; she is so utterly unlike either of her brothers and very quiet and matter-of-fact. We dined at six-thirty and got to Hendon at eight, just as the dance commenced. I had any number of capital partners and enjoyed the whole thing immensely. I had a very pretty black dress and my flowers were lovely. I danced very often with a barrister named Gill, an amusing man, and a very good talker like all barristers.

I danced right to the end and was not a bit tired; it was very jolly, only the worst of it is that good times go so quickly. Edith looked lovely in white and Eva in blue. We were a large party, four girls, Mrs Bishop and three men, and we all crowded into two broughams.

*Friday 3 February, Trebovir Road* We dined early and went off to the Globe to see Wilson Barret in The Golden Ladder. I was very much disappointed in him, he seemed to me very stagey, and I do not think the part suited him. Miss Eastlake I did not like at all; she has a very monotonous voice which she invariably raises at the end of every sentence, and she was much too old for her part. We had a very comfortable roomy box. The play was awfully sensational, with a murder and a very harrowing scene in a prison that made everyone weep.

*Wilson Barrett (1846-1904), actor/manager whose productions were often based on religious themes and often ridiculed by the critics.*

*Wednesday 8 February* We went to tea with Mrs O'Donnell to meet her daughter Annie Lempriere, who has just come back from India, looking just as she did when I last saw her nearly ten years ago. She saw Adelaide Corballis some months ago at Poonah, and thought she was looking old and not over-happy. Poor Adelaide; she used to be one of the brightest happiest girls I knew, and it is too sad to think of what a muddle she has made of her life.

*Mabel later tipped in the following note*: Adelaide Corballis was one of my girl friends in Dover. . . . She married Colonel Corballis when she was about nineteen and went to Gibraltar with him. I heard that she eloped with a young man. Years after I heard that Colonel Corballis forgave her and took her back. I heard nothing more until I saw a notice of her death in The Times about a year ago. It read as follows: 'The Mother Superior of a convent in Devonshire, Adelaide Corballis, widow of Colonel Corballis.'

*Saturday 11 February* Mamma and I dined with Duncombe-Shaftoes. It was a very large, smart party, Lord and Lady Brougham, Sir Julian and Lady Pauncefort, Colonel and Mrs FitzGeorge and a crowd of others. Mrs Fitzgeorge is lovely and he is the image of his father the Duke of Cambridge. The women were nearly all extremely pretty and covered with diamonds. I was the only girl present. It was rather dull; after dinner Sir Julian discoursed to me on China.

*George Duke of Cambridge, Queen Victoria's first cousin and for many years Commander-in-Chief of the army, had two illegitimate sons by his mistress (later wife) the actress Louisa Fairbrother. They took the surname FitzGeorge.*

*Tuesday 14 February* There was a lot of snow last night and the streets today were in an awful state, ankle-deep in mud. I did not go out until the afternoon when Mamma and I went to tea with Mrs Chesborough. She is a very pretty little American, her husband is secretary to the Legation and she seems to have a very good time. She has a lovely house and was rather over-dressed in light green plush. She thinks I will enjoy life in New York, but I am doubtful: I hate leaving London and cannot yet realise that we are really going.

*Wednesday 15 February* We went to a very nice dinner party at the Glynns; there were only four women and eight men, who entirely carried on the conversation, and it was very amusing in consequence. I have never heard so many funny stories before, there was a constant fire of them.

*Friday 17 February* I lunched with Kate Borthwick at the School of Cookery where she is learning. We had a capital lunch, cooked by the students, and afterwards she took me all over the Schools. The buildings are not very good or well-arranged, but everything is beautifully neat and clean, and there were rows and rows of copper pans shining like gold. Kate was funny in describing her experiences. She paid a lot to learn, but she says she has taken it out in the things she has spoilt. She dropped a huge rabbit pie yesterday, smashed the dish and of course ruined the pie. It is so useful to know how to cook.

*Sunday 19 February* I dined with the Roses and had a very jolly evening. There were no other women but Mrs Rose and myself, and six men, the Spiers among them. Mrs Rose was in great glee as her mother had just given her a magnificent solitaire necklet of diamonds.

Willie Eden told us a very funny story. When he first went on the stage an old uncle, a country clergyman, was dreadfully unhappy. He had never been inside a theatre in his life and was not comforted until Willie assured him he was not in the ballet!!

*Sunday 26 February* Mortie arrived at the unearthly hour of 6.00am in the very best and most riotous of spirits. He is looking very well and it is wonderful how he has brightened us all up. I have never seen anyone so funny as he is; we never stop laughing while he is with us.

I lunched with the Shaftoes and said goodbye to those dearest old people; I do hope they will live until I come back. I got home early and all the afternoon we had a crowd of people to say goodbye: Mrs Montefiore, Mrs Henriques, Jack Burne, Kate and Grace Borthwick, the Moreleys, Mrs Veal and Mabel Senior. There was rather a rush and I had not time to speak to anyone quietly. It was a very tiring day and I feel too dazed to think of anything. I *cannot* realise that we are leaving all our friends.

*Thursday 28 February* This was wretchedly unsettled day. There was a great deal to do and we all felt miserable and were horribly quarrelsome and snappy to each other in consequence. In the evening Mamma and I went to say goodbye to the Glynns, we also went to the Fred Edens and the Chatfields. It is dreadful saying goodbye to all these friends. I am leaving so much behind me and I do dread the new life in America, with all the new friends we shall have to associate with.

*Wednesday 29 February, on board the SS Lydian Monarch* We were all up and about before 7.00am, and started for the Millwall Docks at 8.15. six children, two dogs, my bird, Mamma and Harry. It was a cruelly cold morning and altogether very wretched. It was a long journey down to the docks through awful slums and crowds of shipping, but I felt too seedy to take any interest in it all. We got on board at ten and find we have two of the best staterooms on board. The Lydian Monarch is a very good ship and there are only a few passengers; I have not spoken to any yet but Reggie and Sybil are very friendly already. Uncle Andrew and Alice and Charlie Eden came to see us off. We said goodbye to Mortie and Harry and sailed at twelve in a blinding fall of snow. It is a terrible thing to say goodbye to ones best friends.

The captain is very nice and kind. This was a lovely day, the sea as smooth as a lake and the sun so hot that we sat on deck without wraps all day. The children are very happy, they have made friends with all the officers; the Captain gave me a cap like his own with a badge and gold braid. He is quite a character and tells all sorts of interesting stories, and has given us the use of his own cabin; I am writing in it now. The children are all very happy and excited and have a brilliant colour already, but I cannot reconcile myself to leaving England and the Captain makes me feel worse, as he says about twice an hour that there is no country like England or people like the English.

*Thursday 1 March* This was a lovely day, the sea as smooth as a lake and the sun so hot that we sat on deck without wraps all day. The children are very happy, they have made friends with all the officers and the captain is very good to them.

*Thursday 8 March* We had to lay to all day as the storm was so great that we should have gone to the bottom in an hour if we had kept on. A wave forty feet high struck the ship this a.m. washing three sailors onto a winch and seriously injuring them. We had been caught in a cyclone. I was horribly ill all day and wished myself dead. Mamma and the children are perfectly well.

*Tuesday 13 March* Very rough and squally all day. We ought to have got to New York yesterday but we have had head-winds. It is getting much colder; it was freezing today and there were heavy falls of snow.

*Wednesday 14 March* The pilot came aboard this morning and at 3.00pm we sighted land, Long Island. It looked very dreary, covered with snow, but it was a blessed relief to see it after so many days at sea. It is bitterly cold with heavy falls of snow, I expect New York will be wrapped in ice. It is wretched. I did hope we had left all the cold behind us in dear old England. As we neared Sandy Hook we got into a field of ice: the ship cut her way through it right up to Staten Island where we anchored for the night.

Jersey Heights was covered with snow and New York a blaze of light, with Brooklyn Bridge outlined in electric light. The Statue of Liberty looked like a huge white ghost with the electric light streaming on to it.

*Thursday 15 March* We were all on deck by 7.00am to see New York Bay: I think it must be one of the most beautiful places in the world. Even now, covered with snow, the country is lovely.

At 11.00am Mamma and I went ashore and our luggage was examined by the custom house officers. I had rather dreaded that ordeal but they were very considerate and merely glanced inside each box. We expected Papa to meet us but he never came until late in the afternoon. It was impossible for him to come sooner as there had been a terrible storm and the lines have been blocked. The trains are running very irregularly so the Captain insisted that we should remain on board ship all night.

Papa is looking very well and it was very nice seeing him again; he is so bright and cheery and seems so glad to see all his troublesome children again. He and Mamma went off into the city and I was entertained by the Captain and Dr Beaumont. They are the last Englishmen I shall see for some time so I made the most of them.

*Friday 16 March, Newark, New Jersey, in an hotel* We were awakened very early this morning by a great noise on deck. I dressed and went up and found they were beginning to unload the cargo and coal. The ship was crowded with all sorts of queer people and some of them came into breakfast in the saloon, much to the disgust of Dr Beaumont, who had an awful customs officer next to him. The ship was very uncomfortable and I was rather glad to get away.

We started at 1.00pm and I said goodbye to the officers, who have all been most kind and attentive. From the ship we went straight to the ferry. We crossed the North River and I stood on deck all the time; although the river was covered with ice it was quite warm, with a soft, balmy breeze. We landed and went straight to Lake Erie station and took the train for Newark. The trains are so dreadfully overheated I thought I would faint before we got to Newark.

Newark itself is a wilderness, the train runs along the street, there is the merest apology for a station, and the houses look as if they had been put up for a makeshift and were to come down tomorrow to make way for something more substantial. They are nearly all wood, painted very bright colours and with extraordinary ornaments of cut wood. It all looks so new and gimcrack. I feel so horribly discouraged and miserable; I did not expect very much but the reality is worse than I ever thought it could be.

We went to the hotel where Papa has been all the time and had lunch at once, delicious oysters stewed in milk. The hotel is overheated like every other place and my throat is getting very relaxed with this tropical heat. At seven we had dinner: the first thing handed to us was a glass of iced water to each person, oysters of course, one has them at every meal, and they are delicious. We had an extraordinary menu, hot bread, cake, preserved pears and all sorts of cold meats, very nice but rather bewildering.

*Saturday 17 March* We remained in the hotel all the morning unpacking. They keep the most fearfully early hours here; most of the people had breakfast at 6.30am and when we came down at 8.30 we were quite the last. We had iced water and an orange first, and then all sorts of meats, eggs etc and delicious griddle cakes with maple syrup. They have very nice things to eat but they mix them up in a peculiar way: at luncheon they gave us apple fritters with roast beef.

After lunch we went for a walk up the principal street: it is very broad and lined with trees. In summer it must be lovely, at present it is hideous as the houses are as ugly as they can be. Each house has evidently been built to the taste of its owner, there is no uniformity whatever. Some are wood, next door is a brick, next door a brownstone, then another wooden one painted pink with green shutters, and so on for a mile or more.

*Sunday 18 March* This morning Maude and I went to church, to a church that is considered very ritualistic in Newark, but to me it seemed a very tawdry vulgar imitation. The service was awfully cut up. They began with the commandments, and sang the creed with a man conducting with a baton like a bandmaster! The sermon was very high-flown but with very little point. The singing was good, but the whole service was so unlike anything I have seen before that I could hardly realise I was in church.

Mr Conant came for us and took us all off with him to spend the day. He lives on Jersey City Heights with a married daughter and son-in-law, the Smiths, and his daughter Helen who seems to be nice, full of energy and very bright and amusing. We dined in the middle of the day, which was barbarous, and then went for a walk. We went to the Roman Catholic church, and it is the one thing that is the same as in England. That is the best of the RC church, it is the same all over the world. There was the familiar smell of incense, and the images and flowers etc, all very wicked no doubt, but they reminded me of England, and I loved them for it.

*Tuesday 20 March, on board the SS Lydian Monarch* Mamma and I went to New York by train and then the ferry. It is hardly fair to judge New York now as the whole place is in such an awful state from the late snow. We went in the elevated railway, which is certainly convenient but it utterly ruins the look of the streets. It is simply hideous, but these Americans have no idea of beauty, and sacrifice everything to utility. Their finest streets are ruined by a network of wires and the masts that support them.

We went to the pier to see Captain Huggett on board the Lydian Monarch, and I stayed to dinner on the ship, and then went to see Faust with Irving and Ellen Terry. It seemed almost as if I was back in London, only the theatre was different. Everyone wore hats or bonnets instead of evening dress, and it did not look so bright as our theatres, but Faust was just the same as in London, and I did enjoy seeing it again. Irving acted magnificently, he makes a perfect Mephistopheles.

After the theatre we went to a very nice restaurant called O'Niells and had some delicious oysters. It all seemed very foreign, the streets and shops were brilliantly lighted and crowded with people, many of them German or French. I slept on the ship as it was too late for me to get back to Newark. I had the deck cabin and was very comfortable.

*Friday 23 March, Newark, New Jersey* I went with Mamma to look at some houses in Newark, but none of them would suit us. I remained in the hotel all the afternoon; it was very dull and I felt desperately homesick.

*Sunday 25 March* We lunched at the hotel and then went to Jersey City Heights. We first went to a boarding house, where we saw some rooms that we took, as we are tired of living at Newark and hate hotel life.

*Monday 26 March* Harry Lewis sent me a long letter and rather an annoying one, for he asked me to marry him, and it is impossible for me to accept him. It will be so dreadful to write and refuse him, he is so good and I hate to hurt his feelings. What a nuisance it is, and how silly people are to fall in love, I do hate it so, it annoys me more than anything.

*Tuesday 27 March, Jersey City Heights, in a boarding house* We did not leave the hotel until past four. There was an unaccountable delay and a good deal more trouble about our luggage than there was when we left England. There were dozens of small parcels, the dogs and my bird to be looked after, and we made a procession, each one loaded with parcels, 'the Eden family on the move'. We got to Jersey City at five. There were no cabs or conveyances of any sort, so we had to walk to the boarding house through a perfect sea of mud.

*Friday 30 March* After lunch Mamma and I went to Newark to see Mrs Gillette. We went to the works and saw Papa; he showed us all over. Some of the machines are beautiful, especially one very clever one for covering or rather braiding the wire with thread. We spent a long time in the works and saw everything. Reggie was on a high stool in the office looking idle, as if he wanted to get away. He has only been at his work for two days.

*Saturday 31 March* I went for a walk with the children; the scenery all round is lovely, there are a great many woods and the whole tract of country is very wild and uncultivated.

At night we went to a reception and private view at the Academy in New York; it opens to the public on Monday. The rooms are very small and few, and they were closely packed with a very funny-looking lot of people, artists and their friends. There were not many pictures and only one or two were good, they all showed a want of finish. The cattle pieces were the best, the portraits were very bad and were criticised by the press.

*Sunday 8 April* We went to service at a very nice church this morning and heard a capital sermon that delighted me. The singing was very good, the choir was composed of ladies and it was rather like a concert as they had solos, choruses etc. It was altogether a very nice service, quite the most homelike we have yet been to.

*Monday 9 April* Nearly all the people here are Methodists or Baptists, and tremendous fanatics. All over the town they have written up texts and denunciations; on the kerbstones, fences and buildings one reads: 'Repent or go to hell', 'Prepare to meet thy God', and other awful sentences. It seems shocking and irreverent, and I am afraid it does not do much good.

*Wednesday 11 April* This was the day of the church fair that Miss Conant has been working at for the last month or two. I went to the schoolroom attached to the church where I found the Conants and lots of other girls, all busy at their stalls. There were three of us on our stall, Helen, Miss Dremus and myself; we only sold fans and sachets. All the girls were dressed very gorgeously but there were no particularly pretty ones. They are very odd in their manners and very familiar: one girl whom I was introduced to hardly said 'how do you do' before she said, 'My! What beautiful hair you have!!'

*Sunday 15 April* I went to church this morning with Mamma; we went to Christ Church, where I saw many of the people I was introduced to at the fair. They all bowed to me in the church just as if we were in a concert room or hall, and many of them carried on animated conversations. They show little reverence for a consecrated building.

*Tuesday 17 April* Mamma and I went into New York by the ten o'clock train and spent the whole day there. We first went to some shops to look at furniture for our new house and found it much cheaper than England.

We walked right down Fifth Avenue and saw the celebrated Vanderbilt palaces. I was very much disappointed in them: they are brown stone and look like clubhouses. We went into Broadway and then to 10ᵗʰ Street to Mr Conant's. He has a studio in a big building where there are thirty other artists. He showed us his portraits and they are very good; one of Henry Ward Beecher is capital.

*Wednesday 18 April* I went all over a chemical factory this morning. The man it belongs to, Mr Milke, is living in this house, and his wife went with me. It was very interesting but the smells were appalling. We saw the preparation of the new anaesthetic, cocaine; Mr Milke was the first to make it in America. In one room they were making tartar emetic, and it was lying about in beautiful crystals. The smells are terrible and the work very unhealthy: in the antinomy room the men can only work for two hours at a stretch, and one of them is very ill with lung disease brought on by the particles getting into his lungs.

*Saturday 21 April* At night I went to a party at Miss Fenn's, the girl I met here the other night. It was a very quiet affair, only a few people, and we all played a game called angling, with hooks and little brass fish, and I got the second. It was rather nice and I enjoyed it. We had a light supper with the inevitable ice cream; making it must be the staple industry of the country.

*Sunday 22 April* I went to St John's again for evening service; Papa, Mamma and Maude came too. The singing was even better than in the morning, and during the offertory a girl with a magnificent soprano sang a duet with a tenor, it was rather like an operatic duet, but it was simply perfect, sung with exquisite feeling and two highly trained voices. We had a nice walk home by moonlight. Papa was in capital spirits; we laughed all the way home.

*Friday 27 April* I stayed at home all day, although the weather was lovely; I got entranced over my point-lace and worked so hard at it that I did not care to go out. After dinner we all went for a short walk. It was a lovely night, with a glorious full moon shining on the bay, and the lights of New York like diamonds.

*Sunday 29 April* It was a baking hot day. It is wonderful to see how the trees have budded: yesterday the chestnuts were covered with little round buds and today there are quite large leaves.

After lunch we went to the station to meet Mr Byass who arrived from New York by the 3.15 train. We took him for a walk and heard all about his trip. We had a long talk about the Baglan people but he never said a word about Edith, and I was rather disappointed. I hoped to hear they were going to be married after all.

*Monday 30 April* I spent most of the morning packing up as we move into our new house on Wednesday. I am very tired of moving about and will be glad to be settled. After dinner we went to our new house to carry some china etc that would be broken if sent with the other luggage.

*Tuesday 1 May* We went into New York very early this morning and got to the pier where the Lydian Monarch is lying at ten o'clock. She only came in this morning. Captain Huggett was very well and all the officers. We stayed an hour or two on board and then went to Liberty Street to meet Mr Byass. We went straight to the Brunswick Hotel; Mr Byass is staying there with the friend who has been travelling with him, a very nice man named Inglis, and *so* English. It was nice having a long talk with one's own countrymen again.

After lunch we walked from the hotel right up to Central Park. We stopped at the cathedral and went in; it was so deliciously quiet and dusky after the glare and noise of Fifth Avenue. We stayed there for some little time, and Mr Byass told me that he was afraid things would never come right between Edith and himself. He was terribly agitated when he spoke of it, and I am afraid it has been as overwhelming a blow to him as to poor Edith. I am *so* sorry for them, they are so devoted to each other and it is awfully sad that things should be as they are.

We spent a long time in Central Park which is perfectly lovely: it is full of flowering shrubs and trees, and there are miles of little paths that windin and out among rocks covered with trees and creepers. The Park was infinitely prettier than the London parks but we were much too British to acknowledge it.

*Wednesday 2 May, Jersey City* This was a wretched day: we moved into our new house and all was in confusion. The furniture we ordered days ago did not come till past 8.00pm and then of course there was a great hurry to get it all arranged. How I hate moving, and we seem to have more of it than anyone.

I think we shall like this house: it is rather small but very pretty and the garden is very nice. The first of May is the great moving day in America, and as Americans are always changing their houses, the streets are full of carts of furniture and people carrying all sorts of things. In one street a house was being moved bodily, the great unwieldy thing had been rolled out into the road and there it stood, stopping the traffic right in front of the railway station.

*Thursday 3 May* We were all very busy all day unpacking and arranging our things. Everything was in the wildest confusion and our meals were like picnics. I unpacked all my pictures and photographs and nailed them up, and my room begins to look rather nice. It is quite a small room, with two windows, and a lovely view of New York Bay. The house is a very nice one. There are a good many rooms, but all small, there is a delightful piazza opening out of the dining room, and another out of the front drawing room. Papa has a cosy little room as a den, where he keeps his tools etc.

*Saturday 12 May* I learned how to make bread today and feel awfully proud, because I made five large loaves and they were simply delicious. Making bread is delightful work: it is such fun kneading the dough, and punching and hitting. It would be capital work if one was in a bad temper, to work off the steam.

*Tuesday 15 May* This was another hopeless day: I don't think it ceased raining for more than half an hour at a time all day. It is terrible weather and has such a bad effect on one's spirits, as if things were not bad enough already. I hardly know how I shall endure this life much longer; it almost maddens me to look out of my window and see the steamers passing down the bay on their way home.

*Sunday 20 May* Papa likes this life and place and is angry with me because I am not more contented, so I must pretend to like it better for his sake.

*Saturday 26 May* Although it was a pouring wet day I started immediately after breakfast to go to Newark to see Papa. It was the first time I had been out alone, and I made a mistake and got into the wrong tramcar. I got carried right to the other end of Newark before I knew of my mistake, and it took me more than an hour to get at last to the factory. I only stayed a short time and then went to see Mrs Gillette. I remained with her for some time. She was very pleasant and showed me all her new house; it is rather a nice one, but the reception rooms do not seem to be used at all. The Americans always sit in their bedrooms, which are arranged as sitting rooms. I should prefer to keep my bedroom for my own use.

*Monday 28 May* Today there was quite an influx of letters. Mamma had one from dear Peg. She is in mourning, as her great friend and our unknown cousin, Lady Victoria Kirwan, died last Good Friday. She also told us that Uncle George [Dickson] is hopelessly ill. It is very sad; it seems that if we ever go back to England it will be to find everyone dead.

I had a letter from Mrs Lewis in which she blames me bitterly for the way I have treated Harry. I don't think I deserve her reproaches, and she must know how utterly impossible a marriage between us would be. I had also a letter from Harry himself, two sheets full of recrimination and reproach, evidently written on impulse, or he would never have dared to send me such an effusion. I hardly know how to answer it, and it would be insulting to take no notice of it.

*Friday 1 June* Mamma and I spent the afternoon in New York. We went by the ferry to Liberty Street, and from there walked to Trinity Church, which is lovely: the organ loft and reredos are old carved oak, and there is some magnificent stained glass. The graveyard is very well-kept and full of old graves with curious inscriptions. One was to the memory of a man who died in 1762 and 'was born in olde England in 1682'. I wonder what America was like then. I think it must have been rather nicer than it is now, for it had not the awful mixed population of low Irish and Germans, and all the off-scourings of the old world that it now rejoices in.

*Wednesday 6 June* Our pictures, china and books came from the custom house at New York, where they have been lying for nearly three months, and we spent the whole afternoon unpacking them. Some of the china is dreadfully smashed; I am so sorry, for we have had it for years, and most of it belonged to Papa's great-grandfather. A little cabinet, that I prize very much because it is very old and belonged to Lord Grey de Ruthin, is broken to pieces, and I am afraid it can't be mended. It really is too bad, the people at the custom house are so careless, and as they are not obliged to pay for what they break, they don't care how they handle the things.

*Saturday 9 June* A letter came from Mortie to Papa. It is ages since he has written to any of us and we did not know where he was. He writes from Glasgow; he is at the Exhibition there and writes in excellent spirits. I am so glad he is happy and getting on so well. He says in his letter that Nellie Fitzgerald advised him to go to Glasgow, so he is evidently still very much *epris* with her. I wonder if she will really marry him, but it is hardly likely. He never writes to me; he is so angry because I once said something against Nellie and I don't think he has ever forgiven me.

*Sunday 10 June* Mamma and I went to church at St John's this morning and heard an excellent sermon from Dr Stoddart; it was more like a lecture on morals and behaviour than a sermon, but it was so practical and improving. If only one could remember to carry it into daily life.

After lunch I went alone to the Catholic church, for benediction, the old familiar service. When I closed my eyes I could almost fancy myself back in the Carmelite church in Kensington. The Catholic service is the one thing that is the same all over the world, wherever one goes the ritual is the same, and it is a comfort to find something that is the same as at home. I think it is because it is so conservative that I am so fond of it. I do detest things that are constantly changing.

*Thursday 14 June* Mrs Smith came to see us and asked if the children could join a children's society connected with the Sunday School, and she was rather disappointed when Mamma refused. Children are so precocious and brought forward here that Mamma has determined to go to the opposite extreme, and keep Sybil and Maude back, so as to keep them children as long as possible.

*Thursday 21 June* Maude and I went out after tea, up to Bergen Avenue to see the sun set over the Orange Mountains. The scene was lovely, the mountains and the towns of Newark and Elizabeth were quite indistinct, in a pinkish-yellow luminous mist, then the river, with the bright rays of the sun, and right at our feet the beautiful woods looking black against the distant landscape. It was exquisite, and we could stand on the hill and see it all spread out beneath us. The sky was magnificent, brilliant crimson and golden clouds on a deep blue sky that toned into a lovely tender green as it neared the horizon. It was beautiful beyond words, but even the cleverest painter could never catch those colours, not even Turner.

*Tuesday 26 June* This evening I went with the Conants and a lot of others for what they call a straw-ride. We started from the Conants' house at 7.00pm, about thirty of us in a huge hay cart with straw and seats. We took what is called the plank road, as it is made of planks on piles, and leads right through the marshes and over the Hackensae and Passaic rivers. We got to Newark about ten and went straight to Papa's works, where there is a very large hall with a glorious floor. We meant to have danced, but no music arrived, so we had to do without it. We brought supper with us and had a sort of picnic. Helen Conant was in great spirits; the other girls were detestable, loud and vulgar and horribly fast.

We started for home at about twelve. There was a bright moon, and the drive was delightfully cool and pleasant until we got into the marshes, where we were nearly eaten up by mosquitoes. We did not get home till 2.00am, and so ended the last straw party that I think I am likely to attend.

*Wednesday 4 July* This was the Glorious Fourth and we were not allowed to forget the fact, for all day long guns were being fired, crackers going off, bells ringing, and everyone shouting and yelling. Every man and boy had small pistols or rifles which they fired constantly about the streets or in their gardens. I saw one intelligent youth sitting with his back to a pump calmly firing a revolver into the air, and this performance lasted the best part of the day.

All along the Brooklyn shores right across to Staten Island there were rockets. Both were brilliantly illuminated, and the effect was as if a shower of coloured fire was falling all over the vast stretch of country. All the ships in the bay were also illuminated, and as they moved quickly past added much to the extraordinary beauty of the scene.

*Saturday 14 July* I had a letter from Eva Bishop today, full of news. Her brother Harry has been gazetted to the 20th Lancashire Fusiliers, and is going to Glasgow. Edith Richards is in town enjoying herself very much. She is going off to Norway so West Cross will be shut up this summer; what a change from last year. I wonder if she has forgotten Sidney Byass yet; it does not look like it, as she is evidently unwilling to go down to Wales and run the chance of meeting him.

*Tuesday 17 July* This afternoon Mr Glynn calmly walked in and startled us out of our lives. We had no idea he was in America, but he has been here for six weeks and has been all over the country. He came out to see Jack, who is on a ranch in Wyoming. We were *very* glad to see him, and had a long talk about Earls Court and all the people there. It was very nice seeing an old friend, and he seemed glad to see us.

*Sunday 22 July* We all went to evening service at Christ Church, where we heard the most extraordinary sermon. The preacher had a lot to say about the Garden of Eden, and said that the memory of its beauty had such an effect on humanity 'that whenever the name of Eden was mentioned, a rapturous thrill of ecstatic joy was felt in every breast'. Of course all the people we knew in the congregation looked at us and smiled, it was very funny.

Mr Glynn came to dinner and had a long talk with Papa about the American war. Papa very seldom talks about it, but when he does tell his experiences, it is awfully interesting and I could listen for hours.

*Robert Eden had fought in the American civil war on the side of the North.*

*Tuesday 31 July* Mrs Smith called for me after lunch and took me to a meeting of the St Agatha's Guild, held in the room adjoining Christ Church. The members of the Guild are young girls, and in a weak moment I consented to join. There were about thirty girls present this afternoon, and the rector, Mr Moody, whom I do not like. The Guild does parish work, and at present is trying to raise 25,000 dollars for a new church, and for this purpose a bazaar is to be held in October and concerts are to be given all through the winter. The proceedings opened with a prayer, and then different modes of raising money were suggested. I rather dislike mixing up religion and money in this way, but I suppose it is inevitable.

Rather a funny thing happened today. Sam went into the garden and eat some horrible decayed matter that smelt fearfully. When he came back to the house he was unbearable, so Reggie and Sybil took him into the kitchen, and Mamma caught them in the act of pouring Condy's fluid down his throat. Of course the poor thing was nearly poisoned.

*Tuesday 7 August, on board the SS Lydian Monarch* Mamma and I left Jersey City at two o'clock and got to the Lydian Monarch at three. We found Captain Huggett very well. I like going to the ship; it feels as though a little bit of England has floated over here, and we always feel at home on board her. At four-thirty we took the boat to Coney Island. Our party consisted of the Captain; Mrs Garland, an English woman whose husband is secretary of the Savage Club; Mr Kenealy, who is sub- editor of the Morning Journal; our two selves, and the doctor, who is in the service, and bound for Aden.

We had a very jolly trip down to the Island. It is rather a vulgar place but very amusing: lots of people were bathing, men and women together. There were dozens of booths and merry-go-rounds, and all sorts of stalls of refreshments etc. It was just like a huge fair. I enjoyed myself immensely. I talked to Mr Kenealy most of the time, and was charmed with him. He is very clever and amusing and very flattering, as he listens to all one says and talked to me in a delightfully sensible way. Mr Sargeant was rather nice too, but I didn't speak to him very much.

*Wednesday 8 August, Jersey City* We remained on board until twelve and then said goodbye as they sail tomorrow. Mr Kenealy saw us into our train. That ridiculous Mr Sargeant has taken a violent fancy to me and wants to marry me, Mamma told me. He said nothing to me, I am thankful to say. It is very funny. He is rich and rather nice and came out with the ship for the sake of the voyage, as he has been invalided home from India. Luckily he will sail for England tomorrow, so I shall not see him again. It is very strange that he should care to marry me after only a few hours' acquaintance.

*Sunday 12 August* After lunch I went to the Conants and met Mr Chesley there. He played to me for a long time, Chopin, Beethoven and Weber. I liked Chopin best, I never tire of his beautiful melancholy music, with its curious modulations and exquisite chromatic passages, that sound like the wind in the trees.

*Monday 20 August* Dear old Mrs Duncombe-Shafto sent me two papers today, the Queen and the World. I had a long letter from Sara Owen with the account of the wedding of an old schoolfellow, Annie Jones. Mamma had a letter from Peg, full of news. She is at Waldershare where she and Gac have had a houseful of visitors, including Prince Adolphus of Teck, whom Peg raves about as he is so handsome and well-mannered. Kate Lancaster-Lucas is going to be married to a Major Williamson; I feel rather sorry for him. Dear Peg wrote a very sweet letter as usual. I do wish I could see her again. She and Mrs Shafto and Mabel are the three people I miss more than all the others, and I would give anything to see them.

*Friday 24 August* Mamma and I made a delightful expedition today to Bergen Point; it is about five miles from here and we went by streetcar through very pretty roads. It is pretty at the Point only rather built over, and there is a good view of Staten Island. The houses are very big and pretentious, with large gardens. One of the best was utterly ruined by big painted iron deer and dogs that were dotted about among the tress to represent the real thing. It was horrible, in the worst possible taste. We walked about a good deal, had some tea and ices at a dreadful little eating-house, and finally took the cars home.

*Tuesday 28 August* Maude and I went for a long delightful ramble today, all through the woods and along the sand hills. We took the dogs with us and enjoyed ourselves immensely. Sam had one little adventure: he attacked a cat at a farmhouse we passed and got the worst of it. The woods are beginning to put on their autumn tints, and look lovely; many of the leaves are bright crimson and yellow. The view over the Hackensac and Passaic was more beautiful than ever.

*Thursday 30 August* Papa went to a meeting of electricians at the Hotel Brunswick in New York. I sat up for him until past midnight and was the first to wish him many happy returns, as tomorrow is his birthday.

*Monday 3 September* We went over to New York at ten-thirty this morning. Mr Kenealy met us at the ferry and we lunched, or rather breakfasted at the Astor House, such a funny old-fashioned hotel, like Claridges or some of the older hotels in London.

We took the ferry to Staten Island, landed at St George, and then took the train to Stapleton, where we went to the New York Canoe Clubhouse, of which Mr Kenealy is a member. There was a race to choose the man to try and beat the English champion who is coming out. There were a lot of people. We were introduced to the Commodore, Mr Munro; his wife was charming, and although we had not been introduced she gave me some bon-bons and offered me a chair and field-glasses in the kindest way. We stayed at the Club until past four and narrowly missed our train. We got back to New York at five, had tea at the Astor House, and so home after a very pleasant day.

*Friday 7 September* We got up and breakfasted at the unearthly hour of 6.30 this morning and made our way into New York, arriving at 22$^{nd}$ Street pier at 9.00, where we met Mr Kenealy. It was bitterly cold and although we were wrapped in winter cloaks we shivered. We got on board the Albany boat at nine and went up the Hudson as far as West Point, where we landed. It is quite useless to describe it. The view from the hotel where we lunched was wonderful beyond expression and the scenery all the way up from new York is exquisite. We spent three hours at West Point and saw the cadet barracks and all the various buildings. The place is very well-kept and very picturesque.

We caught the returning boat at 2.50 and got back to New York at 6.00. It was very nice coming back. There was a good fresh breeze that sent everyone below, and Mr Kenealy and I found a delightfully sheltered place behind the smoke-stacks, where we sat all the time, getting a glorious view of the scenery. Mamma grew sleepy and went below. The boat was full of people coming back from Saratoga and the mountains. There were children everywhere, who behaved worse than I should have thought possible. I pitied their wretched parents and nurses who were perfect slaves to them.

*Wednesday 19 September* Captain Huggett and Mr Kenealy dined with us and we had a very good time. After dinner the children, Mr Kenealy and myself went into the garden and for a little walk down the lane. It was a delightful night, no mosquitoes and not too hot, so we spent most of our time out of doors. Mr Kenealy was very bright and amusing. He brought me a case of Eau de Cologne in payment of a bet I won on the canoe race at Staten Island. We had a long talk about different things, chiefly myself, which is always an absorbing topic with me. He told me I was a cynic. It is so odd to hear different people's estimations of one's character. Mr Kenealy is very nice; I like him immensely. He is very clever, can talk on any subject, and I should think he was bound to rise in his profession.

*Friday 28 September* I got up at five this morning and went with Papa to the factory, where I spent the whole day. At first it was very nice for I looked at all the machines and talked to Mr Braddell etc, and watched Papa, but about 3.00pm it began to get rather dull and by 6.00, when we went home, I had a raging headache and was too tired to speak. They were insulating a large piece of cable with bitumen, which was very interesting, and I also tried to wind some cotton on one of the winding machines. Although it looked ridiculously easy I could not do it, but broke the cotton all the time. Papa was making experiments with a new invention he has for winding cotton, and I watched him for a long time, but he made it answer eventually.

*Sunday 30 September* Mr Kenealy came to lunch and went for a walk afterwards with Papa and Fitz and I. We went across the fields, down a breakneck path on to the line, crossed a crazy bridge over a canal, and had to go through a horrid marsh on rickety stepping-stones. We went some way along the towpath of the canal. It was a very good walk, only we had to cut it short as Mr Kenealy had to catch a train back to New York.

*Sunday 7 October* The Conants gave me a newspaper with a most flattering notice of Mr Kenealy in it, calling him a rising young journalist, good, honest etc, and one of the most eligible bachelors in New York. I had no idea we had been entertaining such an angel unawares.

*Wednesday 10 October* I was all day at Bergen hall helping to arrange the stalls for the bazaar which is to open tonight. All the girls round here are helping. My spinning wheel is on a rug against the wall, and I have a very old chair in keeping with it. The bazaar opened about six and I was there shortly after in my Marguerite dress. It is rather pretty, all brown, a serge shirt, velvet bodice slashed with white, a little brown velvet cap, a silver chatelaine, and Grand-mamma's wedding veil as an apron. I made quite a sensation, had hundreds of compliments and an admiring crowd round me all the evening. I spun a good deal and gave away the thread I made.

*Thursday 11 October* At home all the evening, when we went down to the hall to the fair. There were *tableaux vivants* during the evening, got up by Helen Conant. They were very good indeed: I was in one of them as one of Bluebeard's wives. There were six of us, and we all stuck our heads through holes in a sheet to look as if our heads were cut off; our faces were powdered white and a green light thrown on us. We looked ghastly and would have appeared quite dead, only we unfortunately laughed when the curtain went up.

*Friday 12 October* This was the last night of the fair and I enjoyed it so much that I am sorry it is over. I got to the hall about six, and Mamma followed with Mr Kenealy. I did not spin very much as there was such a crowd, and every time I started the wheel there was a throng round me which was embarrassing. Mr Chesley and Mr Hall were there and I had a long talk with both, and was introduced to dozens of other men besides, and I had a delightful time altogether. My dress was very much admired and I had heaps of compliments and overheard many pretty speeches, all of which charmed me. I do love flattery.

*Monday 29 October* At home all day practising hard at Mendelssohn's rondo in B minor that I hope to play at the concert tomorrow. At night I went to a meeting at Mrs Sperry's house to arrange about the set of dances that are to be given through the winter by the society I have joined. All the usual set were there, Helen Conant, the Michaels, Halls, Priors etc. It was rather dull. I had a talk with Mr Sperry about the new tunnel they are building under the North River, and when I admired the Brooklyn Bridge he electrified me by saying we had a better bridge in England, the Forth

Bridge. It is so seldom an American will own the superiority of anything outside his own country.

*Tuesday 30 October* I played at the concert tonight and it was not nearly as bad as I feared it would be. I had an encore and lots of compliments.

*Monday 5 November* I had a letter from Mabel. She says she has heard that Mortie is on his way out to America to marry Nellie Fitzgerald, who landed here last month. We have not heard from Mortie for ages and I can hardly believe it is true. He knows we do not approve of his marrying Nellie.

*Monday 19 November* I went to our rector's house today and he took me to the church and introduced me to a lot of girls who form a society called the Guild of the Holy Cross. Under the church there are several rooms used for parochial purposes, and in one of those this Guild meets every Monday to work for the poor. The girls were very nice and cordial; we all sat round the room talking and working. They are getting up a box of Xmas presents to be sent to a very poor parish, somewhere in the backwoods. I remained sewing hard until five.

*Wednesday 28 November* Mrs Chesborough wrote from London to say she would be out here before Xmas. I am very glad as she may introduce me to some nice people in New York. Our old maid Caroline also wrote to say she would be here by the Umbria on Sunday.

*Sunday 2 December* Caroline came by the Umbria. She had a very good passage and looked well. We were all very glad to see her again. She has been so long with us and we were very sorry to leave her behind when we left London.

*Monday 3 December* I was solemnly received into the Guild of the Holy Cross today. All the members assembled in the church; I sat in the front pew. Mr Stoddard read a short service and gave a very nice address, then asked me a few questions and I made some promises. Then he took my hand and formally received me into the Guild. It was an ordeal, and I was glad when it was over.

*Wednesday 5 December* This morning a girl belonging to the Guild went with me to Newark to attend a mission meeting. It was held in the chapel of Trinity Church; it was attended solely by women. Delegates represented the various missions, and one after another got up and pleaded for money for her special project. Several missionaries had sent appeals for things they wanted: one had sent a long list including black lace mittens and muslin trimming; of course his appeal was rejected.

One disagreeable-looking old woman stood up and pleaded for money to buy the mortgage of a cathedral in Mexico; it is feared the Catholics will get it, and I sincerely hope they will. They have done more in the mission field than the Protestants. She seized the opportunity to make a long tirade against the Catholics, called them pagans etc, and was altogether narrow and unchristian. The meeting lasted for nearly two hours and I was glad to come away.

*Thursday 13 December* In a weak moment I consented to teach a class in the Sunday school. Mr Stoddard asked me and I could not refuse, although I hate the idea.

*Sunday 16 December* I went to St John's to Sunday school this afternoon. It was an awful ordeal, I felt so afraid of my pupils. There are eight of them, all under fifteen, girls I am glad to say. I had to ask my pupils questions which none could answer, and this lasted for an hour.

*Tuesday 25 December, Christmas Day* This was a wretched day, so unlike last Xmas. I did not go to church. I had two letters: one from Eva Bishop, and a long one from Edith Richards full of the kindest most loving wishes from all the dear people in Wales.

*Monday 31 December* Tonight we went to a dance at the factory at Newark; they asked us a week ago. There are about sixty men, most of them are British and exceedingly respectable and superior. The affair began at eight with a 'grand march'; each man took his especial girl and marched and counter-marched for nearly fifteen minutes. Papa brought one of the foremen up to me and I had the best waltz with him I have had since I left home, he really danced beautifully.

### 1889
*Friday 4 January* I went to a meeting of the Holy Cross Guild. We had a short service in the church, prayers, psalms, and the usual address from Mr Stoddart, which I like so much. He has started a new plan of answering any questions any girl may want settled. The questions are written and put on the reading desk before the service, and he answers them after he has given his little sermon. It is an excellent idea as there are so many things one wants to know.

*Tuesday 15 January* The minister of the Universalist church came to see Mamma today and talked rank blasphemy to her, until she got so angry that he calmed down a little. I did not go into the drawing room at all as I hate religious arguments at any time. The children resented him as well, and when he was in the hall going away they set the dogs on him, but he got away all upset. I laughed but Mamma was awfully angry.

*Friday 25 January* In the evening I went to a dance at the Halls, which I enjoyed immensely. There were a lot of very nice people. I danced a with a man named James, who knows a lot of English people. He was the only American I danced with; my other partners were all English.

*Wednesday 30 January* I met Miss Chesley, and she asked me to go to Boston with her and her father in March; of course I shall be delighted to go.

*Thursday 31 January* Helen Conant came to see me today, and three of the girls belonging to St John's Guild, Miss van Elder, Miss Collard and Miss Drayton. They were all very nice, but it seemed so funny for three girls to come without their mothers to call on a perfect stranger, but mothers are not of much account in this country.

*Saturday 2 February* Mamma and I walked to Newark this morning; there was a bitter wind against us and made the six miles very tiring. We lunched with three old maids named Dodwell, which was still more exhausting. They were very kind, but fearfully slow and so painfully neat. When they left the dining room for the drawing room each put on a little shawl, and wanted us to do the same. We spent the afternoon with them and I nearly went mad: the strain of keeping up the conversation was severe.

*Tuesday 12 February* I paid calls all the afternoon. It seemed so strange to be making calls without Mamma. I went to Miss Drayton first and sat some time with her, she is very bright and nice. I then went to Miss Collard's where I spent some time. She has been a great deal in England, so has not the extraordinary false ideas of it that most of these people possess. I stayed so long at the Collards that I had time to pay only a flying visit to Miss van Gelder. I rather enjoyed making these calls; it is such a comfort to think I am making acquaintance at last.

*Thursday 21 February* Mamma and I went over to New York and called on the Hewitts. They have a gorgeous house on Lexington Avenue, a marble hall and staircase, and four huge drawing rooms opening into each other, and crammed with all sorts of pretty things. Mrs Hewitt is a nice woman and gorgeously dressed; the daughters are nice too. One is strong-minded and goes in for farming, the younger one is the nicer of the two.

*Saturday 23 February* Mamma spent the day at Newark house hunting. She found one she liked and has taken it. From all accounts it is very nice, but I loathe the idea of moving again.

*Tuesday 26 February* I called for Carrie Chesley and went with her to the hall to try the piano for tonight's concert. It is such an infamously bad one that I could not play the concerto of Mendelssohn's I had been working so hard at. I called for Carrie MacMichael and then for the Chesleys, and we all went together to the concert. It was dreadfully dull, no good music, and my solo was a dreadful failure. I played an arrangement of Faust, and only two or three pages of it, as it was impossible to play on that piano. On our way home we saw Mr C. Hall who had been sitting at the back, and he paid me some pretty and very welcome compliments about my music.

*Tuesday 5 March* I went to a very nice dance at the Halls. All the English colony were present, and the MacMichaels, Helen Conant and a few others to represent the Americans. Everyone was in the best of spirits and I enjoyed it immensely. We danced right into Lent, which some of the people were shocked at; it was understood that dancing was to stop at twelve. I danced with all the Halls, including the sailor, who is delightful. Charlie Hall was not very bright: the near approach of Lent had affected him, I think. Helen Conant was radiant; it was difficult to realise that in a few weeks' times she is going into a New York hospital to train as a sick-nurse.

We stopped dancing at twelve-thirty, when I sang two songs and got a lot of applause. It is very funny how I am asked to sing and play at every entertainment I go to, no matter if it be a dance or concert, but it is very flattering and I like it.

*Saturday 9 March, on board the SS Dimoch* I met the Chesleys at 3.00pm at the station, and we went to New York, where we got on board the Boston ship, and sailed at 5.00. Her name is the Dimoch and she is a very fine ship of 2,700 tonnage, and beautifully clean. We have a large stateroom, very much better than I have seen on the ocean steamers, and the saloons are very nice too. We had dinner at 6.00, and as it was light until nearly 7.00

we saw the East River and part of Long Island Sound. Carrie and I went to bed quite early as the sea air made us sleepy.

*Sunday 10 March, Roxbury, near Boston, staying with Mrs Chesley* We were up early and had our breakfast at 8.00 and went out on deck. It was blowing very hard and the vessel pitched a good deal. I was so sleepy that I slept nearly all day. There was not much to see as we were out of sight of land until nearly 2.00pm when we sighted Boston in the distance. We were a long time getting in as the harbour is a dangerous one, full of shoals and rocks on which many ships have been wrecked. We got alongside our dock at 4.00pm, and said goodbye to the ship with many regrets for she was very comfortable.

We went to Mrs Chesley's to spend the night. She lives at Roxbury and we had to pass through the old part of Boston. I could not see much of it, but it seems old and very English, and the people are not so conspicuously dressed as in New York. We were very tired and it was a dreadful effort to sit up and talk, and we did not get to bed until past 10.00pm. When we went to bed we slept as though we were dead.

*The next twenty pages of Mabel's diary are concerned with energetic sightseeing and socialising in and around Boston. She enjoyed it 'immensely'. The girls sailed back to New York on Monday 18 March; their ship had been delayed a day by rough weather. They had an uncomfortable voyage, arriving on 19 March. After breakfast with the Chesleys, Mabel went straight home.*

*Tuesday 19 March, Jersey City* After lunch I went with Mamma to have a look at our new house. I do not care very much for it, but the grounds are very nice.

*Friday 5 April* I did not go out at all, although it was a lovely day. Mr Kenealy came to tea but I did not go into the drawing room to see him. I am getting tired of him: he comes too often. Miss MacMichael and Mr Hall (the sailor) came after dinner and spent the evening with us. They were very bright and amusing and I enjoyed having them.

*Friday 19 April* This was Good Friday. I went to morning service at Christ Church and sang in the choir. Helen Conant came in very late with Nellie Fitzgerald to my surprise, and after service they waited and I had a talk with Nellie. I last saw her in London three years ago. Since then she has been in Germany and Italy, and is now in New York for some weeks. She is looking very well, not much older, and still pretty. I asked her about Morton and I do not think they are engaged.

*Wednesday 24 April* I went to the Chesleys this afternoon to practice my songs. I rushed home to dress and then back to the Chesleys and went with them to St John's, where the Guild gave the concert. It was a great success. Carrie and I played our duets and got lots of applause, and I sang and was not a bit nervous, although it was my first appearance in public. There were two other girls, Miss Green and Miss Smith, who sang beautifully, and we had a lot of instrumental music.

Supper was served in one part of the hall and at ten o'clock our party, consisting of Helen, the Chesleys (3), Carrie MacMichael, Mr F. Hall, Mamma and I had supper. We were very jolly and had great fun: everyone was in such good spirits and so nice. We stayed until quite the end, and then all walked home together, and I felt quite sorry to think it was probably the last time I would be with the same party.

*Thursday 25 April, Newark, New Jersey, in the new house* This was a horrible day of confusion and discomfort. I do loathe moving and we are always doing it. The vans came at 9.00am and took away everything but the piano. At 4.00 we made a little procession, all of us, dogs included, and went to Newark. Our new house seems nice and I think we will like it. Mamma and Papa stayed with us for dinner, and then went back to the old house.

*Friday 26 April* I was busy arranging things, and got most of the things unpacked. When Mamma comes the house will be nearly straight. I made my room and the children's look lovely. Mine is a dear little room with windows opening on to a balcony that overlooks the tennis lawn. The garden is lovely and there are huge maple trees that send their branches nearly into my windows. The house is a very old one, and all the better on that account. I think we will be happier and more at home in it than we were in Jersey Heights.

*Monday 29 April* I was up and out in the garden with Papa at 6.10 this a.m. I hardly knew myself up at that unearthly hour, but it was very nice, and I shall try and get up early always. It is much better than the late hours I used to keep in London. I spent the whole day in unpacking.

*Sunday 5 May* This was a glorious day, very warm and sunny, the garden looked lovely and the air was quite heavy with the scent from the pine trees and pear blossom. Mamma and I went to service at a church called the House of Prayer. The service was dreadfully ritualistic, an exact copy of the Roman Catholic service. The singing was good but the whole thing terribly overdone.

*Tuesday 7 May* The people who live opposite called, but we were out. Their name is Ogden, and they have a lovely old house that has been in their family for generations.

*Thursday 9 May* This afternoon Mamma and I went to call on the Ogdens. She is a young woman, newly married, and is a daughter of Judge Depue's. She lives in the oldest house in Newark, directly opposite ours, a quaint old wooden building, with lovely old furniture She is a very nice woman.

*Saturday 11 May* Mabel is dead. I had a letter from Maude this morning. It was written on the twenty-third and Mabel died on the twenty-second April. There were no particulars; just the bare announcement. I cannot realise it; it is like some dreadful dream. I was always thinking of what we would do together when we met again, and now I shall never see her. In all my plans and hopes for the future she was the principal figure. I loved her for years, more than anyone else, and always looked to many more years we would spend together. Now she is dead, and things will never be quite the same again.

Maude enclosed a letter Mabel wrote but forgot to post. It seemed such a terrible mockery reading a letter from the dead, and it was full of accounts of some balls she had been to and the dresses she wore, and how much she had enjoyed herself, and she said too how much she wanted to see me again, and how often she thought of me. If I could only have seen her once more to say goodbye. I loved her so dearly. For the past eight years she has been so mixed up in my life that I can't realise how I shall get on without her. My darling Mabel. She was always so sweet and generous and always the same to me. We never quarrelled although we were so much together. She has always been delicate but I never dreamed of death in connection with *her.* She was so young too, in the very prime of her youth and beauty. No one can ever be to me what she was. I have heaps of friends but none like her. There seemed to be some affinity between us that drew us together from the start. I wonder where she is now and if she can see me, or if I shall ever see her again. Now that she is dead I don't think I shall be as afraid of death as I have been. She has gone before me and perhaps when I die she may be the first to meet me

*Sunday 12 May* All day long we had people here today. Mrs Ogden came in after church and sat talking for some time; she is very nice. Mr Conant came to lunch. Mr Sinton, an Englishman, spent the evening, and Mrs Gillett brought two friends after dinner. So there was I chattering away with my thoughts full of Mabel. I have tried hard to realise she is dead but I cannot do it. I cannot believe it. It seems impossible that *she* should die. It is so dreadful not knowing how it all happened. I do wish Maude would write and give me all the particulars, then perhaps I might be better able to believe it was really true.

*Saturday 18 May* Mortie had been spending his time in New York with the fair Nellie. Until Monday he had not seen her for nearly three years, and is as infatuated as ever.

*Sunday 2 June* This was dear Mabel's birthday, her twenty-third.

Mamma and I went to morning service at St James's. After lunch Mortie, Maude and I went for a walk round the cemetery, which is one of the prettiest I have ever seen. I went to Evening service at St John's, where I met Miss Parker. She is very nice, and introduced me to the vicar Mr Durand. She plays the organ for service, and as she is going to Europe on Saturday has asked me to take her place, and I rashly consented, although I know next to nothing of the organ.

*Monday 3 June* I spent the whole afternoon in the garden with Papa, working hard. Everything looks so well, the cherries and strawberries are all ripe, and we are besieged by small boys on the look-out to steal. I like this place so much. I am beginning to like America after all.

*Friday 7 June* I went to tea at the Parkers and met a crowd of girls. I wonder if I shall ever be intimate with any of them. I felt rather afraid of them all. I am such an utter stranger and all their conversation was about people and things I know nothing of. Everyone is very kind, but they are strangers, and I hate strangers, especially girls.

I saw Mr Courtland Parker for a moment.

*Sunday 9 June* Miss Ogden came to tea; she told me a lot about the Parkers. Miss Parker is looked upon as a sort of goddess. Everyone adores her, and the brothers are all very nice and gentlemanly.   They are not very young: Courtland Parker is thirty-one. I did not think he was so old, but like him all the better, for very young men are always so conceited and uninteresting.

*Tuesday 11 June* Late in the day there was a very bad thunderstorm. Mamma was in New York, and as it grew very late and neither she nor Papa came home, I began to get alarmed. At last at 8.15 she rushed in with the news that the factory had been struck with lightning and was in flames, and that Papa had had a narrow escape. The two boys flew off without any dinner, and Mamma and I bolted a chop and followed them with some food for Papa, and I with a bottle of Benedictine. There was no train, so we had to walk.

The factory was blazing when we got to it, such a scene of desolation. Papa was dripping and black with smoke, and Mortie nearly as bad. The lightning struck just over Papa's office, and the place was in flames in a very short time. The firemen worked hard for two hours before they could get it under control. All the furniture in the office was saved, and all valuable papers. It was a very hot fire and the men got exhausted, and later on very drunk.

We had to stay until past 12.00 and missed the last train and had to walk back, Mamma, Reggie and I. It was an awful tramp, we were dog-tired and there was no chance of any sort of conveyance.

*Wednesday 12 June* I woke very late and got down to the factory as early as I could. Mortie told me some funny stories about the firemen. There were two brigades that came up first, Kearny and Harrison; one of the Kearny men tried to get in by a window; the Harrison men were already inside, and one of them in a fit of 'professional jealousy' turned his hose on the Kearny man and routed him, and then went on with his work. There were four brigades altogether, and I believe the greater number of the men got drunk. It was certainly a bad fire and they had some severe work, but it seems awfully bad management that they should have had so much drink about.

*Friday 14 June* In the evening we went to a meeting at the church for the purpose of making this part of Newark into a parish. I saw Mr Courtland Parker and he introduced me to yet another brother, named Robert. This makes the fourth Parker I have met and it is rather overpowering, especially as they are all so nice that it is difficult to know which one to like best; so far I cannot decide. Courtland is the best-looking, but I fancy he is conceited. Charles is very sensible but I think dictatorial, and the twins, Chauncey and Robert, are both very nice with delightfully courteous manners. We walked home with the Ogdens and sat for some time on their piazza, where I was introduced to Mrs Ogden's brother, Mr Depue. He was very pleasant as nearly everyone is here; I wonder if they will all be so amiable when we know them better. I think knowing people intimately is a fatal mistake.

*Friday 21 June* Mrs Ogden came and spent an hour or two with me this morning, and we had a long talk about all the Newark people. She gave me various hints as to how to behave etc. Everything is different here, and things that are thought shocking at home are quite correct here and vice-versa. As far as I can see girls seem to have a much better time here than they do at home, they seem to be able to do exactly what they like.

*Wednesday 17 July* After lunch I went to the church and played on the organ while Mamma pumped for me.

*Tuesday 23 July* Arthur Eden sent me a paper with a long account of Uncle George's death . He died at Stratford Place, London, on the third, from internal cancer. He was buried at Glemham near poor Flo. In the same paper was an account of Ada Pitt's marriage to Mr Horace Mann at Maidstone. It was a very brilliant affair: the Archbishop of Canterbury and half the peerage were present.

*Tuesday 30 July* Mamma had a letter from Mr Kirby with an account of Mabel's death. She died of a tumour. She had had attacks of pain that were all put down to internal neuralgia. I remember the first was when I was with her in Dover in '87. Lately the attacks had been more frequent, but she was able to get about and went to balls etc up to the last. She always looked pale and ill, but no one ever suspected she was dying. She died very peacefully and painlessly.

*Friday 16 August* Mrs Ogden came to see me. She came back on Wednesday and went off again after lunch. She is going to Seabright. After lunch Reggie and Mortie rowed us up the river Passaic as far as Belleville. The scenery is lovely; the banks of the river are well wooded. After I came back I played tennis with Reggie. Choir rehearsal at night.

*Friday 23 August, Seabright, staying with Mrs Ogden* I went down to Seabright today with Mrs Ogden's brother Mr Depue; I met him at the station. It rained all the way down so we could not see much of the scenery, but talked instead. Mr Depue is very nice and says funny things that make one laugh. Mrs Ogden is living in her father's cottage at Seabright; her father and mother are away and she and an older sister and her brother are alone. We arrived in time for dinner, and as I was tired I went to bed soon after.

*Saturday 24 August* After lunch a man named Young came down from Newark to spend Sunday, and we all went for a drive. We drove to Long Beach which is a horrible shoddy place. I never saw such wonderful dresses before; many girls were in ball dresses and all were covered with diamonds and they were all driving in gorgeous carriages. It was like a circus. On the way home we stopped at Huglers and got a lot of bon-bons, such good ones. The horses shied and tried to bolt, but we got home all right and found Mr Depue and a college friend named Jackson, and Mr Ogden and his sister, all come to spend Sunday. We had a jolly dinner party, and afterwards sat on the piazza singing college songs to a guitar.

*Monday 26 August* There was a high tide, so after dinner we took off our evening dresses and I dressed myself in some waterproof things, and the others did the same, and we all went out to see the fun. We got drenched: the sea washed right over us. When we got home we changed all our things again, and as the servants had gone to bed, we all went down to the kitchen, and I made some mulled claret, while the others all waited on me, and fetched and carried. We drank it in the kitchen round the fire, and as there was a very sanctimonious old maid present, a cousin of the Depues', we all pretended to be drunk, and shocked her. Mr Depue was splendid; we were all ill with laughing.

*Tuesday 27 August, Newark* I was up early this morning and went back to Newark. Mr Depue and Mr Jackson went up on the same train. At Perth Amboy Mr Charles Parker got in and I had a little talk with him. At Newark I said goodbye to them all and drove home alone

*Thursday 5 September, Haverstraw, state of New York, staying with Mrs Filer* I went over to see Mrs Ogden and at twelve we started for Haverstraw, Sybil, Fitzroy and I. We had to go to New York and from there to Weehawken, where we got the train. The line goes through pretty wooded country, and after leaving a long tunnel comes out on a glorious view of the Hudson. Mrs Filer met us at Haverstraw with her youngest child. She is a widow with seven children. We had a drive of about two miles to her house which is very high up. The house might be a nice one, but it is over-run by the children, five of whom are boys, and all are spoilt and noisy.

*Monday 9 September* After lunch we went to call on the Wests, a formal ceremonious call, which I loathe. We all sat round in the drawing room with our best manners, and it was too silly. Dear Peg visited the Wests some years ago, and it made me feel more at home to think she had been here.

*Tuesday 10 September, Westmere, Haverstraw, state of New York, staying with the Wests* There was a perfect hurricane today, and in the midst of it Gerald came and drove us over to Westmere, the name of his father's house. It is a very nice place; I took a fancy to it at once. There are four West boys: Gerald and Willie and two small ones, Fernando or Fernie as he is called, and Harry. Fernie has wonderfully good manners for such a small boy. I feel more at home with the Wests than I have done with anyone else; they are so kind, and then our very distant relationship is a bond of union.

*Thursday 12 September* It rained harder than ever, and in spite of the rain I went for a walk with Gerald and got soaked. After lunch we played billiards, looked over some books, and tried some songs, and after dinner whist as usual. The day slipped by very happily; I am enjoying my visit so much.

*Monday 16 September, Newark* We left Haverstraw by an early train. I was awfully sorry to go. Mrs West and Gerald saw us off and I hated saying goodbye. I always have to part from all the nice people I meet.

*Wednesday 25 September* Morton said today that a person would have to know me at least six years before they understood me, or knew all my different moods, as I was so awfully changeable.

*Tuesday 8 October, Edgehill, near Poughkeepsie, New York, staying with the Denslows* Mamma and I left Newark this morning at eight and caught the Albany boat in New York at nine. We went up the Hudson as far as Poughkeepsie to stay with the Denslows. The river scenery was lovely; the maples looked as if they were on fire and the pines make a beautiful dark green contrast.

Mr Denslow met us at Poughkeepsie and drove us out to his place, Edgehill. It is right out of the town, a very pretty place with a good view of the river. The Denslows are quite old people, rather saddened by the deaths of their two children. They are all alone and spend most of their time travelling. They have just been round the world in their yacht, the Coronet.

*Wednesday 9 October, Newark* We had an early lunch and caught the boat back to New York at one o'clock. I sat on deck nearly all the time watching the scenery. We got to New York at five-thirty and to Newark in time for dinner.

*Tuesday 15 October* I dined with the Ogdens this evening and had a very jolly time. Mr Courtland Parker was there. I have not seen him since the spring and he did not seem as nice as he used to be: I think he is rather conceited and blasé , and he put on all sorts of English affectations.

Some cousins of Mrs Shaftoe's named Hanson came today. I did not see them, but they left a parcel from Mrs Duncombe-Shaftoe for me containing two lovely diamond stars and a curious old silver bracelet. The stars are really exquisite and I am in ecstasies over the first really good diamonds I have ever had. Those in the opal ring Peg gave me are small, but the stars are large and like spots of fire.

*Thursday 17 October* Mamma and I went into New York this morning and did some shopping, we then had lunch, and walked to Rutherford Place where the Hansons are staying. We found Miss Hanson at home and liked her extremely. She seems very English to us as she is the first newly-landed English girl we have seen.. She is charmingly pretty with a complexion that will make a sensation in New York this winter. I hope I shall see a good deal of her.

*Sunday 27 October* Mortie went off to New York tonight to live, but he is coming home to spend every Sunday. I am very sorry he is going, I shall miss him, but it is better for him to be in New York where his work is.

*Wednesday 30 October* Last night, about one-thirty, I was aroused by some stones thrown against my window. I was too lazy to get up and see what it was, and thought it might be the branches of the trees blowing against the glass. Ten minutes later I heard a man's step on the stairs, and Mortie rushed into my room. I thought there was something wrong, but he had taken the idea suddenly into his head to sleep out here, and had come out from New York by the last train. I think he does the maddest things of anyone I know. He stayed all day and went back to New York after dinner.

*Monday 4 November* Mr and Mrs Ogden came after dinner and spent the vening with us. Mr Ogden told me that Mr Courtland Parker said I was a very smart girl, which pleased me very much, as it is almost the first pretty speech I have had since I came to Newark.

*Friday 15 November* We went to a reception at the Depues where we were introduced to all Newark. There was a great crowd, all talking at once. Miss Ogden was there of course. Miss Lewis and six other girls, including Frances, were in evening dress; it did look so funny but is the correct thing.

*Tuesday 19 November* I spent the evening with Mrs Ogden, and talked about housekeeping and neighbours etc and all sorts of things. She gave me a lecture on being stiff: she says I am 'stand-offish' and do not meet people half-way, who are inclined to do all they can for me.

*Wednesday 20 November* This afternoon I went with Mrs Ogden to Temperance Hall in Belleville Avenue where the fair was held for the benefit of St James's Church. There was a very good attendance but it was terribly slow for me. Mamma and Sybil came at 7.00 and had supper too, and we all remained until the very end at 11.00. Mr Courtland Parker and his brother Robert were there, and I had long talks with them both. They were both charming, and Courtland a great deal more cordial than he has been to me before. He gave me bon-bons and flowers and a very pretty work-basket, and was altogether very nice. I saw a few people I knew but no one I cared about except the Parkers and the Depues. Sherrard Depue gave me a severe reproof because I complained that some horrid common people came up and spoke to me familiarly. He is horribly republican in his ideas

.

*Saturday 7 December* Mortie came home from New York in time for dinner. Sherrard and Frances Depue came afterwards, and we all went into the kitchen and made toffee. But that proved too slow for us, so we went into the garden and played prisoner's base on the lawn in the moonlight, and made such a noise that a policeman took up a position on the fence. Then we played at soldiers and stormed a fort, which was defended by Mortie and Sherrard. In the melee the fort, which was the garden seat, was completely smashed, but we won. We also played at football, rugby rules. Frances's gown was badly torn and we all got rather muddy, but it was glorious fun.

*Saturday 14 December* It snowed hard all day. At 5.00pm I started out well wrapped up for the station, where I met the Depues and we went together into New York. We met Mortie at the ferry and took the elevated to Forty-ninth Street, where we had dinner at an Italian restaurant. It was a very nice dinner and we had great fun. We were all in the best of spirits, and said such funny things that the servant who was waiting on us had to retire to laugh. We then went to the Bijou Theatre to see the Brass Monkey. I did not think it at all funny, but everyone laughed so I did too. After the theatre we walked to Maillards, where we had the best coffee I have ever tasted, and ices, and then we walked slowly down to the ferry.

*Wednesday 25 December, Christmas Day* We started for a walk with the Depues but on crossing the bridge the river looked so tempting that we went for a row as far as the Erie Bridge. It was as warm as a spring day. After our row we got home in time for a late lunch. We had a family dinner party at 7.00; Mr Sinton and Mr Braddell were the only strangers.

*Friday 27 December* Mrs West wrote this morning and asked Maude and I up to Haverstraw. I shall go next week, I think. It will be delightful going back there again, and I think Maude will enjoy it.

*Saturday 28 December* I went down to the library this afternoon and saw all the papers. On my way I met Mary Ogden. Her husband is ill with *la grippe*, the terrible influenza that has been raging in Europe and has at last come to America. In Paris half the population is laid up with it, and on Xmas day there were 308 deaths in Paris alone.

*Tuesday 31 December* I had a long letter from poor Mr Kirby telling me all about Mabel's death. She was ill ten days, and only at the last they knew she was dying. She did not know it herself as the doctors kept her under the influence of opium to deaden the pain. She died unconscious and painlessly. If she had lived a terrible operation would have been necessary and perhaps invalidism for life. It is so strange and as unreal to me as the first day I heard of her death.

### 1890

*Wednesday 1 January* Frances and Sherrard Depue came this morning and sat for an hour or two, and then we all, including Mr Braddell, went down to the factory where we spent the afternoon. After lunch we played cricket and hide and seek through the factory, making the most fiendish noises and yells. Sherrard drove me round the biggest building in a sort of trolley and nearly upset me, then we had theatricals and sang comic songs until I thought the roof would fall in. We kept up all this noise and frolic until nearly 4.00pm when we were completely exhausted. I could hardly walk home, where we found the Hansons who had been waiting ever since 2.30. They remained for dinner and we had a very jolly evening.

*Saturday 4 January, Westmere, Haverstraw, staying with the Wests* At 2.00pm Maude and I started for Haverstraw. Mamma went with us as far as Jersey City and saw us into our train. At Weekhawken, where we had to change, Gerald met us and made the rest of the journey with us. Mrs West met us at the station and drove us home; it was quite dark so Maude could not see much of the scenery. It was very nice going back to Haverstraw, almost like going home. Willie and a cousin, Miss Johnson, came up by a later train. She seems a very nice girl. After dinner I played a little on the piano and talked a great deal and Maude played games with the little boys. I went to bed very early as I was tired.

*Sunday 12 January* I did not go to church, but instead Gerald and I went for a long walk and climbed to the Lower Tor. The trees were so thick that we did not get much of a view until we got right to the top, and then it burst upon us. It is useless to try and describe a view. It is easy enough to talk about a stretch of river and rolling thickly wooded country, but it conveys nothing.

There was a slight haze that softened the distant hills, the river was like a sheet of glass, with just one white sail reflected in it. Haverstraw lay at our feet like a toy village, the little quaint wooden houses dotted here and there. We were so far above them we could hear no sound. We were out of the world, and I felt a great deal nearer heaven than if I had been in church.

*Monday 20 January, Newark* We got up very early this morning, and after a hurried breakfast rushed off to catch the train. Haverstraw looked very dreary with a thick mist hanging over it, but I was sorry to leave it. We got home at lunch time and found Sybil and Fitzroy down with *la grippe*. All the others were well. There were letters for me from Mortie and Maude Kirby. She is alarmed about her health, as her lungs are so delicate.

*Thursday 30 January* I spent about two hours at the library reading an article in the Encyclopedia Britannica on philosophy. It was very hard and I did not understand a word of it. I wish I had someone to help me in these things. Papa is the only one I can ask, and he always laughs at me or gets angry if he hears I am going in for anything apart from piano-playing or embroidery. He thinks women should read nothing but novels.

*Friday 7 February* Mr Hanson and Mortie came from New York for dinner, and afterwards we all went to the Bachelors' Ball. I danced nearly all the time with George Hanson, and three times with Courtland Parker, also with Mr Charlie Parker and the eldest brother Wayne, whom I like so much.

*Sunday 9 February* I went to St James's this morning and sang in the choir as usual. I saw Mr Court Parker and had a short talk with him after service. Mortie and I went to the Ogdens; we saw Mr Ogden and the new baby was exhibited. It is rather pretty and has very fine features for so young a thing. In the afternoon I read a good deal and played comic songs on the piano for Mortie's benefit; his musical taste is decidedly low.

The Depues came to see us and we discussed Friday's ball. We walked home with them. I am sorry to be fickle, but I really am getting a little tired of Mr Depue; Frances I like as much as ever. I don't know how it is but I always tire of men; I like them immensely at first, but afterwards they bore me.

*Wednesday 12 February* I went to see Miss Tiffany who lives in Belleville Avenue. She was at home and very nice and kind. She is very musical and asked me to go and practise duets with her, which I know I shall enjoy. She had a great deal to say about the Parkers; she has known them all her life and thinks a great deal of them, especially of Courtland Parker. She considers him almost perfect.

*Sunday 16 February* After lunch I went for a short walk with Mortie and then to the Ogdens. Mary was downstairs for the first time, and was holding quite a reception. Mr Courtland Parker was there, and some people named Vanderpoel. Mrs Vanderpoel is Miss Tiffany's sister. Of course the new baby was exhibited; it is rather a pretty baby, but it made a mistake in being a girl.

*Wednesday 19 February* Sybil distinguished herself today by buying a packet of cigarettes and smoking them in the garden in full view of all passers-by on the road. She smoked five before she was discovered by Caroline, who came to me almost in hysterics. I gave Sybil a lecture, but she took it all as a joke and can see nothing out of the way in smoking. She has been practising it for some time past, I believe. She is the strangest girl I ever met: she does such unheard-of things, and she is so amusing and pretty that it is impossible to be angry with her for long. She is certainly the beauty of the family.

*Saturday 1 March* Mr Hanson dined with us and we all went to the theatre to see a play called Mr Barnes in New York; we met the Depues there by appointment. The play was very funny; Mortie and Mr Hanson did all the laughing though. The Depues were unusually silent. These Newark people are so prim and stupid. They are all alike, and every day I feel less inclined to associate with them. As Mortie says, 'only a few years ago the best of them were mere tradespeople, so they have to be very careful of their dignity'.

*Wednesday 5 March* After dinner I went over to the Ogdens to attend a rehearsal of a play Mr Ogden is getting up for the benefit of the church. I am cast for a very good part, and Mortie also has one. I am to be a young girl, Mr Chauncey Parker is to be my lover, and Mr Robert Parker, Mr Ward Campbell, Frances Depue and others are to fill the cast. The play is called Champagne, and I think it will take very well.

*Saturday 8 March* After dinner the Depues came for us, and we went coasting on a hill quite close. It was grand: the hill was like a sheet of ice and we came down in a flash, but it was rather dangerous; we were all upset several times. We then went into the Ogdens' garden where the hill was not so steep. We stayed there nearly an hour and then went into the house, where we found Mary singing love songs to a guitar; such a contrast to us. She was in a gorgeous tea gown, we were in our oldest rags, covered with snow and generally disreputable, but she did not seem to mind. We sat down and had some cake and sang college songs. After a while we migrated to our house, and about eleven the Depues went off and I went to bed, dead tired. It was a glorious night, the air very cold and crisp, and a bright full moon.

*Sunday 9 March* After lunch Mortie and I went down to the Depues and walked up with them to Mary Ogden's, where we had tea. Courtland was at the Ogdens too, and after much trouble I induced him to talk a little. He listens to what one says but hardly ever talks. I do not think he likes me much and I am sorry, for I like him immensely, and he was so nice to me when we first met last June.

*Tuesday 11 March* After dinner I went over to the Ogdens, and Mr Ogden gave me a private rehearsal, and then we all went down to the Giffords together, and had a rehearsal of the whole cast. It was dreadfully stupid, no one knows their lines, and no one can act a bit. I never saw such stupid people. I am as bad or worse than any. I can make nothing of my part, and between us all we nearly drove Mr Courtland Parker mad. He is stage manager. He acted with me again as Mr Chauncey Parker was as usual absent, and has only been to one rehearsal. They say I am not animated enough but how can I be, surrounded as I am by such a chilly crowd. I never saw such stiff cold people, they freeze me up. Mr Court Parker looks at me as if I was an infectious illness.

*Tuesday 18 March* At night I went to a rehearsal at the Parkers. I thought it went very badly but the others were very much pleased, so I evidently know nothing about it. It was very amusing as we talked and laughed; by degrees I am becoming more intimate with these people. The Parkers will bear knowing, but the others I am afraid are hopeless. Chauncey Parker is very nice, but his brother Courtland is the nicest of all.

*Sunday 23 March* A full account of our cast in the forthcoming play was published in today's paper. Frances Depue gave me the first words of praise I have had: she said that the cast all thought I did my part well. They have a strange way of showing their approval, for each individual finds constant fault with me, and Mr Court Parker always has a contemptuous look on his face when I rehearse that is far more expressive than words.

*Friday 4 April* After dinner I went to a choir rehearsal; we had a very long exhausting practice of two hours and a half. We sang all the Easter music, anthems, chants and lots of hymns. Mr Court Parker was present and helped very much. He sings bass but Miss Tiffany says his voice is really a very sweet tenor.

*Saturday 5 April* At night we went to a rehearsal at Library Hall. It is rather a nice little theatre, with quite a large stage. We got on much better than usual; Sherrard Depue, Mrs Gifford and Mr Charles Parker made an audience. I do wish I was acting with people I knew better. It is so hard to do anything with a crowd of strangers, and it makes me feel so horribly nervous and self-conscious.

*Sunday 6 April, Easter Day* This was a lovely Easter Sunday. It was gloriously fine and warm, and everyone turned out to go to church. There was a tremendous show of new bonnets, and I never saw such an extraordinary variety of hideous artificial flowers before. At St James's we had the music we have been practising for so long, the whole choir including Mr Court Parker were present, sixteen voices in all. We got through the programme without a hitch, thanks to Miss Tiffany's careful drilling. I remained for the sacrament, and Sybil also for the first time.

Mr Court Parker walked home with me. He was very nice, as he always is when one is alone with him; it is when other people are about that he is so chilling and distant. I like him so much, and think he is one of the best men I ever met.

*Tuesday 8 April* At night Mortie and I went to a rehearsal at the Hall and for once the entire cast was present, and the play went better than it has ever done before. Everyone was in a good temper and seemed to really enjoy it. Miss Campbell, the girl Mr Court Parker is said to be engaged to, was present. She seems rather nice, but not nice enough for him. She and Mary Ogden and her husband made our audience. Mr Ogden told me I did very well, and I really think I did, better than usual, but I loathe my part. I have to make love to Chauncey Parker, and it is so silly.

*Thursday 10 April* At night we went to the last rehearsal; Mamma and Fitzroy went down to the Hall with me. We had quite a large audience, who were very critical as they were all the relations of the cast. Everyone told me I did very well and seemed surprised at it, as I have done so badly at the former rehearsals. I had a long talk with Mr Court Parker and he said I did well, which pleased me, for I know he never says things he does not mean.

Mr Chauncey Parker electrified me by asking me if I was not engaged to George Hanson, and would hardly believe me when I declared I was not. I am sorry such a report should have got about.

I had a letter from Maude Kirby today with a description of her fiancé: he is tall, an Oxonian and - a doctor, which I am horrified at. I hardly look upon doctors as gentlemen, and with a few exceptions, they never go into good society.

*Friday 11 April* After lunch we went to see Frances Depue and Agnes Gifford; both were getting ready for the theatricals, although it was only four in the afternoon. I began to dress at 5.30 and was down at the Hall by 7.30. I went straight to the dressing-room and waited for Frances and Agnes, and then we all admired each other. Agnes looked lovely; Frances wore black and red, her hair beautifully arranged, and lots of diamonds. We all three had our hair powdered and we were painted within an inch of our lives.

The theatre filled up very quickly and at 8.10 we commenced. The first play was Book the Third, with Mr Court Parker, Mr Ogden, and Miss Ogden, who looked lovely in pink silk and was as good as a professional. It was very well received with thunders of applause. It took an hour to act.

Then our play, Champagne, came on. There are fifteen characters in it, twelve men and three girls. It is supposed to be a comedy but it is not very funny. The two Parkers did very well: Robert was my father and Chauncey my fiancé. Frances Depue was my mother, and she did very well, better than any except Mr Frank Gifford, who took the title role of Champagne, a comic servant. I don't think I ever felt cooler or more composed in my life. I did not miss any of my lines, and was not nervous for an instant, even when I was all alone on the stage.

I enjoyed it immensely and was awfully sorry when the curtain fell. Frances was the star, but I had a lot of compliments too, and they all said I did better than expected. Mr Court Parker was invaluable, stage-managing and seeing that we were all in our proper places. Without him we would never have done so well. Everything he does is well done. Mr Hanson gave me a bouquet of roses, which I carried in the second act, and at the end Mr Court Parker gave me a lovely basket of roses that I was very much pleased with; it was so nice of him to think of me.

After the play was over our special friends came crowding on to the stage to congratulate us. Sherrard Depue came on between the acts and made me some very pretty compliments. I do love getting compliments, and I do think that sometimes people mean them. Mr Court Parker said some charming things to me, and I know he is too truthful to tell a story for the sake of flattering one. Frances Depue said I looked like a picture by Lely. It is horrid of me to write all this down, but really it pleased me so much that I must.

It was a lovely night as we walked home from the Parkers and sat up until past 2.00am talking it all over. I was too excited to go to bed.

*Saturday 19 April* Mortie and I went to the Depues and spent the evening with Frances, who amused us by telling our characters and fortunes by palmistry. She told me I was nervous, emotional, fickle, obstinate and greedy, also that I should have a very eventful life, would be married twice and was very susceptible. On the whole I think her estimate of my character is a perfectly true one. I forgot to add that she also said I was snobbish and vindictive.

*Tuesday 22 April* I went to a dance at Mrs Rowland Keasby's, Mary Ogden chaperoned me. There was a great crowd, most of them strangers. The Parkers were there, but Chauncey was the only one I spoke to. I think Mr Court Parker is offended with me for some reason, for he never came near me, and I wanted to speak to him very much.

*Monday 28 April* It was a glorious day and I spent the greater part of it in the garden. It is horrid of me to be unhappy and discontented in Newark as long as we have this delightful garden. I really ought to be happy.

*Thursday 15 May* I went to see Mrs Hitchcock, and to my surprise I liked her. I disliked her when I first met her, and have allowed myself to dislike her ever since, although I knew nothing against her. It was merely the prejudice of a first unfavourable impression. I wonder if I shall ever get over the folly of judging people by a first interview. I have made such astounding mistakes: I thought Mr Court Parker fast and rather impertinent when I first saw him. I now know that I was utterly mistaken and that he is one of the best of men.

*Sunday 18 May* Mary Ogden came over for tea, and we walked round and round the lawn and had a long talk, or rather she gave me a long lecture. She was very kind and sweet, and told me I must make some advances towards the various people I have met. She does not seem to understand how hard it is to make friends with all these strangers. When I talk to any of the people here I feel as if a thick wall of ice rose up between us, effectually shutting me out, and all the time I am so shy and nervous that I hardly know what I am saying. It is horrid and it gets worse every day.

*Wednesday 11 June* At night I went with the Ogdens to the Foster Home, where there was an entertainment in aid of the funds of the Home. Nearly everyone I knew in Newark was there, and I talked to them all and found it very amusing. At eight the operetta L'Africaine began. It was all the wildest burlesque and really very funny. Mr Court Parker was dressed as an Indian and looked simply diabolical; I did not think such a dignified man as he is could look so awful. I have always admired him very much, but after this exhibition tonight I shall not like him half as much. He certainly did it very well and his voice is beautiful.

*Sunday 15 June* After Sunday school I walked home with Agnes Giffard; I have not seen her since our theatricals. She does not strike me as being very interesting, but then I think you have to know a person very well to be interested in them. There are three stages of a friendship: the first, when you think you are going to like the person in question very much; the second, when you begin to discover his or her faults and are so disillusioned that you hate him or her; and the third, when you learn to forgive the faults and discover the virtues, and when you reach the third stage you are safe to become intimate friends.

*Tuesday 24 June* This was a glorious day. Frances Depue came to play tennis, and after she left I played with Morton until dusk. The garden was beautiful today. The lawn has been enlarged and lots of flowers are in full bloom. I think we are so lucky to have such a pretty place.

*Thursday 3 July* Mary Ogden wrote and asked me to visit her at Milford on Monday, and Mrs West wrote and asked me to go to Haverstraw on Monday too. I shall go to Haverstraw I think, and to Milford afterwards, if Mary will have me.

*Friday 4 July* Sherrard Depue came up after breakfast, and actually inveigled us into celebrating the Fourth by setting off a lot of crackers in the garden. We also fired a little cannon of Morton's, but the best fun of all was in a little mine we dug. We put nearly half a pound of gunpowder in it and covered it with large stones. When it exploded it sent the stones about twenty feet into the air. When we had used up all the gunpowder and crackers we played cricket, although the grass was very wet and a slight rain was falling.

*Monday 7 July, Westmere, Haverstraw, staying with the Wests* Maude and I went up to Haverstraw today to visit the Wests. It was very hot travelling. The country looks beautifully green and fresh, and we found all the Wests well.

*Wednesday 9 July* I spent the greater part of the morning lying in a hammock while Gerald read poetry to me. After lunch it was too hot to do anything much, so I only played a little on the piano. In the evening when it was cooler we drove down to the village. The horses were fresh and jumped about a good deal, but Gerald drives well and kept them in hand.

*Sunday 13 July* It rained hard all the a.m. but cleared after dinner, when Gerald and I went for a walk through the woods and had a long interesting talk. I like talking to him so much: whatever he says is worth listening to. We talked about ourselves nearly all the time. He thinks I am very much changed since he first knew me, that I have lost many of my British prejudices and am more liberal, but I don't think I am.

*Tuesday 15 July, Newark* We left Haverstraw by a late train. We had a long journey, reaching Newark at 9.00pm.

Morton has gone to Boston to look after an appointment he has been offered been offered. I hope he will get it, although I will miss him rather, but I think he is better away from home. He is so imperious and dictatorial that he does not get on with any of us very well.

*Saturday 19 July, Milford, Pennsylvania, staying with Mary Ogden* I came up to Milford today, and now I am in the wilds of Pennsylvania. I left the train at Port Lewis, a place on the Delaware river. There were stages to meet the train and I took one for Milford. There were a lot of other people in it, and among them a very affable young man who talked a great deal, and when we stopped at a half-way house to water the horses offered me something to drink.

At night Mary and I went to see some friends of hers who are staying at one of the hotels here, and we also walked through the village. There are no small poor houses in it; they are all villas, and look as if they were all packed up and put away in a box when the season is over.

*Tuesday 29 July* After dinner we went for a long walk up a lovely lane, one of the prettiest walks we have yet taken. I shall be very glad to get home again, but I am a little sorry to leave this lovely place. We are all going back together on Thursday.

*Thursday 31 July, Newark* We all left Milford together at 2.30pm and drove to Port Lewis in the stage. We all got on the train and enjoyed the first part of the journey, but after a while the heat was too much for us, and about six o'clock we got dreadfully tired. We had to change at Paterson and wait an hour for our train, and finally reached Newark at eight o'clock.

*Sunday 10 August* Today for the first time I began to see some silver lining in the cloud that brought us to America, at least as far as I am concerned. If I had remained in London I would never have read or practised half as much as I do here, for I would not have had time, but now that I am among strangers and thrown entirely on my own resources I can learn far more than I would ever have done in dear old London, where I always had so much to do. I shall begin to look upon my life in America as a sort of schooling, and my return to England will be my great holiday.

*Wednesday 20 August* Papa, Mamma and I went down to Staten Island today to see Miss Edsall's marriage to George Hanson's friend Mr Willis. It was such a rainy morning that I could not wear a lovely pink muslin gown that I had got on purpose. We had to go to New York and from there took the boat to Staten Island where we found a special carriage in the train waiting for us. We went to Fort Wadsworth and from there drove to the church at Rosebank.

The church was beautifully decorated with flowers, and we had not been seated long when the wedding party came. There were no bridesmaids so Miss Edsall was all more effective in her white gown. She was very simply dressed in the usual white satin, with a very long train and yards and yards of white tulle veil. She had some lovely diamond butterflies.

After it was all over we all drove to Miss Edsall's sister's house, Clifton Towers. The sister is married to a Mr Alexander, an immensely wealthy man, and their house is lovely. I had a long talk to Mr Willis. I think he was glad to have us there for we were the only English friends of his present. We spent some time looking at the presents, and were then introduced to dozens of the guests.

We had lunch at one o'clock and then lounged about till three, waiting for the bride to change her wedding gown. There was great excitement when she at last appeared. She looked very sweet in a grey travelling gown. She was very nice to me and invited me to visit her when she returns from her wedding trip.

*Thursday 21 August* I went down to Perth Amboy this morning to see Miss Parker's wedding. A lot of people went down in the same train with me, Mr Ogden among them. We reached the church in very good time. Chauncey Parker met me at the door and put me in a pew with Miss Dodd which was very nice. The bride was very punctual, and by the time she arrived the church was quite full. There were six bridesmaids, all little girl nieces of Miss Parker's; they were in white and pink. Miss Parker looked charming in the usual white, with a large diamond star in her hair, and a sapphire necklace that I think rather spoilt the effect.

I walked to the house with Miss Dodd and Chauncey Parker. Mr Court Parker met me at the door and took me right to the bride who was very sweet to me and kissed me. She looked radiant, so happy and self-possessed. Her husband Mr Parkman is not at all handsome, but seems very nice. I had a very nice talk with Mrs Parker and dozens of others, including Wayne Parker, who as usual told me I was an American. I made a great mistake telling these people I was born in the USA.

I talked to everyone but the one I most wanted to see, and that was Mr Court Parker. He came up several times to see if he could do anything for me, but was as monosyllabic as ever. I wonder if I shall ever get him to talk to me as unconstrainedly as he did the first time I met him. I can't imagine what I have done to offend him and wish it could be cleared up.

*Monday 8 September* Frances Depue came to see me today. She came back to town last Thursday and her parents arrived from Europe on Friday. While they were in London they met some people who told them all about us, and gave them a very liberal dose of all our 'titled relations', as Frances called them.

*Thursday 25 September* I met Frances Depue in the library. She always amuses me so much when I am alone with her. She thinks I am clever in a literary way, and she tries to talk up to what she imagines to be my standard. It is very odd, but Frances, who is a good judge of character, thinks I have no heart at all but a great deal of brain; of course people never know themselves, but it seems to me it is just the other way round. I believe I have more heart than most people but I have never had a chance to show it. We are not a demonstrative family, and it must appear to outsiders as if there wasn't an ounce of affection among us.

*Saturday 27 September* I spent an hour or two at the library reading the papers. I got the life of George Sand for myself, and some of Miss Alcott's books for the children. I was very much interested in George Eliot's life, and think what a lucky thing it was she met George Lewes: without his advice she would never have become an author and their union was such an ideal one.

I have been thinking a great deal about it and have made up an ideal husband for myself. He must be willing to listen to all my ideas and not to laugh at me if I try to write them down. My head is so full of thoughts that I am sure I could write if someone would only help me, and not make fun of me. He must love music, especially Chopin's nocturnes, and he must love to listen to me play. I am never so happy as when playing Chopin to someone who enjoys it. And finally, he must be very clever. At present I don't know any such man, and I doubt if I ever will.

*Sunday 28 September* I went to church this morning and sang in the choir. It was very trying, I sat between a soprano who sang false and a tenor who shouted, and I found it impossible to sing at all. Mr Durrand gave us a very good sermon on judging our neighbours, and condemned unjust criticisms. I do wish I could give up saying sharp things about people.

*Thursday 2 October* I went to choir rehearsal after dinner. I have not been for a long time so I rather enjoyed it, although it seems rather unreal. I never feel quite myself when I am singing in a choir or teaching in Sunday schools. I think  that when people change all their surroundings and assocciations they must in time change their characters as well. I have no doubt that that transformation is taking place in me now, and that is why I am so unsettled and depressed. I wonder what sort of person I shall be when the change is complete.

*Sunday 12 October* I lunched with the Depues. Frances's parents are away so we had things to ourselves. We had a long talk after lunch, about books as usual, and also gossip. Frances told me that my engagement to Mr Court Parker was announced. This canard has been started by the Ballantines and makes the fifth man the Newark people have engaged me to. Frances told me lots of nice things different people said about me, which was delightful. She also said I was looking prettier than ever which was more delightful still, as lately I have fancied I was getting rather ugly. I don't want to go off just yet.

*Sunday 19 October* Frances Depue came and I went for a short walk with her. She does not look at all well, but she takes so much medicine it would be strange if she did feel well. I think medicine-taking is the great vice of the American people, as Maude says 'they eat pills by the teaspoonfull, ordering several hundred at a time, and drink tonics etc as we do wine'. It must ruin their digestions. At home in England I never thought about such things, but I am now proud of not being able to remember when I last had any medicine and I am certain I have not taken more than three pills in all my twenty-four years.

*Sunday 26 October* After lunch I went for a walk with Frances Depue. We walked round and round the Park until it got dusk, talking and saying horrid spiteful things about everyone. How I do wish I could control my tongue better. I don't mean half the things I say, they slip out almost without my knowledge. I met Mr Court Parker and did my best to bow pleasantly to him, but ended up being as stiff as ever. He must think I hate him, but I can't control my smiles any better then my tongue.

*Monday 27 October* I met Frances Depue in the reading-room and went with her to her house, where I saw her mother, who is ailing as usual, this time from the effects of a heavy supper the previous night. Oh! have no pity for people who makes themselves ill by injudicious feeding. Frances was very sweet and amiable; she is nicer every time I see her, I really believe I am beginning to like her. After lunch she came to ask me if I would help at a fair to be given in the rink next week. I am to wear a Spanish dress which is rather a bore, but I think the fair will be amusing. .

*Wednesday 5 November* Frances Depue was there [at the fair] and all the others, so it was very jolly. We had not very many customers but hope to do better tomorrow night. We danced a little and managed to have a very jolly time and I got really excited and felt young again for the first time for months. I think a judicious course of excitement would make me quite juvenile again.

*Friday 7 November* This was the last day of the fair. I spent the whole afternoon there with the Kinneys and Mrs Campbell Clarke. In the evening we had the same lot with the addition of Frances Depue and Mary and a lot of out-of-town men. Mr Wayne Parker and his wife were there; I had a very long talk with him in which we compared English and American society, as we always do. I like to hear him talk, he throws so many new lights on familiar customs, and sometimes I almost see ourselves as others see us. I also had a talk with his wife. I had never spoken to her before and was surprised to find how nice she is. The more I see of the Parkers, the more I like them. I talked to Mr Will Jackson and liked him too; everyone seems nicer nowadays, perhaps it is because I am growing nicer. Mary Ogden says I am very much softened. I certainly don't hate people now as I did when I first came to Newark.

*Sunday 9 November* After lunch I started to go to the library, but half-way met Agnes Giffard who made me turn and walk back with her as far as St James's, where she was going for Sunday school. A little farther on I met Frances Depue, who turned and walked a little way with me. In Broad St I met Mr Court Parker, who came up to me and shook hands and was as cordial as on the first day I met him. He has evidently forgiven me, and I am so glad, although I don't know how I could have offended him.

*Tuesday 25 November* Miss Griffith came to see me. I think she is a very nice girl, but the people here in Newark seem to think she is not good enough to know, and why, I can't imagine. She is lady-like and refined and knows people in England who belong to *our* set. I intend to cultivate her, whether the people here do or do not.

*Tuesday 16 December* I went to a tea at the Whiteheads that I enjoyed very much, for I had Chauncey and Court Parker to talk to nearly all the time. The latter has just got back from Washington, and says he is all right again. He looks very well and is nicer than ever.

Chauncey Parker gave me a long lecture and told me I must be more worldly, and put my overweening pride in my pocket. He also said I was very ingenuous, and talked to me all the time about myself, which was delightful, and made me like him more than ever. Certainly the Parkers are a charming family

*Wednesday 17 December* I had a letter from Edith Richards today, the first for a whole year. It was all about herself. She spent the season in London, was presented, rode every day in the Row, and had a very good time. She said she has just been to see Madame Patti at Craig-y-nas, and found her rather disagreeable, putting on the airs of a grande dame.

*Friday 19 December* I went to the book club this morning. It met at Mrs Guy Edwards' and the only members present were Mrs Hitchcock, Mrs Lewis, her sister and myself. We were to have read Spenser, but were all too frivolous and instead we talked scandal. I heard one very good story of a man who came here to visit some relations; they asked him what he thought of Newark society, and he said 'it was his idea of hell'. I should like to meet that man.

*Saturday 20 December* I went to a tea at Mary Ogden's. Chauncey Parker was there and talked to me nearly all the time. Mr Court Parker was there too. He came to speak to me, but Frances Depue was sitting beside me and said something rude to him, so he went off.

*Sunday 21 December* Nellie Parker came to tea with me and talked and amused me very much. I like her, she is so unaffected, and seems very sincere and honest. She gives a sad account of Court Parker. He is in the lowest of spirits and nothing seems to cheer him. At night she hears him pacing up and down his room, never resting, so absent-minded that he never seems to know what is going on, and often not answering when spoken to. Oh how I wish I could do something for him, but what is the use of wishing: a girl is tied hand and foot and can do *nothing*.

*Thursday 25 December, Christmas Day* At five o'clock we went to a Xmas tree at the Ogdens. Miss Tiffany was there, and we got some presents: Mary gave me a photograph frame, and Frances a silver and turquoise pin. At seven we had the usual Xmas dinner. Mr Braddell was the only stranger present. Afterwards I went to a dance at the Whiteheads that I did not enjoy very much. I can't dance with the men here, their steps are so odd and there was no one nice to talk to but Mr E.Durgee. I sat on the stairs with him for about three dances, and he quoted poetry and paid me compliments and was altogether charming.

*Saturday 27 December* Frances Depue came this afternoon and took me for a ride in their sleigh. We went up Mt Prospect and towards Belleville, and had a very jolly drive. It is the first time I have been in a sleigh since I was four years old, and of course I don't remember it.

I went to a tea at Mary Ogden's where I received and had a very nice time. There was a great crowd, most of them people I knew. Papa and Mamma came, also Morton. It was the first tea Papa had ever been to in Newark and he really enjoyed it He took a great fancy to Mrs Roland Keasbey.

### 1891

*Saturday 3 January* I went to see Nellie Parker and chatted with her for a few minutes. I met Morton and Frances Depue together as usual; they are getting themselves well talked about.

*Friday 9 January* I lunched with Mary Ogden and as usual we talked scandal and dress. We talked a great deal of Mr Court Parker, and of his reported engagement to Miss Anderson. He is so intensely melancholy that one can hardly believe he is engaged, but Mary says he is the sort of man who would make himself very unhappy over the thought that he might not be going to be a good husband.

*Monday 12 January* I had a long letter from Alice Eden this morning urging me to go to England at once and stay with her. It has unsettled me very much: it is so hard to know what to do for the best. Mamma wants me to go as she thinks it would be a good thing for me to be among people of our own class again. With the exception of the Parkers there is no one here of our own rank, but I hate the idea of leaving home. The very idea of a change has made me miserable. I don't know my own mind; one day I am pining for England, and the next day feel that under certain circumstances I could spend my whole life happily in Newark.

*Saturday 17 January, Clifton Towers, Staten Island, staying with Mr and Mrs Willis* In the afternoon I went to New York with Mamma. We met the Willis's at South Ferry where she left us, and I went down to Staten Island with them. It was a dreadful day, all the cars were hung with icicles, even horse's manes and tails were frozen.

The Willis garden looked lovely but so cold, and the sea at the end of the lawn looked so grey and dreary. We got to Clifton Towers in time for dinner, and afterwards sat around a big wood fire in the drawing room and talked over all our friends in England. Mrs Willis has never been there but her husband has told her all about them. He was about town in '83, '84 and

'85, and belonged to a very fast set: Lord Grey de Wilton and kindred spirits were his great chums. He knows nearly all my relations, and strangely enough, poor Harry Hastings was his godfather.

*Harry Hastings, the third marquess, eloped with his best friend's fiancée. He subsequently lost a fortune on the turf and drank himself to death. His father had married Mabels' half-aunt, Barbara.*

*Sunday 18 January* Mr Willis and I talk about England all the time, about the schools, especially Eton and Winchester, and the different people we have known. I almost feel I was at home again.

This house is kept so hot that I feel faint; at night my room was so warm that I had to throw the windows wide open, although it was all a mass of ice outside.

*Monday 19 January* After dinner Mr Willis taught me the noble game of poker, which we played until bedtime. I like Mrs Willis very much; it is rather a dangerous experiment to be shut up in the country with a girl one does not know well, but I really think she and I will like each other.

*Tuesday 20 January, New York, staying with Mr and Mrs Slocum* Mrs Willis and I went into New York this a.m. and lunched with her sister Mrs Alexander at 16th Street. Mrs Slocum was there to meet me, and another woman named Cowden. I like Mrs Alexander, she is very fashionable in the New York sense of the word, and very rich, with a lovely house. Everything was overwhelmingly grand and expensive; money here is so much more in evidence than in England. We dined at the Slocums house in 40th Street and slept there instead of going back to Staten Island.

*Wednesday 21 January, Clifton Towers, Staten Island* Mrs Willis and I did a little shopping and then to see Dr McBurney as she feels ill. We had to wait a long time in his consulting room. There was a horrible smell of drugs, and a child who was being operated upon in some way was shrieking all the time. The table was covered with copies of Punch and Life, like all doctors' and dentists' tables. We took the midday boat to Staten Island and arrived at Clifton Towers in time for lunch

*Friday 23 January* This was a glorious day. Mrs Willis was ill in bed the greater part of the day and her husband went to New York, so I was left to my own resources. In the morning I went for a delightful walk. Of course I don't know my way about, so I explored and lost myself, but finally reached the house in time for luncheon. Afterwards Mr Willis came home and took me for a long drive in a conveyance called a buckboard, a very ugly but comfortable sort of cross between a dog-cart and phaeton. We went to the top of a high hill, where we got a glorious view of Sandy Hook, Coney Island, Brooklyn, New York and Elizabeth, and the little villages of Staten Island lying at our feet. We drove home through a filthy little village rejoicing in the name of Tomkinsville!

Mrs Willis got up in time for dinner but went to bed soon after. Mr Willis and I sat up as usual playing cards; I taught him bezique.

*Saturday 24 January* We all breakfasted early this morning and went to New York by the 9.30 boat. We went first to Dr McBurney's on Thirty-eighth Street. Mrs Willis is alarmed about herself and has great faith in this doctor, who is apparently a great swell. There were lots of people and we had to wait our turn; we waited just two and a half hours. I read every paper and book in the room and Mr Willis and I swore.

Finally Mrs Willis emerged from the consulting room and we all three went off to lunch with the Slocums. There were some girls named Willard there to meet us, and we had a very jolly little lunch. Afterwards Mrs Alexander came in looking very gorgeous in blue velvet and black fox; she asked us to a lunch on Tuesday.

From the Slocums we walked down Fifth Avenue, did some shopping, and then found our way to South Ferry, from whence we took the boat back to Staten Island. I was dead tired and did not recover until after dinner and a glass of green chartreuse, which is a capital pick-me-up. Mrs Willis was quite done up and went to bed leaving her husband and myself to play cards until 11.00.

*Sunday 25 January* It snowed hard all night and when we awoke this morning it was about three inches deep. We couldn't go to church; we spent a horribly wicked Sunday. We did not breakfast until past ten, and from then until lunch time read the papers and mixed drinks. I invented a very good one: the ingredients are equal quantities of gin, maraschino and anisette. Mr and Mrs Slocum came to lunch in spite of the weather; we gave them a very good lunch with champagne as a reward.

*Monday 26 January* We spent the afternoon quietly at home, working and talking. Mrs Willis gave me her views on a variety of subjects. I rather distrust people who have views, they so seldom carry them into practice. She thinks I would be happier if I were married. I think so too, provided I married the right man. But alas for married happiness! Directly her husband came home she quarrelled with him about something and retired to her room, leaving Mr Willis and myself to dine alone and spend the evening alone. If I marry I shall try not to quarrel with my husband, especially before strangers.

*Tuesday 27 January* When I came down to breakfast this morning I found the Willis's on as good terms as ever, much to my joy. Mrs Willis and I went up to New York and lunched with Mrs Alexander. We had a very nice lunch and then went to a piano recital at Chickering Hall by Vladimir de Pachman. He played Chopin music entirely, and kept me entranced for an hour and a half. It was rather a relief when it was over, if it had lasted much longer I would have cried or done something equally silly. I can't begin to describe his playing, his touch was exquisite, so soft and clear, and yet strong as only a man's can be. He has less affectation than any pianist I have seen, but all the time he is playing he smiles and talks to himself, as if he enjoyed it more than anyone, which is very attractive.

*Pachman was considered mentally unbalanced and would sometimes appear on stage with two warders*

We went to tea at Mrs Reeve-Merritt's. She is a very pretty woman; she was beautifully dressed in a white gown, embroidered with moonstones and diamonds, and sat in a big carved chair and looked like a picture. I met crowds of new people. We did not stay long at the Merritts as we had to hurry off to a dinner at the Slocums. General and Mrs Slocum from Brooklyn were there. He is a quiet old man who hardly spoke at all, but she is charming. After dinner I played to her, and she sat by the piano and listened in a most flattering way.

   We left early and got back to Staten Island by 10.00pm. The trip down the bay in the ferry boat was enchanting; there was a bright moon and all the lights on shore shone and sparkled like diamonds. I was dead tired and had an awful headache, the result of drinking Benedictine after lunch, sherry at the Merritts, and Créme de Menthe at the Slocums. I deserved to have a head after such a mixture as that.

*Wednesday 28 January, Newark* I went back to Newark today. I was very sorry to leave Clifton Towers; I like the Willis's so much and they have been very kind to me. I got home about 3.00pm, they were all so glad to see me that it was quite a pleasure coming back.

*Thursday 29 January* Mr Wayne Parker told Mamma the other day that he considered me the lightest-hearted girl he ever met, which seems to me a most extraordinary idea of my character, for I am sure no one can be more subject to blues than I am.

*Friday 6 February* I went to the last Bachelors' Cotillion at night with Mary and Mrs Hitchcock and two men from New York, with one of whom (Mr Smythe) I danced the cotillion. It was the nicest dance I have had since I left London; I enjoyed every moment of it. I wore my 'lucky gown', a black one in which I invariably have a good time. It has never failed me and is the prettiest I have. Mr Court Parker was there, and I danced with him and talked to him a little. He looks much better; this is the first dance he has been to this winter. Everyone was very kind to me and I was so happy that I was sorry it was over. We stayed until the very last dance. It seemed quite odd for me to be happy tonight; I could hardly realise it was me.

*Wednesday 11 February* This was Ash Wednesday. I did not go to church until the evening, when I went with Sybil to the House of Prayer. Sybil loves the service there, only she has an odd way of speaking of it. She calls the vestry 'the greenroom', the congregation 'the audience', and the service 'the performance', and she does it quite seriously. I don't think it ever occurs to her that it is not quite a concert.

*Thursday 12 February* We went to see Mrs Depue who is ill, and being dosed by the whole family. They delight in illness in that it gives them a chance of trying all kinds of new medicines. Judge Depue gets wildly excited over a new pill, and Miss Depue is never happier when she is pouring patent tonics down her own or someone's else's throat.

*Saturday 21 February, Clifton Towers, Staten Island* I got to Clifton Towers in time to have some tea and unpack comfortably before dinner. Mrs Willis is much better, and he was very cheery. After dinner I played some of Chopin's nocturnes to them, and Mr Willis played bezique with me until 11.00 p.m.

    The Willis's and I have cemented our friendship by agreeing to call each other by our Christian names: henceforth it will be Gordon and Gertrude.

*Wednesday 25 February* After dinner Gordon and I played bezique and I lost so much that I don't believe I shall have money enough to take me back to Newark. Gertrude went to bed early as usual, she tires herself out by housekeeping and fidgeting about with her servants. I think she is too particular.

*Saturday 28 February, New York, staying with the Slocums* Gertrude and I went to New York by an early train and went straight to the Slocums, where we lunched and talked about dress with Mrs Slocum. It seems to me that women think about nothing but dress and I never thought so much of it before, but I begin to love it now.

After lunch we went to Mrs Alexander's, where we met Mrs Blacque, and where Gordon joined us. We went and did some shopping, into all sorts of shops, it did not bore me at all. Gordon bought me some of my favourite scent, Chypre. Then we went back to the Slocums and dined with them and played cards after dinner. I was desperately tired and went to bed early, but could not sleep. The Slocums live on 40ª Street and I think it must be the noisiest in New York.

*Sunday 1 March* The Willis's took me to lunch with some very nice people named Chapman who live in Lexington Avenue. Mr Chapman is a lawyer and a perfectly charming man; she is also very nice. They are rather Bohemian: she smoked after lunch and talked slang. She has written a play and some books and owned that she couldn't sew, but in spite of all her peculiarities she was nice, and had a dear little boy.

*Monday 2 March, Clifton Towers, Staten Island* We went out immediately after breakfast and did some shopping, and then to Mrs Alexander's, who was almost too busy to breathe. She is off to Florida tomorrow, and was telling her maid how to pack her clothes, and giving dozens of orders at the same time. I went out with her and did some shopping, and went to her house to lunch, to meet Mrs Jack Bloodgood, rather a fast woman. I thought her very bad form: she told coarse stories and talked herself blue in the face. We did some shopping afterwards, and finally took the boat back to Staten Island, both very tired and irritable.

*Wednesday 4 March* We spent the afternoon very quietly working and talking and Gertrude surprised me by telling me she was very fond of me. Of course I knew she liked me, but I never supposed there was any affection in the case, and it does seem so odd. I can't understand anyone being fond of me, for I never feel a spark of affection for anyone. I think Peg and dear Mabel are the only two people I ever really cared for. Gertrude is very sweet and kind, and I feel like a wretch for not having warmer feelings towards her.

*Saturday 7 March* After lunch Gordon went for ride on a beautiful chestnut Mrs Alexander sent down yesterday, and Gertrude and I went for a drive in the pony cart. The little fiend of a pony was as vicious as could be, he kicked as hard as he could, and put his head down and bolted, and I had to pull as hard as I knew how to stop him, my arms ached so I could hardly hold the reins, and I would have had to put my feet on them and try to stop him in that way. Luckily we had a clear road so there was no danger, and we rather enjoyed it. It was so ridiculous to think of that tiny thing having the cheek to deliberately bolt.

*Tuesday 10 March* Gertrude was busy so I took the pony and went for a long drive alone, through the villages and a back road that was nearly up to the axles in mud. The pony went at a gentle walk all the time; nothing would induce him to go faster.

*Wednesday 11 March, Newark* I spent the morning sitting with Gertrude sewing and left Clifton Towers after lunch to go home to Newark. I had a very pleasant journey home, it was a lovely day and Newark looked at its best. I was really glad to get home, it looked very pretty and nice and they were glad to see me.

*Friday 14 March* We heard today that we are to leave this house and perhaps Newark. I do wish I could harden myself so as never to become attached to anyone or anything, for as soon as I begin to like anything, it is taken away. I love this house and feel as if I knew every twig and blade of grass in the dear old garden, and now we have to leave them all. I am so tired of changing and did hope that at last we had settled down, but it seems to me that it is our fate never to settle, but always to be wandering from one place to another. In a month the garden will be at its loveliest, just when we are leaving it. I suppose everything is for the best, but it is very hard to realise it.

*It appears from later comments in her diary that Mabel and her family had moved house (and sometimes country) some twenty times before she was twenty-four.*

*Friday 20 March* This was my twenty-fifth birthday; I am getting very old. The girls say I am an old maid. I spent the day fretting and fuming over a banner I am to embroider for the Sunday school. I had to make the design and found it difficult and tiresome, but I finally managed it. The banner is crimson silk, in the centre is to be a wreath of laurel leaves in natural colours, above it a crown in gold, and beneath it the words Class of Honour in gold. I do hope it will be a success.

*Tuesday 24 March* Mamma looked at a lot of houses today and selected one in an avenue near here, so now we have the prospect of being utterly uncomfortable for some months to come, first of all moving and then settling into a new house, which is always misery. I hate new things and I have so much of it; the others all like moving and changing about.

*Friday 27 March* George Hanson wrote today and offered Papa an appointment in Tacoma, and Papa wrote at once to enquire about it. It will be very strange if we go so far away, and I don't think I shall like it. I wonder if we will ever settle down anywhere.

*Friday 3 April* I went to a dance at the Kinney's tonight. There were a great many more men than girls which made it go off very well. I wore a white gown with a scarlet ribbon across the bodice like an order, and was asked by nearly every man I danced with what order it was.

*Sunday 5 April* Gertrude and Gordon Willis lunched with us and stayed until late in the afternoon, both were very charming. They sail for home on the 18th of next month. Gordon is wildly excited, Gertrude is rather nervous at the prospect of meeting so many strangers.

*Wednesday 15 April* Packing has begun, the carpets are up in every room, and we begin to move into the new house tomorrow; it is like a bad dream. I did hope we were settled in this house but I don't believe we will ever settle anywhere: Mamma is too fond of change.

*Monday 20 April* I went to see the new house today; it is worse than my worst anticipation. It is a horrid modern vulgar villa, built last year I should imagine, and with not the shadow of an old association about it, and to think we have to live a whole year in such a hole. To make things worse, the house we are in has never looked more charming: it is old and seems full of old memories, and the two years we have spent here has made the house seem like our home, and I have grown to love it.

*Saturday 9 May, Staten Island, staying with Gordon and Gertrude Willis* I practised in the afternoon until three o'clock when I took the train for New York, and from there to Staten Island. It was a broiling hot day and the journey was tedious and uncomfortable. Staten Island looks delightfully pretty and spring-like. The Willis's are in their new house but are barely settled. It is a nice house and will be lovely when it is all arranged. Mr and Mrs Edsall, her father and mother, are living with her. I sat on the balcony with Gordon for a long time talking about his trip to England. He and Gertrude sail on Wednesday, and he is very much excited about it.

*Sunday 10 May* After lunch Mrs Slocum came. I was rather amused today by seeing how Mrs Edsall and Gertrude both go for their respective husbands; of course, it is understood in this country that man is an inferior animal, but all the same, I don't see why he should be so constantly jumped upon.

 I think it is a pity that American husbands should be so very submissive. It says a great deal for their chivalry, but it does strike me as being rather weak, and I would prefer a husband who would assert his independence. The women here are spoilt, they are selfish and inconsiderate, and very unreasonable.

*Monday 11 May, Newark* After breakfast I drove Gertrude down to the village where she had countless errands and bills to pay before going away. It was a broiling hot day, very dusty and dirty. We took the little beast of a pony. He walked all the way to the village, no amount of whipping would make him go, but as soon as I turned his head towards home he went off at a gallop, and nearly tore my arms out of their sockets trying to keep him in. He also shied at everything and behaved like a fiend all round. I lunched with Gertrude and took the 3.30 train back to Newark.

*Tuesday 19 May* After dinner I went to a concert given by Miss Tiffany's choral society in the vestry room at St James Church. Mary Ogden sang in it and I ought to have, but I gave my old excuse of a bad throat and got off. I sat beside Mr Court Parker which was not very pleasant as he was cross and rather rude. He evidently dislikes me very much. When I told him I could not sing because of my throat, he said that he 'would have supposed that a person of my originality might have invented a better excuse', which was an unnecessary sneer.

*Wednesday 10 June* Mrs Williams and Mrs Edwards called for me this morning and drove me out to Belleville. It was a perfect morning and the country did look so beautiful, so fresh and cool and clean. I think people in the country are better than town people, they do not have so much to unsettle them. Life in a village in England must be a good preparation for Heaven. I should like to marry my ideal man and go and live in a farmhouse like Mr Poyser's, and make butter and preserve the fruit and look after the chickens. I don't wonder that Marie Antoinette loved the Trianon.

*Monday 22 June* I practised and worked all the morning, and after lunch Maude and I went for a walk and took the dogs. We went to my favourite old Bloomfield road, and walked on until we were almost too tired to get home again. Maude loves the country as much as I do, and we gushed to each other all the way, and built castles in the air consisting of plans for a lovely old farmhouse we would have some day. We stopped at a bridge over a little brook and watched some bare-footed boys playing about. They did look so happy that we longed to take off our shoes etc and paddle about as well. Everything looked so beautiful today, the boys in the brook, an old horse standing under some trees, and cattle lying in the sun.

*Wednesday 8 July* Mr Miller came to call and I had to entertain him. He is the rector of the House of Prayer, the church Sybil goes to, and he came to see her, but immediately she heard that he was in the drawing room she went to bed and sent down word that she had a bad toothache. Of course there was nothing the matter with her, and as soon as he left she got up. The house is overrun with parsons. We all attend different churches and the respective parsons all call, and I nearly always have to entertain them.

*Monday 13 July* I read a book of Kingsley's today called *Prose Idylls*. It was full of lovely descriptions of English scenery, so vivid that I shut my eyes and could see all the places before me, and it did make me so homesick and long more than ever to be back in dear, damp, cool England again. There are lovely places and charming people here, but for English people there is but one place in the world, and that is - England. I remember Cecil Tattersall telling me that long ago and I only half agreed with him then, for in those days I had never been away for long, and did not know what it was to be expatriated. I wonder where Cecil Tattersall is now; I have not seen him for eight years. I hope I shall meet him some day to tell him how true a prophet he was. He told me so many things that have come true, and gave me many warnings that I neglected. He told me never to let people turn my head and make me conceited, and I have let them do both. I am afraid he won't like me when he sees me again. He said that I would not be as nice at twenty-five as I was at seventeen, and he told the truth. I am not nearly as nice as I was. Tonight I feel that I want to go home and marry Cecil and live in that beautiful old place of his near Canterbury. I think it would make me very happy.

*Saturday 1 August, Staten Island, staying with Gordon and Gertrude Willis*
I went to Staten Island by a late train in the afternoon and found Gertrude waiting for me; Gordon was playing tennis. Gertrude was very kind and sweet and made me feel very much at home. At dinner I saw Gordon. He is very blue about coming back to America and completely unsettled.

*Tuesday 4 August* We lunched at the Alexanders today After lunch I talked to Mrs Alexander about books. She has always some hobby, and just now she has a craze for books. We all sat in her room and Mrs La Montaigne told stories, all funny, and all rather broad. The people in this set are all broad and I hate it.

After dinner we girls changed our dinner gowns and put on plain cottons and went off with the men to a place called South Beach, where there are toboggans etc, a sort of miniature Coney Island. The greater number of the shows were closed because the lights had failed, so we went for a long walk on the beach instead of going on the toboggans and things. I walked with Mr Cornfoot and we got on very well. He has a little yacht and he proposed all sorts of excursions in her. After we had walked until we were tired, we went back to the house and talked until we were still more tired. I like Mr Cornfoot.

*Tuesday 11 August* I had a letter from Mamma. She says that Mortie may sail for Spain tomorrow, as Mr Moodey wants him to go there for three years on business connected with the Brush Co. I feel very blue about it. I hoped Morton would come back to Newark, or at any rate be near us. I miss him so much.

*Thursday 13 August* Gertrude and I went up to town early this morning; we went to some offices to find a cook as Gertrude discharged hers yesterday. I have never been to a servants' office before and it was rather amusing. There were disconsolate mistresses sitting in rows waiting for servants to be trotted out, and the servants were the most villainous looking persons I have ever seen. The servant question seems to be a very serious one. I don't believe the coming generation will have any.

*Saturday 15 August* After dinner we went to a servants' ball at Clifton Towers. It was given in the stables, which had been swept out and elaborately decorated with flags. Mrs Alexander had a house party consisting of ourselves and Mrs Lloyd-Aspinall, Mr Blague and some others. We made a little procession into the ball, I leading with Mr Alexander. I don't know why they made me the guest of honour.

We opened the ball with the lancers; I danced with a groom, who knew a great deal more of it than I did. Mrs Alexander danced with the head coachman, her husband with the cook, and Gordon seized a very pretty housemaid. After that came a waltz and then an Irish gig, beautifully danced by only four couples. After that we left them to enjoy themselves, which Gordon said meant unlimited beer and whiskey.

*Thursday 20 August* This was the first anniversary of Gertrude's wedding, and she and Gordon went up to town and dined at Delmonicos. Mr Alvarez came to see me in the afternoon and paid me a great many high-flown compliments. After dinner Mr Cornfoot came and we sat on the piazza in the moonlight until the Willis's came home at midnight. It was a perfect night, a brilliant moon in a cloudless sky, and just one bright star. We talked about many things. Mr Cornfoot is an artist in every sense of the word and goes into raptures over beautiful skies, and I think he loves the sea even better than I do. He is very nice. I wish he were not going back to England so soon. I hate being great friends with people and then losing sight of them.

*Sunday 23 August* We all went to church this morning. Gordon and Gertrude drove but I walked with Mr Cornfoot. It was damp and hot but I enjoyed the walk. The fog turned into heavy rain, but in spite of it Mr Cornfoot came to see me and must have got drenched for his pains. We sat on the piazza sheltered from the rain but where we could smell the cool fresh earthy odours that rose from the meadows all round us. It was rather sad to think we were having our last long talk.

*Thursday 27 August, Newark* I had a very nice letter from Mr Cornfoot this morning, it was a very flattering letter, and as honest and sincere as he is himself. I answered it at once, and sent him a little sketch that I had framed for him.

   A great change threatens us. Papa has just had an excellent offer to go out to Tacoma, and tomorrow he intends to telegraph and accept it conditionally. If he really goes the family is to follow in the spring and I am to go home to England. It seems too good to be true. It will be such a wonderful change and I am sure it will be for the better. I am the only one who can tolerate Newark, and lately even I have grown very tired of it.

*Saturday 29 August* Mr Cornfoot sent me an etching of the yacht Chiquito done by himself, it is very pretty. He sent a nice letter with it. He is rather a surprise: I had no idea he liked me so much.

*Wednesday 9 September* I had a letter from Mr Cornfoot; he sails tomorrow on the Fuerst Bismark and this was his goodbye. I suppose we shall meet again some day. I am very unhappy. Mamma does make it so hard for me, nothing that I do pleases her, and she gets so angry at the slightest thing.

*Tuesday 15 September* Papa decided today to go to Tacoma at the end of October. I don't know when we shall go, most probably next year. What a wandering restless family we are! I wonder if I shall ever settle down; there does not seem much chance of it for a year or two at least

*Friday 18 September* I went out with Mamma immediately after breakfast, househunting. If Papa goes to Tacoma we think of leaving this large house and taking a flat. Mamma loves househunting, and today she was in her element. She loves it as much as I hate it. We must have walked through miles of rooms we looked at so many different houses, some of them very nice, others just the reverse, but we did not decide on any, and finally reached home in time for luncheon utterly exhausted.

*Saturday 19 September* Papa got his marching orders today. He is to start for Tacoma on Wednesday, and I am trying to realise that I may not see him for about two years. He is delighted at going: he loves the West and travelling is his hobby. I sat up until very late poring over maps with Papa, planning his route and finding out exactly where Tacoma is. It is a long way from here, nearly 4,000 miles.

*Tuesday 22 September* A deputation of some of Papa's best men at the factory came to him today and presented him with an address and a really beautiful meerschaum pipe and a stick. It was very touching, they were all so much affected at saying goodbye to him that Papa said it was very moving; his men adore him and many want to follow him out to Tacoma. He is glad to get away from Newark but very sorry to leave his workmen who have all been so faithful to him.

*Wednesday 23 September* We dined at five o'clock and then went with Papa to the station; on our way we called at the Ogdens for him to say goodbye to them. Papa  went by  the  Pennsylvania  railway. We met Mr Braddell at the station and he went as far as Philadelphia with Papa. They went by an express train that does not stop at Newark unless it is signalled; it stopped for Papa and for a second or two there was great bustle and excitement, and then he was gone. Mamma and the two girls cried. I did not. I must be very hard-hearted. I never cry. I am glad Papa has gone: it will do him good, and he will be very happy in Tacoma.

*Saturday 26 September, Westmere, Haverstraw, staying with Mr and Mrs West* I took an afternoon train to Haverstraw. Mrs West met me at Weekhawken and we went on together. Mr West met us at the station and drove us home. Gerald is away in Nova Scotia but Willie is here, and Mrs Walls and her daughter, and a man named Johnson comes tomorrow. The Wests are all very much as they were last time I saw them. I missed Gerald very much.

*Friday 2 October* After lunch Miss Wattles [another guest], Willie and I went for a drive with Garner West. We got home shortly after five and very soon Gerald made his appearance, back from Nova Scotia at last. I was very glad to see him; the house was dull without him.

*Monday 5 October, Newark* I took the 1.48pm train back to Newark. Mr West and Gerald went to the station with me and I said goodbye to all the others at the house. The Wests sail for Europe on the fourteenth, so I am not likely to see them again until we meet in London next year.

*Wednesday 7 October* We went into New York very early this morning and shopped for about three hours. At 2.00pm we met Mr Hanson at Delmonicos and had luncheon, and talked until it was past four. We had so much to say that I thought we would never end, we discussed all our mutual friends in London, New York and Newark, and he told us all about Tacoma. I am afraid we will not like it; it must be a very wild place full of rather a queer set of people.

*Saturday 17 October* Mamma had rather a discouraging letter from Papa; he does not seem to think Tacoma will do for us, and talks of coming back. We will all be very disappointed if he does, as we want to go out there very much.

*Saturday 31 October* I practised for a long time in the morning, and after lunch went to the church and practised on the organ for more than an hour; after that I got the dogs and Sybil and went for a walk to Bloomfield. It was a perfect day, the Indian summer has come. There was a lovely blue haze that hung over everything and softened the bright tints of the foliage, and at sunset made the sun look like a globe of red fire as it sank down behind the blue Orange mountains. The leaves are falling away fast, in many places we were ankle-deep in them and as we walked they rustled and made a noise like the sea. I love walking in dead leaves, they have such a delicious smell.

*Saturday 21 November* Caroline our old maid who has been with us for so many years went away today, and I miss her more than I can say. She was so faithful, and the best friend one can have is a faithful servant. Mamma sent her away as we are going away and could not take her with us. I was very sorry to part from her.

*Saturday 5 December* This afternoon I went with Mamma to a reception at the Ballantines that was a perfect example of *nouveau riche* entertainment. It was quite the most gorgeous affair I have ever been to either in London or New York: everyone was attired in Worth gowns, there were several hundred cut roses and stacks of other flowers, an orchestra, and a collation fit for a ball supper, and all this for an afternoon tea. There was such a crush that it was almost impossible to speak to anyone, the noise drowned ones voice and was so great that the music could only be heard by gusts. I managed to speak to a few people I knew, and shook hands with Chauncey Parker across half-a-dozen dowagers who wouldn't move.

*Tuesday 8 December* I lunched with Mrs Edwards, or Rose as she has asked me to call her, and played with her beautiful baby for a long time, he is a darling. Rose and her mother were both very nice, and I would have enjoyed myself very much if they had not persisted in discussing their servants all the time. Wherever one goes it is the same topic: servants. The topics no well-bred woman should bore her friends with are: servants, her children or her health.

*Thursday 10 December, Staten Island, staying with Gordon and Gertrude Willis* I went down to Staten Island this morning and got to Gertrude in time for lunch. A friend of Gertrude's, Miss Jacob, also arrived in time for lunch, and early in the afternoon Mr Ellen one of Gordon's oldest friends came. He is an Englishman and is out here for a visit. He took Miss Jacob and myself for a drive in the buckboard. There was a lovely orange and scarlet sunset that we saw through the leafless trees; it was a perfect evening with a clear cold air that was delicious for driving.

*Friday 25 December, Christmas Day, Newark* I dined with the Ogdens, they had dinner in the middle of the day on account of the children. I stayed with them until about four o'clock, and then went home and had to eat another Christmas dinner at seven. Turkey and plum pudding rather palled on me today.

*Tuesday 29 December* I had a lot of letters this morning that made me happy for the whole day. There was a lovely card from Morton and letters from Edith Richards, Mrs Lewis and Will. He also sent me a card, he has never forgotten me at Christmas; he and his people are among my most faithful friends. Harold Cornfoot sent me a letter and a beautiful card painted by himself which pleased me very much, for it showed that he had taken some trouble for me. I think I have some of the kindest friends in the world.

### 1892

*Monday 18 January* This was one of the most miserable days I have ever spent. On Saturday Mamma and I had one of our too frequent quarrels. I have no doubt I was greatly to blame, but she was very unjust. I was out all day and saw nothing of her, but today she recurred to it again and nagged so dreadfully that I could hardly control myself, but I am glad to say I did not lose my temper. At dinner there was a dreadful scene. Sybil is also in disgrace, and she was very rude and was ordered away from the table. She went to her room and cried, and then to my horror Mamma cried too, and Fitzroy in sympathy. Reggie was rather upset and I was the only calm one. I am utterly hard-hearted; I did not seem to care in the least, but went on eating, or rather pretending to. I gave everything to the dogs.

*Tuesday 19 January* I spoke to Mamma this morning in the hope that she would make up but she would not answer me, and during the day I only saw her at mealtimes, when she spoke to everyone but me. It is utterly wretched.

*Thursday 28 January* I had a letter from Harold Flower today, such a nice letter. Although I have not seen him for nearly five years he is as faithful to me as ever, and wrote as if we had just seen each other. Seeing him again will be one of my greatest pleasures when I go back to England.

*Tuesday 2 February* Reggie has been ill for some days but of course we did not send for a doctor; we never do. However today he was so much worse that we sent for Dr Underwood, and he pronounced Reggie's case to be a very severe one of influenza. He said nothing about pneumonia but I am afraid of it. Reggie has utterly collapsed as most male creatures do when they are ill, and until the doctor came I was awfully nervous about him.

*Sunday 7 February* I went to Mary Ogden's but had only been there a short time when Mamma sent for me as the doctor had just said that poor Reggie has typhoid fever. It is a dreadful shock, for we all know what typhoid is. I went home and sat with him until 10.00pm when Mamma took my place. He sleeps nearly all the time and is delirious on awakening.

*Friday 12 February* Up at 4.00am again. Reggie is much better. The attack of fever is a very light one, and his good constitution has pulled him through splendidly. He has been ill for more than two weeks now. Of course he is much reduced and very weak, but the fever has left him. He is rather cross which is an unfailing sign of convalescence, and he swore a little because he had to drink so much milk.

*Tuesday 23 February* Reggie was better and sat up for the first time, but only for a short time as he was very weak. His appetite is truly remarkable. There is a constant procession up to his room of steaks, chops, omelettes, bowls of bread and milk and other little trifles, and he drinks about a bottle of port a day.

*Friday 4 March* I played the organ at service this afternoon and had a terrible breakdown in the first hymn. My choir is composed of very raw material, consisting of Sybil and a few others who know nothing of music, only sing by ear, and lose their nerve at once. The first hymn was one they did not know very well, consequently they were all afraid to try it and kept dead silence, while I was pounding away at the organ trying to encourage them, but it was no use, they would *not* sing and the congregation was almost in hysterics. It made me so nervous that I had a wild longing to get up and leave the church.

Morton wrote to tell the sad news of D'Arcy Kirby's [Nassau's] death, but gives no particulars. Mabel was his favourite sister, and I think that her death and his wife's must have changed him very much. Poor D'Arcy, he was one of my oldest friends, and it will seem so strange without him in London.

*Thursday 10 March* I had a letter from dear old Kate Borthwick this morning, the first for over two years. I would like to see her again; she was such a nice girl. I also had a letter from Harold Cornfoot, rather a silly one that I shall not trouble to answer.

*Friday 18 March* At home all day. Six inches of snow fell last night and it is horribly cold. Mamma has decided to leave this house on the first of April. Ever since Reggie had typhoid she has been anxious to get away from it, but moving is even more detestable and I dread it.

*Wednesday 30 March* We went to our new house today and things were in the usual state of chaos. I do think that moving is an invention of the devil, and our movings must be worse than any one else's because we do it in such an erratic way. The house we have moved to is more in the country and has a lovely view of the Orange hills. My room looks towards Orange on one side and New York on the other, the view was really worth moving for.

*Sunday 17 April, Easter Day* I went to see Rose Edwards and then to the church, which was not open, but I got the key and went in and practised. The school children arrived early and the church was soon crowded with them and their parents and friends. I felt horribly nervous when I began to play, then I suddenly calmed down and went through the service without a hitch. I played the Ave Maria from Mozart's twelfth mass for an offertory. The children sang the carols very well, the banner I worked for them last year was presented to the class that had done best.

*Monday 25 April* Papa wrote to say that he has decided to leave Tacoma and go to Boston, where I suppose we will have to join him. It makes my heart ache to think of leaving Newark just when we are beginning to like it, and go among strangers again.

*Tuesday 22 April* Mary Ogden came to see me and was kinder and sweeter than she has ever been before. We talked a great deal about Mr Court Parker, and she stood up for him so well and made such kind excuses for the odd manners and peculiarities that I positively loved her.

*Wednesday 4 May* Papa came back from Tacoma today; it was a great pleasure to see him again. He was looking very well, but of course tired after having spent six days in the train. He will stay with us until Saturday, when he goes to Boston.

*Sunday 8 May* We all went to service at St James's. Afterwards Papa spoke to everyone he knew in the congregation, which was a very limited number: Mr Durand, the Ogdens and Mr Parker. It was so nice going to church with Papa again. We discussed the sermon, and Papa looked up the text in a Greek testament and refuted some of Mr Durand's arguments. In the afternoon he went off to Boston where I expect we will follow him.

*Monday 13 June* I left the Ogdens [where she had spent the night] early and went up to the woods in West Prospect Avenue to help arrange a fair for the benefit of the creche. A lot of tents were dotted in among the trees, and tables etc formed the booths. They hung several hundred paper lanterns up and made the place look very pretty.

*Tuesday 14 June* I went to the fair grounds and found everyone arranging their booths. I made several large bowlfuls of Russian tea and the others cut sandwiches, but a sad fiasco occurred. At 6.00pm it began to grow very dark, the sun went down fiery-red into a bank of dark clouds, and all around were flashes of the most vivid lightning I have ever seen.

We hoped against hope the storm would pass, but it did not The rain suddenly came, and then there was a rush to save all we could. Many of the booths were mere tables with no roofs, and the unfortunate people who owned them had nowhere to put their things. We ourselves rushed about dragging in the rugs etc we had spread on the grass, and we had all to crawl into that little tent: the Hitchcocks, Tilfords, Mr Knapp, Mamma and the girls, the two Gifford boys and myself, twelve in all.

The tent was open at either end and we had to crowd up to keep dry, then it began to leak and the men had to pile up rugs over the leaks, and still the rain came in. It rained harder and harder and we watched as it put out all the lanterns and destroyed the paper ones, but we did not miss their light, the lightning was illumination enough. The thunder crashed and we expected to be struck any minute. The rain became so heavy that the tent caved in and threatened to collapse, and the men had to steady it up as best they could, and we had the additional excitement of wondering how long it would be before we were buried under a load of saturated canvas. This lasted until 10.00pm when the rain paused a little and we made a dash for home. When we emerged from the tent the sight was a sad one, the ground was a vast puddle, and all the lanterns, bunting etc beaten into the mud. The booths were all a wreck.

*Thursday 30 June* I got *The Life & Philosophy of Giordano Bruno*, and shut it up  after I  had read  about two chapters.  I don't know whether my faith is shaky or I am only very impressionable, at all events I have no one to talk over such books with, and they unsettle me so much. And after all religion and faith are about the only things worth living for, and it is a pity to risk losing them, and at times I come very near it. I wish I were an ignorant peasant kneeling in blind faith before a Madonna; anything would be better than these doubts and puzzling questions that are always rising in my mind.

*Giordano Bruno founded the Carthusian order in 1084. The first house was the Grande Chartreuse in the mountains north of Grenoble*

*Monday 11 July, Glenside Park, Summit, New Jersey, staying with Mary Ogden* I went up to Glenside Park today to stay with Mary Ogden. She has a house there and the Depues are with her. I met the judge and Mrs Depue at the Newark station and went up with them. Glenside is in the hills near Summit. I got to Mary's in time for dinner. She and Frances were very sweet and seemed delighted to see me. Glenside is rather a large park and there are about a dozen cottages in it, all occupied for the summer by visitors. One house is reserved as a sort of restaurant where everyone has all their meals, so there is no cooking in any of the houses, which is a great advantage in hot weather.

*Saturday 16 July* A great many people came to spend Sunday at the Park and dinner was very lively. Afterwards there was a dance that I enjoyed so much that I almost forgot that it was cross blue 'me'. There was an Englishman there named Bingham with whom I danced, it was a great treat. I so seldom waltz now as no one can do my step and I can't do theirs.

*Wednesday 20 July, Newark* I got up and breakfasted very early this morning, said goodbye to everyone, and left Glenside. I was sorry to go. Mrs Depue drove me to Fenwood station and I came to Newark by way of Elizabeth, which is quite the worst way of approaching Newark. It did look so ugly and dirty after the country.

I found all well at home, and the dear puppies grown a little and much stiffer than they were. When I went away they were very limp and their legs gave way under them, now they look as if they had been stretched.

*Thursday 26 July* I have at last found a name for my pug puppy; I am going to call him Teddie. We used to call Mortie that in the dear old days at South Kensington. Harry Lewis or Tibbie gave him the name and it stuck to him for a long time. It will remind me of the jolly time we used to have when Mortie and Tibbie were nothing more than wild school boys, and before Harry Lewis spoilt our friendship by falling in love with me.

*Sunday 7 August* Morton has come at last. I was lying down this a.m. and heard a step on the path that I knew at once. I rushed to the window and there he was; he is looking very well. He came into New York last night and stayed at the Brunswick until this morning. We talked all the morning, we had so much to say. He has been at Glemham with Aunt Charlotte and dearest Peg, and he saw Gac and Muriel and the Macgregors and Hansons, and talking to him about them all was almost as good as being back in London. He seemed to bring a breath of British air with him that made us all feel English again. I am afraid some of us are beginning to forget it.

*Monday 8 August* Morton went off this morning to see Frances Depue at Glenside. Last night he gave me a packet of letters written to him by Mabel Kirby and today I read them, and for a moment was carried back to those old days when she and I were so much together. Morton was very fond of her and has many relics of her in his desk, such as dried flowers, a little tulle veil etc. I never thought men kept such sentimental trifles.

*Thursday 11 August* Morton has an appointment that will keep him in Newark, I am glad to say. He began his work today. I don't know yet what it is but it is something to do with electricity.

*Wednesday 24 August* The whole household was depressed and gloomy; Mamma and Sybil were the cause as usual. Dinner was late which made Mamma cross, and if anything goes wrong we all suffer for it, even if none of us are to blame. Tonight Sybil had to bear the brunt of it, incessant nagging and fault-finding, until at last she began to cry at the dinner table, and even then she was not left alone. I feel so sorry for her. We have a miserable home; I wish we were all out of it. We shall never be happy until we all have homes of our own.

*Monday 29 August* The day after tomorrow we move into a flat in Bellwich Avenue for the winter. I will be glad to be settled there but how I do dread the move. We have so many delicate fragile things in the way of china and pictures that a move with us is a very serious thing. Nomads such as we are should be always in light marching order, nothing but necessaries and no impedimenta in the way of ornaments or luxuries.

*Thursday 1 September*  We were very busy all day getting settled in our new house. I think we will like it; the drawing room is pretty and I have a lovely room, so has Morton.

*Saturday 10 September* I had a letter from Edith Richards full of news, the most important of which was that Harry Lewis was engaged to Maude Flower. It is the oddest feeling to realise that a man who once swore that I was the only woman on earth he could ever marry has transferred all his devotion to someone else. I remember him telling me of Maude Flower, how utterly uninteresting and plain she was - that was before I saw her. Afterwards I thought her a very nice girl, and I think she and Harry are exactly suited to one another. The most startling piece of news was that Hal Flower is supposed to be devoted to Miss Mellen. I don't mind Harry's defection, but I do feel sore about Hal. I still have a sneaking fondness for him, and although I can't marry him I don't want him to marry anyone else just yet.

*Saturday 17 September* After lunch I went to a regatta with Morton and Maude. I talked nearly all the time to Mr Franklin Phillips, and Maude listened and afterwards told me I was too clever, and that people would like me better if I pretended to be stupid. She said I snubbed Mr Phillips by letting him see I knew more than he did on every subject that came up. I wonder if I did, I was not conscious of it, I only meant him to see that I was interested in what he was saying. It is a misfortune for a woman to be clever, it makes her so unpopular. A man told Mary Ogden I was so clever he was afraid to speak to me.

*Sunday 18 September* I went to evening service. I do feel so well and happy, I can't understand myself. I don't think I ever felt as I do now before, it is a wonderful feeling and makes me feel as if I owned the world.

*Sunday 25 September* Morton and I went to supper with the Hitchcocks, a miserable farce of trying to enjoy ourselves. They had just had a terrible row, she has threatened to leave him and go back to her mother. She told me all about it, and at supper when we were all together it was hideous trying to talk and behave as if nothing were wrong.

*Sunday 2 October* I took the dogs for a walk - it was a lovely day, clear and bright with a tinge of cold in the air that made one feel strong and untiring as an immortal, and I feel so happy that nothing can depress me, and hopeful and confident about the future. I have not felt like this since I left England. I am at last getting over my utter misery at leaving my dear old home. I feel as if I were seventeen again, and tonight when I looked in the glass I looked the image of a photograph that was taken then.

*Sunday 30 October* Tuesday will be All Saints Day and we celebrated it today, singing all the beautiful All Saints hymns. It is my favourite festival of the whole calendar, and the communion of saints is the most beautiful feature of a beautiful religion. Mr Parker was in church. I spoke to him after service. I had almost hoped I would never see him again, now I am unsettled.

*Saturday 5 November* Mamma went off to Boston to stay with Papa and left me as housekeeper, so after lunch Sybil and I went down town and gave all the orders to the tradespeople. I hated it, especially the butchers. I am sure they thought I was an idiot and palm off all sorts of bad meat on me. I went to choir practice at night, but had to leave early because I suddenly remembered an order for the grocer I had forgotten, and we had to rush home to arrange it before the shop was closed.

*Monday 14 November* At night I went with the Ogdens to hear General Custer's widow lecture on Garrison Life on the Frontier. It was very interesting and she is a charming woman with a very expressive face. It is said she never got over the shock of her husband's massacre by the Indians. She spoke of him a great deal; I rather wondered how she could to a roomful of strange people.

*Monday 21 November, Staten Island, staying with Gordon and Gertrude Willis* Mamma came back from Boston this morning very benefited by the change, but it was a great trial leaving poor Papa there. I went out with her to do some shopping and then took a late train for Staten Island, arriving there in time for dinner. Gertrude is looking very well, much fatter than she was, which is a great improvement. Gordon is well and they are all much more cheery than when I was last here.

*Monday 28 November* We had a very riotous dinner, quite the noisiest I have been at and quite the most risqué things were said. It was altogether a queer sort of spree. We women were all gorgeously dressed. Mrs Alexander had a necklace, tiara, bracelets and innumerable pins of diamonds on a white satin gown, Gertrude in mauve satin, Grace in green ditto, me in grey velvet and silver. I sat between Rene la Montaigne and Mr Jacob, the latter flirted with me so outrageously that I was frightened. I have never been with so fast a set before. I don't like them; they make me feel degraded and vulgar afterwards, but I am afraid that at the time it excites me in an unholy sort of way.

We were rather late in getting to the ball; it was given in an hotel called the Castleton. I danced with the men of our party and all the men who were at our tea yesterday, and sat out some dances with Mr Jacob, and he did his best to make a fool of me but didn't, because when men tell me my eyes are the loveliest etc and that I am so original and hard to understand and interesting and the rest of it, I always remember what Cecil Tattersall told me so long ago, ie 'never to let my head be turned or allow myself to be spoilt by flattery', and take that trash for what it is worth. Sometimes I would like to believe a little of it because it really is awfully nice to know that one is pretty, and I do love people to admire me.

*Sunday 11 December, Newark* I went to supper at the Ashmores but did not enjoy it very much because we were all so depressed about the Hitchcocks. Some time ago she said she would leave her husband if things did not improve, and yesterday she went back to her mother at Cambridge, and they say she will never come back again. She is seriously ill and they seem to think she is dying.

I saw Mr Hitchcock, he was at the Ashmores. He was making a brave show of indifference, but he must feel it dreadfully as he adored Carol. I think she was too hard on him; he was jealous and she provoked him. It is terrible for him to be left alone in that big lovely house, for Carol has taken her boy with her, and left her husband utterly alone.

*Sunday 25 December, Christmas Day* We all gave each other presents this morning for Christmas. I had some very pretty things, and useful ones too. Mr Braddell gave me an umbrella.

After luncheon I went to the Ogdens. The Depues were there and there was a great display of presents. Mary gave me a silver pin for my hair and Frances a photograph frame. I went to church in the afternoon to practise on the organ. We had the usual Xmas dinner, rather duller today than it has been: Morton was dining with Mr Hitchcock and Papa away.

*Friday 30 December* I lunched with Mary Ogden to meet a relation of hers from Perth Amboy, a Miss Paterson, a very nice woman and very good-looking, and an old maid. I wonder why the most attractive women one meets are so often old maids, while such utterly objectionable women marry charming men.

*Saturday 31 December* I did not sit up to see the New Year in but heard the bells when I was half asleep. I used to be sentimental about it, and might be now if I had any encouragement. This last year has been a slight improvement on the first I spent in the States. I am beginning to be a little more reconciled to being away from home, and *all* my thoughts are not centred in England as they used to be; it seems rather disloyal.

## 1893

*Tuesday 10 January* I had a letter from Peg this morning that took me back to Ealing eight years ago, because she told me of Captain Tattersall. I had sent her my photograph and it arrived at Waldershare when he was visiting there. He saw it and Peg wrote and told me *all* he said about it, and about me. I have not seen him since that June day at Ealing in 1885, and it is strange to hear that he remembers me and still admires me. He has been in India with his regiment but has left the service now, and is living at his place in Kent. He was so nice to me and helped to make my first season the happiest I ever spent.

*Thursday 12 January* It snowed steadily all day, there is about two feet of snow on the ground. I grew tired of needlework etc so I ploughed my way through the snow to the Ogdens, and lunched and spent the greater part of the day with Mary. We had a very cosy chat, only she told me something that annoyed me. Frances Depue is making an utter idiot of Morton, meeting him by appointment and writing to him. Her father threatened some time ago to disinherit her unless she gave Morton up, and she is seeing more of him than ever *sub rosa*. I consider Frances to be a thoroughly unprincipled girl, because she does not care for Morton but is only amusing herself.

*Monday 30 January* Maude and I went to Mrs Williams this morning to help make clothes for destitute Italians, of whom there are 16,000 in Newark. The pastor of the Italian mission was also present. He looked like a washed brigand in clerical dress and spoke villainous English; he is a Presbyterian and in his address seemed to glory in the fact that his congregation was made up of converted Catholics. I don't see why one church should enlarge itself at the expense of another.

*Friday 3 February* I went to see Frances Depue and Miss Seely; Frances was unusually charming. Miss Seely gave me a severe rebuke for my snobbishness, or exclusiveness as I like to consider it. From her point of view I am a snob, but she sees no class distinction. I dislike people below me because they are narrow very often and always seem to have unpleasant peculiarities. It is not because they happen to be tradespeople or work for their living that I don't like them, but because they are not congenial nor do they like me. At home in England I never thought of this question because it was never brought up and never would have been, had I been happy enough to remain there.

But here it is so different. Here one has to be a snob to keep dysfunctional people from intruding and I feel so ashamed and sorry that I should ever deserve to be called one. All this discussion arose from a remark I made about the choral club I belong to. The people in it are all belonging to that lower middle class I do so hate; they are well off shopkeepers many of them. They dress twice as well as I do and have every advantage, yet they are vulgar and grate upon me, and I have to be almost rude to them, and Miss Seely thinks I should be friendly with them.

*Saturday 11 March* I had a letter from Gertrude asking me down to Staten Island for a long visit. I think I shall go, I want a change badly.

I went to choir rehearsal; neither the organist nor leader appeared until late and the choir very flatteringly asked me to train them, which I was delighted to do. I am always glad to have a chance of laying down the law.

*Sunday 12 March* I went to morning service and sang in the choir; Mr Parker was in church as usual, under the same roof but as far away from me as if the Atlantic divided us. I wonder if we will ever be friends again, and whose fault it is that things are the way they are.

*Saturday 8 April* I practiced for a long time. I do love my music dearly better than anything else. I would like to go to Germany and study hard for some years. When I sit down at the piano it is like opening a book and going back over my whole life, for everyone I have ever cared for I have played to, and they have all had some favourite tune I have always played to them. When I play these old tunes now, all those dear people come back to me. Nothing in the world is as reminiscent as music; scent of flowers brings back old associations sometimes but music always does. In my music world my friends are all known by the names of their favourite airs.

*Tuesday 2 May* We went to live in a new home today; I don't know whether I like it or not. We have drifted about so much within the past years that it seems as if we would never have a settled home again, and it is a dreadfully tiring sort of feeling. We are such wandering badly regulated sort of people.

*Wednesday 3 May* We were very busy all day arranging the things in our new house. I like it very much, better than any houses we have had in America. It is well arranged and quite large enough to be comfortable. My room is lovely with the branches of two beautiful chestnut trees almost touching two windows and wisteria twined round the third. I am sure we will like this house and be happy here. I feel more settled than I have done since we left England and I do believe in presentiments. It was a dreary day, raining incessantly, but we were too busy to be affected or depressed by it. I had not time to practice.

*Sunday 21 May, Staten Island, staying with Gordon and Gertrude Willis* I missed morning service and went to Staten Island by an early train. It was awfully hot; I was exhausted by the time I reached the Willis's. They have a new house, a larger one than the old one and very nice and pretty; the Slocums are to spend the summer with them.

We spent the afternoon in trying to keep cool on the lawn but it was awfully hot and the mosquitoes were out in thousands. Late in the afternoon we went down to the sands, the whole crowd of us, Gertrude and Grace gorgeously dressed as usual and in the very bright colours that are the fashion now. I never saw such colours before, vivid purples, yellows, greens all mixed up together. One's eyes ache with the glare and everyone wears them.

*Monday 22 May* After lunch Gertrude showed me her new gowns; down here they talk and think of nothing but dress. Certainly her things are lovely, but I get tired of them. In the afternoon we walked down to the sands and sat watching the sea. It looked lovelier than ever today but then every time I see it, it seems more beautiful. I do love the sea. We talked scandal about New York people: apparently they are all bad. Grace says the young drink and the women are utterly immodest and bad, while the men are worse. I think the fast set in New York is worse than in London.

*Thursday 25 May, Newark* I went to see Mary Ogden and dined with them; they go to Glenside for the summer on Saturday. I shall miss Mary very much and I always feel lonely when her dear old house is closed. I have so many happy associations with it: it was the first house in Newark I ever felt at home in, and we have drifted about so much in last few years that it seems more like a home to me than the house I live in. I have had such good times in it. The few pleasant talks I have had with Courtland Parker have been there and on that account alone I would like it.

*Sunday 28 May* I went to morning service at St. James's. After the service I heard that Miss Klemm the organist had resigned. Mr Ogden and Mr Parker are the vestrymen who have charge of the music, and as they seemed to be in difficulty about finding an organist I offered to play for a month or two, and they accepted and asked me to become the regular organist, but I don't quite care about doing that. Mr Ogden and Mr Parker walked home with me.

*Sunday 25 June* I played for morning service, the music went very well. I like being in church, all but the sermon. I thought today during the sermon what a wonderful proof of our civilisation it was that a whole crowd would sit patiently on a hot day and listen to such trash as the sermon was. The remote barbarian ancestors of this congregation would have risen with one accord and slain a man who dared to bore them as poor Mr Durand did today. I don't blame the savages for eating their missionaries.

*Monday 3 July* I went to the library to get a book for Fitzroy. I have made a list of books for him, and am putting him through a course of reading. I am so afraid he will forget he is an Englishman and has actually bought a camera and a quantity of gunpowder to fire off tomorrow: fancy a brother of *mine* celebrating the 4ᵗʰ July; some of our ancestors were killed in the War of Independence, and it is enough to make them turn in their graves.

*Tuesday 4 July* I hardly slept an hour last night because these patriotic Americans began to fire off cannons early yesterday, and kept it up all night. A boy next door has a cannon that burst and hurt him badly, and Fitzroy dropped a light into a box containing cartridges and half a pound of powder; he was not hurt. I went out in the afternoon at the peril of my life for the streets were full of boys throwing crackers in every direction.

*Tuesday 8 August, Westmere, Haverstraw, staying with the Wests* I went up to Haverstraw today by a late afternoon train. It was horribly hot and dusty, and I was glad to get to cool green Westmere. The Wests do not seem to have changed much in the two years that have passed since I last saw them. They are all at home but Gerald, who is at the Exhibition in Chicago. Fannie has grown very much and Willie is improved by his year in Europe; they all as kind and nice as ever.

*Tuesday 15 August* We went to the village as usual, the carriage making a cloud of dust as we went. After lunch we went for a long drive, up hill and down dale, through beautiful country that looks dreadfully dry and dusty. In the evening we played croquet with the Reicks until it grew too dark to see the balls. I don't like croquet, it is so mild and reminds one of meek young curates.

*Friday 18 August* In the morning we went to the village, at least the others went and left me at Mr Gordon Peck's brickyard, where he met me and took me all over the yard, and told me all about brick making. It was very interesting. He took me into the engine room and showed me the engine, which was a beautiful one that I seemed to fully understand after he had explained it. I love machinery, it always seems to be alive. Mr Peck has a railway from the brickyard to the river to carry the bricks to the barges. There is a little engine and he took me to the river and back on it, about two miles. It was great fun. The engine is so small that there was room for only Mr Peck, myself and the engineer, and it bumped along as if it meant to jump the track. Mr Peck was very kind, and showed me everything and explained all I wanted to know.

*Wednesday 23 August* There was great excitement and bustle this morning, cutting sandwiches and packing the luncheon baskets. Half of our party drove to the picnic, which was at a place farther up the river called Tomkin's Cove, a hideous name for a lovely place. Mrs West, Willie and I drove down to the village where we asked Mr Peck to the picnic, and then we took the train to the Cove, and he drove up later.

In the afternoon we went down to the river and fished for crabs. Some of the others went out in a boat and canoes, and some of them bathed, but I caught crabs with a line, and Mr Peck stood by with a net to get them in. It was great fun and I enjoyed it, but like all good things it passed too quickly. At five o'clock we all started for home, some driving, some by train. Mr Peck drove me home with a very fast horse that went at full speed up or down hill.

*Friday 25 August, Newark* We got up at 5.30 this morning as we were going home and wanted to go by the boat that leaves Haverstraw at 7.00am; the trip took three hours and we had a lovely view of the river banks, only it was rather misty. I was sorry to leave Haverstraw. We did not get to Newark until luncheon time, and we were very tired and hot, and Newark was so dusty and stuffy after the country.

*Sunday 3 September* I went to vespers at the Roman Catholic church; it is a long time since I have been in a Catholic church. I love the service, it seems to suit me better than our own. Mamma says that as I don't understand a word of the service she wonders how I can like it, but that is the very reason it appeals to me; it is just as hard to put one's prayers into words as it sometimes is to find expression for one's thoughts, and in a Catholic church I can kneel and listen to the music, and send vague wordless prayers to Heaven that are so vague that they are hardly thoughts, and yet they are as fervent as any words could be. I like the lights and flowers and ritual; I am sure that in Heaven there will be plenty of music and flowers, and why not have a foretaste of it here?

*Saturday 9 September, Glenside, staying with Sydney and Mary Ogden* I went up to Glenside by an early train. I met Agnes Gifford at the station, and we went up together. She has just come back from London and talked of it all the time. We drove to the Park: she is to stay with her sister-in-law, who has a cottage there this summer, and I to Mary Ogden's.

Mary looks better than I ever saw her before, she is very fat and rosy, and looks years younger. The new baby, a son, is a beauty, and very good. We spent the morning wandering about the grounds with Frances [Depue]; she looks very well and is very nice, much nicer than usual; I felt quite fond of her.

*Sunday 10 September* We went for a glorious drive with Mr Ayres, Mary, Frances and I, his horses go like the wind. We went to see the view we saw this a.m. but from another point, and then we went by a lovely road through the woods, the trees meeting overhead and the sun shining through.

*Wednesday 13 September, Staten Island, staying with Gordon and Gertrude Willis* I went down to Staten Island to stay with the Willis's, I got there in time for luncheon. Gertrude had some people to meet me, Mrs Ogden Fowler and Mrs Laurence, both rather nice and very smartly got up. Grace was there, with a dear baby of four weeks.

*Friday 15 September* We spent the evening in addressing invitations for a tea Gertrude intends to give on the 27$^{th}$. She may have to put it off as Mr Alexander is very ill and may not recover.

*Thursday 21 September* We went and called for Nathalie Alexander this morning and went for a walk in the woods. We gathered a lot of ferns and talked and laughed, and poor Nathalie said it was quite a holiday for her as she spends most of her time in her husband's sickroom.

*Friday 22 September, Newark* I left the Willis's today after luncheon. I was very sorry to go and they wanted me to stay, but I promised to get back today for choir rehearsal. I got to Newark in time for dinner, and then went off to the church.

*Wednesday 27 September, Staten Island, staying with Gordon and Gertrude Willis* I got up very early this morning, did some shopping and then caught the 9.00 train for New York, then changed for Staten Island and finally reached the Willis's at 11.30. I found them all very busy getting ready for the tea this afternoon. The house looked very pretty, decorated with golden rod and other autumn flowers.

After luncheon Mrs Edsall and I walked to the woods to get some ferns for the tea-table. We got back in time to get into our smart clothes, and about four o'clock the people began to come. Gertrude had Nathalie, Grace and I to receive, and her mother and Mrs Norman Walker to pour tea and chocolate. There was a great crowd and the usual babble of voices. I enjoyed myself very much and met lots of new people.

*Monday 13 November, Newark* I had a charming letter from Eva Bishop today, but it had the usual effect that all letters from England have, it made me dreadfully homesick and more conscious than ever of what an intolerable misfortune it is to be so far away from all my old friends, and with so faint a prospect of ever getting back among them.

I went out this morning very early and did some shopping. I met two of the Parkers, Court and Wayne. The latter stopped and talked and was charming, Courtland Parker looked crosser than ever.

*Tuesday 12 December* We had a letter from Reggie to say he was coming home on the 21ʳ; I shall be so glad to see him again. I went out in the afternoon and bought a lot of Xmas presents, and now I have provided for the whole family and have only outsiders to think of.

Sybil and I went to a very jolly party at the Wrights. I enjoyed it very much and did not feel a bit shy or dull once. For the first time since I came to Newark I felt at home among the people, everyone was very nice. My only disappointment was in not seeing Court Parker; he was not there. Mrs Keasbey asked me after him, which I thought odd. She told me she never saw him now: he seems to avoid his old friends and never goes anywhere.

*Friday 15 December* Sybil and I went to a tea at the Jacksons, a very small one. I talked to Edward Jackson nearly all the time, he was very interesting. We began with horses and got on to the higher education of women, and also discussed the sort of women men liked, and his ideas were quite different from most men. He likes women who can discuss politics etc, and I don't think men as a rule like that. I remember once saying at a dinner that I did not believe any man was ever much interested in a woman's conversation unless he was in love with her or flirting, and every man at the table agreed with me.

*Monday 25 December, Christmas Day* We all went to the theatre to see a comic opera. On the way we passed a Salvation Army girl, standing in the cold street. We heard her voice, rather an attractive one, and very earnest. Ten minutes later we were in the theatre watching a ballet and listening to a love song, certainly a dramatic contrast. This was a very jolly Xmas, it was so nice having Reggie here.

*Thursday 28 December,* We went to a very jolly dance at the Kinneys. Their house is so pretty and well lighted that everyone looks well in it, plain girls look pretty, and pretty ones beautiful. I met a great many men from New York and they were all very nice, one man especially was charming, an artist named Marble. He was good-looking with the most beautiful hands I ever saw, and he was delightful to talk to, so delightful that I am anxious to meet him again. There were lots of nice people and I enjoyed every moment, and was sorry to come away. I had a lovely gown and knew I looked well, and so did Sybil.

### 1894

*Tuesday 2 January* This was a very stormy day indoors, the angelic (?) Eden temper was in full play, we were all as irritable and cross as we could be, all fighting and hating each other. On days like this I long to go away and never see any of my family again. I think we have the worst tempers of anyone living.

*Saturday 13 January* I went to choir rehearsal after dinner; it was a great effort but Miss Tiffany has an uncanny influence over me, and having promised to go whenever I have nothing else to do, I feel I must. But I am tired of it, and of everything else. Sybil is such a responsibility that I feel weighed down, and wish I could go away and leave everything. I would like someone to look after me for a change, and not feel that I am always the one to plan things. I have no doubt I interfere a great deal; Papa says I am a 'managing woman', his pet aversion.

*Thursday 18 January* Mamma and I spent the afternoon paying calls, the first time I have ever done so with her. Hitherto she has utterly refused to know the people here and has held aloof from them, but now I am glad to say she is thawing a little.

*Thursday 8 February* It seems to me rather silly and useless to keep a journal of such a life as mine, when for weeks at a time the only and daily entry is, 'read, practised, worked, went for a walk'. I don't think I would keep it if I had anyone to talk to intimately: as I have no such friend it acts as a safety-valve when my feelings are too much for me, and I always have the hope that someday someone I care for will read this diary. In that hope I often find myself writing as if I were talking to that beloved and unknown 'someone'.

*Wednesday 21 February* I went out early with Papa this morning, did some shopping, and spent about an hour in reading at the library, and the rest of the day was the same as usual, with no one to talk to but the family. I am not intimate with one member of my family, to Sybil and Maude I have always been too much the 'elder sister' to ever be an associate, and I don't get on with the boys because I am too dictatorial, another disadvantage of having for almost as long as I can remember had more or less charge of them all.

*Monday 12 March* I went out shopping this a.m. and met Court Parker and tried to bow amiably to him and only succeeded in grimacing. Ten minutes later I met a man I don't care a sou for, and he got the sweetest smile with no effort.

*Sunday 18 March* After lunch I went for a walk and met Court Parker, and I actually had the courage to stop and speak to him. I was so nervous that I hardly knew what I said. I only know I talked very fast, and he was very nice, and it was a great pleasure to see him again.

*Tuesday 27 March* In the evening I sang at a little concert Miss Tiffany got up as an entertainment for the choir. It was rather a nice little party. I stayed there until 10.00 pm then I rushed home and dressed and went off to a dance at Oraton Hall. I enjoyed myself very much, and danced until I was exhausted; my partners were all very nice. Court Parker was there, but he left early. I had a lovely white gown and felt at my best.

*Monday 9 April* I went up to the Ogdens; I love their dear old house, for its own account, and for the sake of happy times I have had in it. Mary read a letter to me she had had from Morton, and in it he says he has seen Nellie Fitzgerald again, and he gushes over her for about two pages. I do hope he is not going to marry her.

*Tuesday 17 April* I went out immediately after breakfast and did some shopping. I met Court Parker looking so old and grey, and he gave me the gravest bow I have ever had. He has changed dreadfully since I first saw him.

He was then rather bright-looking and young, and now his face and hair and eyes all seem to be one colour, grey, and he stoops. All the same I admire him as much as ever, nothing can spoil him in my eyes.

*Monday 7 May , Staten Island, staying with Gordon and Gertrude Willis* I went down to Staten Island today. I met Gertrude in New York and went down with her. I had not seen her since her return from Paris; she is looking very well, and so is Gordon. The country is lovely, and it is such bliss to be in it again. I really think I would like to live in Staten Island.

*Thursday 10 May* After lunch [in New York] we went to two shops and chose wallpapers for Gertrude's new house. We went to see the Jeromes and found a whole crowd of people there, so we did not stay long. We drove in the park for a little while, it looks lovely with all the lilacs in blossom, and the trees are all a clean fresh green. We dined at the Alexanders; the house has been partly done up since I was last there. Nathalie's boudoir is oppressively gorgeous, the walls covered with pink silk, and a big plush divan filling one side of the room, pink silk curtains over every door and window, and pink shaded lamps.

*Monday 14 May* I went alone to the pier where I walked up and down for a long time looking at the sea and building castles in the air, castles where Court Parker was always the central figure, that strange unreal Court whom I have created out of my own fancies. I hardly know him in reality, and wonder if he is half as perfect as I fancy. Someday I will write down his character as I have imagined it, and then if I ever know him better it will be interesting how near the truth my intuition was.

*Friday 18 May* I had a letter from Morton that was a tremendous shock: it announced his engagement to a Marie Stuart of Dansville. At first I felt wretchedly unhappy about it, we know nothing of her, but on thinking it over I came to the conclusion that Morton's taste is too good for him to marry any second-rate person. I am awfully sorry, for I think he is too young at twenty-seven. It seems so unreal and impossible that one of our family should ever marry. He has spoken very little about Marie Stuart. He saw her in church at Dansville about two years ago. I believe he wrote to her, and she wrote back and said that if he could get a formal introduction, credentials etc she would be glad to meet him.

Morton asked me to write to Marie Stuart and I did so, but it was a very difficult letter to write, and I made a miserable failure of it. I ought to have told her I would welcome her as a sister, but as I did not feel that at all, I *couldn't* say it. How could I tell a girl I knew nothing of that I wanted her for a sister. Impossible! I do hope I shall like her and that she will like me; if she does not make Morton happy I shall loathe her.

*Tuesday 12 June, Newark* I went out early this morning to do some shopping. I met Court Parker and spoke to him about some of the church music that Miss Tiffany has asked me to see about. He was so rude and ungracious in his manner that I have been wondering all day why I don't hate him. His face was as hard and expressionless as a rock, and yet not altogether expressionless. I hardly know how to describe him: if any other man were as rude to me I would cut him dead, but I forgive anything in Court. It is not lack of pride, for I believe I am the proudest woman living, but I do admire him and can find excuses for all his faults.

*Thursday 14 June* I was at home all day, practising, reading, working. In the afternoon I helped to make some strawberry jam and preserves, it makes me feel like one of our dear old ancestresses, who used to potter about in their stillrooms and make all sorts of conserves and essences. They must have been much happier than we are, they had no advanced education or upsetting views and theories to make them unsettled and discontented; their aims were within their scope, to be what every woman can be: ie good housekeepers, good wives and loving mothers. Surely that is enough to fill any woman's life, and more than enough to make her happy.

*Tuesday 3 July* I went out very early to do my shopping. I saw Court Parker looking so handsome and cool in a very light tweed suit and straw hat. I never saw him look as well. He did not see me; I crossed the street to avoid him because I was hot, and felt untidy and ugly, and did not want him to see me to such disadvantage. What a fool I am about that man. It would not surprise me in the least to hear that he never wasted a thought on me, and yet beside him everyone else is absolutely insignificant as far as I am concerned. I have not a scrap of interest for anyone: it is all concentrated in him.

*Friday 6 July, Glenside, staying with Sydney and Mary Ogden* I went up to Glenside today to stay with the Ogdens. I love Glenside, it is right in the heart of the country, I would like to spend the summer here. Mary met me at the station; she looks blooming. The Depues are up here. Frances looks as if she were dying; I never saw her look as ill before.

*Friday 13 July, Newark* A man named Stuart Edgar drove up from Newark to lunch, and went back with me when I went. He is a cowboy, and very nice, with better manners than anyone I know in Newark. He was so attentive and looked after me so well on the journey, that he reminded me of one of the chivalrous Americans of fiction, and I actually asked him to call, about the third man I have asked since I have been in the country.

Last night Mr Ogden told me there was a vacancy among the aldermen, and that he had a great deal to do with filling it. He suggested Papa, but I did not think he would care about it, and suggested some others, among them Court Parker, but Court was vetoed because he was so 'indifferent and disgusted with the world and mankind'. That remark threw a new light on Court, and made me wonder why he is so changed; everyone discusses him in the same strain.

*Monday 16 July* I had a letter from Mrs West asking Sybil and myself up to Haverstraw, but Mamma does not want us to go. I am very sorry to refuse, I like being with the Wests.

*Tuesday 17 July* I wrote to Mrs West, Morton and Marie Stuart. I am very anxious to meet her; considering what an important part she will probably play in our lives, it is remarkable how little interest we take in her.

Sybil lunched with Mrs Gifford today and came back with the news that my engagement to Court Parker was again rumoured. I can't imagine how such a thing could get about, and it annoys me more than I can say.

*Thursday 19 July* Papa had a letter from dear Peg today, one of those letters that carries me straight back to the old life at home, and makes me forget America and everyone in it. She mentions having seen Cecil Tattersall. He is looking very ill and altered, and I thought of him all day and *longed* to see him again. Of course I have idealised him, but he did make a tremendous impression on me, one that lasted until I met Court Parker, which was years after I had seen Captain Tattersall. Both are so shadowy in a way, for I have so little of them both; it seems strange that the two men who have most impressed me have been the two I have seen least of, and men who as far as I know have never thought twice of me.

*Thursday 2 August* Papa had a letter from Morton; he is going to visit Marie Stuart's people for a fortnight. I do wish I could meet that young woman. I want to know for certain whether I shall like her or not. She has one very bad habit: she does not answer letters very promptly. I wrote to her some weeks ago, and she has taken no notice of it, which is rude.

*Wednesday 15 August* I had a letter from Mrs West. Gerald's marriage [to a Swiss girl] has offended his father very much, and the subject is not to be alluded to. Marie Stuart also wrote, a very nice letter telling me all about herself; she seems to be very jolly and very young. I can't understand why I am not more anxious to see her, but I really feel very little interest in her.

*Friday 24 August* I have been in bed since Monday, ill with dysentery. I got up after lunch today, feeling horribly weak. Morton wrote and astonished us all with the announcement of his marriage. He wrote separate letters to Mamma, Papa and me, all more or less apologetic.

He had been visiting Marie's people, and when the day came to leave Marie drove him to the station where they found it too agonising to part, so they drove to a parson's, got married, and went off together, her people as ignorant of the whole affair as we. I can't altogether believe the affair was quite so impromptu; what an odd girl she must be. I wish they had waited and been married properly with us all present; it seems a pity to do anything under the rose, especially when there was no earthly reason for it. I was deeply disappointed at not being at my brother's wedding, the first in the family too.

Morton and Marie are coming to visit us on the 14th; I am longing to see them. It is extraordinary how quietly we take things: at dinner tonight the subject was hardly mentioned, nor has it been much spoken of at all. I am afraid the truth is in our family we take very little interest in each other's affairs.

*Tuesday 11 September* This was a very long busy day. Morton and his bride are coming on Saturday, and we are making great preparations. We are dying to see Marie and feel rather afraid of her, it will be awful if we don't like her.

*Saturday 15 September* Marie has come at last and we all like her immensely. She and Morton came in time for breakfast, having travelled all night. Marie did not seem at all shy, although it must have been rather a trial meeting us all at once. I felt horribly frightened. She has not at all a pretty face, but a good figure and she is very jolly; we felt as if we had known her for years after a very short time. Morton is very happy, in better spirits than I have ever seen him before. He and Marie are more like an old married pair than a honeymooning couple, which is a great comfort. I would have hated it if they had been sentimental.

Mr Braddell came up from Philadelphia to spend Sunday, and we had a very uproarious evening, singing and laughing, all stiffness gone. Marie is up to any amount of fun, just the wife for Morton, but it is funny to think of him as married.

*Sunday 16 September* I like Marie better every day. I don't quite understand her yet, but I am sure there is a great deal in her. We are very lucky to have such a charming sister-in-law, and I am delighted for Morton's sake.

*Tuesday 18 September* This was a very quiet day. Marie was a little dull because Morton was away, and it rained so fast that we could not go out with her. We sat and worked all day. Morton came back in the evening in boisterous spirits; he is wonderful, he laughs all day. I never saw anyone so happy; how lucky he is. Marie is so sweet, and he is so prosperous, it seems almost dangerous to be so happy.

*Wednesday 19 September, Haverstraw, staying with Mr and Mrs West*          I spent the morning with Marie, and then went up to Haverstraw. I was sorry to leave Morton and Marie, but they leave tomorrow and I promised Mrs West to go today.

*Sunday 23 September* Carrie and Garner West came in the afternoon, also my devoted admirer Mr Gordon Peck, looking very much older than when I last saw him. He came in the afternoon and stayed until past ten. He is a nice man, who thinks of little besides hunting and shooting and managing his big estate.

*Saturday 29 September* Mrs Peck, Gordon Peck's sister-in-law, came to call on me. She is a nice woman, just a little bit vulgar and loud.

I had a letter from Gertrude insisting that I should go to her as soon as possible. I must go, but I am very sorry to cut my visit here short, I am enjoying myself so much.

*Tuesday 2 October* We went to call on Mrs Peck and stayed a very long time, much longer than I cared about. Her house is very nice, and they have a great many good books and pictures and seem to be people of refined tastes. They are a little bit incongruous. I can't exactly make out what set they belong to, but on the whole they are very nice, especially

Gordon Peck. I fancy he gives himself airs, but of course that does not affect me

This is my last day at Haverstraw, and I am horribly blue at going away. I don't want to go to Staten Island, I would rather stay here. I do love the country more and more every day, and yet I don't know if I would consent to settle down in it for the rest of my life. I might on impulse, but I have an idea that I would regret it after a few years.

*Thursday 4 October, Staten Island, staying with Gordon and Gertrude Willis* I was very busy all day. I had so much to do, letters to write, bills to pay and lots of shopping, all my plants to pot and put in a little greenhouse we have arranged. I was afraid to leave them until I came back on account of the frost. Late in the afternoon I went down to Staten Island and got there in time for dinner. I found the Willis's in great confusion as they go to their new house on Monday. Gertrude is fairly well, Mrs Edsall tired out, and her husband dying slowly of consumption. Nathalie Alexander is here for the night. She is in excellent spirits and very slight mourning. Her husband has been dead two months; he has left her very rich.

We were all very jolly at dinner, in spite of all that has happened. Nathalie told fast stories, so did Gertrude; in between the laughing we could hear Mr Edsall coughing upstairs, and I thought of calm, peaceful Haver-straw and contrasted the West's ménage with this. There is a good deal of fascination about Gertrude's set and the life they lead, luxurious, fast and reckless, but I think I like the life at the Wests better, quiet as it is, it is more wholesome.

*Saturday 6 October* In the evening Gertrude went to bed early, Mrs Edsall was up with her husband who hardly ever leaves his room, and Gordon and I were alone, which was very nice. Apart from our mutual liking for each other, we have a tremendous bond in our nationality, and we talk about dear old England always. I have no doubt we both exaggerate our homesickness, but I don't think either of us care at all for America, much as we may like some of the people in it. Gordon likes very few, but I know that I have some *very* good, kind friends here, and for their sake I am not going to abuse America any more.

*Monday 8 October* Today was one of the most hideous I have ever spent: we moved into the new house. Gertrude went away so as to be out of the bustle; Mrs Edsall went to the new house to superintend the arrival of the furniture; Gordon and I stayed behind to superintend its departure. We were all very cross and tired at night, Gordon was the only amiable one.

*Tuesday 9 October* We were awfully busy all day putting the place in order; the servants and people worked splendidly, and by dinner time the house was fairly comfortable. In the midst of the confusion the cook suddenly announced the intention of leaving, and promptly left. No one in the house could cook, so I offered my services and had great fun cooking a very nice little dinner. We telegraphed to New York for another cook, meanwhile I shall do it.

*Saturday 13 October* This was the longest day I have spent for some time. It rained so heavily that I could not go out, Mrs Edsall went to New York and left me with Gertrude ill in bed, very low-spirited, and Mr Edsall creeping about the house with that terrible cough of his, and in a terribly depressed state. He talks constantly about religion, and seems to doubt everything. I don't quite understand him. He knows he will soon die and he does not seem to believe there is any future life, so he lives in fear of impending annihilation. He talks to me about it and I try to comfort him, but I feel so helpless. I am so full of doubts myself that I don't know what to say. I can only tell him that I instinctively believe we shall have another chance in another world.

*Sunday 28 October* After tea I went for a walk with Mr Martin along the sand to the salt marshes, and there we had a view that made me cry out it was so exquisite. It was rather dark, there was a flaming yellow sunset, a glare of gold in a dark misty purple sky, the salt marshes all dark and mysterious-looking in the haze, the trees bare and black against the sky, and right at our feet a pond that reflected the golden sky and seemed to be a patch of the sunset. It was glorious, the most beautiful of all the beautiful views I have seen this lovely day, and I was with a man who gushed over it as much as I did.

*Wednesday 31 October, Newark* I got home in time for luncheon, they were all very glad to see me. I went out after lunch to do some shopping, and spent the rest of the afternoon in unpacking and putting away all my things. It seems odd to be at home again, and it will take some time for me to settle down and get back to the old routines again, but I hope I won't go back into the old groove.

*Wednesday 21 November* I went to New York and lunched with Grace Slocum. Grace looked very pretty in grey silk and the house is more charming than ever. She showed us all her new clothes and we talked scandal, and enjoyed ourselves thoroughly. In the evening I went to hear Father Huntington preach on the renunciation of the world; my mind reels at these extremes. He is a wonderful man, handsome, magnetic, eloquent, I can imagine impressionable young girls, and even level-headed women, falling at his feet and confessing to him, and fancying themselves carried away by religious fervour, while all the time it was merely his charm that held them.

I hope it is not wicked to say this, it was how it struck me. I did not agree with half he said, but he was so terribly in earnest, so handsome, that I longed to believe in him and be led by him. They say he is idolised wherever he goes, and I can understand it, for he has so completely fascinated me that I shall keep out of his way. It is a bad thing to go to church on account of the clergyman.

*Friday 23 November* I went to church at noon to hear Father Huntington, and after service was over I spoke to him, and asked him for the names of books that will help to turn me back to the church again. I told him I had become unsettled by promiscuous reading. He was very kind, and did not appear to be shocked, as I half expected. I think he must be one of the best men living. I don't wonder that people rave about him, and that he is famous everywhere. He has the best manners of any man I have ever met.

*Saturday 24 November* I spent nearly the whole day in church. It was not from religious fervour, it was love of excitement, nothing else to do, and a great admiration for Father Huntington. Poor old Mr Durrand is probably as good a man, but it is irksome to listen to him once a week. Father Huntingdon preaches the same religion, and I could listen to him every day, the difference is in the men. I am not moved by real religious feeling, and I feel as if I were sinning in going to church with such motives. At noon I went to Trinity where he gave a short address, very good.

*Sunday 16 December* I went to Woodside church this morning to hear Father Sergeant who was preaching there. It was a very good sermon, but much as I admire both Father Sergeant and Father Huntington they make me feel that they are narrow, because they almost persuade one that the only way to heaven is through the Episcopal Church, and that is rather a confusing idea.

*Sunday 23 December* Father Huntington preached at Woodside this morning and I went to hear him. It was wonderful, most impressive, because of his earnestness and hope, and the bright view he takes of religion. His face becomes transformed when he preaches, and the expression changes every instant. He is a wonderful man.

Morton and Marie came in the afternoon. They changed their minds at the last moment and came for Xmas. Mr Braddell also came.

*Monday 24 December* Papa and I got up at 5.00am and took the first train into New York to meet Eva Bishop who was coming from Montreal by the night express. We were to meet Eva at the Grand Central, but she was not there. We spent an hour hunting for her, and at last gave it up and came home very disappointed. We had hardly taken off our things when a telegram came for us to say that she had arrived and was waiting for us at the Murray Hill. We went back at once to New York and found her at the hotel. She is very much changed, during her illness her hair was cut, but she is as sweet as ever, and it does seem too good to be true that one of my old friends is here with us.

*Tuesday 25 December, Christmas Day* Eva and I got up early and went to early communion at the House of Prayer, a very ritualistic service, and very pretty, the altar covered with flowers and candles, and the church rather dark. We came home to breakfast, and gave and received all our presents. I had a great many, chiefly books, all nice ones that I wanted. In the afternoon Mary and Frances Depue came to see Marie. It was rather a funny meeting, Marie knows how fond Morton was of Frances, and she was not at all cordial in her manner. Frances was very nervous and talked fast, and Morton sat quietly by and did not say a word. The whole thing was a little comedy, and we were the audience.

*Sunday 30 December* Eva and I went to supper with the Ogdens and had a very good time. It is such a pleasure to me to have Eva here, and to have her meet all my Newark friends. Seeing her again is like taking up my old life again, and it makes the world seem so much smaller, and London so much more get-atable. If a London girl can find her way out to a place like Newark, surely I will some day be able to get back to London.

*Monday 31 December* I had a letter from dearest Peg; her letters make me blue. I always long to see her so after reading one of them. She gave me a lot of news of the family and of Captain Tattersall, who is out of spirits, cynical and looks old. I did not sit up to see the New Year in, this last year has been such a happy one that I did not want to see the last of it.

*1895*

*Saturday 12 January, Staten Island, staying with Gordon and Gertrude Willis* Eva and I went down to Staten Island to stay with the Willis's. I was very glad to go for it was all new to Eva, and Newark is very dull. Eva was delighted with Gertrude and Gordon, and we had a very jolly evening. Gertrude is looking very pretty.

*Wednesday 16 January* In the afternoon we went to a children's party that was great fun, it was at the MacFarlands. There were a great many children, most of them very unattractive, but one or two dear little things. Some of their mothers were with them, they were also unattractive, only more so, but I tried to forget their bodies and believe that each had a beautiful soul, and that all were probably vastly my superiors. It was rather difficult; perhaps in time I shall learn to be humble.

*Saturday 19 January* Arthur Blake, a great friend of Gordon's, came to stay until Monday. I met him once before, he is very nice, good-looking, clean, and plays and sings. The Walkers dined with us and we had a dinner party of ten. After dinner Gordon and Arthur Blake sang comic songs, one funnier than the other, and imitated concert and operatic singers; we laughed ourselves tired. It was a very jolly party; so many of us were English, which made it very homelike and like old times.

*Tuesday 22 January* I had a long sad letter from Mr Kirby that brought the tears to my eyes. He said for the two years following D'Arcy's death he nearly went mad, and then he bought another yacht and went to sea, and felt happier at once. Now he never comes ashore unless obliged to, and feels that alone in his yacht he is nearer his dead children than he is to those who are still alive. Dear kind Mr Kirby, he has had the saddest life of any man I know.

*Later on the diary reveals that Mrs Kirby was in a lunatic asylum.*

*Wednesday 23 January, Newark* We left Staten Island today. We were very sorry to go, we had had such a good time, and the Willis's seemed sorry too, but I hope before long we shall go to the Island to live. We met Mr Wayne Parker in New York and he came all the way home with us, talking in a very interesting way, as he can do if he likes. We got home in time for dinner, found all well, and were really glad to be at home, although it was so jolly at the Willis's.

*Wednesday 30 January* After dinner Papa took us up to the riding school to see the troop drill. I enjoyed it very much. Court Parker was there, he looked very cross and frowned instead of smiling when he bowed to me. Eva thought him disagreeable; so he is, but all the same the nicest man in the world for me.

*Sunday 3 February* In the afternoon I went to Sunday school and took Sybil's class, as she was not well enough to go. It is a class of boys and they behaved like demons, one of them threw a hymn book at my head.

*Friday 8 February* I had a letter from Mamma. She has found a house in Staten Island that will suit us, so I suppose it is almost decided that we shall go there to live. I am delighted, I am utterly tired of Newark.

*Friday 16 February* I went to choir rehearsal. I have not been for so long that I was half afraid to face Miss Tiffany, but she did not scold me at all.

I had a long talk with Leslie Baker. I like her better every time I see her and would like to know her intimately; perhaps it is better not to, for it really seems to me that I never like anyone when I know them very well. At this present moment I truly believe there is not a single person outside the family that I have any real affection for. I *like* almost everyone I know, but I don't *love* anyone. I wonder if I am a very cold person, or if I have a sort of latent affection waiting to be stirred up. I hope I have. I hate to think of myself as a heartless person; it is repulsive.

*Tuesday 19 February* Sybil and I went to a very crowded fashionable tea at the Wrights, where there were lots of people I did not know. Court Parker was there, looking older, graver and greyer than ever. I shook hands with him and tried to analyse my feeling for him. I am not as wildly unhappy about him as I was, but that is because I have so many other things to think of now; he still has the power to spoil everything for me. I was enjoying myself this afternoon until he came into the room, and then I grew restless and distrait. The best thing for me is never to see him, and that is one reason I am glad we are leaving Newark.

*Tuesday 26 February* Mamma came back from Staten Island. She has found a house at New Brighton that she is very much inclined to take. I hope she will; I am longing to get down there to live.

*Friday 1 March* Eva and I went into New York to lunch with Miss Mott-Lord. We met her mother, such a dear old lady, a real *old* lady in a cap, not an imitation young one in dyed hair and youthful clothes as so many old women are nowadays. The Lords are Quakers, and it is very pretty to hear them 'thee and thou-ing' each other. I have never heard it before.

*Friday 29 March* I saw Father Huntington this morning at the House of Prayer and had a long talk with him, and he gave me some very good advice, and was kind and nice as only he can be. He is the most interesting man I have ever spoken to, full of fun, gay and light-hearted, and the next moment serious and grave, talking with his whole heart and mind about religion.

He gave me a very different impression of my own character from any I have ever had before. I used to think myself rather clever; I now feel as if I hardly knew the alphabet, all my old ideas swept away and no new ones come to take their place, and he gave me a little praise that embarrassed me and made me feel I had misrepresented myself, so hard and cold and self-contained, no one is necessary to me. I always want to be left alone, and that surely is an unnatural state of mind, even the old friends whom I have been longing for ever since I left England are nothing to me.

*Tuesday 9 April* We started very early for Staten Island, and went to see our new house. I like it very much and look forward to living in it. I am sure we will be happy there. We lunched with the Willis's, and then went to New York to tea at Delmonicos.

*Saturday 13 April* Eva sailed for home today. Mamma and I went to New York to see her off; she went on a steamer called the Massachusets. Eva was sorry to go, and it was dreadful to have her go; I shall miss her.

*Friday 19 April* We move to Staten Island next week, and there is a great deal to do. This house is being gradually packed, every day something disappears. The china went last week, today the books, tomorrow it will be the pictures. It always seems during our numerous moves as if things would never be settled again. But I am *very* glad to leave Newark. I have been miserable here, and I want to make a fresh start in a new place.

*Monday 22 April* This was the last day in Newark. People were coming all day to see us, I had no idea we were so popular. I am sorry to leave some of them. I heard that Court Parker is getting on well [from a riding accident], the papers had grave accounts of his accident, much exaggerating it.

*Tuesday 23 April, New Brighton, Staten Island* Maude and I with two of the dogs went down to Staten Island early this morning, later on in the day the rest of the family arrived - that is all but Reggie, who is going to stay in Newark. I like the new house very much. It is larger than the old house, with a pretty drawing room and a very large hall and staircase. I have a delightful room, facing the west, so I shall have the afternoon sun and see the sunset. It seems so quiet here after Newark; we are right on the top of a hill, and it is half country and half town.

*Thursday 25 April* I like this house better every day. It is so homelike and suited to us in every way, and it is such bliss to be in the country. Today the birds were singing as we had almost forgotten they did sing, all the trees are budding, and summer seems to be coming at last.

In the evening Gertrude and Gordon and Mrs Edsall came over to see us, it is so nice to have them near enough to come and see us, it makes it so homelike. I already feel more settled here than I ever did in the house in State Street. I can't help feeling that we are going to be very happy and prosperous here.

*Friday 9 May* This was a lovely day - hot, with a deep blue sky, and all the trees fresh and green. I feel inclined to walk round the place all day admiring it. We are all so much better and happier since we came here, our dullness and bad tempers seem to be left behind in Newark, even the dear dogs are improved, and scamper about to their heart's content.

*Monday 20 May* I was at home all day. At home does not necessarily mean in the house for I was in the garden a great deal with the girls and the dogs. We are a very happy family on the whole; of course we quarrel, but I don't think I am ever so happy as when I am with Maude. She is so amusing and original that I can sit with her all day.

*Sunday 26 May* I went over to the Willis's in the afternoon and stayed for dinner. I heard rather an interesting story about Mrs Langtry. Mrs Sedley sat near her at Delmonicos the other day, she (Mrs Langtry) was with a man to whom she was explaining that it was impossible to write her autobiography because it would betray too many people, so she had written a novel, which was in fact a history of her own life, but she said that to publish it she needed 5,000 dollars. The man made a fuss, said no, and argued a good deal. Finally he said, 'you have just fifteen minutes to get to the theatre for rehearsal'. She put her elbows on the table, leaned her face on her hands, and looking him steadily in the face, said, 'and *you* have just fifteen minutes to write that cheque'. He wrote it, and they went straight to the bank and cashed it, and now we are all waiting for this wonderful novel to appear.

*The actress Lily Langtry ( 1853-1929) did write a novel, 'All at Sea', but it was not published until 1909.*

*Sunday 9 June* I went to morning service at St Paul's with Sybil. Mr Wood gave a very good sermon on the atheistical tendencies of the age. Nearly all his sermons are on that subject; it seems to me to be almost too deep and dangerous a theme to be treated in a short sermon. Some of my most disquieting thoughts have been suggested by arguments against Christianity that clergymen have introduced in their sermons with a view of confuting them, in many cases the quoted arguments against it have been far more conclusive than the ones pleading for it.

*Sunday 23 June* Gertrude's baby was christened today at St John's, Clifton; her name is Kate Gordon, and her godmother is Mrs Dinsmore and Mr Reeve-Merrit her godfather. The christening took place in the morning, Grace's child Nathalie was baptised at the same time. Afterwards there was a luncheon party of about thirty. The house looked lovely, full of flowers that kept arriving nearly every hour. Everyone was beautifully dressed and there were lots of nice men. The amount of scandal that was talked was amazing: Mrs Reeve-Merrit said the most damaging things about almost everyone; having no reputation of her own she tries to ruin everyone else's.

*Wednesday 3 July* At home all day, alone and delightfully quiet: Fitzroy went to Newark, Maude and Mamma to New York, Sybil to the dentists. It was a lovely hot still day when everything seems busy growing, all the plants beginning to blossom. I have been going out every morning to count the new buds on the geraniums and nasturtium, soon there will be too many to count. I love this place. I feel so much happier than I did in Newark, my life has broadened out enormously. A year ago I thought of nothing but myself, now I have new ideas in every direction, some of them due to dear Father Huntington and his teaching.

*Friday 19 July* I was very homesick today. I read some old letters, some from Mabel and some from Harry Lewis, two of the best friends I ever had and both lost, Mabel dead, and Harry, after hating me for years, is probably perfectly indifferent to me now.

*Friday 26 July, Staten Island, staying in the Willis's house with Mrs Edsall* Mrs Edsall came to tea this afternoon and asked me to go and stay with her until Monday. I was very glad to go: her house is so quiet and it is a change from our noisy establishment. Mr Edsall is very ill in bed, so we dined alone and sat on the piazza after dinner.

*Sunday 28 July* Mrs Edsall and I went to service at St John's. Dr Eccleston preached a very good sermon. He has a very fashionable congregation, and he always gives sermons on fashionable vices, and they are sometimes very exciting, and often hit home.

*Tuesday 13 August, New Brighton* I went to New York to do some shopping; it was very empty, I suppose everyone who can has gone away. I went into Grace Church to see it; I was rather disappointed. I had heard it was so fine, and it struck me as being rather commonplace. It is beautiful outside, but seems too narrow and crowded inside.

*Monday 26 August* My days all pass so quickly now that there is nothing to write about, so I am going to describe my doings today as it is a typical one, and may interest me years hence when things will probably be a little changed:

I got up at six and breakfasted with Papa, coffee, brown bread and butter; then I watered some of the plants - my begonia cuttings are getting on splendidly - then I read the paper, then a murder story in a magazine, then I did some lacework, tidied my room and washed the five dogs, which was a tremendous business and nearly flooded the bathroom. After that luncheon. All the afternoon I sat and worked and talked to Mrs Sheldon. After dinner we went to South Beach to show Mrs Sheldon the sights. I hope she was edified. It was a glorious moonlit night.

*Tuesday 3 September* I went over to the Castleton and got Grace [Slocum], and we went together to the club to see a cricket match between New York and an eleven from Oxford and Cambridge, who are here for a month to play. They landed on Saturday. They play splendidly. It is eight years since I saw a good game of cricket, and I enjoyed this more than I can say. Of course they beat the Americans, who had their second innings today.

After the play was over the men came over to our club and drank tea and made themselves very agreeable. One of them, Mr Mitchell the captain, was introduced to me and we had a delightful talk, delightful because he talked of London and last season, Henley and the Canterbury week, as if we had been in England, and I almost felt as if I was there. He knew Tibbie, had played cricket with him and gave me the latest news of him.

I enjoyed talking to him so much, his voice and accent were so English, so homelike, *how* different Americans are. Surely there are no men in the world like Englishmen, and no country like that blessed land.

*Wednesday 2 October* I have been ill in bed for weeks with malarial fever, a most horrible illness, raging fever and aches and pains. The weather was very hot all the time, and I was so hot and thirsty and miserable tossing about on a bed like an oven. To make it worse there was a scare of typhoid, and the doctor had to pull me about to find out.

Marie's baby was born during my illness on 16th September. It is a boy, said to be a very fine baby, but Morton and I think him hideous, he makes such faces.

*Sunday 6 October* This was a long dull day, and I felt tired and weak. The baby went out for the first time, a grand procession, Mamma carrying him, with Morton following and all the dogs. The baby is very good, he doesn't cry much. He is very big and strong but ugly, even Morton acknowledges he is hideous. He has a look of Morton, but his eyes are blue.

*Thursday 17 October, Staten Island, staying with Gordon and Gertrude Willis* We went to a dinner party at the Sports to meet some English people named Laurence; they live next door to the Bishops in Lancaster Gate. Mr and Miss Laurence are on a trip to this country. He took me in to dinner and talked to me all the evening; he is quite young, still at Cambridge, and very nice for a Cambridge man. He said I had not a trace of American accent, and thought it wonderful after having lived here for so long. I do try my very best to speak real English, but I am always afraid of picking up Americanisms.

*Saturday 19 October* In the afternoon we went for a long drive through the woods, the foliage seems more beautiful every autumn. All this is so beautiful that I begin to wonder if I appreciate it as I ought. I think all the time of going back to England, all my plans are made, and I am even laying aside my prettiest clothes to wear there. But today it occurred to me quite suddenly that I did not appreciate all I have here, the beautiful scenery, and all the *very* good friends I have, and perhaps after all I am happier here than I would be in England.

*Tuesday 22 October, New Brighton* I left Gertrude today and came home and was *so* glad to get back to the dogs and my flowers and the rest of the family. Marie looks very well and the baby has grown, he is very pretty now.

*Wednesday 30 October* At home all day. I sit with Marie now, she hardly ever leaves her room. I am beginning to know her better, she is very reserved, a difficult person to know, but I like her better every day. The baby is a darling, growing so pretty and very bright.

*Friday 1 November, Newark, staying with Sydney and Mary Ogden* I went to the Ogdens for the night; it was very nice and homelike going back there again, everything the same as usual, the only things changed being the children, who have grown. Mary looks very well; she says she misses me very much.

*Saturday 2 November* This was All Souls Day. Miss Ogden went with me to early communion at the House of Prayer. Father Huntington celebrated and said a prayer for the dead, giving a list of names of those who died during the past year. It was a very impressive service.

We went back to breakfast, and I sat for an hour or two with Mary. She told me the very sad news that Court Parker was drinking. I am more shocked than I can say: it seems impossible that he of all men should sink so dreadfully.

*Friday 15 November, New Brighton* At home all day. Morton was very jolly, nicer than he has ever been before - when he is like this I love having him here. He asked me to be godmother to the dear baby; it is to be christened on Advent Sunday.

We went to see a football match between Yale and Princeton, it was at Manhattan Fields, a place at the upper end of New York; it took hours to get there. The football was most astonishingly unlike our game, it is awfully rough, and at first I thought a fight was going on, at times it was brutal. I got very much excited as I began to understand it, but it is a very difficult game to follow. One man was so hurt he had to leave the field, and lots of them were stunned for a few seconds, it really was not a nice sight. Yale won. There were about 30,000 people there, and they shouted and yelled all the time.

*Sunday 1 December* This was Advent Sunday; we all went to church to see the baby christened. I was his godmother, and he was called Robert Henley Stuart, Robert after Papa, Henley after our great grandfather, and Stuart after Marie's brother. The baby behaved like an angel, smiled when the water was poured on him, and looked lovely. It was the prettiest christening I have ever seen.

*Saturday 7 December, New York, staying with Harry and Grace Slocum* I went up to New York this afternoon to stay with the Slocums until Monday. Grace was at the opera when I arrived; she came in about six o'clock, looking very pretty. She is very happy, with lots of money and everything she wants.

*Wednesday 11 December, New Brighton* I lunched with Minnie Walker today. Gertrude was there, and we had a very cosy time, only they would talk about their babies all the time. I envied them a little, it must be very nice to have husband, children and a house of ones own. I think I have been stupid not to marry, unfortunately I did not care for any of the men who asked me.

*25 December, Christmas Day* After lunch I went over to the Willis's; they had an Xmas tree and lots of presents. The Slocums came late in the afternoon, also our entire family, and we all dined together, twelve of us. The table was all holly and red ribbons and looked lovely, and we had a pudding on fire, and drank the health of absent friends, which was a sad reminiscent toast, the absent friends always are the most longed for. What bliss it would be to have all the people one cared for together, never to be separated. I suppose heaven will be like that.

*Tuesday 31 December* We all sat up to see the New Year in, and see the last of good old '95. It has been such a happy year, the brightest we have spent in America. It really seems now as if the tide had turned, and we were going to be happy and prosperous again. I begin the new year feeling well and happy, so young that there must be some mistake about my age: it is not possible that I am thirty next birthday.

### 1896

*Friday 3 January* I paid calls this afternoon, and found no one at home but Lily Walker. I stayed a long time with her, she is such a nice girl. I am very lucky to have such good friends. She tried to persuade me to get a bicycle but Papa hates them, thinks they are unfeminine, and says if I ride one I will get all hot and dusty and look hideous.

*Friday 17 January* At seven o'clock I went to Minnie Walker's and dined there. Gertrude and Gordon were there, and we all went to the Leap Year Ball. I had a lovely dress, broad black and white stripes. I did not enjoy the ball at all. Things were exactly reversed: we had to ask the men to dance and to hunt them up; there was such an enormous crowd that it was very tiring. I was furious with myself for not being up to the mark. We stayed there until nearly three.

*Thursday 30 January* I went to the last rehearsal [of the Pirates of Penzance] at the club. We have two more rehearsals but they are to be at the theatre. We went through the opera splendidly tonight, we had both coaches, the musical one and the stage manager. There was a great discussion about the dresses. The stage manager insists they shall be nine inches from the ground, and very few of us can wear such short ones. My feet are too big for such an exposure.

*Tuesday 4 February* We all met at the hall where we are to have our performance, and rehearsed at 2.00pm with the orchestra. After the rehearsal we remained for dinner, and until it was ready we danced in the dark hall, dark except for the lights on the stage. At six o'clock we all dined together in a restaurant below the hall and I have never enjoyed myself more. We all sang during dinner, chorus songs first, and then solos. Mr Griffiths, who has a splendid voice, sang some of Whyte Melville's hunting songs, and the men made speeches and drank our health, standing one foot on the table and one on a chair. The three English people, Mr Griffiths, Gordon and I, sat together and got very excited and sang the British Grenadiers as a trio, and all the Americans cheered us and sang the Star Spangled Banner, and we cheered them.

*Wednesday 5 February* In the evening the performance of the Pirates came off. We all dressed in one big room, the girls looked lovely in light summer gowns, all the colours of the rainbow, and a great deal of white. The men were splendid as pirates, it was almost impossible to recognise them. It was more like a professional show than an amateur one.

*Thursday 6 February* We had another performance of the Pirates. We had a very full house, not a seat to spare; Papa and Mamma and Sybil came. The opera went off as well as it did last night, and we had a great deal more applause. When we were not on the stage I sat in the wings and talked to Mr Griffiths, we are great friends. After the play was over we danced in the hall. We did not stay late as I was rather tired; Mr Griffiths came away with us.

*Tuesday 11 February* Mr Griffiths is going to give a tea in his house in my honour. I am to ask the people; it will be very jolly. I really am becoming very popular, and I enjoy it. Fitzroy told me today that his friends had been guessing my age, and they agreed it was twenty. I shall be thirty next month. It seems absurd because I feel younger than I ever did. Perhaps it is a final flicker up before I sink into middle-agedom, a sort of Indian summer in my life.

*Thursday 13 February* I spent the whole day with Gertrude Willis. I took my work with me and sat very quietly talking. Gordon came in in time for tea and we discussed the Pirates, I had not seen him since the show. He rallied me gently about Mr Griffiths, and said his attentions were very marked. I think it is rather a pity to ascribe 'intentions' to any man who is civil to one.

*Saturday 15 February* I went to see Mrs Wilmerding this morning. She received me in her room in a dressing- gown, she had been smoking and reading Town Topics. She told risqué stories and talked scandal and with it all was attractive, so much so that I feel priggish and dull beside her.

*Thursday 20 February* Gertrude and I went to Mr Griffiths, to the tea he gave in my honour. He has a pretty house in Livingston, fitted up with the greatest taste. He made a charming host, and looked after everyone well. The people were all my friends. I poured tea, and felt myself to be of the greatest importance. After tea Mr Griffiths sang very well, hunting songs chiefly. Gordon sang too, and a man named Messel. I played the accompaniments. It was a very jolly little party, and I enjoyed it so much that I was sorry when it was all over.

*Tuesday 3 March* Mr Griffiths came in the evening. My friendship with him is such a sudden one; I have known of him only since Grace was at the Castleton last summer. I like him very much, he is so gentlemanly and so thoroughly English and manly, going in for all kinds of sport and wearing such good-looking tweed clothes, he is just like the men I used to know at home. I had a prejudice against him before I knew him so well on account of his supposed flirtation with Mrs Wilmerdine, people talked a great deal about it, and one or two have actually dared to ask how I like having a married woman for a rival. That is the sort of gossip Staten Islanders indulge in.

*Wednesday 11 March* Mr Griffiths came to see me after dinner, which was very good of him as the storm was dreadful at night. He stayed for a long time and we had a delightful talk. What I like about him so much is his intense Englishness.

*Sunday 15 March* Rather a funny little incident occurred this morning. Mr Griffiths and I decided to go to service at St Mary's this morning, we were to meet anywhere between our house and the church. Just as I was dressing Mrs Wilmerding sent her maid over to ask if I were going to church and if she might go with me; of course I at once suspected that it was an arranged thing between herself and Mr Griffiths. Emily Vyse had almost persuaded me that they were carrying on a desperate flirtation, and I jumped to the conclusion that I was to be used as a sort of chaperone or bluff. I was rather puzzled how to behave, but I decided to see only what was on the surface, so I called for Mrs Wilmerding. She was a long time dressing and made me late.

Mr Griffiths was in the church and the service half over. After service he joined us, and then I knew that all my unworthy suspicions were absolutely unfounded. Mrs Wilmerding was absolutely furious, because I had not told her that Mr Griffiths was to be there, and assured me she would never have come had she known it. Mr Griffiths was angry with me for being late, and not particularly civil to her. In fact there was a nice little fracas, in which I was the only one who kept calm. It was really funny, but I am glad that the two are not making fools of themselves.

We drove home leaving Mr Griffiths in rather a bad temper, I think, and on the way home Mrs Wilmerding relieved her feelings by blasting his reputation; she repeated that old, old scandal that I am so tired of, and that does not in the least alter my feelings towards him because it is all past and over, and she also said that he was mean and bad-tempered, at which I grinned, because her own temper was shaky, to say the least. Finally she said he wasn't a gentleman. I consider I am as good a judge as she, and I think him emphatically a gentleman. I am anxiously awaiting further developments in this little romance. It is delightfully funny.

*Friday 20 March* Today was my thirtieth birthday; comment is needless. I am trying to persuade myself that my girlhood is years behind me but I can't believe it, I feel younger every day, it is no vanity to say I look young, for everyone thinks I am about twenty-four. I wonder if I am really an old maid, thirty is certainly a dubious age.

*Sunday 22 March* I went to Christ Church for service. Miss Davidson came and sat with me, and we walked home together. After lunch I went over to the Willis's and had a delightful afternoon. Mr Griffiths rode over and put his horse up, and then we went for a walk. Mr Griffiths was nicer than ever; we get along so well together. I like him better every time I see him, he always has so much to talk about.

Just as we were leaving Gertrude's we met the Wilmerdings, and Mrs Wilmerding gave me the coldest bow, almost a cut, it is evidently war to the knife. I don't mind the loss of her friendship, but I hope she will not make mischief between Mr Griffiths and myself, a spiteful woman can do so much harm.

*Tuesday 24 March* I met Mrs Edsall at the ferry this morning, and went up to town with her to shop. She talked a great deal about Mr Griffiths, and amused me very much by warning me not to fall in love with him. She thinks him a very flirtatious person, and is afraid he may break my heart. I am not afraid.

*Wednesday 8 April* I had a letter from Mr Griffiths to say he would be at the rehearsal of the Pirates of Penzance tomorrow. It is to be given again on the 16ᵗʰ, and we begin to rehearse tomorrow. I am going to act with Mr Griffiths this time; last time I acted with Mr Miller.

*Thursday 16 April* This was one of the happiest days I ever spent. Early in the afternoon I went to see Mrs Wilmerding, and went with her to the opening of the golf club, which was a very mild affair. There was no one there I cared about and we did not stay very long. I went on to a tea at the Walkers, where I met a great many very nice people. I stayed long after everyone had left, talking to Lily and Edith, then I hurried home, and eat my dinner while I dressed for the Pirates. I wore the same dress as last time, all white with a pink hat. I got to the hall very late but in time to be made up.

Mr Griffiths came back from Boston in time. I saw him from the wings when the opera began, and whenever either of us was not on the stage, we sat in the wings and talked. I acted with him, and we talked all the time. I was in wild spirits and enjoyed myself immensely, but alas, it was all over so soon. I suppose that is what we will think when we are old: how soon it is all over. Afterwards I had my paint washed off, and went out into the hall to see my friends. I had a talk with Gertrude and Mrs Edsall who were charming, and told me all sorts of pretty things about myself and made me feel so happy. I love to be admired.

Gertrude went home and I joined the Wilmerdings and waited for Mr Griffiths, who took ages to wash off his paint and change his things, but the result was so good that we forgave him for keeping us waiting. He came down looking exquisitely clean and well got up; he is not exactly good-looking, but so well turned out that he is more attractive than many really handsome men.

We four went off to Hugo's for supper, getting there so late that we had to wait for a long time for a table. We sat on the stairs and watched the people, all Staten Island seemed to be there. Our table was in the piazza, and we sat out there at midnight in the thinnest clothes and ate our supper. The Italian singers were singing, and we had the piazza all to ourselves. Mr Griffiths and I danced; it was great fun, I was very happy, and I did not get tired until quite the end, when we were driving home, and then I collapsed and could hardly say goodnight to Mr Griffiths. He is so amusing, up to any amount of fun, and so gentlemanly, that I never feel afraid of him as I sometimes do with other men. I am so glad I know him, and I hope we will always be friends.

*Thursday 30 April* I spent the afternoon with Emily Vyse. She invited me to her wedding on 2ⁿᵈ June. I don't believe she is very happy, she is not much in love with Roquey Lyon, and I think she is marrying him for very much the same reason that I will eventually marry, i.e. because there is nothing else for a woman of our class to do. Very few of us are lucky enough to marry the men we care for.

*Friday 1 May, Staten Island, staying with Gordon and Gertrude Willis* I went over to Arrochar in the afternoon to spend a few days with Gertrude. I am rather glad to get away from home for a little while; I get narrow and morbid sometimes, and when I go away I seem to look at things from all sides and not so much in detail

*Tuesday 5 May* Gordon went to see Mr Griffiths and brought back very sad news: he is very ill and going back to England in a few days. Ever since I have known that man I have had a feeling that our friendship would be a very short one, to be ended by some such contretemps as this. I don't in the least expect to see him again, and I am very sorry I ever met him. He will probably die in England, he has looked like it for some time. What a twisted, tangled world it is.

*Sunday 10 May* This was a dreadfully hot day, the house was like an oven, and I longed to be at home in our cool big house, where there is always a draught. Mr Griffiths lunched with us, I enjoyed that very much. After lunch we had a long talk about his trip home etc.

*Wednesday 13 May, New Brighton* I worked and practised very contentedly until late in the afternoon, when I got restless and went out for a while in spite of the weather. I am no longer content to lead a quiet domestic life, I have a craze for excitement and dissipation. As I see myself at the present time I am utterly frivolous, I care for nothing but dress, going out, any amount of admiration and excitement. The books I used to like bore me; I hardly ever read. I don't even like the same music. I could never tire of Chopin, but all the same I enjoy waltzes better, and I feel I could dance until I died. I feel as I grow older I take everything more intensely, and if only I had the chance, no one living could be happier or enjoy life more acutely then myself.

*Sunday 24 May* I went to church this morning, and then hurried over to the Willis's afterwards for luncheon, but was half an hour late. I did not enjoy myself because Gertrude attacked me about something Grace repeated to her that I had said. Grace totally misconstrued it, and Gertrude seemed to be only too ready to think I meant to be unkind, and it has hurt me more than I can say. I always thought she had more confidence in me than to believe I would say anything against her. This is a most difficult world to get on in, everything one says is misconstrued, and even ones so-called dearest friends are ready to doubt one. The only safe course seems to be to have no intimate friends, and never on any occasion to express any opinion, good, bad or indifferent.

*Wednesday 27 May* I had a telegram last night to say the ship the Macdonalds are on would be in today at dawn, so I was up at 5.00am and got the first boat I could to New York, and found the Comanche [from Florida] at her dock. I hunted all over for the Macdonalds, and found them at last dressing. Kate is so changed I would never have known her. She, who used to be so slender, is very fat, she was casually dressed, and utterly unlike her old self in appearance. Her manner is the same and she is as light hearted as ever, her husband is very nice, and she has two dear little children. We were a long time getting off the ship, and did not get to Staten Island until eleven.

*Thursday 28 May* It rained hard all day and there was no chance of getting out; the Macdonalds were rather tired with their long journey, and were glad to stay quietly in the house. Kate and I had a long talk about old times. A great deal has happened to her since we last met, she has been round the world, married and had three children, and lost one. She has not changed much, and she says I am exactly the same. Seeing her has made me feel like my old self, it is like stepping back into the dear old life in London.

Her husband is very nice, he is her cousin, a son of Lord Kingsborough's, very poor, and I'm afraid rather useless, like so many nice men [Lord Kingsborough was a senior Scottish judge].

*Saturday 30 May* We had a very busy morning packing up and getting the children ready, and at 9.30am we went to town straight to the Anchor line pier, and on board the Ethiopia. She is an old ship, rather small, but beautifully kept and smart, and the officers are all in bright fresh uniforms, such a contrast to the North German Lloyd. Kate was delighted to be going home again, but very nice and sympathetic to me, saying she wished I were going. She found out that one of the stewards had been a butler of Lord Kingsborough's and knew them well so she will be well looked after.

*Tuesday 2 June* We went to Emily Vyse's wedding today. She was married in her father's house by Father Ducey. I was so late that I did not see the ceremony, but I was in time to congratulate her. She looked very handsome, but pale, and rather sad. She had a lovely gown, white satin and point d'Alencon.

*Mabel spent ten days with the Wests at Haverstraw, which was quiet and restful but not exciting.*

*Wednesday 17 June* I took the early boat to New York; Mrs West drove down to the dock with me. I was sorry to leave them, they have been so kind to me. I like the quiet of their house, but I am always glad to get home again; I got there in time for lunch. Sybil goes to Providence, Rhode Island, on Saturday to spend the summer at a convent there. It will do her good as she is in very bad health.

*Tuesday 23 June* At home all day. A very funny letter came from Sybil; she says the solemnity at the convent is terrific. I think she is beginning to feel homesick already. I miss her so much that I am depressed.

*Saturday 27 June, Kingsbridge, near New York, staying with Dr and Mrs Fordham Eden* I went to Kingsbridge today to say with the Edens. I got there in time for luncheon; Maude met me at the station. They have a very nice house with small grounds, and very nice horses and carriages; everything is very well done. Dr Eden is a good looking man, and Mrs Eden is very kind. Maude is rather a spoilt young person; it seems so funny to meet another Maude Eden.

In the afternoon we went to a tea that was rather stupid. There was an Englishwoman there, a Miss Hobhouse, a strong-minded woman who told me she was a Socialist. She landed only this morning and is out on a mission of some sort. She was introduced to me with great *empressement* as being 'a niece of Lord Hobhouse'.

*Thursday 1 July, New Brighton* I went to see Grace Slocum today, she is at the Castleton for the summer. Mrs Edsall and Gertrude were there, also Lillie Walker. I was glad to see them all again, it seems rather a long time since I saw any Staten Islanders. The only thing I did not like was that they all talked scandal, and it made me miserable. It is a habit the people here have. I don't believe they mean to be spiteful but they do say the most damaging things about everyone, as if no one were genuine.

*Friday 3 July* I lunched with Mrs Wilmerding, and had one of our queer talks. She mixes up all sorts of ideas, surprisingly intellectual and exalted ideas with most shockingly improper ones. She is all extremes, doing the most imprudent things, and getting herself so talked about that it would not surprise me at all to hear that everyone had cut her. Effie Macfarland came, after which I left. I like her, but she and Mrs Wilmerding together are too much for me. They are fast, there is no doubt about it, and when they get together they discuss all sorts of things that are best left alone. I hope I am not a prude; I like to think I am fastidious.

*Tuesday 14 July* Sybil came home looking very well, and rather tired of the convent where she had vowed she would spend the whole summer. She is very amusing, telling funny stories about the nuns, and mimicking them. She is glad to be home again and I think she has had a lesson, and won't be quite so anxious to leave home again.

*Monday 20 July* I had a letter from Peg today, it chilled me a little. I wrote to her asking her and others if the family would receive the Fordham Edens well if they went over to London next season. In this letter she is very stiff about it, and evidently does not want to meet them. I have been so long in this country, and grown so used to meeting all sorts of second-rate people, that I had forgotten how intensely exclusive and caste-ridden my relations are. I used to be so myself, living here has deteriorated me. I suppose I have not associated with my equals in actual rank since I left England, but I know that most of the people I have met are my superiors as far as morals and intellect go. However that would have no weight in my class, nothing but birth counts there.

*Saturday 25 July* Miss Laurence took me for a drive in in the afternoon, and Mr Goldmann went with us on horseback for a part of the way. Miss Laurence told me that he admired me immensely, and spoke of trying to marry me, which startled me so much that I could hardly speak. I am glad she has told me, as it will put me on my guard, but it infuriates me that any man should speak of me in that way, even to such a friend as Miss Laurence. I suppose he wanted to find out about me and sounded her on the subject, and she very wisely told me, but the whole thing is too humiliating, he has only seen me a few times.

*Sunday 26 July* I went to the Castleton after lunch to see Grace and sat with her for a little while, and then we went to Arrochar to see her father. Mr Jerome died last night and they are all very much grieved. This death will affect a great many people, Mr Jerome was head of a big family scattered far and wide and the last of a set of famous brothers.

*Thursday 30 July* I spent the afternoon at the Castleton helping Grace with her mourning; she has been obliged to get everything in a great hurry. I stayed there until five, when I went home and rested for an hour, and then dressed and went back to the Castleton to dine, invited by Mr Algernon Bell. The Slocums were there of course, and Mr Parke Bell. I ought to have enjoyed myself, but I felt tired and ill, and could not talk much. After dinner we sat on the piazza for a while, and then went up to the Bells' room for the usual drinks, and at eleven they all walked home with me.

*Wednesday 12 August* It was just a shade cooler today. I went over to Arrochar and spent the day with Gertrude. She and I and Gordon dined with the Lyons and had a very jolly little dinner in the new house. It is lovely, so cosy and comfortable, and I never saw a happier pair.

*Friday 14 August* I walked over to St George early this morning to meet Mary Ogden, who came over from Perth Amboy to see me. She had a great deal to say about Court; he is as sombre and quiet as ever. She says he is terribly sensitive, she thinks he has never forgiven me for having (as he thought) once made fun of him. I never meant to, and wish I had a chance of telling him so; everyone seems to put the blame for our coolness on me, and it makes me blue to think that I was ever unkind.

*Monday 17 August* I spent the afternoon at the club A great many girls go there every day and sit on the piazza, drink tea and play tennis. I saw several girls I know and had a very good time, the grounds looked lovely and the girls were all very friendly and nice. I get fonder of Staten Island every day, and more at home in it.

*Wednesday 2 September* Gertrude and I went up to town by an early boat. Almost the first person we saw on board was Mr Griffiths, he came back from England two weeks ago. He joined us and told me about his trip. He is looking very much better, and I am glad he is back again.

*Friday 4 September* I met poor Mrs Wilmerding, and went home with her. She has just come back from Naragassett where she was the heroine of a terrible scandal; she is tabooed here and is awfully depressed. She told me all her troubles; of course she is to blame, she is a silly little thing, but I am very sorry for her, it is dreadful to see her going straight to the devil, and not to be able to do anything for her. I can do nothing for her. I suppose it is bad for me to be seen with her, everyone has warned me not to go with her, but I cannot bear the idea of cutting her, and I don't mean to do it.

*Monday 7 September* The county fair and horse show opened today, and I went to it with the Willis's. Mr Griffiths was there, and we walked home together very slowly, and had a nice long talk about his trip home.

*Wednesday 23 September* I went for a long drive in the morning with Mrs Laurence, right out into the country. It is blazing with golden rod and autumnal tints, most lovely, but rather depressing because it means the end of summer. I am growing so fond of Staten Island, and like everyone here so much, that I am afraid that I shall soon be going to leave it. I am always afraid to grow too fond of anyone or anything, it always seems a premonitory symptom of loss.

*Friday 25 September* This was the last day of the tennis tournament, and a gala occasion. There were a great many people at the club, and I had a delightful time, enjoyed every minute of the afternoon. Tea was going on all the time on the club piazza, and I gave tea to all my men friends and played hostess. I was sorry when it was over, I had such a good time. I am so happy now, it is such a novel feeling to be so popular and have so many friends, it reminds me of the old days in England. I like almost everyone I meet, and really (without being conceited) I think everyone likes me. They are all awfully nice to me.

*Saturday 26 September* I had a most delightful afternoon. Miss Laurence drove me out to the country club, the hounds met there at 3.30pm. Mr Griffiths met us, he was riding of course, a very good-looking horse. We all followed by the road, and saw a good deal of it. It was very pretty and exciting, even if it were only a drag; there are no foxes here.

In the evening I went to the Castleton with Nina Fowler. Mr Griffiths was there. I danced with him twice, and spent the rest of the time on the veranda talking. I do like Mr Griffiths very much. I hope I won't make myself unhappy about him.

*Friday 2 October* I went over to Arrochar late in the day. Mr Edsall was very much worse. Grace was crying her heart out, but Gertrude did not seem to be much affected. Nathalie was expected every moment, and relations kept coming so I went away soon. I could do nothing [Grace, Gertrude and Nathalie were the Edsalls' three daughters].

*Monday 5 October, New York, staying with Grace Slocum* This afternoon I got a note from Grace to say that Mr Edsall died this morning at seven o'clock. She came down from town and found him dead. She begged me to go up to town and spend the night with her, so I went, getting there in time for dinner. It was a depressing evening, she is very much overcome, and talked about her father all the time.

*Tuesday 6 October, New Brighton* Grace and I spent the morning in shopping; she had a great deal to get in the way of mourning. Late in the afternoon I went down to Staten Island to see Mrs Edsall. I hardly expected that she would see me, but she did, and told me all about her husband's last moments. The house was all dark, and there was an oppressive smell of flowers, and a deadly silence, his room door closed, and over all that ghastly flavour of death.

*Wednesday 7 October* We went to Mr Edsall's funeral today at St John's church. There were very few people there, just his immediate relations, the Harry Alexanders, Walkers and Mr Reeve-Meritt, and a few others. The service was very short, but with a great deal of lovely music. The coffin was hidden by flowers; it was hard to realise that Mr Edsall was lying in it, so quiet, who had always been such a nervous restless man..

I had not meant to have gone to the cemetery, but Grace asked me to just as they were leaving the church, so I went with Harry and herself. It was a long dreary drive in the darkened carriage. The cemetery looked lovely, the sun was shining on the autumn leaves, and the service at the grave was very short and simple. It did not seem at all sad or dreadful. There were so many flowers, and it was such a calm bright afternoon, that it did not seem such an awful thing to leave him there all alone

*Monday 11 October, New York, staying with Grace Slocum* We went to morning service at St Bartholomew's, the music was very good but I don't like the church, it is so rich that it is oppressive, there did not seem to be a poor person in the congregation. We had a very hurried luncheon, and caught an early boat to Staten Island. I went home to see them all, and then joined Grace at Arrochar. We found Gertrude and Mrs Edsall looking much better, they are beginning to recover from the shock of Mr Edsall's death.

*Monday 12 October* I have enjoyed this visit to Grace in spite of all the trouble and woe there has been; she has made me feel so much at home. I sometimes feel almost overwhelmed at the kindness and attention I receive from all Mrs Edsall's family. They hide nothing from me, I know all their family secrets and affairs, and they ask my advice about everything they do. It puts rather a heavy responsibility on my shoulders, and I am so afraid of saying more about them than they would like, that I don't care to talk about them with anyone

*Tuesday 13 October, New Brighton* I stayed at Grace's until late in the morning when I came back to Staten Island. I unpacked and then went to see Mrs Edsall. She was very quiet and sad, but if possible more loveable than ever, interested in me in spite of all her grief. I am very lucky to have such a friend. I believe she really loves me, and that is a great deal for me. I had tea with her, and then went to the Lyons where I dined. I like being with them, they are so happy, and their house is so pretty. I would like to be married and in a pretty house of my own.

*Mabel spent the next two weeks with the Fordham Edens at Rye, Long Island Sound, which was very uneventful.*

*Thursday 5 November, New Brighton* In the evening I went to a rehearsal [of Iolanthe], a very long one. Mr Griffiths was there; he came up directly the rehearsal was over and we had a long talk. We have not seen each other for nearly six weeks, and a good deal seems to have happened in that time. He walked home with me. We found a poor little dog that had been starved, it was nearly dead. Mr Griffiths went into a hotel nearby to get some milk for it, and we went home and left it with him. It could not be in better hands; he loves animals.

*Monday 9 November, Arrochar, Staten Island, staying with Gordon and Gertrude Willis* I spent the morning in getting ready to go away. I am going to spend a week with Gertrude. I like being with her, but I would rather be at home. I have made up my mind to go everywhere I am asked, and to try and get as much out of life as I can.

*Tuesday 10 November* In the evening I went with the Lyons to *tableaux vivants* at the Castleton. The first person I saw was Mr Griffiths, and he stayed and talked during the entire show. Of course I enjoyed it immensely.

I think Mr Griffiths is a very remarkable man. He is very clever, has read a great deal, and does many things well. I don't know whether I understand his character or not, but at present I consider him extremely kind and courteous, extravagant, a little bit selfish, and vain in a sensitive, diffident way, the sort of vanity one can forgive. He talks a great deal about himself, but is always interesting. At times he has a vague, absent-minded manner, and with all my cleverness I can't find out what he thinks of me. He never pays compliments or makes personal remarks. I danced a good deal with him tonight, for there was a dance after the show was over. I enjoyed the evening, as I always do when I am with him. He interests me more than any man I have met for a long time.

*Thursday 12 November* I went for a short walk with Gertrude this morning and then to see Emily, who is ill in bed. I sat with her for some time and we had a long queer talk about love, a topic I don't often discuss. I did not discuss it much today, but listened to Emily's views: she says people can be in love once only in their lives. I don't know whether I agree with her or not. I was certainly terribly in love with Courtland Parker, and I have not cared for anyone since in the same way, and I am thirty now, and ought to understand myself.

*Wednesday 18 November, New Brighton* I left the Willis's today to spend two days at home. Gertrude is very kind, but I was glad to get home again. I have promised to go back to her on Friday. I went to see Nina Fowler, Elinor Sedley was there looking rather frowsty in a wrapper. I don't like girls to come down to breakfast in a wrapper. After lunch I went to the Castleton to help at a big fair for the benefit of the SI Hospital. I poured out tea at the refreshment table all the afternoon, which was rather slow.

*Friday 20 November, Arrochar, Staten Island, staying with Gordon and Gertrude Willis* I left home this morning and went back to Arrochar for one night; tomorrow we expect the Macgregors who are coming from

England, and I must be at home to see them. I got to Gertrude's in time for luncheon, and spent the afternoon in the house with her, reading and working. In the evening we all went over to Emily Lyons. Mr Griffiths was there; he rode over on one of his polo ponies, and was looking very nice and smart in his riding things.

*Saturday 21 November, New Brighton* I spent the whole morning with Gertrude, and after lunch I came home. The Macgregors came in the afternoon, just landed from the St Louis. They had a horrid passage and were very tired. They were full of news of London, and spoke of it so enthusiastically that I long more than ever to get back there. Philip looks better, but is unhappy at leaving England.

*Tuesday 24 November* Mr Griffiths wrote and asked me to a hunt breakfast in New Jersey on Thursday, but as there is some difficulty in getting a chaperone I am afraid I will not be able to go.

*Wednesday 25 November* I went up to town by an early boat. I met Mr Griffiths on the boat, and decided to go with him to the hunt breakfast tomorrow. Mrs Fowler will chaperone me but will go on a late train. I don't suppose it is quite the correct thing to do, but Mamma does not object, and if I did not go early with Mr Griffiths I would not see the run, so I am going up at the unearthly hour of 7.30.

*Thursday 26 November* I got up early this morning, dressed under great difficulty by lamplight, drank a cup of coffee, and rushed to the station to catch the 7.44am train. I met Mr Wilmerding there, and Mr Griffiths was on the train, both were very smart in pink. There was a thick fog in the bay which so delayed the boat that we were afraid of missing the train at Hoboken, but we caught it all right, and met a large party going up to the meet from town.

We went to a place called Gladstone, beyond Summit. The horses were all there, and traps for some of the women to follow by road. There was a field of about eighteen. The run was very slow and we could not see much of it from the road, but I liked the drive in the fresh damp air. The finish was at 2.00pm, about three miles from the kennels.

There is a charming little hunting box where the master, Mr Messervy, lives. It is very prettily furnished with a large square hall. We all went back there to breakfast, which we had at little tables, and then afterwards went to the kennels to see the hounds and the horses. Mr Griffiths and I played about there for a long time, then we went back to the house, and sat in the hall and sang songs, danced and had a glorious time. There was a big wood fire that blazed, and all the pink coats looked very picturesque in the firelight.

We sat there until six o'clock, when we all got into various traps and drove to the station, where there was a special train to take us back to New York. We did not get to Staten Island until nearly ten. Mr Griffiths was charming and looked after me well, and I was awfully sorry when it was all over, but it will be something nice to look back upon.

*Mabel has tipped in a lengthy newspaper cutting, signed 'Purler', which included Mabel's name among those present, and from which the following two excerpts are taken:*

'Owing to our late arrival hounds did not make a move until 12 o'clock, with the result that the drag, which had been laid with the idea of hounds following it an hour earlier than they did, was almost cold, and what might have proved a good gallop across a fair line of country gave but very little satisfaction or pleasure to the large field that turned out to have a day's sport, and promote a good appetite to do justice to the good things we knew would be provided for us at the hunting box at Gladstone, by our hospitable master, Mr George Messervy.'

'The breakfast was everything a hungry man could desire, and the magnums proved a great consolation to some of us. Whatever may be said of the day's sport, I am sure that everyone who was at the breakfast will agree with me when I say our kind and genial host gave us a right royal good time, and that his speech was very much to the point, and that the few words upon hunting spoken by Mr Benjamin Nicoll, were worthy of the great and immortal Jorrocks.'

*Saturday 5 December* I went up to town this morning to see Mrs Wilmerding. She has left her husband, and is with an aunt in Madison Avenue. She has quarrelled incessantly with her husband, had been terribly talked about, and now there is talk of a divorce; she told me all the story. I like her and am very sorry for her, but she is very much to blame. I am sorry I went to see her, it left a bad flavour. I wish I never came into contact with divorce cases or people who have ugly stories, but it seems to be my luck to have a great many friends who have been talked about.

*Friday 25 December, Christmas Day* Xmas Day, and not very exciting. We were all alone, which is a great mistake if one wants to be festive, an outsider always gives 'go' to anything, but this year there was no one we cared to ask. I was in the house all day; Mr Griffiths sent me a pretty little antique silver tray, but I was in an ungracious mood, and rather wished he had not sent it.

*Sunday 27 December* I went to service at St Mary's. I met Mr Griffiths and he went with me. I am sorry to say he does not behave well in church, he did not kneel or make the responses, but he sang the hymns he insisted on having before the service was over. We went for a walk, but it was so cold that we did not enjoy ourselves, although I always like being with him.

*Tuesday 29 December* I went up to town this morning. I lunched with Grace Slocum, Mrs Edsall was there, also a Mr Pope who said nice things about England and English people. I stayed at Grace's until five o'clock; she had a great many callers which made it amusing. Mr Griffiths came for me at five, and we went to call on the Battleys, Mr Battley is an old friend of Mr Griffith's. They have a pretty set of rooms in 33rd Street, and we spent a very pleasant hour with them and had tea. She looked lovely, but was rather overdressed.

We caught a very late boat back to the Island and were late for dinner. Mr Griffiths went to the Wilmerdings, and I went after I had had dinner at home. Marie has come back to her husband, their quarrel is patched up, and I hope everything will be all right. We had a very jolly evening, and Mr Griffiths brought me home at 10.30pm. I had a happy day, and I am sorry it is all over.

*Wednesday 30 December* I lunched with Marie Wilmerding. She is in a very repentant mood, determined to behave herself very well, and to live down all the scandal she has caused. I am sure she is not nearly as black as she is painted.

*Thursday 31 December* I went to the hunt ball with the Macfarlands, and did not enjoy it at all. Very few of my friends were there, and a horrid set of people came down by train, most of the men had drunk too much, and I did not like any of my partners. Mr Griffiths made me furious by not going into supper with me, he said he was obliged to go with the party he dined with, but I know he could have got out of it. I had rather a bad headache, and was so angry that it got worse, so I sent for my cab, and went home without saying a word to anyone but Mrs Macfarland.

*Wednesday 6 January, Arrochar, staying with Mrs Edsall* Gertrude has been ill for some time, and has decided to have an operation performed. She will remain at Nathalie's house for it, and Mrs Edsall came back to Arrochar today with the children. She has asked me to stay with her until Gertrude comes back. I cannot refuse, but I do hate leaving home. I came over to Arrochar in the afternoon, and was in time to receive Mrs Edsall. She is so sweet and kind, that I like being with her.

*Monday 11 January, New Brighton* I came home today to stay until Wednesday. I dined with the Wilmerdings, the Lyons and Mr Griffiths were there. I did not enjoy it much. There was a good deal of risqué talk and innuendo that embarrassed me horribly. The other women drank B&S and smoked, and I felt like a prig because I did not

I felt rather quiet and out of my element, and there is really a sort of coolness between Mr Griffiths and myself that has existed since the hunt ball, it is my fault, and I must try and overcome it. I am so desperately exacting. We stayed until very late; it was 1.00am when I got home. Mr Griffiths walked across the park to our house with me. He is *very* nice; I am so stupid ever to be angry with him.

*Saturday 16 January, Arrochar, staying with Mrs Edsall* I went home for about half an hour to see them all this afternoon, and at 4.30pm I met Mr Griffiths on the boat, and went up to town to meet the Lyons, who asked us to dine at Le Chat Noir. Le Chat Noir is a queer little French restaurant in Sixth Avenue, rather a Bohemian place, but the dinner was not bad and it was very amusing. We were a very congenial party and had great fun. After dinner we went to Durlands to see the Rough Riding Club. Mr Griffiths and Mr Donetil were both in it, tent pegging, bare-backed riding etc, it was rather an 'off' night for them both, they did not do well. Afterwards we went to a café and had supper.

I went back to Arrochar with the Lyons, and the men went to Livingston. It was a very jolly evening. I had a funny sort of time; I always do when Mr Griffiths is with me. I cannot understand what my feelings are towards him. I think he likes me, but it would be impossible for me to say whether I cared for him or not. I like talking to him because his manners are so good, and he flatters me by the interest he takes in me. I like being with him, but I know that I don't like him half as much as I did in the spring when I nearly fell in love with him. I begin to think I am not capable of being in love with anyone.

*Wednesday 20 January* Mr Griffiths came over to dine with us, and we had a charming little dinner, just the three of us. The table was lovely with pink candle-shades and orchids, and there was a very nice menu. He was charming and Mrs Edsall talked as brightly, and much more sweetly, than any girl. After dinner she sat with us for a time, then went to bed, and we had a nice long talk. I enjoyed every minute of it, and it was all too short.

*Thursday 28 January, New Brighton* In the evening we gave the first performance of Iolanthe. The whole evening was rather like last year when we gave the Pirates, but tonight it seemed to lack the 'go' and excitement of the Pirates. We all wore fairy dresses, blue and pink covered with silver, our hair down and silver stars in it. We were all very elaborately made up. The play went fairly well.

*Thursday 4 February* At home all day, a very nice quiet day; home is a delicious place after all. Mr Griffiths spent a long evening with me, coming very early and staying until nearly twelve o'clock. We had a delightful cosy time, sitting over a big log fire, talking. He told me all his plans for the future and some of his past life, all of it very interesting.

*Friday 5 February* Mr Griffiths came for me at 8.30pm with a sleigh, and we drove over to Emily Lyons. We went by the country way and had a delightful drive. We spent about an hour at Emily's, Gertrude and Gordon were there, and we had great fun. We drove home, back through the country, the sleigh bells jingling, the only sound to be heard in the dark snowy lanes.

*Tuesday 9 March* I went up to town early, and spent the morning at the Museum with Grace Slocum. We looked at the casts and models of old buildings in Europe, and tried to imagine ourselves in some sear, old, quaint town in Germany. It was rather a shock to come out into the vulgarity and garishness of the New York streets. I lunched with Grace.

*Wednesday 10 March* This was a warm rainy day. Mary Davidson came to see me, and I went for a short walk with her. Mr Griffiths spent the evening with me; he has been ill and looks more delicate than ever. He seems to have very little constitution, but a great deal of muscular strength. He was very interesting, he talked about his affairs, which are very flourishing, he is very clever. I never tire of him. I wonder he is not more popular, people who know him well like him, but he does not seem to have many friends.

*Sunday 28 March* I went over to Arrochar after lunch, and found the Willis's and Lyons playing golf on links they have laid out near their houses. The Busks joined us, and I walked round with them all, and then Mr Griffiths came. He drove over, his arm in a sling, quite useless; he cannot ride or take any exercise; he is very plucky about it, and does not grumble at all. We all had tea at Gertrude's, it was very jolly. I love their Sunday teas in Gertrude's pretty rooms, with nice, interesting people, and lots of fun and laughter.

Mr Griffiths drove me back, rather an exciting drive, for the pony galloped all the way, kicked for the last mile, broke a trace, and we were at the last gasp when we met one of the stablemen who rushed to our help. Mr Griffiths had only his left arm, and was getting awfully tired. We had to get out and walk the rest of the way.

*Saturday 10 April* I went up to town this afternoon. I met the Busks and Mr Griffiths at the station, and the Lyons at St George, and we all went to the Chat Noir and dined. After dinner we went to the riding school and saw the rough riding club give a show. Mr Griffiths took part in the event, but could not do much on account of his arm. He sat with me nearly all the time.

After it was over we went to a restaurant for supper, which was very jolly, and we caught the one o'clock boat home. I left my chaperones at the station, and Mr Griffiths saw me home. We reached the house at 2.00am!! I enjoyed myself so much I am sorry it is all over.

*Monday 12 April* I went to New York and lunched with Marie Wilmerding. Miss Bradhurst was there. Marie was in very low spirits, she hates her husband, and says so frankly. Of course she is unhappy but she ought to keep it to herself.

*Sunday 18 April* Soon after lunch I went over to the Willis's, where I had tea. While I was there Jack Wilmerding rode over to ask me to dine at the country club, so about six o'clock I made my way out there, and was met by Mr Griffiths and the Wilmerdings. It was very jolly. I don't know when I have ever enjoyed anything more. We were all four in very good spirits and I felt very happy. I knew I was looking well and got heaps of compliments; I do love admiration from the right people.

*Friday 23 April, New York, staying with Mrs Pfizer* I went up to town in the morning and went to Grace Slocum's. Gertrude and Mrs Edsall were there, and there had been a family fight, and there was such a chill in the air that I wished I had not come. They left soon after luncheon, and I went out with Grace. We went to see Mrs Jerome, who is at the Fifth Avenue, and went up to Mrs Pfizer's in 30° Street. She had asked me to dine and stay all night.

The Pfizers have a very large luxurious house, but it is not very comfortable or homelike. We dined at eight, ten of us, Miss Sickles among the number, a very pretty girl, and an artist named Muller-Ari, Mr Hecksher, and Mr Griffiths, who took me in to dinner, which in a way seemed all wrong. We know each other too well to be paired off at a formal dinner; we ought to have gone in with strangers. It was a very gorgeously appointed dinner, beautiful plate and glass, but the service, as usual in American houses, not good, with long waits between the courses.

After dinner we all went into a very cosy smoking room, the nicest room in the house. We had some music, Mr Griffiths sang and I played a little. All the people but Mr Griffiths went away at midnight, and the rest of us sat talking until past 1.00am. I would have enjoyed myself immensely but for my throat, which kept me in constant pain.

*Sunday 2 May, New Brighton* My cough seems to get worse every day; it keeps me awake at night and bores me all day. I ought not to have gone out as it was a cold damp day, but the Willis's are going away and I wanted to see them, so I went over to Arrochar. The Busks were there and it was very jolly, the Slocums were there too. Everyone was very jolly and in good spirits, and I would have had a very good time if I had not punctuated all my remarks with a cough. I dined at home. Mr Griffiths spent the evening with me, which was very nice. He is a charming man; I like him better every time I see him.

*Thursday 6 May* Mamma and the others all went to town to see Buffalo Bill's show, leaving Papa and I alone. Mr Griffiths dined with us, and we had a most delightful time, just we three. Papa was at his best, which makes him the most brilliant man I know, and we talked and laughed all the time, and I enjoyed it so much that I forgot I was ill until I was nearly choked by a fit of coughing. Papa talked about his old Oxford days, and was as jolly as a boy.

After dinner we sat in the library and smoked for an hour or two, and then left Papa to read the papers and went into the drawing room, and Mr Griffiths talked about all his people and his affairs until past twelve, o'clock, but I was not at all tired, and enjoyed every minute of the evening.

*Saturday 15 May* I went to a dinner of twenty given by Mr Rokeby at Hugots, chaperoned by Nina Fowler. The men were chiefly Englishmen, the girls the usual set, Bonners, May Boyd, Miss Sedley etc. I sat between Mr Ripley and Mr Boyd, men I don't know well, but I got on very well with them. Mr Griffiths came in at the end, and we met some other people on the dock, and all went off for a trip on the quarantine launch.

We went as far as the Palisades, it was a lovely moonlight night and the river looked glorious. I sat with Reggie Walker in the stern, and he talked sentiment to an alarming degree; he is one of those queer shy men who are rather afraid of women, but who expand amazingly if they meet one who will draw them out. He wants to come and see me, and if he means all he says, will be rather troublesome. I am afraid I like to have men friends, but I don't want them to make love to me. I talked to Mr Griffiths on the way back, *not* sentiment, but a good straightforward talk about his new house.

*Friday 28 May* I went to the opening of the Ladies' Club this afternoon. There was the usual crowd of very well dressed pretty women, a few, *very* few men who seemed rather bored, endless tea, cakes and ices, and a band. The scene was very pretty, all the bright-coloured gowns on the lovely green lawn, and the western sun shining on the trees. I met nearly everyone I knew, but I never enjoy a crush.

Just as I was leaving Mr Griffiths came, looking very ill, but as smartly dressed as ever. He left the club with me and we walked slowly home, and then suddenly decided to go to the stable to see the horse Rough-and-Ready. He was trotted out; he is a beauty.

Mr Griffiths feels as ill and depressed as I do; there is more the matter with him than with me: he is very ill. I am merely very tired and discouraged, and in a horrid sensitive mood that makes me exaggerate people's indifference to me, and underrate their many kindnesses. Lately I have been utterly self-absorbed, scheming and planning my own happiness and advantage and not thinking of anyone else, so it is no wonder I am not very happy.

*Sunday 30 May* In the evening Mr Griffiths came for me, and we went to service at St Mary's, a very pretty choral service with an anthem. He drove me home and left early, telling me frankly that he had a book to read, that he wanted to finish. I was rather disgruntled with him for preferring a book to me.

*Thursday 10 June* Mr Griffiths rode over to tea on his beautiful hunter. He was very happy over a letter he had just got from his brother in London offering him a place in the London office, to be a partner, beginning with a good income and unlimited possibilities in the future. He will not go for some months, perhaps not for a year. I shall miss him, we have become such friends that his going will leave a great blank. We sat talking over his affairs for a long time, and then went to the stable and admired the horse, and then he rode off looking very smart.

*Saturday 12 June* This was a delightful day. I met Mr Griffiths at the ferry, and we went up to Orange. We got there about four o'clock and drove to the country club, where we waited for the rest of the party, Mrs Pfizer and the Wilmerdings. They finally arrived, and we at once drove off to the field. The polo was not very brilliant, the men had not played much together, and it is still early in the season, and the ponies were green. But polo is always the prettiest game in the world to watch. There were a lot of people looking on, in all sorts of traps, coaches, phaetons etc.

After the match was over we all went back to the club and had tea, that is Mrs Pifzer and I did while the men changed for dinner. Mrs Pfizer sat at the head, and put me at the foot of the table with Mr Griffiths on one side, and a very nice man named Kissel on the other. It was a very jolly dinner; I enjoyed it because everyone was so nice to me. We got the 10.00pm train back to town. We went down with the Pfizers and Wilmerdings, but left them in town, and Mr Griffiths and I came on to Staten Island, *sans chaperone*, by the 12.20am boat, very shocking. We were both terribly sleepy but it was a glorious day and worth all the fatigue, and Mr Griffiths was charming from start to finish.

*Thursday 8 July* Sybil and Maude are going away this week, and I was very busy all day helping them to get ready. Mr Griffiths came in the evening, we sat on the piazza for a long time; it was moonlight and deliciously cool after a long, hot day. He talked about going back to England. As usual that is his one topic, he is building all sorts of castles in the air, arranging where he is to live, and the clubs he will belong to, and the horses he will keep. He is very boyish.

*Tuesday 13 July, Bernardsville, New Jersey, staying with Mr and Mrs Pfizer* I was very busy packing all the morning. In the afternoon I made my way to Barclay Street station to meet Mr Griffiths, who promised to take me as far as Hoboken, where we were to meet the Pfizers. As usual he was late and I had to go alone. I met Mr Pfizer all right, and Mr Griffiths appeared just as the train was starting. We had a long wet journey up to Bernardsville and a wetter drive to the house, so I saw nothing of the country. The house is a very pretty one, and the party consists of the Pfizers (2), the Taylors (2), and Mr Griffiths and me. We dined at eight, and sat rather stiffly in a little drawing room afterwards. I was tired and went to bed early.

*Wednesday 14 July* I was late for breakfast, positively the last to appear, but only a few minutes behind Mr Griffiths. I practically spent the whole day with him; Mrs Pfizer leaves her guests to themselves in the most delightful way. After luncheon we sat on a very pretty piazza, and talked and worked until four, when we women went for a drive, and the men rode beside us. After the drive I got on a pony, and Mr Griffiths gave me a riding lesson, which I did not enjoy much because I was really frightened, but he took great care of me, and I wasn't killed, and we went down a lovely shady lane with a little brook near it and lots of ferns.

We dined at eight. After dinner the others disappeared and Mr Griffiths and I sat on the piazza in the moonlight and went for a little walk down the drive. We are certainly left very much to ourselves, and it is very nice.

*Saturday 17 July* We all went for a stroll in the woods, lovely paths leading to a brook. We lost the others and sat by the brook talking, and then went back to the house and sat under the trees until luncheon time. Mr Griffith was in a very lazy mood, and it seemed to be absolutely pain to him to walk, so I had pity on him and we sat under the trees on the lawn. Late in the afternoon we drove over to Morristown to see the polo. It was only practice play but very exciting at times, and they play it properly here with lots of ponies. We drove back in the evening; we divided the party and Mr Griffiths came back with me. We dined very late. After dinner we sat on the piazza, and Mr Griffiths and I went for a short walk. There is a sort of honeymooning atmosphere about this place. The Pfizers are very much in love with each other, and the Taylors have not been married long, and they all far prefer each other's society, so Mr Griffiths and I are left very much to ourselves, which is very nice. He is just the man for a country house life, always ready to play at anything and doing most things well.

*Sunday 18 July* Mr Griffiths and I went up to the stables, and played about there. One of the men polished my belt buckle which Mr Griffiths declared was disgracefully dirty, and then we watched one of the grooms plait straw, and tried to do it ourselves. There are eighteen horses here, and at the kennels there are several hunters, and polo ponies at Morristown.

After dinner they played poker on the piazza while I looked on, and so ended the last day of a *very* happy visit. We took a little walk down the drive and agreed we had been very happy, and it was a pity it was all over.

*Sunday 25 July, New Brighton* I went over to the Willis's in the afternoon. Gertrude is not well, and 'received' in her bedroom. Mary Busk and Emily Lyon were there, and Grace and Algernon Bell. After they went I sat with Gertrude, and she made me absolutely miserable by repeating a whole volume of scandal and gossip that has been going the round of the Island about Mr Griffiths and myself. I feel as if I hated everybody, and would like to go away tomorrow and never see any of them again. I keep so aloof from everyone here, never interfere with them in any way and say so little, that it amazes me to find that anyone can have anything to say about me. I am reported to have boasted that I have refused him three times, another report is that I am crazy about him, and that he is amusing himself with me, and I am defenceless against all these lies. I can do nothing. It is malice from beginning to end.

*Thursday 5 August* Mr Griffiths and I dined with the Willis's tonight; we went over together. It was a very nice quiet little dinner. Gertrude was charming and Gordon at his best, and I had a very good time. Mr Griffiths paid me the first compliment he has ever been guilty of (he never pays compliments), he said he thought I was the 'goodest' person he ever met. Mr Rose once told me how good I was; it pleases me very much, although I know how faulty I am, but when I know people think me good it spurs me up to deserve their good opinion.

*Sunday 15 August, Arrochar, staying with Gordon and Gertrude Willis* I went to Gertrude's early in the day to stay until Tuesday. In the afternoon we went out with the Alexanders in their steam yacht Sappho. We did not go out of the lower bay. It was very rough with a good stiff breeze, and we shipped a good deal of water, and were nearly thrown out of our chairs. It was delightful, I would like to have stayed out for days and the rougher the better; she pitched and danced about like a cork. I used to be a very contented person and not long for anything, but now I want a yacht and horses to ride and to play golf all day, and be always in the open air.

*Sunday 22 August* I went over to Gertrude early in the afternoon to find that they had all gone off in the Alexanders' yacht, so I took a book and waited. Mr Griffiths rode up about four o'clock. The Willis's and Roquey Lyon got back about six, and asked us to stay to dinner, which we did and had a very jolly time. I am so happy with these people and they are so good to me, that I sometimes wonder if I am not making a mistake in going back to England. I never seem to know when I am well off, but am always longing for something else.

*Sunday 5 September* Fitzroy and I went to Midland Beach this morning; everyone goes there on Sunday morning to bathe. I met Gertrude and Emily there, their respective husbands were bathing, and we sat on the sand and criticised. Most of the women looked hideous: bathing suits are not becoming.

*Friday 17 September* I went up to town to lunch with Marie Wilmerding; she is living alone at the Garlach with a French maid. She has left her husband and is waiting for a divorce which is to be granted at once, without any publicity. She intends to go abroad immediately afterwards, and wants me to go with her, to winter in Rome and get to London in time for the season, but nothing would induce me to. I like her very much, but I don't believe her conduct is above reproach, and I am afraid that sooner or later she will be more talked about than ever, she is awfully imprudent.

*Saturday 18 September* Morton and Marie and the baby came this morning to pay us a long visit. The baby is the most bewitching thing I have ever seen. He was two years old yesterday but he looks like four, he is very tall, straight as an arrow, with a very haughty way of holding his head. It seems ridiculous to say it of a baby, but he is really distinguished looking. Marie is the luckiest woman in the world to have such a boy, if he were mine I think I would be half insane with happiness.

*Wednesday 6 October* I went to town today to lunch with Marie Wilmerding. Emily Lyon was there and Nina Fowler and Mrs Taylor came in afterwards. Marie sails for Europe next week, and this was a sort of farewell. She goes to escape all the scandal of her separation from her husband. She is not going to divorce him, but there is to be a legal separation. I wonder what will become of her. She is so utterly without ballast that I don't see how she can keep straight.

*Thursday 14 October* I went into New York early this morning to say goodbye to Marie Wilmerding. She sails on Saturday for Naples to join her father, and I don't expect her ever to cross my path again. I am not sorry although I like her, but I have parted from so many people I like that it is losing its sting. I think very soon I shall have no feelings left; faculties that are not exercised become weakened, and my affections are seldom called into play.

*Thursday 21 October* I lunched with May Busk today, and spent the whole afternoon with her. Emily came in late, and we all went to a tea at the

Bonners, which was duller than most teas, which is saying a good deal. There was an intolerable crowd, everyone was distrait and bored. I saw everyone I knew, Mr Griffiths among others, but he was so indifferent and disagreeable that I said as little to him as possible. I believe we are getting tired of each other.

*Saturday 23 October* Sybil and I went with May Busk to the Polo Club to see the Gymkhana games; they were very good indeed. Mr Wilmerding and Mr Griffiths were in them. There were a good many people on coaches and various traps. The events were the usual gymkhana games, Jack Wilmerding won the mallet and ball race, and Mr Griffiths won the hunt cup forhigh jumping with a new chestnut he brought back yesterday.

Mr Griffiths came to see me in the evening; I did not see much of him during the afternoon because he was like all men, more interested in the horses than in the women present. This evening he brought me some photographs that were taken during his trip to Nova Scotia, and also the diary he kept while there. He was very nice, and I have forgiven him for the indifference that I believe now only existed in my imagination.

*Sunday 24 October* I read the diary Mr Griffiths kept in Nova Scotia. It is very amusing and very frank, showing his character in every line as I suppose all diaries do, and it shows his greatest fault, ie his utter self-absorption. I don't think it is inherent selfishness, but an unmarried man of thirty-six, who has lived for years away from his family and anyone who has a claim on him, and who has plenty of money, is almost sure to become superficially selfish and rather self-engrossed. He is the kindest of men really, but he is constantly showing in little ways, such as lack of attention and forgetfulness of promises, that no one exists for him but himself.

*Wednesday 10 November* I was frightfully annoyed by being told that Mr Griffiths was going to take May Boyd in to dinner tomorrow at the club, leaving me to Mr Witherspoon, whom I hardly know. They all spoke as if it were rather a slight, and made me so angry that I went home and wrote a note to Mr Griffiths to say I would not go to the dinner, which had the effect of bringing him up to see me. He explained his reasons, which were satisfactory to a certain extent, but still I feel annoyed and wish I could get out of going, but I cannot now. This dance and dinner are being given by twenty men, each one of whom asks a woman, and I consider that as Mr Griffiths has asked me, he ought to take me in to dinner. Mr Witherspoon is charming, but he is not my host on this occasion.

*Thursday 11 November* In the afternoon I had a long singing lesson, and hurried home from it to dress for this dinner. I rushed into my clothes and got to the Parkes early. I was to go with them; the stage was to call for us and it came at seven with Mr Griffiths and a lot of other people. We called for about half a dozen more, and finally got to the club at 8.45pm. There were about fifty people altogether, and we all sat at a table very prettilyarranged in the shape of a 'T'. I sat between Mr Witherspoon and Mr Griffiths.

The dinner was not particularly exciting, but the dancing afterwards was great fun: there was not too great a crowd, and lots of very nice men. I danced until I nearly collapsed; in the Virginia reel I had to stop or I know I would have fainted. It is the first dance in Staten Island I have really enjoyed. The girls were all very pretty and well dressed, some of the men, Mr Griffiths among them, were in 'pink', which looked pretty, and we all danced with a great deal of spirit and go. We did not break up until 2.00am. We came back in the stage as we went, but at the Castleton Mr Griffiths and I left the others and took a cab to our house; it was quicker and more comfortable. On the way home we sang hunting songs until we were hoarse. I was very sorry when it was all over, but there are to be more of these dances.

*Thursday 2 December* I played golf this morning with Nina Fowler, and made the best score I have had. It was such a glorious day that I could not help playing well. Later I went to a large tea at the Walkers, everyone was there. They were all very nice and I had a lot of invitations, most of which I had to decline because I am going to the Alexanders tomorrow.

Mr Griffiths made a long call in the evening, he has not been here for three weeks so he had lots of news. He gave a hunt breakfast at the Club to men, and he has asked us to another dinner dance next week. He is really very good about entertaining.

*Friday 3 December, Stamford, Kentucky, staying with Nathalie Alexander and her husband* At five o'clock I met Gertrude and Gordon at the station, and went up to Stamford to visit Nathalie in her new house. It was quite dark and deep snow on everything, so I could not see the house from the outside, but the inside was charming. It looks wonderfully cosy and complete for so new a house, there is a big hall, all palms and big divans and lots of pretty luxurious chairs and cushions, and crowded with Nathalie's pretty things, bronzes, china etc. The dining room is rather small, there is a billiard room and some other small cosy rooms, and the bedrooms are nice. There is no one here but the Willis's.

*Sunday 5 December* After lunch I went for a long walk with Mr Boyd; I did not like it much. I do not care for him, and of course he brought the conversation round to Mr Griffiths. He seems to be trying to make mischief, he certainly has made me uncomfortable, but I am a disloyal friend to believe his insinuations, or even listen to them.

When we came in Mr Abbott was there, and we all had tea together in the hall round a blazing log fire in a huge fireplace, there was everything to make me happy except the right kind of people. I like so few people, and cannot adapt myself to everyone.

We dined very late. The others played pool afterwards, and I looked on and longed for someone nice to talk to. I am utterly out of my element here. I don't like the everlasting cocktails, staying in the house playing pool when we ought to be out in the open air, and above all the risqué stories and loose conversation.

*Tuesday 7 December, New Brighton* I got up very early and came as far as New York with Gordon, and then on to Staten Island alone. I was rather glad to get home, although I think a good long change of air and scene is what I want to make me quite well in body and mind. I have got deep into a groove, my life is empty and dull, going out and seeing people, and planning my clothes does not satisfy me, and I don't know what to take up.

*Monday 13 December* I went over to Emily's very early this morning. She was in bed but dressed and breakfasted, and we went up to town together. We met May Busk and Edith Walker on the boat, and had the usual gossip. They left us in town, and we went to be photographed in Harlem, Emily in a lovely white satin gown, and I in a hat. We arranged each other, and she looked very pretty. Afterwards we explored Harlem; it is a horrid place, with cheap shops and gaudy common people. We lunched and shopped. I had to get a new gown for a dance on Friday, and had a lot of trouble over it. We got home early tired out, a day in town gives me a headache nowadays.

*Friday 17 December*    In the evening Sybil and I went to a dinner dance given at the Country Club. Mr Griffith took us out, and it is a long drive, and I was talked out before we got there, besides being very tired. There were thirty-nine of us, we all sat at one table shaped like a T, and very prettily decorated with pink flowers. There was a very good dinner. I sat with Mr Griffiths, and Mr Wilmerding on my other side.

We began dancing at ten o'clock, the floor was not very good, which was horribly tiring. I danced with Mr Griffiths very often, and Mr Stoddart who is very nice, and a lot of others. No one seemed to dance particularly well except Mr Hopkins. I did not really enjoy the dance at all. I was very tired and rather irritable and thoroughly dissatisfied with myself, and everyone else. I do need a change so badly, and not see or hear of anyone here for weeks. I am tired of them all.

*Saturday 25 December, Christmas Day* This was a very happy Xmas; I enjoyed it more than any Xmas for some time past. I went to church alone in the morning; I would have liked to go with someone, but the girls went off to their very ritualistic church that I dislike, and the others don't care much about church.

I love the Xmas service, with the dear old hymns that always make me feel like a child. Holly berries and an old church, Papa and Mamma, Xmas trees, and Hark the Herald Angels Sing, are all mixed up in a vague way with all the Xmas recollections I have. Someday I hope I shall have a child to make happy Xmases for, so that it may have many happy memories to look back upon. I can remember the Xmas Morton and I spent at Eythorne with dearest Grandmamma and Peg, our stockings were simply crammed with the most delightful things. I can remember them now, and we went to dine at Waldershare, Aunt Charlotte in a lovely gown, and diamonds that seemed to shine like fire, and Uncle George, Flo, Morton and Cecil and Guilford, they are all dead now.

We dined in the state dining room and I was afraid of the powdered footmen (I was only four years old). After dinner the room was made quite dark, and we had snapdragon, and the brandy burned blue flames, and the portraits on the walls looked like ghosts, especially the great big Vandyke at the end. Waldershare always seemed full of ghosts, it was so big and shadowy and full of portraits, but that was a happy time, the poor North boys were all so kind to me, now they are all dead, and we are out here miles away from it all, the whole party broken up before they ought, because they were all young, and had a right to expect to live for years.

*Monday 27 December* I had a long letter from Eva, rather an upsetting one. She says her relations with her mother are so strained that she intends to leave home, and become a hospital nurse, and begs me to go as soon as possible, as she will not begin her training until after my visit. I feel now that I must go as soon as possible, but somehow or other I dread leaving home. I long to get back to England, but I have a presentiment that if I go I will never come home again. It is a morbid feeling, but it spoils all my pleasure in going. I feel unhappy about poor Eva: in spite of all her money and brilliant position she is miserable, what a pity it is she does not marry.

## 1898

*Friday 14 January* I spent the morning and lunched with Gertrude. I came home early in the afternoon. I used to love coming home after being away but now I hate it, things seem to have changed so, or I have. The girls never seem to care to be with me, Mamma is utterly indifferent, and I really am apart from them all. I wish I knew whether it were entirely my fault.

*Sunday 16 January* May Boyd's engagement to Mr Stoddart is announced. I fancy Mr Griffiths was very fond of her, and wonder if he is at all unhappy about it. I have not seem him for an age, he seems to have quite lost interest in me. I am sorry because I like him so much, and do not like to lose any of my friends.

*Tuesday 18 January* I went up to town to a tea at Mrs Hallett Burrow's, she has a pretty apartment in Central Park. She was extremely cordial and nice; there was a great crush of people and I had a very good time. I had a letter from Mr Griffiths; he thought I was away.

*Wednesday 19 January* I went up to town and lunched with Mrs Pfizer. She is settled in her town house now, and very pretty and comfortable it looks. We had a nice little luncheon together, and a long confidential talk about Mr Griffiths. She fancied there was something between us, but I undeceived her. I don't want anyone to think we are in love with each other, for that would utterly spoil our friendship, and he is not the sort of man I would like to marry.

*Friday 28 January* I had a letter from Mr Griffiths that has made me very anxious and uneasy: I can make nothing of it. He hints that he is in some great trouble that is nearly driving him insane, but he gives no clue as to what it is, and says he will come and tell me all about it. In the meantime I am imagining the very worst, and am miserably anxious and unsettled.

*Saturday 29 January* I had a note from Mr Griffiths asking if he might come and see me, also saying that his mind is at rest. I strongly suspect he is engaged to someone, and that it is all settled.

*Tuesday 1 February* Mr Griffiths came in the evening and told me all about his affairs. He *is* engaged, to a New York girl, a Miss Treddick, whom he met at Portsmouth last summer. He told me all about her, but was very restrained in his expression of admiration; he did not seem to me to be very much in love. The affair is not quite settled, but he hopes to be married before he sails for England in June. It seems so odd to think of him being engaged; he has only known her a few months.

*Sunday 13 February* I walked over to Arrochar alone in the afternoon. I found Gertrude thoroughly unhappy, she who has everything to make her happy, husband, children, a devoted mother. The trouble is that she is so enveloped in love, and so carefully protected from all trouble, that the slightest thing that goes wrong makes her wretched. She is very discontented, and dissatisfied with Gordon, whom she does not understand. No one can understand an Englishman but his own countrywomen, and I do not know of a single marriage between an Englishwoman and an American that has turned out well. The question of nationality is always a disturbing element. Englishmen are selfish, American women are exacting and selfish too, a bad combination.

*Thursday 17 February* Mr Griffiths came in the evening and talked all the time about his engagement; it does not seem to be going very smoothly. Miss Treddick's people are raising objections, and he is very low-spirited about it. He brought her photograph, she is pretty. Her name is Gertrude. He wants us to be great friends, but - I don't know.

*Sunday 27 February* After lunch I went over to the Willis's, all the old set were there, the Lyons, Busks, Mr Griffiths and me, but it was all so changed. It was very jolly in a way, we all laughed and talked, but I was very uncomfortable: it was the first time I have met the old set since Mr Griffith's engagement; they all know of it. He was very nervous and unlike himself, and they were all watching us to see how we behaved to each other. It was a very difficult position, all these people, in fact everyone thought we were engaged, and would not believe we were only very good friends. And now they are all puzzled and surprised, and are probably pitying me. It is all very tiresome; it seems impossible for a man and a woman to be friends without some such complication arising.

*Monday 28 February* I took an early train to Newark, and got to Papa's office before noon, and we went out together and bought a trunk for me to take to England. I really begin to feel now as if I were going.

*Sunday 6 March* We [the Lyons and Mabel] went over to the Willis's for tea. May and Billy were there, the old set all together once more, and I am sure for the last time. Emily and Roquey go away tomorrow, Mr Griffith's fiancée will be back from the South in a month and he will devote all his time to her, and in eight weeks I shall be gone, and the dear old set will be broken up for ever. We have had two years of it now, which is a long time, but it makes it all the harder to end it. We have had such happy times together, so many different 'sprees', but I think the jolliest of all have been the Sunday teas in Gertrude's dear little red drawing room, everything so pretty and homelike.

*Wednesday 9 March, New York, staying with Mr and Mrs Pfizer* I went up to town to dine with the Pfizers and spend the night. I had a long talk with Mrs Pfizer before dressing for dinner, it was chiefly about Mr Griffiths' engagement. She thinks he is marrying for money.

The dinner was a great success, one of the jolliest I have been to this winter. The table was lovely as usual, and the people very nice, and I felt at my best. I had a lovely grey gown and had heaps of compliments, and my spirits rose with each. I am so doubtful of myself nowadays that compliments do me good. Mr Champney told Mrs Pfizer that my get-up was perfect.

*Sunday 13 March, New Brighton* I went over to May Busk's for tea; I had not been there for an age, it was very nice. May was charming, and gave us a delicious tea with nice buttery crumpets. Mr Griffiths was there. We talked very cosily, we four, we discussed the relative merits of English and American women. Billy [Busk] admires Englishwomen, but Mr Griffiths did not commit himself. We walked home together, rather a long walk, but it was great fun. He mentioned Miss Treddick's name casually once or twice, but his conversation was chiefly about himself.

*Friday 18 March* Sara Johnson and Edith Fosser came to tea. They are dear girls, but everyone seems nice now that I am leaving them. It makes me shudder to think I sail in six weeks. I hate the idea of going and leaving all these dear kind people. It seems awful not to want to go back to England, especially after having longed for it all these years, but it seems to have come too late.

*Thursday 7 April* I got a telegram from Emily Lyon with the news that she and Roquey sail for England at the end of the month. I am delighted to hear she is going; I am so fond of her.

I had a long letter from Mr Griffiths; he is in town, staying there for this month. He wants me to meet Miss Treddick, and asks me to decide whether I would like to have a dinner or luncheon at the club to meet her. I don't much care about either. I am rather tired of him and his affairs.

*Saturday 9 April* I went up to town early this morning to see Emily; she is not very much excited about going to England, but Roquey is delighted. We lunched at the Waldorf, May Busk and Gordon came too. I saw lots of people I knew. Carolus Duran the French painter was walking up and down the corridor staring hard at everyone, evidently getting impressions. He is a handsome man, not tall, with a white beard, rather shabbily dressed, but no theatrical artistic make-up, he might have been anything from a dissenting parson to a broker. He does not label himself 'artistic'.

*Saturday 16 April, New York, staying with Dr and Mrs Eden* Another letter from Mr Griffiths begging me to be at his luncheon party, but I have quite decided not to go. I went up to town to stay with the Edens; I got there in time for dinner. Mr Cushman dined with us, and we afterwards went to the Comedy Club to see some amateur theatricals, which were fairly well given. Seated very near me were Mr Griffiths and his fiancée . I did not see him for a long time; as soon as he saw me he came to speak to me. It was rather a curious position: this is the first time I have ever seen Miss Treddick, and the first time I have ever been with him when we were not in the same party. I have grown so used to his attention, that I felt it unnatural that he should be with anyone else. He never mentioned her at all but talked just like old times, but I felt the oddness of it all, and was rather bored and I am afraid awfully rude.

Miss Treddick is exceedingly pretty, young and very fresh-looking. He is a lucky man to get such a charming girl. He came back to me several times during the evening; I wonder if he really cares for me. Everyone seems to think he does, and my intimate friends have the impertinence to tell me so. He asked me again and again to come tomorrow. What a queer little romance it is; it is lucky for me I never fell in love with him, or it might have been a tragedy.

*Tuesday 19 April, Newark, staying with Sydney and Mary Ogden* I went to Newark today to spend the night with Mary Ogden. It was a pouring wet day and the place looked very unattractive, but I felt a little sentimental interest in it. We spent the afternoon in paying calls, and dined quietly at home. I was very unhappy in Newark, but there are a few pleasant memories of it: it always suggests Court Parker at every turn. I think of him constantly, and would give almost anything to see him again. Mary says he looks very old. I wonder if I shall ever see him again, and why it was that things went so wrong with us.

Mary's children are very sweet and she is perfectly happy. She is deeply interested in her house, and goes out a great deal, but she is narrow, and probably all the happier for it. I don't think people with broad views are happy. She goes to church, does her duty, and is as simple as she ever was, but I have outgrown her.

This visit has unsettled me, and brought up all the old longing for Court Parker, and revived that miserable thought that our misunderstanding might have been explained if I had not been so stiff and shy. Looking back now I can see that I was in the wrong all through, but I was young and silly, and the infernal pride which is the bane of my life kept me from seeking any explanation.

*Friday 29 April* I was up at six o'clock this morning. I sent off all my luggage, wrote a lot of letters, and was off to Arrochar to see Gertrude before ten o'clock. I paid her a very short visit, just to say goodbye, and then rushed home again and put things away that are to be left behind. All the afternoon people kept coming to see me to say goodbye: May Bush, who really seemed sorry I am going, and Mr Griffiths, who said he was coming to see me off. Frances Depue came at five o'clock for the night

*Saturday 30 April, on board the SS Mobile* I was up this morning at five o'clock; there were a few things to be done. It was impossible to realise I was leaving home for so long. I would have given anything to have given up the whole trip.

Papa and Mamma, Frances and Fitzroy came up to see me off, and Mr Griffiths met me on the ship. We sailed at nine o'clock. The ship seems very comfortable, and there are not too many people on board. Papa and Mamma stood at the end of the dock and saw the last of me, it was dreadful leaving them. I wish I had stayed at home.

I sat on deck all day and saw Staten Island, it seemed so funny to be going away from it. It was a very warm day, the sea like a mill pond. There seem to be very nice people on board; a man from Staten Island named Whitelaw is among the passengers. He is an Englishman and devoted himself to me all day, and sits next to me at mealtimes.

*Thursday 5 May* We have had head winds ever since we left New York, and have made no speed at all. We are off the Newfoundland Banks today, and it is awfully cold and rough. Nearly all the passengers are ill. I was on deck all the morning talking to Mr Whitelaw and Mr Allen, and a very nice woman, Mrs Moore.

*Friday 6 May* It was not quite as rough today, and warmer, and we amused ourselves on deck all day. We have such a nice party at the table I sit at. I am at one end and the Fourth Officer at the other, Mr Whitelaw at my right, and the Moores, who are very nice, next. The other three people are not of much account, they don't talk much. We all talk a great deal about what we eat, meals are the great excitement on board. We see an occasional ship, and we discuss the day's run, play ship's quoits, and I tried golf. The officers are all very kind, and do their best to amuse us. After dinner we went to the Fourth Officer's cabin again, and talked and drank ginger ale and ate apples.

*Saturday 7 May* This was a glorious day; it was like yachting, the ship was so clean and steady, and even the sea-sick old ladies poked their heads out of their cabins and revived a little. I always have plenty to amuse me: Mr Whitelaw is always at hand to do anything I want, he is so kind and will do everything I ask, and the Fourth Officer is most devoted, and always is suggesting something for me to do. I am enjoying this voyage immensely and don't mind its length a bit; the people on board are so amusing. There are some girls with lovely voices, they are professionals, and are always practising in the saloon.

*Sunday 8 May* After lunch the Fourth Officer took Mr Whitelaw and myself right aft, and we sat behind the steering gear all the afternoon. He showed me all the machinery, and how to take soundings, and answered every senseless question I asked. We sat there until teatime, when I went to the saloon, where the company was very incongruous. I had tea with a very nice nun, her companion, a priggish young woman, an actor who is going to London to play in a comic opera, and a woman who looks like a women's rights lecturer, and we all agreed splendidly.

*Tuesday 10 May* I feel rather stupid today. We went right forward after breakfast and spent the morning there, lying on rugs and eating apples. The Fourth Officer had his pockets full, he always carries a lot for me. I slept all the afternoon. I am leading a very animal existence, sleeping and eating, but it has done me good, I feel like a different person.

*Thursday 12 May* All day we were in sight of land, and I sat on deck and looked at the Devonshire coast. I would like to be on one of those bluffs, and see the big Atlantic waves break against the rocks. We went aft after lunch, and sat there until teatime, those two devoted men, Mr Whitelaw and Mr Allen [the Fourth Officer], have made this voyage very pleasant for me. I have always had one or the other to wait on me. I have made friends with two very nice ladies, Miss Livingston and Miss Tracey, and another girl, Miss Hutchins, I like very much. I am such good friends with these people that it is hard to realise that our friendship is so soon to end, but I hope to see more of Mr Whitelaw and the Fourth Officer.

*Friday 13 May, Lancaster Gate, London, staying with Mr and Mrs Bishop* I got up very early this morning so as to see all the coast, for we were in sight of land all day. I saw Dover distinctly, our dear old house, and the Parade and castle, it made me rather sad to think of how few friends there were left in what used to be our home. It was a lovely day, and the country looked its best. We saw the Goodwins, Deal, Ramsgate etc, and then the Nore and Thames.

We passed a great many steamers. We came very slowly up the Thames, the custom house people came on board and examined our baggage. It was dark by that time, so they had to do it by electric light, and the confusion was awful, but it was all very interesting. We were ages getting into the Albert Docks.

We stuck on a mud bank just inside the dock and could not get alongside; another boat had to be shoved in, and we walked across her, and at last stood on English soil. Back again after ten years! By this time it was ten o'clock, and I wondered how I was going to get to Lancaster Gate alone, but Mr Allen as usual came to my rescue, and went all the way with me. We had a special train to Liverpool Street; all the passengers and luggage got in and off we went. I said goodbye to all, and promised to see some of them again. At the station there was trouble over the luggage, I was so tired that I could not pick mine out for a long time. Mr Allen did everything for me; I could not have managed without him. We finally got everything settled, got into a hansom, and got to Lancaster Gate at 12.30am. Mrs Bishop and Dolly were sitting up, and were so glad to see me as if I had been their dearest relation. They gave Mr Allen some supper, but he had to hurry back to the ship. I can never be grateful enough to him for his care and attention throughout the voyage. Eva was at a ball but came back early, and we talked until nearly three o'clock.

*Saturday 14 May* I slept very late this morning. I sleep in Eva's room; it is very nice, looking out on the park. The house is a huge one, very comfortable and home-like, as only English houses are. I had a lot of letters that I read in bed, everyone seems so glad I have come back. I got up about twelve o'clock, and went to walk in the park with Eva. It is simply lovely, such masses of flowers and green grass and beautiful healthy children with red cheeks. I thought the women rather dowdy and badly dressed.

*Monday 16 May* I went over to Bailey's Hotel this morning to see Emily Lyon, she and Roquey landed last week. It seemed so strange to see Emily in London. She was in bed looking very unhappy and lonely, she feels perfectly lost and nearly cried when she saw me. I don't think she likes London, but she was too nice to say so. I walked across the park home again, it looked lovely, full of flowers, and such quantities of beautiful children playing in Kensington Gardens. London *is* the nicest place in the world. I love it.

*Tuesday 17 May* This morning I went to the City all alone, to my bankers in Austin Friars. It was an awful place to get to and I was afraid of getting lost, but I managed all right. The City looked very dingy but delightfully old and interesting, full of dear little pokey alleys where I am sure there were all sorts of old historic houses and interesting remains. I came back by Charing Cross and Victoria, all the old familiar places, it does seem so homelike. I feel as if I knew and liked everyone I met in the streets.

I lunched with the Montefiores, who have a house in Belgrave Road for the season. Mrs Montefiore looks much older; she and her husband were charming. I am inexpressibly flattered by everyone's kindness; I hoped people would be glad to see me, but their kindness has been far more than I expected.

I had a letter from Mamma today; they are all well at home. I do wish they were all here.

*Wednesday 18 May* I spent the whole morning writing letters. I wrote to lots of people here to say I had arrived. After lunch Eva and I went to a new picture gallery on the Chelsea embankment, it is called the Tate Gallery. There are some lovely pictures in it, many of them I remember as being at South Kensington. At five o'clock we met a Canadian friend of Eva's, a Mr Redmond, and we had tea at a tea house in Bond Street where an Indian opened the door, and delicious tea was served by Indian girls in a room like an Indian bungalow. It was very pretty and quaint.

*Thursday 19 May* I went to see Aunt Mary this morning. She has a dear little house in South Kensington. She was writing at her desk in the drawing room, just as she has done every morning of her life, and as all my aunts do; immediately after breakfast they all go and answer their letters. She looks just as she did ten years ago, she reminds me so much of dear old Grandmamma. She was very sweet to me, kissed me about a dozen times. We had a long talk about the family, the accumulated news of ten years. There have been many deaths, but the ones I like best are left.

Aunt Mary has the sweetest voice and the most gracious manners of anyone I know, except of course dear Peg and Aunt Charley. My aunts are really the best-bred ladies I have ever met, it is an education to be with them.

*Monday 23 May* I lunched with Aunt Mary; she was so kind, and we had a delightful quiet little luncheon together. She treats me as if I were a child, someone to be taken care of and advised, and I enjoy it. I have been so independent and self-reliant for so long, that it is a comfort to lean ever so little on someone else.

After lunch we went to see dear old Mrs Duncombe-Shafto, whom I always look upon as one of my dearest friends. She is in a lovely house, full of old china and old furniture. She was sitting in the drawing-room, so blind that she could not recognise me until I spoke, and then I thought she would never let me go. She is a wonderful woman; in spite of her great age she is as up to date as anyone, she knows everything that is going on, entertains everyone, and is the most interesting and brilliant talker.

I got back to Lancaster Gate just in time to dress for an early dinner and go to the opera. It was a very gay night because the state ball of tonight has been put off on account of Gladstone's death, and everyone went to the opera instead. The opera was Die Walkyrie, very long and heavy. I don't appreciate Wagner. The boxes were full; every woman was covered with diamonds, tiaras, coronets etc, it was very brilliant. The Princess of Wales was in the Queen's box, she looked lovelier than ever, in black with diamond wings in her hair. She was the prettiest and sweetest-looking woman in the house, and she seemed not the least bored, she talked and nodded her head in the most animated way, and looked about twenty-eight.

*Thursday 26 May, Waldershare Park, staying with Gac, Countess of Guilford* In the afternoon I went down to Waldershare to stay with Gac Guilford. I went by the boat train from Victoria, the old familiar line I have so often gone to Dover by. There were some friends of Gac's named Farnham, mother and son, who went down with me. The brougham met us at the station, and we all drove up together. Mr Farnham was very stupid and did not talk a bit, but his mother was very nice. Waldershare looked like home; it was so familiar after all these years, and Gac not a bit changed, as kind as ever. Muriel is a great big girl.

The house is lovely, so stately after the American gimcracks I have been to, the lovely old pictures, old furniture, everything old. We had tea, then dressed for dinner. My room is a big one, with some splendid old pictures and a huge bed and a looking glass with an earl's coronet over it. We all made grand toilettes for dinner, Gac with a big diamond necklace, and met in the oak room, a room panelled with oak and a Canaletto over the mantelpiece. We dined in state in the big dining room, where there are more pictures, including the glorious Vandyke that the Queen wanted.

*Friday 27 May* Waldershare is said to be haunted, and I lay awake nearly all night expecting to see the ghost, but she never came. I spent an hour or two this morning wandering over the house and renewing my acquaintance with it. The library is the best room, full of china and some beautiful pictures, Knellers and Lelys, all of dead and gone Norths.

Gac and Mrs Farnham, her son and myself, walked up to the kennels. The hounds are not there now, and only five horses in stables built for twenty-seven. Guilford is in South Africa, and when he comes back the stables will be filled again. Mr Farnham went with me to the top of the hill whence we saw dear old Eythorne House; Gac is going to take me to see it. The deer in the park are quite tame and followed me about. The park is lovely, full of very fine old trees. Mr Farnham knows all about trees; he is much nicer than I thought. He has found out we are cousins, his aunt, Lady Hartopp, was Grandpapa's sister.

After tea Gac, Mr Farnham and I went for a ramble through the gardens and the Wilderness. That is the loveliest part of the park, it is full of flowers, bluebells and primroses, and there are hundreds of birds. Gac knows every bird and where lots of their nests are. She and Muriel are thorough country people, they understand everything connected with it.

*Saturday 28 May* After lunch we went to call on the Narborough D'Aeths, who are living in Grandmamma's old house. It was the first time I had been in it since I was a mere child. The house of course looks altered without the dear old furniture, but the garden is just the same as when Grannie walked in it among the flowers she loved so, the same Banksia roses climbing up the walls, and the stone trough for the birds to drink in. The bees used to fall in and drown themselves, and Grannie used to put in pieces of wood for them to climb up on and be rescued.

We then went to a cricket match in the park. Guilford has built a new pavilion that was opened today. The match was between the workmen on the estate and the house servants, and a team from the artillery at Dover: the soldiers played best. We had tea in the pavilion, ourselves, the D'Aeths and the Atwoods, a very uproarious meal it was, we really romped. I eat a great deal of cake as usual, and Captain Clough-Taylor made a caricature of me that was really very funny. After we finished Gac asked all the cricketers to come up and gave them tea, soldiers, servants and labouring men, and it was wonderful how nice their manners were. She talked to them and they all seem to adore her, she is so kind to everybody; being queen of Waldershare suits her.

*Sunday 29 May* I got up early and had a walk with Mr Farnham before breakfast. We went to the gardens and picked lilies of the valley. It was a lovely morning, and the birds were singing loud enough to drown our voices almost, the woods here are full of nightingales. We went to service in the dear little church, we in the front pew, the servants immediately behind us. The butler sang everything in a very loud good tenor.

*Monday 30 May* I walked over to Eythorne with Gac, the dear little village seemed like something I had once seen in a dream, so familiar and yet so vague. We went to see Mrs West; she was Grandmamma's housekeeper from 1858 to her death in '75, when she married the estate carpenter. She used to be so good to me when I was a child. She was very pleased to see me today, she kissed me and held my hands and examined me closely to see what I was like. And she talked about dear Grannie and Grandpapa and the old happy days. When I went away she kissed me again.

A whole crowd of people came to lunch, Lord and Lady Forrester, their daughter and son, a Mr Wanklyn, MP for Bradford, and others. We all went down to the pavilion afterwards to see another cricket match. A lot of people joined us there, and quite late in the afternoon who should appear but Captain Tattersall. It was odd to meet him again after all these years. At first I was decidedly disappointed in him; he is of course much older, rather grey and very quiet. There was such a crowd that I had not much chance of talking to him until tea time, when he came and sat beside me and we had a long talk, and he told me as much as he could in that short time about himself and his doings.

I have so often wondered if I would ever meet him again. He is very nice, I like him immensely, but I could not help wondering what it was about him that made me fall in love with him for so many years. It seems so strange to think I made myself unhappy about him. Alas for realisation: I have longed so often to see him again, and the meeting gave me very little more pleasure than any casual acquaintance. We had a little walk through the park and then back to the house, where he got my address in London and asked if he could call, so I shall see him again.

*Tuesday 31 May, Lancaster Gate, staying with Mr and Mrs Bishop* I got up early and went for a walk with Mr Farnham. He is so nice and good-looking, and likes me very much. I left Waldershare by a morning train and went up to London with the Farnhams. I got to Lancaster Gate in time for tea. Although I was sorry to leave Waldershare, it was a great pleasure to get back here where they are all so good to me.

*Wednesday 1 June* I went over to Aunt Mary's to see dearest Peg, who has just come back from Italy. I went into the room unannounced, and for a minute she did not realise who it was, and then she was really quite hysterical. We both laughed and cried and kissed each other a dozen times, she is the dearest woman in the world. I am more than happy to have seen her once more; we talked as if we were wound up. I had a thousand things to tell her, she is the one person whom I don't mind telling everything. She is just as funny and witty as ever, just as stately, in fact perfect as ever. All my aunts are charming, but she is the best.

*Saturday 4 June* It is all nonsense to say that it is a mistake to 'go back', and that things that have pleased one in childhood seem changed for the worse when one is grown-up. I have been 'going back' ever since I have been in England, and everyone and everything is better than my wildest expectations. My only disappointment was in Dover, everything else has been perfect, and I have never been happier than I am now.

*Thursday 9 June* Some people came to tea, and rather late came Captain Tattersall. He looked very well, his hair is very white, but it goes well with his dark eyes and moustache, he is very distinguished looking. He gave me a brief sketch of what he himself has done during these last twelve years. He is very cynical and rather conceited and does not seem happy. I don't know whether I really like him or not, he is not like he used to be. He thinks I am just the same, but I don't quite see how he can tell. I think he is spoilt.

*Thursday 14 June* Mabel Bishop announced her engagement today, to a barrister named Richardson. The whole family is jubilant, much more pleased than she seems to be. We had great fun chaffing them in our elegant way.

*Thursday 16 June* Harry Bishop came very late last night, too late for me to see him, so we met at breakfast this morning. When I last saw him he was at a crammers, now he is Captain Bishop. He is very good-looking, very tall, an enormously big man. He is rather quiet and shy, but he seemed to be as nice as the other Bishops which is saying a good deal, for they are all charming.

Eva and I went to tea with Mrs Duncombe-Shafto. She had a lot of people there, a very nice woman Lady Elizabeth Williamson, who comes from Durham and knows all my relations; it is so nice to come back to England, and feel what an important family I belong to after living among Americans who don't know anything about it. I hope I am not a snob, but I do love being important.

*Friday 17 June* I spent the morning sitting in the park with Harry talking. He is rather a silent young man; Eva says he is shy, so it was rather uphill work talking to him, but he is so good-looking that I can forgive him a lot.

*Saturday 18 June* Harry is improving. I think he *was* shy, but I am thawing him. We again spent the morning in the park, we walked across to Hyde Park Corner by easy stages, stopping to sit down whenever we felt inclined, which was very often. We sat in the Row until one o'clock, when I went to lunch with Gac and he to the 'Rag' to lunch there. Gac had a man from Dorset, a Mr Dale, rather a bore. Muriel was there of course, and she and Gac were so charming that it almost compensated for Mr Dale's stupidity.

After tea I went with Harry to Kensington Gardens, and we sat under the trees until it was time to dress. After dinner we did not quite know what to do with ourselves, so Harry got a hansom and I put a cape over my dinner dress, and we drove about for an hour or more. It was a very absurd way of spending our time, but it was very jolly, and Harry is improving at an alarming rate. He certainly is as nice as he is good-looking.

*Wednesday 22 June* Harry is a funny person. The last two days he has been very quiet, hardly saying a word, in fact I have not seen much of him, and began to fancy he thought I did not improve on further acquaintance. But this morning Dolly called me into her room mysteriously, and gave me a little blue jeweller's box from him, and it was a dear little gold safety pin for my tie. The other day I said to Eva in his presence that I wanted a new pin, and he remembered it, and got it for me, but it was so funny not giving it to me himself, and he did not give me a chance of thanking him for it until the evening.

We dined early, and Harry and I went to the Gaiety to see a very pretty play called The Runaway Girl. It is one of the prettiest dressed pieces I have ever seen, and it was so funny we laughed all the time. After it was over we drove back, went in for a second, and then went on to a dance next door, where the others with Eva had preceded us. We were very late of course. I danced twice with Harry, went into supper with him, and sat on the stairs where we had a quarrel. He said I had been treating him very badly these last two or three days, and he is offended and looks as if he were going to sulk.

*Saturday 25 June* Eva and I went down to Ranelagh in the afternoon. We met Colonel Henriques there, and spent a long afternoon watching polo-racing and the very smart clothes. Ranelagh is much prettier than Hurlingham. We had tea in the pavilion, and stayed until nearly seven o'clock. On our way down we passed the York children, our future king, little Prince Edward sitting beside his nurse, a dear little fair boy.

When I got back from Ranelagh I went upstairs. Just when I was changing someone knocked at the door; it was Harry to ask me to go to the play. So I dressed up, and we hurried through dinner, and went off together, and had a most delightful evening. He was quite at his best, and our little chilliness is over. He is so nice and kind, and pays me all the little attentions that I love. I was rather shivery driving to the theatre, and he took off his coat and wrapped me up in it. I love being taken care of. We got back very late and sat up talking alone for nearly an hour, which was of course very improper, but *very* nice.

*Sunday 26 June* We were all very late this morning; I never breakfast before ten. After breakfast I tried to write letters and my diary but Harry kept interrupting me, so I gave it up. Out of compliment to him I put on what he thinks is my prettiest dress, a black and white cloth, and with Eva we went to walk in the park. They took me as far as Hyde Park Corner, whence I drove to Eccleston Square to lunch with Mrs Farnham. I was sorry to go because Harry's leave is up today, and he said it was horrid of me to be away for his last meal.

Mrs Farnham's luncheon was very nice. Miss Peel, a very nice woman, was there, also Miss Hanbury-Tracy, Lady Augusta Farnham, and two other ladies. Mrs Farnham was so kind to me; she makes me feel she loves having me there. I got back to Lancaster Gate just in time to say goodbye to Harry; he went back to Preston, where his regiment is quartered.

*Saturday 2 July* In the afternoon Eva and I went down to Ranelagh to see the polo. We watched it all the afternoon, with a short interval for tea and strawberries under the trees. There was an immense crowd of wonderfully well-dressed people, hundreds of smart carriages, coaches etc, and great show of polo ponies, altogether a very expensive affair: only a very rich country could have produced such a show. With all the luxury, there was an utter absence of ostentation, everyone seemed to take it all as a matter of course.

*Monday 4 July* I met Gac in the park early this a.m. and sat with her until lunchtime. Muriel was riding, and came to the rail to speak with us several times. We saw lots of people we knew: Florrie Hastings, who is still pretty, although she is an old woman now, but she is still known as the 'beautiful Marchioness of Hastings'. [see note 17 Jan 1891] Gac knows everybody, so it was very nice being with her. I lunched in Eccleston Square with Muriel, who was in great form. I think we would be great friends if we saw more of each other.

I went back to Lancaster Gate and called for Eva, and we went to a reception at the American Ambassador's. They have a house in Carlton House Terrace, and it was literally crammed, it took us about ten minutes to get upstairs. We were very graciously received by their 'Excellencies', Colonel and Mrs Hay. The crowd was a very smart one, and very American. It wasn't pleasant to hear the old familiar twang.

In the evening I had rather a blow. Harry wrote to his father to say his regiment was ordered to Malta on the 26th of next month, en route for India; it is very unexpected and a disappointment. I hoped so much to see a great deal of him next winter. He will come up for Mabel's wedding, after that I shall probably not see him again. I shall go to America and be buried there for the rest of my life, and he will be in India for the best part of his life probably. It is rather a horrid old world sometimes.

*Saturday 9 July* I spent the morning with Aunt Mary, who gave me a little lecture on the way *ladies* should behave. I don't think she actually believes I don't behave myself, but she has doubts, I am sure.

*Tuesday 12 July* Eva and I went to see an aunt of hers who lives at Heston, a dear little village just out of London. Her husband Mr Sharpe is rector, and they live in an ideal rectory, a very old red brick house facing on a village green, and it is now a large rambling place with mysterious little passages and thick walls. There is a lovely old garden that was a blaze of flowers, literally thousands of roses, and an old lawn and splendid old walnut trees.

The rector is a dear old man, he took me into his study and showed me all his books, and read me part of his sermon for next Sunday. I felt as if I were in another world. I so seldom hear anything about religion now, but in the country among the flowers, and in the perfect quiet and peace, God always seems so much nearer.

The church is a very old one, the tower is a thousand years old. We went to the top of it, up a narrow spiral staircase, stone steps that are much worn; fancy the people who have gone up those stairs, Saxons, Normans etc. I think if I could go up them alone and dream, I could almost see those old people, charm up their ghosts.

We went back to the rectory for tea, a regular old-fashioned country tea, with places laid at the table, loads of cake and strawberries, it was very jolly, the kind old rector making mild jokes. Eva said she had never seen him so animated before. I was sorry to leave the garden, it did look so peaceful in the sunset; the rector went nearly all the way to London with us. We were loaded with roses, and rather sunburnt after a long happy day. A day spent in the country suggests the Nunc Dimittis, one seems to take some of its peace away.

*Monday 18 July* We spent the whole day at Lords watching the Gentlemen v Players. It was W.Grace's fiftieth birthday. The place was packed full of people, they were sitting ten deep all round the grass, and Grace was cheered every time he appeared. He plays a wonderful game still, but he was very lame today. We saw Gunn make 139; all the best players were playing, the fielding was magnificent. We had seats in the luncheon pavilion (on the roof) and got a capital view; we stayed until nearly seven,when the score was 309 runs for five wickets for the Players. It was as good cricket as I have ever seen.

*Wednesday 20 July* I went with Mrs Bishop to have her dress for Mabel's wedding tried on; my old dressmaker Sykes is making it, as well as all Mabel's things. The wedding is the one topic now, presents come pouring in, and everybody is discussing what to wear. Even the men of the family are as much concerned as the girls, and bridegroom and best man are simply racked by anxiety about the fit of their coats and their ties etc.

*Thursday 21 July* In the afternoon Eva and I paid calls, and ended up at Mrs Duncombe-Shafto's. She was in great form today, and as her reminiscences go back for over sixty years she has a great deal to talk about. She told of how she posted from London to Paris in the early '30s, she and her husband in one carriage, and in another was their great friend Henry

Lord Brougham. He used to bitterly resent the extortionate charges at the hotels, and used the most frightful language before everybody. Mrs Shafto said they were often detained on their journeys while he disputed charges. He eventually had always to pay.

*Henry Lord Brougham (1778-1868), anti-slave trade campaigner, parliamentary reformer and Lord Chancellor. He popularised the compact four-wheeled one-horse carriage named after him.*

*Sunday 23 July* There was a bustle all day, even Sunday did not stop the wedding preparations, new clothes and guests are the only topics; really getting married seems to be entirely a matter of clothes. Mabel has had heaps of presents, seven jewelled bracelets, some brooches, and quantities of silver things. The engagement has been so short, and she has had so much to do, that she is half dazed.

At five o'clock we went to the tea garden in the park. Dorothy and her young man, Mrs Richards, and Mabel and her fiancé met us there, and we had tea together under the trees. It was a very pretty scene, lots of people, all well-dressed, a lovely bright day, and the park looked its best. I was very happy.

After tea we separated. I don't know what became of the others, but Harry and I sat under the trees and talked until eight o'clock. He said all sorts of pleasant things. He is a very observant person, he notices everything I wear, every fresh dress I come down in he says something about, no one has ever admired my clothes so much before, and it really is an incentive to make myself look nice. As a rule I never believe any compliments I get, but Harry is so sincere and honest that I know he means every word he says. I have enjoyed meeting him again so much, and now he will go away to Malta, and before he comes back I shall be in America, and I don't suppose we shall ever meet again.

*Wednesday 27 July* Everyone woke up at an awfully early hour, and at once began to be busy. There seemed to be a thousand things to do, all the presents to be arranged in the drawing-room, flowers to be put in vases, and the wedding favours and rice to be put in readiness. The bride's bouquet and ditto for the bridesmaids came early, also a lovely one of yellow roses to match my dress. A lovely big wedding cake came, it was about five feet high, all covered with white flowers.

We all began to dress before lunch; I was about the last to be ready. Mabel came into my room while she was dressing, she was very nervous and tired out with all she had had to do; getting married must be an awful ordeal. Mrs Bishop was the prettiest woman present in black and pink. The two bridesmaids, Dolly and Dorothy Richards, were in blue and white, and all the others in white. My dress was a bright canary yellow; I did not like it very much.

We were almost the last to arrive at the church, which was full of people. I sat in one of the front pews with 'the family'. The church was beautifully decorated with white flowers and palms. The bridegroom appeared looking very nervous and waited close to us, the organ played soft music that got on my nerves and made me feel as if I could cry, the bride came preceded by the choir singing a hymn. Mabel was as white as her dress, trembling like a leaf, and her head drooping as if she would faint, but she looked lovely.

The wedding service is an ordeal. The choir sang very pretty hymns, Mrs Bishop cried, and even dear old Darrel looked weepy, but it was all over soon, and Mabel looked quite happy and smiling as she left the church to the wedding march. We all trooped after her as quickly as possible, and got to the house in time to receive the guests, who streamed in, kissed the bride, examined the presents, and then rushed downstairs to tea, where they spent the rest of the day.

There was a lovely tea, the bride cut the cake, her health was drunk and a few speeches made, and then she rushed away to change. She was tired and bored by all the fuss, she did not seem to enjoy it a bit. The people stayed until she came down, they ranged themselves in the hall with handfuls of rice, and she was thoroughly well pelted, the bridegroom too. Hugh tied a white shoe on the carriage and the top was simply covered with rice; we all stood on the porch and gave a cheer as they went off. Mabel looked very pretty. Most of the people left immediately and we had the place to ourselves.

We had just time to change into our smartest clothes, dine very hurriedly and go off to the Gaiety where we had two boxes thrown into one. The entire wedding party went, the two bridesmaids, the best man, all the Bishops, some extra men, and me. We all went in hansoms, I went with Harry, our last jaunt together I am afraid. We had seen the play before, so we did not hurry and were the last to leave the house. We all took our bouquets and our box must have looked very gay and smart.

We came home as we went. It was very cool and nice in the hansom driving through the dark streets, but I was very tired, too tired to say all I wanted to dear old Harry.   A whole crowd of people came to supper,  and we sat up until two o'clock, drinking healths, laughing and talking. I was so tired I could hardly speak, but Harry sat next to me and made me drink champagne until I revived. I talked to him all the time, and we said good-night alone in the boudoir.

*Thursday 28 July* I went to the park with Harry in the morning to have the customary glass of milk. We fed the sparrows and talked as if things were going on like this for ever. After lunch he went away, he goes back to Preston for a few weeks, and then to Southampton to sail for Malta. Exit Harry!

*Tuesday 2 August* I went to see Aunt Mary this morning; she has just come back from Devonshire and looks years younger and better than she did when I last saw her ten years ago. She was very kind and delighted to see me, and I had a very nice talk. I am to go and stay with her on the 18ᵗʰ. I think I shall like it, only I am afraid Aunt Mary will expect me to talk to her about all my affairs. I have not anything particular to talk about, but I hate discussing myself with anyone. I am not sure whether I have any feelings, but if I have they are buried so deep that it hurts to dig them up and expose them to view.

*Thursday 4 August, Sutton, Surrey, staying with Colonel and Mrs Monte-fiore* I was very busy all the morning packing, such a tiresome business. Mrs Bishop told me she thought I cared very little about Harry's going away to Malta. I do care very much and told her so. Eva thinks I am flirting with him, and did her best to keep us apart during his last leave: it was very silly, but she is so fond of him, and sisters always think their brothers are in danger.

I was so sorry to say goodbye to the Bishops, it was like leaving home, and they were all so kind and said they would miss me. Sutton is a very short way from town, the Montefiores met me at the station. I was here years ago one summer. They have a nice house with a garden and tennis lawn. The family consists of Dita and her two small brothers, both destined for Woolwich, and their tutor, a quiet young man. Colonel Montefiore is charming; he talked politics; of course he thinks the country is going to the dogs, every Englishman of a certain age does. It is quiet here; the silence seems deadly after London.

*Tuesday 9 August* I had a short letter from Mamma; Sybil and Maude were expected home the day after she wrote. I am very glad; I did not like to think of Papa and Mamma being alone. I had a very amusing letter from Eva with no mention of Harry in it, she is so afraid I am flirting with him and does her best to keep us apart. What a goose she is, it is just the way to make us flirt with each other.

*Thursday 11 August* We played tennis for a little while but it was too hot. We went for a long drive after lunch through Cheam and Ewell and Epsom to Ashtead woods, where we had tea and spent an hour or more in the woods, very idly looking at the view, and not exerting ourselves much. It was a lovely view, cornfields all yellow, little patches of dark woods and a few red-roofed houses, all very peaceful, contented and *good*, it seems as if no evil could be in an English country landscape, it is too quiet. But it makes me sad; I love it from the bottom of my heart, and I shall have to leave it all again, and go to that America I hate. It suits me so well, this quiet peaceful country life. I cannot explain the fascination it has for me.

*Monday 15 August* I had a long letter from Eva, a very frank nice one. I knew she was worried about Harry and me, so I wrote and asked her to be quite honest and tell me what she thought about it, and her answer was just what I expected. Harry cannot afford to marry me. I have no money, and he must marry someone who has. Eva thinks I don't care for him, but is afraid it is serious with him, and as she sees the hopelessness of it wants to keep us apart. She says that if he married me he would be obliged to leave the service, and thus spoil a very promising career. He would have to give up polo and hunting and lots of other things. We both have extravagant tastes, and would be miserable after a year or two. It does seem hard but I am a very sensible person, thoroughly worldly, and even if I chose to sacrifice myself, I would not let Harry give up everything for me. We are both very modern, selfish and luxurious, and love in a cottage would not suit either of us, but oh, if it could only have been different, how happy and good I could be. Dear Harry, with his splendid looks and sterling character is a typical Englishman, a very king among men, I shall never know such another. I wish I had been born a dairy maid, they don't stop to consider ways and means.

*The following four pages have been torn out; the next page begins:*

. . . . is gone, Harry is gone', until I almost went mad. After dinner I had to sing and play. I did not mind much; I would have liked to have gone to a dance or play and laughed and flirted with anyone; there is sometimes something rather amusing about a great trouble. Dearest Harry, I am so glad we have parted with the kindest thoughts about each other.

*Friday 19 August, South Kensington, staying with Aunt Mary* This was rather a difficult day to get through. It is so quiet here that I am rather thrown back upon myself, and I need noise and gaiety now. Everyone here is so old and sleepy.

Aunt Mary is very sweet, and dear old Fraulein their old governess is staying here, and they all talk about old days. At any other time it would interest me very much, but just now it irritates me. There is such an air of having done with youth and all its hopes that makes me shiver.

I suppose it is good for me being here; Aunt Mary is so stately and punctilious. I must not put my elbows on the table or talk slang or go out much alone. I feel as if I had never behaved properly in my life before. Dear Peg came in time for dinner. She came from Waldershare where she has been ever since I last saw her. She was very tired and overcome by the heat, and did not talk much.

I wrote a long letter to Mamma today, my weekly letter.

*Saturday 20 August* It was very hot today, and the house was so cool and dark that I did not go out. It was a very quiet day. Aunt Mary was busy, fussing about. I can see that my restlessness and nervousness is a family failing. Dear Peg is calmness itself. We talked a great deal today about the old days; I have been so little with the 'family' that I really know very little of it. Aunt Mary was talking about Aunt Barbara (13) and what a wonderful woman she was. She did everything well, spoke languages, painted, was up to date in everything, and sang so well that the Queen was constantly sending for her to sing.

*Saturday 27 August* I had a letter from Aunt Charlie asking me to Glemham next week, and thanking me for a photograph. After lunch I went to see Edith Taylor and walked nearly all the way to her house, but she was out. It was a good day for walking, rather chilly with a wind and occasional showers.

*Wednesday 31 August, Glemham Hall, Suffolk, staying with Aunt Charlie* I left Aunt Mary's this morning; I was not altogether sorry to go, she has been very kind but Tit is rather trying, and it is very dull. I am afraid I am spoilt, but I can't bear a quiet life now. I left London at twelve and got to Glemham at four. At the station a trap was waiting for me and I drove myself to the house. It is a great big red-brick house, Elizabethan.

*Glemham Hall in Suffolk was another North property. It had been acquired in 1710 by a younger son of the 4ᵗʰ Lord North. He had grown rich as a merchant in the Levant, but when his line died out in 1821 it was left to the 6ᵗʰ Earl of Guilford.*

Aunt Charlie was waiting in the hall for me. She is still very handsome, her hair is white as snow and powdered, dressed most beautifully in black velvet, and jewels of course. She gave me a most gracious welcome and I sat in the hall and talked, then rested in my room a little, and came down to tea, after which she showed me part of the house.

The hall is a glorious big one, with a quantity of pictures, all portraits of dead Norths, and some very old furniture. There is a piano, and an organ at the foot of the grand staircase. There is armour on the staircase, and such a quantity of china that it is like a museum; the whole place looks as if it had been untouched for a hundred years. Aunt Charlie took me everywhere and talked incessantly. I think she must have been unusually nice, everyone says she is so queer and uncertain.

At six Peg came in with Bobbie [Dickson], and Lord and Lady Monson who are staying here. Lady Monson is as beautiful as ever, although she must be nearly sixty. Aunt Charlie came down to dinner looking like a picture of Pompadour, with her white hair piled high, and a long flowing silk gown. Lady Monson was perfectly lovely in black with a diamond necklace. We had a very good dinner, the table beautifully arranged and four men servants. Aunt Charlie keeps up more state than Gac does.

*Thursday 1 September* This house is simply perfect, and so huge I shall never see the end of it. In one wing are a library, drawing-room, two boudoirs, a hall and a staircase. There are seven staircases in the house. In the drawing room are chairs that were in the room Charles II occupied.

After lunch I went for a long walk alone, the country is lovely, very well-wooded and prosperous looking. A lot of people came to tea, Mrs Lowther, the Duchess de Sermenita, Miss Lowther and Mrs Mulholland, they were all very uninteresting. At dinner tonight Lady Monson told us about the coronation of the Russian emperor; she is lady in waiting to the Duchess of Edinburgh, and went with her. Lady Monson says the dowager Empress is charming, one of the kindest and most sympathetic of women

*Friday 2 September* After lunch I walked with Peg to the lodge to call on the lodge keeper's old wife, a dear old woman who showed us her flowers, which were lovely, and a jackdaw that talked, a most wonderful bird. I walked through the gardens afterwards: there are four big walled gardens, and a long broadwalk edged with laurel hedges. The Italian garden is the prettiest.

Colonel Parker came today. Aunt Peg warned me against him as being a dreadful flirt. He plays the violin. After dinner the organist of Framlingham came and played on the organ in the hall, it is a beauty. Colonel Parker played on his violin and I on the piano, and then I sang The Lost Chord with organ and violin, and they were all so pleased, and I got compliments enough to satisfy even my voracious appetite.

*Sunday 4 September* I was very late for breakfast, but it takes a long time to put on ones Sunday clothes. I went to morning service with all the men of the party. The butler here, Ash, is the leader of the choir, and he asked me if I would sing in the choir today. Of course I consented, and we had a specially elaborate service. The choir is composed almost entirely of the servants here, with a sprinkling of village children; they sing very well. The church here is very small, a chapel by the chancel is the Glemham pew, it has a separate entrance. The church walls are covered with tablets to the memory of various Norths, for hundreds of years back.

After dinner the organist Mr Wright came, and we had a delightful musical evening. I was too tired to sing more than once, I sang The Lost Chord, with Colonel Parker playing the violin and Mr Wright the organ. Afterwards we had Braga's serenata, Gounod's Ave Maria on organ, piano and violin. It was really almost professional, and the scene was lovely, the organ and grand piano facing the staircase where they were all sitting, the old portraits and armour, and through the arch the big hall could be seen, beautiful crimson satin curtains, heaps of large palms, and the women in their pretty bright dresses, and all very softly lighted by candles. It was really lovely; I am enjoying myself so much.

*Tuesday 6 September* After lunch I went for a walk, through a lovely stretch of the park on to the road, and through lovely leafy lanes to a village called Stratford. There is an old church and a few houses, not many people to be seen, but an old man leaning over a fence who wished me good day, and little girls who curtsied to me. All the farm labourers I met touched their hats, one appreciates all these civilities after living in America; it is wonderful the kindly feeling there is between classes and masses, all the tenants here are so nice, and Aunt Charlie is charming to them, so much interested in them.

*Wednesday 7 September* I played the organ in Bobbie's room for a long time. It has a very sweet tone, it used to be in the church and was brought here when they got a new one. Bobbie's room is full of old furniture and pictures, and a quantity of china, but then every room and corner of this house is like a museum. There is a state bedroom, the one that Charles II slept in, and untouched since his time. The bed has crimson velvet curtains, with white plumes on each poster. In all this big house there is no ghost or legend of any kind.

*Thursday 8 September* After lunch I practised and worked and sat under the cedars on the lawn with Bobbie and Mrs Butler. She is a Russian, very lively and amusing, and utterly reckless in what she says. She talks incessantly; she can jabber in five languages.

Dinner tonight was very amusing. Mrs Butler talked all the time and Bobbie was just as amusing, chaff is the order of the day here, and I get a tremendous share of it, but I love it, it is all so good-natured and amusing. Talk was a bit risqué; it always is when Bobbie meets a kindred spirit like Mrs Butler.

*Saturday 10 September* Captain Shipley arrived, rather late. We went for a walk round the gardens until it was time to dress for dinner. He is very nice and very flirtatious. We played cards after dinner, and Captain Shipley sat next to me, and flirted outrageously right under Aunt Charlie's and Peg's eyes, but they are delightful chaperones. It was a very jolly evening, but I am a frivolous wretch, Harry has not been gone a month, and here I am flirting wildly.

*Sunday 11 September* After breakfast I went for a walk with Captain Shipley. We sat on a log in the park until luncheon time, talking. He told me all about himself: he is devoted to politics, and left the army some years ago. He was to have gone today, but he asked me to arrange that he should stay overnight. I asked Aunt Charlie, and she was charming about it, and at once asked him. She certainly does spoil me.

Dinner tonight was very amusing. Mrs Butler was in splendid form, and talked so loud and fast that no one else had a chance. Aunt Charlie did not like it, especially as she told rather risqué stories and kissed her hands to all the men at the table and punched Bobbie in the ribs to accentuate her jokes. She is dreadful.

After dinner we played cards. Captain Shipley sat next to me; it is a very decided flirtation, and of course the chaff is tremendous, but I don't mind. He wants the Edens to ask him to Eden Lodge while I am there, and has been making himself very agreeable to them. I hope they will ask him, it would be so nice for me.

*Monday 12 September* Mr Howard went away this morning, and the Edens and Minnie Bainbridge in the afternoon. I am so sorry they have gone, they were so nice, and Harry was most amusing and cheering, but I am going to stay with them very soon, and Emily has asked Captain Shipley to come too. After they had gone, he and I went out to the yew walk and sat there until nearly teatime. I don't understand him at all, but I am afraid he is a great flirt: he cannot possibly mean all he says. I like him very much and am glad I am going to see him again. I wish I knew if he likes me as much as he pretends to.

*Tuesday 13 September* There was rather a row today. Bobbie and Mrs Butler chaffed me so unmercifully about Captain Shipley that Aunt Charlie was angry, and spoke to Bobbie; that made him angry with me. I am sorry about it for I did not mind the chaff at all, only Aunt Charlie thought it silly and vulgar. I sat with her all the afternoon and worked at some point-lace I am making.

*Wednesday 14 September* Bobbie is furious with me. He and Mrs Butler are together all day, and Aunt Charlie is so angry with her that she will scarcely speak to her, she thinks her awfully fast. She is going tomorrow and I am glad, because the situation is rather uncomfortable.

*Thursday 15 September* Mrs Butler went away today to everyone's relief. Aunt Charlie would hardly speak to her at the last, and I was afraid there would really be a fuss, but she went off with a slight show of civility on both sides. She kissed me, and I did feel sorry for her although she behaved badly.

After tea I went to choir practice, and worked at the music for the harvest festival on Sunday. Miss Linthwaite the organist is a very nice girl, quite a lady, the daughter of a clergyman; she asked me to go to lunch with her tomorrow and Aunt Charlie will not hear of it: she says Miss Linthwaite is not of our class, and she does not want me to associate with her on terms of equality. It seems rather absurd, but I can't disobey Aunt Charlie.

*Friday 16 September* I went for a walk in the park after breakfast. There is a huge linden tree with a branch near the ground that I can reach and sit on, it is very comfortable, and I sit there and think. It is very quiet now and I have plenty of time to myself, but it would be very nice if Captain Shipley were here. It was a lovely day, with rather a full breeze. I was out nearly all day roaming about the park.

*Monday 19 September* Mr Earle came today. He is an American, but has lived all his life in Europe. He hates America, which I think horrid, no one ought to hate their own country. He is a bookish sort of man, and talks about music and poetry, quotes Italian and collects old silver, also uses quantities of scent. I don't think I shall like him. He has an eye-glass, the third man who has come here with one. Mr Howard and Captain Shipley both glared at me through an eye-glass.

*Tuesday 20 September* I had a letter from Harry Bishop written from Malta; he gives an account of the voyage etc.

After breakfast Bobbie called me into the garden in a very mysterious way, and there told me that he had heard that Captain Shipley was a married man. Bobbie knows very little about him, and his visits here were as a complete stranger. I simply don't believe it, for I liked him too well to be able to believe him such an unmitigated scoundrel. It is beyond belief that he could come to such a house as this, and pay me such marked attention before everyone, if he were married, but the matter is to be thoroughly sifted. Life is full of sensations. I was amused at first, the humour of the thing struck me, but afterwards I felt rather unhappy about it, for if it is true it is so sad to think that so nice a man is such a blackguard.

*Thursday 22 September* After lunch Bobbie went off on his bicycle, and Mr Earle and I drove through the loveliest lanes to a place called Dennington, a quaint little village full of houses with thatched roofs. There is an old curiosity shop there, it is really three or four old barns with lofts stuffed full of old furniture, books, china etc, bought at sales at the farm houses and cottages round here.

Bobbie has found out beyond doubt that Captain Shipley is married, but is on such bad terms with his wife that they each go their own way. I am so sorry for him, and cannot understand why he did not tell us about her. Bobbie is furious and is going to cut him, but Aunt Charlie makes all sorts of excuses for him. So do I, but I wish he had been more honest.

*Friday 23 September* Guilford (65) came in time for dinner. I had not seen him since he was a baby, he is a great tall boy of twenty-one now, rather gawky and not good-looking, but he seems nice, and is quite free from any airs. He is very boyish and jolly, and we had rather a noisy dinner, cards afterwards as usual. Bobbie made some punch which was very strong and good, he made it because I caught cold today like an idiot, and he thought it would do me good.

*Saturday 24 September* I went for a long walk after lunch, across the fields and over fences. I don't like the roads, and it is great fun going across country because you never quite know where you are going. I went through the village, all the little girls curtsied to me and the boys touched their foreheads, nice polite little things. I wish I were the Lady Bountiful of a village.

I shall be so sorry to leave here, it seems like home, such a dear old house, and I am sure I shall never come back again. Aunt Charlie goes to Nice for the winter soon, she has asked me to come to her in May, but I am afraid I shall be in America then.

*Sunday 25 September* I felt quite sad all day because it is my last day at Glemham. I do love the dear old place, and feel as if I were at home here. I have grown so accustomed to the walks and gardens and have my own special haunts. I could never tire of Glemham; I don't believe I shall ever come back to it again.

*Monday 26 September, South Kensington, staying with Aunt Mary* I had a very comfortable journey up to town. I went with Aunt Charlie who was going to Brockenhurst. She took a footman and a maid, and had a compartment engaged, so we had it all to ourselves all the way up. We lunched in the train. It was very pretty country we went through; we parted at Liverpool Street.

*Saturday 1 October* Aunt Mary was talking about her girlhood today, it was very interesting. She was presented when she was seventeen at St James's Palace. The drawing-rooms were held there then, and the great Duke of Wellington came up and shook hands and congratulated her, and she was so pleased and flattered. He lived at Walmer Castle then, close to Grandpapa's house. They were great friends, and Aunt Mary often went to the castle. The Duke was very simple in his tastes, his room was like a barrack room, the only luxurious article in it being a white silk mattress which he always used.

*Monday 3 October* I went to Lancaster Gate this morning and called for Eva, and we went together to Paddington and met Edith Richards, who came up from Wales for a few days. She was looking very well. It is nice to be going back there after all these years, how happy I once was there, and I wonder how it will be now. After we had seen Edith into her cab, Eva and I went off and had some luncheon and did some shopping.

*Wednesday 5 October, West Cross, near Swansea, staying with Mrs Richards and her daughter Edith* The greater part of the morning was taken up with packing. I am beginning to be quite an experienced packer, and don't put my boots on top of my evening dresses as I used to. Aunt Mary and Tit seemed sorry to say goodbye to me, but I was glad to get away from London. I was to have met Edith Richards at Paddington and to have gone down with her, but she never appeared and I had the long tiresome journey to Swansea all alone.

I did not reach West Cross until 9.30pm; there is a long drive from the station to the house and I was dead tired. There was a telegram from Edith to say she missed her train and would come tomorrow. Mrs Richards and Lewis received me, and Mrs Lewis was there. I was too tired to talk much, so I went to bed, in the same room I had when I was here eleven years ago.

*Thursday 6 October* It is very nice being back here after all these years, and nothing seems changed much. Mrs Lewis thinks I am prettier than ever and not much older, which is a great comfort. We drove into Swansea after breakfast to meet Edith, she was very contrite for having missed the train yesterday. After lunch we both were rather tired, so we had deck chairs put on the terrace, and sat there wrapped up in rugs all the afternoon.

We talked over all that had happened since I was last here, and agreed that although we are older, we are happier now than we were as young girls. I certainly enjoy life more every day. We are both boundlessly ambitious and have great ideas of our capabilities. She is very rich and pretty, this lovely place belongs to her, and I think she is quite happy.

*Saturday 8 October* We drove into Swansea to the market this morning. It is quite a sight, the women are dressed in the Welsh dress, and the cockle women wear a white cap with a flat black hat over it.

Mr Bartlett and Hal came to tea. It was strange meeting Hal again, he has changed very much in all these years. He has grown very quiet; he used to be the lightest-headed boy I ever knew, but he has had a great deal of responsibility, and seems to have developed a nervous rather impatient temper. All the same he is very charming, and I am glad to meet him again.

*Sunday 9 October* I did not go to church but went for a long walk with Harold instead, up on to the common, and we had a long talk. There is so much to talk over it is hard to know where to begin. I found out that he thinks I am frivolous, extravagant and totally unsuited for a quiet life. I wonder if that is all true. We had a charming walk, there had been rain in the early morning and it was very green and fresh, and I felt happy to be back again in Wales. I miss Harry and one or two familiar faces, but on the whole it is not as changed as it might have been, and I have not made a mistake in coming back.

*Saturday 15 October* I stayed in bed this morning because my cold was so bad. After lunch I went for a long drive as I thought the fresh air would do it good, but there was a bitter east wind and it made me worse.

Will Lewis came to stay until Monday. He was in excellent spirits and cheered us all up, he is always amusing. I need cheering up; my cold is so bad that it depresses me.

*Tuesday 18 October* In the afternoon we practised duets; I was very bad at it. I never practise now, and my music has gone off very much. I wrote a long letter to Aunt Charlie, my heart went into it. I am very homesick for Glemham. I had a delightful budget of letters from America, Mamma, Sybil and Maude wrote. The girls' letters were charming, full of news about the dogs, and very witty and cheery. I do wish they were all over here.

*Saturday 22 October* Mrs Richards drove me into Swansea this morning; it was raining in torrents, but I like driving in the rain. Swansea is a horrid squalid place, one very seldom meets nice-looking people, they are all from the factories and docks. It is entirely a commercial place, with no good neighbourhood.

*Friday 28 October* The rain came down harder than ever; this weather is certainly an example of perseverance. We went to Swansea after lunch to the opening of a new operating theatre at the hospital. There were a great many people there, and on a dais the mayor, the MP for Swansea, their wives, the donor of the theatre, a tradesman of the town, and Sir William MacCormack who came from town to open the theatre. He is now president of the College of Surgeons, and the foremost surgeon in England. He is a splendid-looking man, over six feet, and with one of the most thoughtful faces I have ever seen. He made a speech, very badly expressed and worse delivery. He seemed to be nervous, and kept rocking backwards and forwards on a chair. The proceedings were very dull. There were long prosy speeches from everyone who had a chance, and I was bored.

*Tuesday 1 November, Baglan Lodge, Neath, South Wales, staying with Mrs Flower*   Miss Way and I went over to Baglan by an afternoon train to stay with Mrs Flower. I was not sorry to leave West Cross. We drove into

Swansea to the station, and Edith and Mrs Richards came to see us off. It is horrid of me not to like them very much because they have been so kind to me, but somehow Edith grated on me; she has changed very much.

It was dark when we got to Baglan, so I could not see much of the dear old place. Mrs Flower gave me the kindest welcome, but I missed her husband; he has been dead seven years. The house is not changed much. Kemmys Lewis lives here; he is rather like Harry, and at dinner Mrs Flower reproached me for not having married Harry. It was rather embarrassing before them all.

*Wednesday 2 November* This is a charming old house, with a long corridor connecting two wings. It is full of old furniture and things, and is very comfortable and cosy. The gardens are in terraces up the side of the hill. I walked up and down in the rain for nearly an hour thinking of all the changes since I was last here. It was then August, a very hot fine August. I used to sit on the south veranda with Mr Flower and eat fruit, and his last letter to me was 'Come back to Baglan soon, and eat peaches on the veranda'. That was ten years ago and I have come back at last, but he is dead, the leaves are all falling and it is almost winter, and everything is as changed as if I had lost my identity But it does not depress me, I am too much interested in everything to feel blue. Harold and Mr Hallowes dined with us; it was very nice being at Baglan with Hal again.

*Friday 4 November* We dined with Mr Bartlett; Mr & Mrs Eaton and Harold were there to meet us. We had a charming dinner, things are always better done in bachelors' houses than anywhere else. Hal sat next to me but he bores me nowadays, he has no small talk. It is impossible that he is stupid, but he is dull.

After dinner Mr Bartlett sang, he does sing so well. I enjoyed the evening. I had on my prettiest dress, I always feel happier when I know I am looking well.

Kemmys had to drive us home as the coachman was intoxicated, and the carriage was rolling from side to side until he got on the box.

*Tuesday 8 November, Cepn Glas, Bridgend, Glamorgan, staying with Mrs Lewis and Will* I left Baglan this morning. Mrs Flower and Dollie saw me off, and Will met me at Bridgend and took me to the house Cepn Glas. I went all over Bridgend, it was a sleepy little country town, deadly dull I should think. Cepn Glas is a comfortable old house, and the Lewis's are very kind, but I am pining to get back to London. I went for a walk with Will after lunch, all through the village. The houses are built of stone, and coloured pink, blue or white, and thatched. They are very picturesque but rather dirty, and the whole place is so dull that I think I would die if I lived here.

*Thursday 10 November* Will drove me to a village on the coast named Porthcawl. It is built on the rocks and surrounded by sand hills, a most dreary spot, no trees or vegetation, and on a grey November day it looked its dreariest. We drove through other villages, collections of stone houses, stone walls, stone roads, all grey and dreary and cold-looking, they seemed to be badly drained, and with none of the saving graces in the shape of gardens, flowers etc.

*Monday 14 November, Lancaster Gate, staying with Mr and Mrs Bishop* I got up very early this morning and caught an early train to London. I was so sorry to say goodbye to them all, it is a very simple quiet life here but there is so much kindness that I am quite happy. All the household were waiting on me this morning, Will drove me to the station, bought me papers etc, and saw me safely off. I got to Paddington at one o'clock. Eva met me and took me back with her. I am going to stay with the Bishops for two days. They were all so nice, giving me such a warm welcome that I was touched. It is very nice to be back again, I always feel so much at home here. They are very busy preparing for Dollie's wedding on the 8ᵗʰ.

*Wednesday 16 November, Eccleston Square, staying with Mrs Farnham* I sat at the breakfast table for a long time talking to Mr Bishop. He is very amusing and so kind to me, as they all are here. I was very busy all the morning getting ready to go away again.

I said goodbye to them all and drove to Eccleston Square to spend a few days with dear old Mrs Farnham. She gave me such a kind welcome, she is a charming woman. Jack was there to my great pleasure. He began to chaff me at once, and called me 'Rebel'.

*Thursday 17 November* After lunch Mrs Farnham took me for a drive and we paid a lot of calls, most of them on people I did not know. We went to see Aunt Mary; Chick Eden (33) was there. I had not seen her since I was a little child, but she greeted me as if we had always known each other, and asked me down to Ticehurst to stay with her and see Uncle Arthur. I shall be delighted to do that.

Mrs Farnham took me to see her sister Lady Shannon. She is the dowager countess now, and has a little house in South Kensington. She is a life long friend of Peg's and was charming to me on her account, but everyone is so charming to me nowadays that I think it would break my heart if anyone were not nice to me.

Mrs Farnham told me all about her two sons during our drive. Jack is the eldest and inherited the property, Quorn. It had been in the family for many generations, but he was extravagant and it had to be sold. The second son George, whom I have only just met, went on to the stock exchange, worked like a slave for years, and finally made enough money to buy the place back. He went down to Leicestershire today to see Quorn; it is a splendid achievement for so young a man.

*Monday 21 November, Worplesden, Surrey, staying with Mrs Willis, Gordon's mother* After lunch I said goodbye to dear Mrs Farnham and Jack and came down to Worplesden via Waterloo. It is a horrid station but it was full of soldiers going to Aldershot. I love soldiers, and never tire of looking at them. It was a most uninteresting journey and a long drive in the dark to the Willis's house, but I found a very warm welcome awaiting me. Mrs Willis is very like Gordon, a very animated talkative woman, she wanted to know all about Gordon and Gertrude. General Willis is away; I am sorry because I wanted to meet him.

The house is a very pretty cosy one, and there are four delightful poodles and two cats, so I shall have lots of animals to play with. Mrs Willis knows lots of people that I do; I don't feel at all shy, although I have never seen her before.

*Tuesday 22 November* We went for a drive to Pirbright in the morning, it is a dear old village with a green and pond with geese, and Kate Greenaway cottages all round. There are no lanes in the world like Surrey lanes, such hedges and trees and glimpses of cosy farms, and fields and woods. The colouring now is exquisite, soft subdued browns and yellows, the trees all in their autumn tints and red-roofed cottages nestling among them, such a beautiful country, and no place in it for me.

*Friday 25 November* In the evening we went to a penny reading in the village; it was a very superior entertainment. There were a few of the old features of the old time penny reading, the vicar who made a speech and announced the different events, the old-maid school mistress who played the accompaniments with occasional wrong notes, and the vicar's son who sang excellent comic songs, and there was also a yokel who sang atrocious comic songs. The audience consisted of almost two rows of 'gentry', and a great many rows of the villagers. They cheered and encored everything.

*Saturday 26 November, Watford, Hertfordshire, staying with Roquey and Emily Lyon* I left the Willis's this morning. Mrs Willis said goodbye most affectionately and asked me to come back in February. I drove myself to the station; it was a cool damp morning. I drove past a lot of men shooting round the coverts and wished I were with them. I had a very tiresome journey to Watford; I had to change at Clapham and Willesden, and it was raining hard when I got to Watford. I found the Lyons installed in a house they have taken for six months; they are not at all pleased with it, but they have arranged a good many of their ornaments, photographs and embroideries about the place, and it looks something like the little house at Staten Island. It does seem odd to be with them here in England.

*Thursday 1 December* Emily and I went for a walk in the morning and shopped in the High Street. After lunch we went out again and went to the old part of the town where there are some dear old houses; it is so old and picturesque that it looks like a street on the stage.

*Monday 5 December* I went out shopping with Emily, rather a stupid way of spending a morning, but the weather is so bad now that I cannot take country walks, the roads are very muddy. I had a letter from Sybil that worried me a little; she seems to be quarrelling with Mamma.

*Thursday 8 December* Today was Dollie Bishop's wedding day. I dressed myself up in my best and went up to town by an early train, and went straight to Sloane Street where Aunt Charlie was staying. I was so glad to see her again, and we had a delightful long talk, about clothes and men etc. She told me that I made a tremendous impression on a man I saw only once, a Mr MacVeigh. I thought at the time I had bored him.

I had to rush away early to be in time for Dollie's wedding at Christ Church at 2.30pm. I was the last to enter the church, but Darrell saw me and put me into the front pew with Eva and Mrs Bishop. Dollie was very late. She looked lovely in white satin, with a Brussels lace veil that covered her train. The church was full; the service was very long, with lots of music. It was a very happy wedding. At the house there was a great crowd, lots of Americans as the bridegroom is American, and on the cake were the English and American flags. The presents were lovely, an immense amount of silver but not as much jewellery as Mabel had.

Everyone was very well-dressed, and all the Bishops looked very well. I missed Harry, far away in Malta. Dollie and Tip went away at five o'clock, showered with rice. I stayed for a little while and talked to them all. I caught the six o'clock train back to Watford, and went to bed early. with a raging headache but it was not too big a price to pay for a very happy day.

*Saturday 10 December, Lancaster Gate, staying with Mr and Mrs Bishop* Emily and I went up to town by a morning train. I left her and went to see Mrs Farnham; she was just going for a drive and she took me with her. We went to see Aunt Charlie and Miss Clements and Aunt Mary. She left me there.

I got to the Bishops in time to dress for dinner. It is like coming home to be back with them again.

*Monday 12 December* I spent rather a quiet day. In the afternoon Eva took me to a tea at a South African millionaire's. They are very new to London, and are trying to get into society; such efforts are rather depressing.

*Sunday 18 December* I did not go to church. Eva and I went to see Aunt Charlie; she was so sweet. Bobbie was there, Mr Higgins and another man. We stayed for a long time and had tea. I shall miss Aunt Charlie when she goes away. I am so fond of her, her manners are perfect and she is such a clever interesting woman to talk to. She gave me a yellow silk dinner dress.

*Thursday 22 December* Mrs Macgregor sent me some lovely handkerchiefs for a Xmas present. I shopped in the morning. In the evening we went to Her Majesty's to see Mr and Mrs Beerbohm Tree in the Musketeers, an adaptation of Dumas' novel. It was a most thrilling piece, beautifully mounted and acted; they have caught the spirit of the book exactly.

*Sir Herbert Beerbohm Tree (1852-1917), the son of a German corn merchant, was not only a successful actor/manager but was, with his wife, received into the best London society.*

*Saturday 24 December* Mr Griffiths [her friend from America] came to see me, which was a great pleasure. He is not looking very well. We did not have much of a talk as there were so many people present. I am so glad he is here in London; I am going to lunch with his wife tomorrow.

There was great excitement today about Xmas, the children all hang up their stockings, and whisper mysteriously in corners.

*Sunday 25 December, Christmas Day* The children all came rushing into my room this morning before they were dressed to show me their presents. They all brought me things and I had presents from Mr and Mrs Bishop; it was like being at home.

I went to see Aunt Mary to take her a present, and then went on to luncheon with the Griffiths; they have a nice little house in Walton Place. Mrs Griffiths is very pretty and nice. She received me as if I were an old friend. Her father and mother, the Treddicks, were there; they are very American. We had a very nice luncheon, and Mr Griffiths proposed Papa's health. He is not looking at all well. I sat with them for some time after luncheon talking; Mrs Griffiths talks a great deal. I think I shall like her very much. Mr Griffiths drove home with me afterwards; it seemed so odd to be in London with him.

We had a great big dinner party, fifteen of us sat down, some cousins and the Seymour Taylors. It was a very jolly party, so many children who talked and laughed and pulled crackers all the time. Darrell kissed me under the mistletoe before everybody as he was taking me in to dinner. After dinner we were rather quiet, no dancing as it was Sunday. It was a very jolly Xmas, but it was a little bit sad being away from home.

## 1899

*Sunday 1 January* A lot of people came to tea, Mr Bartlett and Mr Griffiths among them, the latter to see how my cold was. Dollie and Tip Richards came back from their honeymoon this morning and dined here this evening. They both look radiant.

*Tuesday 10 January* Sybil, Gladys and I went to the post office in St Martins-le-Grand, and were shown all over it by the medical officer. He gave us tea first, and then went to the telegraphy department where we saw three thousand people sending and receiving telegrams. The machinery was explained to us, it is terribly complicated, it takes three years to make a good telegraphist, and the incessant tapping sends some of them insane.

*Monday 16 January, Waldershare Park, staying with Gac Guilford* I was sorry to say goodbye to all the Bishops, but London was so horrid, pouring with rain and muddy streets, that I was glad to get away. I had a very slow train. At Shepherdswell I met Arthur and his wife, and we drove to the house together, up the old familiar lanes. Gac and dear Peg met us in the hall. It is very homelike being here among all my relations, the two Norths, Roger and Hylton, are here, and a boy and a girl named Toynbee came over to hunt tomorrow. All the talk was hounds and hunting; Guilford has his own harriers now.

*Tuesday 17 January* Nearly everyone came down in riding things for breakfast, and at ten o'clock we all started in the brake for St Margaret's Bay where the meet was. Guilford is hunting his own harriers now, twenty couple. Miss Toynbee, her brother and Muriel all followed, and Gac, Fanny and I followed on the road, sometimes on foot, sometimes in the brake. It is such open country that we saw the whole run; they killed three hares while we were there. There was a good field, about forty.

*Sunday 22 January* After lunch I went for a ramble with Muriel. We went up to the Wilderness to get some snowdrops, a few were in blossom; it is quite spring-like, budding shrubs and great clumps of primroses. We wandered through the woods for a long time and listened to a blackbird singing. This is a great place for birds, and there are two rookeries. The park is full of deer now, red and fallow, and there is a dear little doe that follows me all over the place.

We are a very jolly party here, just five of us. I am enjoying myself immensely, and feel ever so much better.

*Wednesday 25 January* I walked to Eythorne this morning with Gac; she visited various poor people and we did some shopping in the village. After lunch we drove to Dover and paid some calls; no one was at home that I knew, except Miss Ramsbottom, whom I had not seen since I was a child. She is very little altered, very kind in her manner. It makes me rather blue going to Dover now, it is so changed.

Muriel came into my room and we had a talk before going to bed. I admire her very much, as much as I disliked her at first; it shows that first impressions are not worth much. She has a remarkable character, more like a man than a woman; she would make a good friend, thoroughly honest and serious.

*Thursday 26 January* I went up to the woods in the afternoon with Gac and Muriel. It was the tenants' shoot, and Guilford was up there with about thirty of his tenants. They had just finished lunch. We did not walk with any of the guns, they shoot rather wild sometimes.

We played cards after dinner. Sometimes we stay in the big dining-room where there is a piano, and I play. There is another piano in the drawing-room, but it is such a big room and so cold it is never used in winter. The oak room is the prettiest, it is panelled with lovely old oak and furnished in red. This is a very comfortable house, but I like Glemham much better

*Saturday 28 January* We went to the kennels to see the stud groom's little girl who seems to be very ill. There was a scare of drains to which we at tributed her illness, and Guilford spent the morning up there flushing the drains with the men. Afterwards he took me all over the place. They make their own gas and I saw the whole process: there is a very neat little house with gasometers in a corner of the park.

We wandered through the woods to the carpenter's shop and timber yard, a big place where we played about for a long time. All the trees that are cut or fall are brought here; it is wonderful how complete in itself an estate of this sort is. Guilford told me he employs fifty-one men, including indoor servants, grooms, wood reeves, shepherds etc, a little village in itself, and this boy owns and manages it all, and does it very well too.

*Monday 30 January, South Kensington, staying with Aunt Mary* This was rather an unsettled morning, packing up etc. Guilford came down early and went off to another tenants' shoot, saying goodbye to us before he went; he is a dear boy. I was sorry to leave Waldershare, I have been very happy here. Gac and Muriel came up to town with me; they went on to Bracknell, to Lady Wilmot's. I said goodbye to them at Victoria and went to Aunt Mary's, where I shall stay for a while. I received a very kind welcome. May (29) is at home now, and I saw her tonight for the first time, she has not changed much. She is a great artist now, and spends all her time and thought at her studio. She cares for nothing else. She is said to be brusque and disagreeable, but she was very kind to me.

*Thursday 2 February* We went to tea at May's studio. She has some beautiful portraits there, her work is very good, and she has a fine big studio; she is going to paint a portrait of me. She has pictures in the Salon and the Academy every year, but she does not seem happy there; there is something lacking. A woman's only chance of real happiness is a husband, home and children, *nothing* else can fill their places.

*Wednesday 8 February* This was a dismal wet day. Aunt Mary took me to a musical party given by Miss Hidden and Miss Heimlicher. There was very ambitious music given by greasy unwashed foreigners, who all seemed very pleased with themselves. There were a great many people, and a very good tea.

*Monday 13 February* I went to the Griffiths for seven o'clock dinner. I wore a black dress because general mourning has been ordered for Prince Alfred, who died last week. I had a long talk with Mrs Griffiths before her husband came in, on America and England. She is very lonely here, and does not look well, but she is very pretty and dresses beautifully.

We hurried through dinner and went to the Shaftesbury Theatre to see the American company in The Belle of New York. I did not like it much, I thought it very vulgar and badly mounted, not to compare with The Runaway Girl. We went back to the Griffiths for drinks, and then he drove me home. It seems so funny being with him in London; he is just as nice as he ever was.

*Thursday 16 February, Ticehurst, Sussex, staying with the Revd Arthur Eden* (17) I took a late afternoon train to Wadhurst. Chick met me at the station, and drove me to the house; there was a glorious red sunset. The rectory is a comfortable house, not very big or pretty, but full of good old furniture, china and plate, most of which belonged to Grandmamma. There are some portraits of the old Henleys and Northingtons. Uncle Arthur reminds me constantly of Papa, although he is not nearly as good-looking. Monkey, as they call the youngest girl, is pretty, and she and Chick are both nice.

*Friday 17 February* They get up rather early here; we had prayers before breakfast, all the servants trooping in. After breakfast we went to the church for a short service. The church is rather a big bare one, I don't admire it much. The curate Mr Knox lunched with us; he is a very dull young man. I don't like curates.

*Friday 24 February* Artie (26) came today to spend a night. He left his wife behind him, and was much nicer without her. I wrote a great many letters today, my usual weekly one to Mamma, one to Lily Walker, Aunt Charlie, Eva and Miss Hanbury-Tracy, friends old and new, no two of whom know each other. It is extraordinary what an enormous number of friends I have.

*Monday 27 February* Monkey and I went into Tunbridge Wells by train, it is only ten miles from here, such a quaint old place, and one of the cleanest towns I have ever been in. It seems to have no slums at all, and each street seems to lead into open country, it is rather like an overgrown village, and at the same time there is a great air of fashion about it, left no doubt by the people who used to come here in powder and patches last century.

*Wednesday 1 March* We went to morning service, being Lent there are services twice a week. Afterwards Mr Knox joined us, and we went for a walk. He is the typical curate, all the young ladies of the parish bow down to him, and he is rather spoilt and conceited.

*Friday 3 March* I went for a walk with a Mrs Birkbeck; she is a South African, and rather unpolished like all colonials. It was a lovely morning, and we went through lovely lanes, and I would have enjoyed it better if I had been alone. In the afternoon Monkey drove me to Hawkhurst. It is a dear old village in Kent, and there is a fine old church..

*Tuesday 7 March* This morning Uncle Arthur took me all over the asylum here; it is intended only for rich people, and is more like a club. The patients were walking about everywhere, quite unrestrained, but there were any number of attendants and servants, and gentlemen who act as companions to the patients. The Duke of St Albans has two companions, another patient, Sir Francis Drake, has two; he is the last of his family, a fine-looking old man, but his brain utterly gone. We met a patient who stopped Uncle Arthur and told him he was dead. The grounds are beautiful, conservatories, aviaries etc and a capital cricket ground. There is a pack of harriers for the patients, and they hunt and exercise all day, everything is done that can be done, but it is a dismal place to me. I have a horror of the patients, they don't seem to be quite human.

In the afternoon I went to quite a different institution, the parish workhouse. Mr Knox took me. We walked to it, about a mile and a half from the village. It really was much more cheerful than the asylum. We went into the infirmary and talked to the poor old wrecks there, old men and women who seemed to be absolutely worn out and spent with the toil of their lives. They were all cheerful and happy, although they seemed to have nothing to live for, come to the end of everything, and they can't have very much to look back upon. It is awful what colourless lives the poor live. There is a pretty little chapel where Mr Knox officiates. We saw the cells where the vagrants sleep, and the stone-breaking machine which I tried, and very hard work it is.

We had a very nice walk back, it was a glorious afternoon like summer. Mr Knox came to tea, also some other people. Edith Eden **(25)** came by a late train; she lives at Southampton now. Since I last saw her she has become a widow; she is very rich, still pretty and young-looking, and with the same sweet manners. I am so glad to have seen her again. We had a very jolly dinner party, and I am sorry I am going away tomorrow.

*Wednesday 8 March, South Kensington, staying with Aunt Mary* After an early tea Monkey drove me to the station. I was so sorry to go, I have been very happy there, but I am to come back in September, or sooner if I can. I got to Charing Cross very late, and to Aunt Mary's just in time for dinner. Dear Peg is here, and Lizzie Sherrard, (28) whom I have not seen since we were in Belgium together. She is fretting very much about her husband who is ill at St Thomas's.

Peg is looking very well, so are all the others. London is very stuffy and noisy after the country. Lizzie lives in Fermoy and knows Lily Walker's sister, Mrs Bryce Stewart.

*Thursday 9 March, Watford, Hertfordshire, staying with Roquey and Emily Lyon* I was very busy all the morning getting out clothes that are put away at Aunt Mary's, and arranging things. I had a long talk with Lizzie. She is miserable about her husband; he is in a private ward at St Thomas's, and next to him is a Captain Arnold who came back from Omdurman with seven bullets in his body, and he has been operated upon. He is all right again.

After tea I went off to Euston, Peg seeing me off, and caught a rather late train to Watford. I am going to stay with the Lyons for a bit. I was very glad to see them again, they are always so cordial and kind. They are looking very well, but Emily is still pining to get back to America.

*Friday 10 March* I had a long letter from Gertrude Willis. She seems to be in the same old groove at Staten Island, meeting the same people, doing the same old wearisome round of amusements (?). I meant to have gone to bed early, but sat up for hours talking scandal with Roquey.

*Thursday 16 March* We went out for a short walk in the afternoon. We dined with the Drews. Mr and Mrs Schreiber were there, very nice people, he was a hussar. It was a very jolly party, I enjoyed it immensely, Emily and Roquey are always so amusing. I played a great deal; it seems to be the understood thing that I shall 'make music wherever I go'.

*Saturday 25 March, South Kensington, staying with Aunt Mary* I left Watford today. I was sorry to leave Roquey and Emily, they are so kind and amusing, although Emily can't find anything good in England. I was very glad to get back to town. I got to Aunt Mary's early in the afternoon: I am going to make her house my headquarters in London.

We started out immediately for a tour of some studios, they are all on exhibition today and tomorrow. We went to May's first, she is not showing as her best pictures went off to Paris for the Salon last week. She and Mr Ward went with us, and we went to studio after studio and saw daubs of varying degrees of atrocity, crowds of people who admired everything they saw, and quantities of tea and cake. It was very amusing; Mr Ward kept by me, and pointed out celebrities. The people were much more interesting than the pictures.

*Thursday 30 March, Waldershare Park* I took a midday train to Shepherdswell. The stations were all crowded with people going away for Easter, and soldiers and sailors and volunteers. Our train was very late, and I did not get there until teatime. I found Gac had gone to the church for choir practice, so I followed her there and learnt some of the hymns etc for Easter Sunday. We got back to tea very late, and found Muriel with Dudley North who is staying here, and Prince Francis of Teck who is quartered at Dover, and spends a great deal of his time here. He is a huge man, very good-looking, and has charming manners, perfectly natural, he is rather amusing and talks a great deal

*Sunday 2 April* We all went to the Easter service, the church looked lovely, so full of flowers it looked like a greenhouse. Mrs Hoskin gave me a bicycle lesson, and I got on very well. We played golf too. Mr Wanklyn and his bride came to tea, and chaffed me a good deal about America; they all call me the 'American cousin' here. After tea we had more bicycling and golf, and then I played duets with Mrs Hoskin.

I sat in Muriel's room until very late after everyone had gone to bed, and we had a long talk, chiefly about Prince Francis. He is paying her great attention, and I am so afraid she may fall in love with him, because he is very attractive. Of course they could not marry, he has no money, and being royal besides is a barrier, but she declares she does not care for him, and will put a stop to the whole affair.

*Friday 7 April* Gac and Muriel went up to town to order their gowns for the May drawing room, and I went into Dover and spent the day with Chippy Bruce. We had a long talk about the old days when we were children and used to play together, and what had happened to us since. After lunch Chippy and I drove up to the Castle to call on Lady Rundle the general's wife, she is rather a pretty shy woman.. Her husband, Sir Leslie, is the youngest general in the army. A lot of people came in to tea, officers with their wives, and they all talked about Cairo and India and Malta as if they were across the way. I would like to marry a man in the army, they seem to have so much fun and change.

*Saturday 8 April* We drove over to the Petos; they live at a lovely old house called Knowlton. We got there for lunch and found a big party, a lot of girls, and officers of the 10$^{th}$ and 15$^{th}$ Hussars from Shornecliffe and Canterbury. After lunch there were foot races, a great many of the farmers and tenants came. Gladys Peto has a pack of basset hounds which she hunts herself. There were races for men, and a steeplechase for the girls with a water jump of twelve feet, they all took it splendidly. After the racing we danced on the lawn, and then had a rest before dinner. We dined in a hall at a long table, a band played all the time, and we sang and made the most awful noise. There were a good many boys and young officers who were just as noisy.

A very nice man, much older, Mr Robertson-Walker, took me in and was very nice to me all day. Suddenly the band played Yankee Doodle in honour of me, and they all chaffed me about being an American. And I got up and bowed and drank to America. Just at the end of dinner the band played John Peel, and we all got up and danced round and round the long table, up and down the hall, tearing along as fast as we could, all singing, one wilder than the other. I danced until I nearly fell. I love these mad frolics. they were all so nice to me. We were dreadfully tired when we left, and we had the long drive home.

*Monday 10 April* This morning we started for Dover, all in our best clothes, and drove to the town hall where there was a big bazaar for the Gordon Boys' Home. We had two maids and Powell the butler with us, and they helped us to arrange Gac's stall. We had a lot of plants, butter, eggs etc, and a crate of pottery that had to be unpacked. We lunched with the Harcourts and had a chance there of tidying ourselves up. At 3.30pm the bazaar was declared open by Lady Rundell, and then the selling began. Prince Francis was at our stall, and it was literally besieged by people anxious to buy from him and Gac. He made a splendid shopman, coaxed people into buying all sorts of things, and laughed and talked to everyone. He can be irresistible.

*Tuesday 11 April* We lunched quietly at home, and drove into Dover immediately afterwards for the second day of the bazaar. We spent some time in rearranging our stall, with Gac's butler Powell to help us. He is a capital man and took care of the money. It was rather an amusing day. The Gordon Boys gave a very good flag drill and sword dance. There were a great many soldiers who seemed to take the keenest interest in the boys, most of whom are destined for the army. They are picked up off the streets, taught, well fed and clothed.

*Thursday 13 April* I went up to Muriel's room and played on her piano and talked, and she told me that she had broken off with the man she is very fond of, but is too poor to marry her. She did it last Saturday, which accounts for the depression I noticed. She feels it most dreadfully, but it was the only thing to do, and she has been brave enough to do it.

*Sunday 16 April* A Mr Prescott who was in the 10ᵗʰ Hussars lunched with us, and Prince Francis came very late. We were a very jolly party, any amount of chaff and fun at luncheon time. I get so much chaff nowadays that I am getting rather quick at repartee, so much so that Prince Francis complimented me most charmingly on my 'wit'.

After lunch we sat in the oak room. It was pouring with rain so we could not go out, so for exercise Muriel and Prince Francis and I chased each other all round the house, up the grand staircase, in full cry down the gallery, and finally landed in her room, where we simply romped. He was just like a boy, tearing round the room, and jumping over chairs and things. Then we played on the piano and sang, and then rushed downstairs again and had a pillow fight in the hall. It was great fun; we laughed until we were weak. I wonder what people would have thought if they could have seen the very dignified Prince Francis rolling on a sofa, with Muriel and me piling cushions on him, and banging him on the head with a pillow, and Muriel, who in public is so stiff and standoffish that few people care to speak to her.

*Wednesday 19 April* I went for a ride on the bicycle this morning, to Eythorne and back, past Grannie's old house. What would she say if she saw her degenerate granddaughter on a bicycle. After lunch I went with Gac to pay calls, rather dull ones. We went to Kearsney Abbey, to the Curtis's. I used to go there as a little child; I seem to be revisiting all the scenes of my early youth.

*Thursday 20 April, South Kensington, staying with Aunt Mary* We got up early this morning to catch an early train to town. We drove to Kearsney where we caught the express, and had a reserved carriage. Gac and Muriel came up to try on their court dresses. I hated leaving them, but I shall see them when they come up for the season in June. I came to Aunt Mary's. Peg is staying here, dear old thing, in capital spirits.

*Friday 21 April* Gac and Muriel came in the afternoon, the latter very depressed because her dresses are a bother and she is deeply in debt, and has a lot of things to get for the season, and it is all over town that Prince Francis is very attentive, which is annoying.

*Monday 24 April* Peg went off to Cologne tonight. May and I went to Victoria to see her off. She has a reserved carriage, and she went off in great state and comfort. The guards and porters at Victoria know us, and we are always well looked after there. We shall miss dear old Peg, but it will be a nice trip for her. She is a wonderful woman, rushing about the world at her age.

*Sunday 30 April* I went to see Lady Shannon and found her alone, so I had a nice long talk with her. She talked about Prince Francis, she has known him and all his people all her life, she says he just the sort of person to 'carry on' with Muriel, or any other girl he fancied. He is fearfully extravagant, and very much in the Queen's bad graces: he was the only member of her family to whom she did not give a present at her jubilee.

*Tuesday 2 May, Bursledon, near Southampton, staying with Edith Eden* In the afternoon I went away as Aunt Mary comes back tonight. I went to Edith's at Southampton, a long journey from Waterloo through lovely country, all green and spring-like. I had to change and go to Bursledon where she lives. Her carriage met me at the station; her house is about a two miles drive, rather a small house, but very good grounds and stables well kept-up. From the windows there is a view of the Isle of Wight.

*Thursday 4 May* After lunch we went for a drive, and then to Netley Hospital to a concert for the invalided soldiers. We went straight to the theatre, it was full of convalescent soldiers, all in pale blue suits with red ties and their regimental caps, which was the only way of distinguishing the regiments they belonged to. They enjoyed the concert immensely, especially the comic songs, and cheered and joined in all the choruses. We were almost the only ladies present, but they seemed pleased to have us, and stared at us all the time.

*Friday 5 May* After lunch we went to a tennis party, which was most dreadfully dull. There were lots of girls, big red-faced young persons, very badly dressed, their mammas terrible old frumps, and exactly five men, the eldest of whom was a clergyman of eighty, the youngest a retired colonel of sixty odd. It really was rather amusing, but I am thankful I am not obliged to live in such society. The girls played tennis, some of them were very good at it. I have no doubt they are very nice girls, thoroughly healthy and strong, not caring much for dress, and good at all sports. They all talked 'horse', the only thing was they might have been a little softer and more feminine.

*Monday 8 May* After lunch we drove into Southampton. Mr Sharp met us there and took me all over the docks; the new dock, the Empress, is magnificent. What chiefly struck me was the order. Although there was a lot going on, there was no noise or confusion; vessels for all parts of the world were loading and unloading, trains going in all directions, but all as calmly as possible. We went over one of the royal mail steamers; she seemed very small after the Atlantic liners. We saw Sir Thomas Lipton's yacht, the Erin, she is a beauty, and laid up beside her was the transport Jelungo, the one Harry Bishop went to Malta in.

*Sunday 14 May* Edith and I went to church; there were hideous hymns and a stupid sermon. The church was full of retired admirals and colonels and their women-folk. This part of the country is populated by them, and that's what makes it so dull: they seem to have done with life.

*Wednesday 17 May* After lunch we went for a long drive and paid calls, the people we called on were rather stupid. This country is lovely, but it has become very suburban. There are lots of brand new villas that look as if retired tradesmen lived in them, and the roads are too well kept. There are no delightful lanes or old houses, everything is new and commonplace.

*Friday 19 May, Hambledon, Hampshire, staying with Jack and Kate Macdonald* I left Bursledon in the afternoon; Edith drove me to the station. I am ashamed to say I was rather glad to go. She has been so kind that it is horrid of me, but there was something depressing about the house and I hated it. I came to the Macdonalds and had a roundabout journey to get here. Hambledon is an old place where no new houses have been built within the memory of man.

     The house is a charming old one, with nice old furniture and some glorious old china, Crown Derby. Kate is looking quite her old self, and as cheery as ever, and her husband looks better than he did in New York.

*Sunday 20 May* This is a charming old village, but I would be sorry to live in it. Kate's house is lovely and so are the gardens. Her husband breeds fox terriers, and they have about thirty of all ages. We spend a lot of time in the kennels.

*Tuesday 23 May* I had a letter from Papa saying it seemed ages since I went away, and an age to look forward to my return. I feel now as if I ought to go back at once.

*Sunday 28 May* We went to morning service. The church is really a handsome one but it is cruelly modernised, lots of embroidery and millinery on the altar, against old oak etc, it is incongruous, like an old woman with dyed hair.

A very nice amusing girl named Wilson lunched with us, she lives in the open air, hunts, has countless pets, and plays games well, just the sort of person I would like to be.

*Thursday 1 June* This was a perfect June day, very hot and bright, the sort of day I would like to spend lying under a tree with a book, dreaming. Kate and I went to a croquet party at the house of an old lady about eighty-six; *she* was playing. She has a dear old garden, and a house full of old things, it reminded me of an old book. I hoped the company would be old-fashioned too, but they were distressingly modern, and jarred. I wanted old maids in mittens like the old dears in *Cranford* [by Mrs Elizabeth Gaskell] but instead of that there were old maids in tailored dresses and straw hats trying to look up-to-date.

*Saturday 3 June, Westminster, staying with Mr and Mrs Mordey* I left Hambledon early this a.m. I was so sorry to go. The children got up early and came down to the door to see me off. I got to town at twelve and went straight to the Walkers; they have been in England for three weeks, and are at St Ermin's. I lunched with them; they struck me as being intensely American, but were very kind and I was glad to see them

I had tea with Lilla Eden, and went for a walk with her, and finally got to the Mordeys in time to dress for dinner. I am going to stay with them for a few days. They are friends of Papa's, and have asked me on his account. They are very nice and kind, and live in a flat in Westminster. Some people dined with us, and we all went to the theatre to see the American play The Belle of New York. I had seen it before; it is very noisy, but pretty, and not *very* vulgar.

*Sunday 4 June* We went for a walk in the park this morning; it was crowded, everybody much dressed up. The women looked as if they were in ball dresses, and most of them were painted. The park is lovely, all the flowers in blossom. I saw a lot of people I knew.

*Monday 5 June* I had a charming letter from Harry, full of polo and his dogs and horses, just the sort of letter I like, and at the end of it he says he wishes he could see all 'the dreams of dresses' that he knows I have got for the summer. No one ever admired me and my clothes as much as Harry.

*Friday 9 June, London, Carlisle Place, staying with Lilla Eden* I left the Mordeys, and have come to stay with Lilla Eden for a short time. We drove all the afternoon; there was a drawing room, and we saw a great many of the people coming back. Town is very full, we were constantly being blocked.

*Sunday 11 June* Lilla and I went to morning service at the Oratory. I did not like it very much, the music was good, but there was too great a crowd of fashionable people. I lunched with Gac and Muriel; they have a house for the season in Rutland Gate, a very pretty house. Muriel is looking unusually well, beautifully dressed and in great spirits, and Gac looked nice too.

*Tuesday 13 June* I had a letter from Mamma with the very unwelcome news that Sybil is engaged to a curate with no money. I cannot imagine a more disastrous marriage for her, and do hope it will be broken.

*Wednesday 14 June* I had an insane letter from Sybil announcing her engagement to Mr Porter. She treats it all as a joke, says she does not care for him, but thinks it time she was settling down. She is very thoughtless, and a bit heartless.

*Tuesday 20 June* Lilla took me to see a collection of beautiful antique panelling belonging to Mr Crafton. We went on to see Ethel Eden and her new baby, rather a nice little baby, the youngest Eden. We went back to tea with Tit. Aunt Mary is away, called down to Beckenham to see dear Peg who is ill. Tit gave a very alarming account, but I allow a great deal for exaggeration. Peg is staying with Mrs Barton, so she is in very good hands.

*Wednesday 21 June, London, staying with Mr and Mrs Macgregor* I went to Aunt Mary's early to hear the latest news of Peg: she has gastric fever, and is very ill. I left Lilla's in the afternoon. She was very kind and urged me to stay longer, but I had promised to go to the Macgregors; I got there in time for tea.

*Thursday 22 June* This morning I had a letter from Alec Barton asking me to go down and see Peg, so I went down in a pouring rain, dreading the end of my journey, not knowing what news I would hear. Mrs Barton was so kind, she told me all about Peg, and then Alec came in and said that on Tuesday he thought there was no hope. I went up to see her; she was so glad, and kept me for more than an hour. She is terribly changed, illness is a most awful and terrible thing; it shocked me to see Peg, so reliant and independent lying there helpless. She is so brave too: she assured me that she did not mean to die this time. I wish I could have stayed to nurse her, she liked having me with her, dear Peg, it is sad that I can do so little for her. She fell asleep and then I left her.

*Tuesday 27 June* In the afternoon Eva, Mrs Griffiths and Lilla came to tea, and were all very charming. Mrs Macgregor did not know any of them, but she allowed me to ask them all. I wore a lovely new blue and white dress; I am getting too fond of dress.

In the evening we went to the Lyceum to see Robespierre; Irving and Ellen Terry were playing. It was a very painful piece, I cried once and everybody else was sniffing suspiciously. I can't imagine why such fearful subjects as the French revolution should be made the subject for an evening's amusement. Irving was excellent, I admire him immensely, and Ellen Terry's voice is as lovely as ever and her acting perfect, she is so natural.

*Monday 3 July, Wilton Place, staying with Charles and Beatrice Eden* After tea I left the Macgregors and came to the Charles Edens, where I shall be for a week. A Mrs Terry is staying with them. We all went to the theatre in the evening to see the Musketeers. Mr and Mrs Tree were excellent in it, and Mrs Brown Potter looked very pretty.

*Monday 10 July, London, Wilton Place, staying with Percy and Gertrude Griffiths* I went to the Griffiths in time for dinner, I am going to stay with them for a week. I like Gertrude Griffiths immensely, she is very pretty and sweet, and their house is lovely. We spent a very quiet evening, Percy sang and I played his accompaniments as of yore.

*Saturday 15 July* The Edwards dined with us; they are rather amusing, but very fast I fancy. We went to the Supper Club after, where there was a very good dance, lots of men, all of whom danced well. I had a delightful time. The Club gives a dance every Saturday at the Grafton Galleries; they seem to be a very fast set. We danced until nearly 3.00am and there was a very elaborate supper; I think there is too much eating in this world. All the women were well-dressed, most of them covered with diamonds. The display of riches in London is bewildering, everyone seems rich.

*Monday 17 July, South Kensington, staying at Aunt Mary's* I went and sat with Gertrude in the Square garden this morning. I like her very much, she is very kind and sincere. After lunch I said goodbye to her and left after a very pleasant visit. I am going to be at Aunt Mary's for a little while, to be quiet and rest. I really am rather done up. She is away but May is here. I had tea with her in her studio, and we spent a delightful quiet afternoon and evening. I always feel at my best with May, and it is a pleasure to be with relations. I love all mine, they are all nice.

*Thursday 20 July, Eccleston Square, staying with Mrs Farnham* I got to Eccleston Square before luncheon, and immediately after Mrs Farnham took me to her niece Ethel Whiteman's wedding at St Peter's. One wedding is very much like another. This was very pretty, and there were crowds of smart people and the bride had a lovely diamond necklace and yards of white satin train. The bridegroom was the younger, which seems to be the fashion. There were six bridesmaids in pale green and white.

I envied the bride because she looked so happy. I always think I would be so happy if I could marry the man I care for, but it would be too great a happiness for this world, so it will never happen.

*Saturday 22 July* Late in the afternoon we went out and paid calls. We went to her sister Lady Shannon, where we heard all sorts of news and gossip. She is such an amusing woman, a very devoted friend and most bitter enemy. The Duchess of Somerset was there, a nice quiet old woman, who wanted to know all about New York. Afterwards we went for a turn in the park. It was rather hot; Mrs Farnham always drives in a brougham, which is stuffy.

*Sunday 23 July* After lunch we drove up to Park Street to see Aunt Charlie, and we were allowed to see Aunt Flo for a little while. She was sitting in a dark room with her eyes bandaged, but she will soon be able to see quite well [after a cataract operation]. She asked me to go and stay with her at Brockenhurst. I promised Aunt Charlie I would go to Glemham on Thursday; somehow I feel depressed about it, as if I would rather not go.

How strangely ones granted prayers turn out. I was longing to go back to Glemham, and when Peg was taken ill would have given anything to have nursed her, and now both wishes are to be fulfilled, and I am feeling wretchedly depressed and unwilling to go. It is a lesson not to desire anything; perhaps even my ardently wished marriage with Harry would be a bitter disappointment.

*Thursday 27 July, Glemham Hall, staying with Aunt Charlie* I came down to Glemham by an afternoon train. At the station, Liverpool Street, there were crowds of poor children going off for their holiday in the country with some clergymen in charge of them. The journey down was very pleasant, the air seemed fresher each mile. It is a blessing to be in the country again.

Dear Aunt Charlie was very glad to see me, and even Bobbie gave me a warm welcome. I did not see Peg; she is very ill, and they thought it too late in the day for her to see me. Glemham looks lovely; it *is* the nicest house I know. We had a very quiet evening; no one is staying here now.

*Friday 28 July* I drove into Saxmundham alone to a concert got up by Mrs Ivo Bligh. Clara Butt sang, and affected me more than I have ever been before by a voice. She is a very tall dark woman, very simply dressed in white, her whole impression was simplicity. She threw her head back a little, and the glorious voice flowed out with no effort, no grimacing. She changed colour, flushing now and then, and her face was quite beautiful; I did not know people could look beautiful when they sang. Her voice is beyond praise, so tender and rich and sweet, and above all so simple, a perfectly natural voice.

Peg is much better but I have not seen her yet. I played to Aunt Charlie on the organ after dinner.

*Dame Clara Butt (1872-1936), a concert rather than an opera singer, was a contralto famous for the richness and compass of her voice.*

*Saturday 29 July* Poor Peg was not so well today, and I was not allowed to see her. Bobbie is with her constantly, such a good nurse.

*Sunday 30 July* I was allowed to see dear Peg this morning. It was very sad, she is too weak to talk much, she just held my hand. I feel as if she could never get better; it seems as if the real Peg had gone and this is some stranger.

I went to church in the morning and sang in the choir, and afterwards walked about with Aunt Charlie, and snipped the dead roses off and pulled up weeds here and there that I am sure the gardeners leave to amuse her ladyship.

*Monday 31 July* Lady George Gordon Lennox came to spend a week or two; she is so handsome, although she is near seventy. Her hair is dyed, but very well done, and she is tall and straight and most beautifully dressed.

*Tuesday 1 August* After lunch Lady George and I went to a tennis party at the Lowthers, at Campsey Ash. There were a lot of people there, the Ivo Blighs, who brought Clara Butt with them. We walked about together all the afternoon. She is an enormous thing, 6ft 2in, her voice is a bit like a man's it is so deep. She is very good-natured and amusing; she picked green apples and ate them, and insisted on crossing the moat in a ricketty old boat. She talked of her own accord about her singing, and said how much she enjoyed singing to a lot of people. She is quite unspoilt, no airs or conceit at all.

*Wednesday 2 August* I went for long walks and rambles in the park all by myself, and those two wonderful old ladies, Aunt Charlie and Lady George, gorgeously arrayed, sat in the garden or walked solemnly up and down the lawns. I was with them for a little while, but they talk of things and people and places I don't know of, and it bores me. I pine for *young* society. If I had a year of this suppressed sort of life I would break out and do something desperate, run away with the butler, who is young and good-looking.

I saw dear Peg for a minute. She looks very ill; it is dreadfully discouraging, she gets no worse, but no better.

*Thursday 3 August* I went for a long walk in the morning, the country is beautiful in every direction, if only I had someone to admire it with, it is an Adamless Eden. I wonder if I really would be happy leading a quiet country life, wearing plain clothes, pottering about in my garden and poultry yard, or if I would long for town and excitement and frivolity. I am so glad I can't choose my lot, I would make an awful mess of it.

*Monday 7 August* I saw Peg today but it was very distressing, her mind is nearly gone, and whether it will come back no one knows. It nearly made me scream when she looked at me, she knew me by name but not the faintest recognition showed itself. She looked at me as if I were a bit of furniture. It seems so strange that we can laugh and joke with such a shadow hanging over the house, but we do, we had a very gay dinner party, Lady George looking most beautiful, covered with diamonds and full of fun. We played cards after dinner and went to bed very late, and all the time dear Peg is lying upstairs in that living death,

*Tuesday 8 August* I went for a long walk before lunch, through the woods and lanes. In the afternoon I sat with Peg; she is wheeled out of her room. Yesterday she was in the ballroom where it is so airy, and today she was in the tapestry room. She looks very ill, but she knew me today and was glad to have me with her.

*Wednesday 9 August* There was a consultation this morning over Peg. The doctors say she can never recover, it is a break-up, she is worn out, which seems incredible. I cannot imagine the world without Peg. She will linger for a long time, so I can't help hoping that she may get better even now. Bobbie spent about an hour in my room talking, we have become great friends.

*Sunday 13 August* I wandered about the dear old gardens this morning for perhaps the last time. I go away tomorrow, and I don't believe I shall ever come back to Glemham, so I went all over it to say goodbye, up the yew walk, and the flower and vegetable gardens, and to dear Peg's rose garden, it is sad to be so fond of a place one must leave.

I saw Peg in the afternoon. She was almost too weak to speak, but she asked me if I were enjoying myself, thinking of others to the very last. I went to afternoon service; Peg was prayed for. After service I went for a long walk with Bobbie, we went into the churchyard. I went in to see Peg for a minute after I was dressed for dinner; she smiled at me so sweetly but did not speak.

*Monday 14 August, Ticehurst, staying with Uncle Arthur* I had to get up very early this morning to catch a train. I went in to Peg to say goodbye to her, she was awake but very feverish. I could not realise that it was for the last time.

I had a very comfortable journey up to town, drove from Liverpool Street to Cannon Street, and got an afternoon train to Ticehurst. Monk met me; I was so glad to see her again. Uncle Arthur and Chick gave me a very kind welcome, and I felt very happy to be back with them again.

*Monday 21 August* Peg is dead. She died at three o'clock yesterday afternoon, Aunt Charlie, Bobbie and Chick were with her. It was very peaceful.

*Wednesday 23 August* Uncle Arthur went to Glemham today to attend Peg's funeral. She is to be buried tomorrow in the churchyard at Glemham; she chose the place herself years ago. We spent a long quiet day in the garden.

*Thursday 24 August* This was the day of Peg's funeral. It was a perfect day followed by a lovely warm moonlit night, and it did not seem so dreadful to think of Peg lying out there in the churchyard. Peg so full of life and so reliant and strong, lying still in the coffin, it seems an incredible thing.

Monk and I went to the station for a message, and while there we saw

Mrs Kirby. She has been mad for years and is at the asylum here, it seemed strange seeing dear Mabel's mother after all these years. She was sent away long before I knew Mabel, and we made friends when we were both twelve.

*Friday 25 August* Uncle Arthur came back from Glemham, Monk and I drove to the station to meet him. He told us all about Peg's funeral. She was carried up the Broad Walk through the gardens and park to the churchyard, and she is buried next to Flo Wilmot. The mourners were Gac, Muriel, Chick, Bobbie, Uncle Arthur, Guilford, Lord Monson, Mr Earle, Mr Brooke, Mr Lowther and Mr Ivo Bligh. It was all very simple, and so Peg passes away from us for ever, one of the wittiest, kindest women that ever lived. Yet she spoiled her own life, and was never happy.

*Saturday 26 August* Monk and I spent the morning in going to see some of the poor people, we went into quite a dozen cottages. The women were all so nice, with such respectful manners, curtseying when we went in and dusting chairs for us to sit on. They are all very poor, and much distressed for want of water. They have only one or two wells among them and depend largely upon rain water; there has been no rain for fifty-five days, and they have not enough for washing. It is sad to think how we waste it.

*Monday 28 August, South Kensington, staying at Aunt Mary's* We all went up to town together. I left them at Waterloo and came to Aunt Mary's for the night. She is away and the others too, and I have the house all to myself. It is horribly lonely - once I loved being alone, now I hate it. Everything here suggests Peg. I can almost fancy her sitting opposite me. I was so fond of her, and relied on her so much. I think the shock of her death has dazed me. I feel quite dull and indifferent to everything, pain or pleasure. Harry Bishop is back in England, but it does not affect me at all. I don't think I would go the length of the room to meet him.

If I lived alone for a year I would go mad; as it is I believe I am a little bit insane. I am so intensely self-absorbed, so selfish and conceited, conscious of it all, and yet powerless to change. I am so tired of my character, if I could only forget myself for a little while. What a fool I am, I only write this because I am thrown back on myself for a while. If someone came along and flattered me I would be in the seventh heaven, and fancy myself the loveliest and most charming of mortals. The crying need of my life is love and sympathy and I have had very little of both. And have given very little!

*Tuesday 29 August, Brockenhurst, Hampshire, staying with Aunt Flo Morant* I lunched early and went down to Brockenhurst; we went via Southampton, Aunt Flo's carriage met me at the station. We drove through beautiful gates at the lodge, along a road through the park, the trees are very fine. The house is a big rambling place. The hall is enormous, wainscoted with oak and full of pictures. Aunt Flo received me very kindly; no one is staying here, so it will be very quiet.

After dinner we sat in a small drawing-room and talked. Aunt Flo is very amusing and talkative. The house is very quiet; at night I opened my window and looked out, the other wing of the house stretched out quite dark, not a light anywhere. Under my windows is a terrace with clipped trees and peacocks prancing about.

*Thursday 31 August* Aunt Flo took me all over the house; it is an enormous rambling old place. I don't like it; it looks haunted. The dining-room is hung with tapestry, there are all sorts of queer staircases and passages. My room is in a wing right away from everyone, to get to it I have to go through an anteroom, down a passage, past the music room and all sorts of mysterious doors, and through two more rooms up stairs. All this is in the dark with my candle guttering from the draughts, some night it will go out and then I shall faint.

Aunt Flo is too stately and magnificent; she oppresses me, but she is very kind. The house oppresses me too, there is a big Rubens in the hall that ought to be in a church. We went into the library this morning, no one ever goes there, it is very big and dull, the books are too old to be interesting. I don't find black-letter light reading.

*Sunday 3 September* I went to church with Aunt Flo. She has a private entrance through the chancel, and the pew is one of the old-fashioned square ones, so high that no one can see into it, and standing right in front of the chancel, blocking out the altar from half the congregation. The church belongs to the Morants, so they can do as they like.

The congregation waited until we left the church, it was almost royal. The Morant arms were in the church with their pretty punning motto *En mourant j'espere* . The family vault is just below the pew, and there Uncle Johnny was laid two months ago.

After lunch I walked to a neighbouring church with Aunt Flo's maid in attendance; she would not let me go alone. The church is simply lovely, it dates from before the Conquest, it impressed me the moment I entered it with the most perfect feeling of peace. It was harvest thanksgiving, the church was decorated very simply with corn, the congregation were all Eddy's tenants and labourers, they seemed to bring the atmosphere of the fields and woods into church with them, the beautiful autumn fields and the woods with the golden sunlight filtering through the trees. The earth is sometimes so beautiful that God might be actually spreading his glory all round.

*Wednesday 6 September* The lanes round here are beautiful but I am glad I don't live here. I dislike the whole place, and I don't like Aunt Flo. She is the most heartless and worldly woman I have ever met, and her pride of birth is almost a mania, it is hard to believe she is my father's sister.

*Thursday 7 September, South Kensington, staying at Aunt Mary's* The morning one leaves a place always seems to drag so. I was never less sorry to leave a place, it has depressed me and I don't like Aunt Flo, so I said goodbye to her without any regret. I had a very nice journey up to town, and went straight to Aunt Mary's. She is away, but May is here and we had a very cheery time.

*Friday 8 September, Waldershare Park, staying with Gac Guilford* I got to Waldershare in time for tea, and found dear Gac and Muriel very well. Harry and Emily Forbes-Eden are staying here, also Mr ffrench-Blake. As usual we had a very jolly dinner, with music and lots of noise afterwards.

*Wednesday 13 September* Guilford had a big cricket match, his yeomanry troop against the Canterbury troop. There was a band and tents and crowds of people and tea in the pavilion; over 200 people came in to tea. The home team was beaten. We all cheered and got awfully excited whenever our side made a run. The ground looked very pretty, and the band played all our favourite tunes. Guilford was very pleased with the day. He had the match for a sort of treat for his troop and their 'lady friends'.

*Monday 18 September* We went into Dover and I went to lunch with Mr Hammond, which made me feel like a child again. Nothing seems to have been changed since I was last here, the same servants -I don't believe the furniture even has been moved, and Mr Hammond is not changed. He asked me innumerable questions about Father and them all, it is delightful to find someone who still takes an interest in them.

*Thursday 21 September* We all walked over to Barfreston to see a most wonderful church. It is early Saxon, very small, but almost covered with most beautiful carvings in which animals play a large part. It stands in a tiny little village in a hollow. The walk was delightful, we came back across the stubble, over the downs.

*Tuesday 26 September* Today I wrote and got my berth to sail for New York on the 7th December, to go back to the country where I was never really happy, the very thought makes me miserable. I have a horrible presentiment that I am going back to America to meet all sorts of fresh trouble.

*Saturday 30 September* Another long wet day, but I suppose we ought not to mind after three months' fine weather. It is very bad living in the house so much, one gets blue and imaginative, but there seems to be a depressing atmosphere now. This horrible impending war in South Africa is weighing upon me like a pall, it feels as if there were going to be some awful reverse, and the thought of our soldiers being defeated is too terrible. In his last letter Harry said his regiment was not under orders but they fully expected to go.

*Monday 2 October* There is great excitement for tomorrow is the opening meet of Guilford's hounds and everybody, hunt servants, Muriel and Guilford are to have new clothes, and nothing else is talked of.

*Tuesday 3 October* This was the day of the opening meet. Everyone was very late for breakfast, and when they appeared they were very gorgeous in new clothes. Muriel came down in a beautiful new habit, a model of a young woman in hunting kit; we cheered when she came in.

It was a glorious day, bright sunlight. After breakfast we stepped out onto the lawn at eleven, the hounds came round, the servants in new clothes looking very stiff and uncomfortable but very proud. The people came crowding in, in all sorts of conveyance, and they all had drinks, and we went out and talked to the farmers. There were a good many officers from Dover, but no one seemed to know them. The run was a very good one; we followed in the brake and saw the whole thing; they found in the Wilderness and killed at Coldred.

*Wednesday 4 October* It rained incessantly all day, it was quite impossible to go out. I sat with dear Gac in her boudoir for a long time, she is the dearest and kindest of women. It does make me so miserable to think this is my last visit here. I shall probably never come again, for Guilford will marry some stranger, and everything will be changed. I love the place, the park is so beautiful, and there is so much life and excitement and happiness here. Dinner last night made such a pretty picture, the big dining-room with Vandyke's King Charles and the Lelys looking down on us. The table had all the gold plate on it, and was decorated with red flowers in honour of the meet this morning. We were all in our best clothes and jewels, all bright and animated. I could not help looking and thinking what a pretty picture it was.

*Thursday 5 October, South Kensington, staying with Aunt Mary* We were all up very early and caught the eight o'clock train to town. Gac and Muriel came up to see their dressmaker. I went to Aunt Mary's, and received the usual loving welcome. She is very much saddened by Peg's death; we had a long talk about her.

*Tuesday 10 October, Lancaster Gate, staying with Mr and Mrs Bishop*       I spent the morning with Dollie, our tongues going nineteen to the dozen. Monk came to lunch; she is on her way back from Scotland to Ticehurst. She was looking very well. After tea I went up to the Bishops to spend two nights, it is very nice being with them again. After dinner we gambled and I sang, with Darrell to play my accompaniments.

*Wednesday 11 October* I had a letter from Harry this morning; he comes back to town next week. After lunch Eva and I went to see the Walkers and Emily Lyon, but no one was at home. We dined very quietly at the Bishops, and I sat up very late talking to Mr and Mrs Bishop.
    The one topic now is the war: it was declared today, no one thinks of anything else, the people one passes in the street are all talking about it and the loafers at the corners. Everyone seems to be with the government, and calling out the Reserves has delighted everybody. To me it is all too horrible for words, the deadly massacre of the flower of our army and the illness and suffering, quite dim all the glory and excitement.

*Thursday 12 October, South Kensington, staying at Aunt Mary's* I had a letter from Mamma to say Sybil's fiancé had been to see them, and they are rather disappointed in him. I do hope she will be happy; I would be miserable if her marriage turned out badly.

*Friday 13 October* I had a letter from Mamma with an account of Sybil's fiancé. She is disappointed in him, he talks incessantly and is not at all good-looking. This is the second letter on the subject in two days.

*Tuesday 17 October* I went to lunch with the Bishops. Harry arrived from Wales just before lunch, dear old Harry, looking so well and sunburnt, he was so nice. I was horribly nervous and could hardly speak, but he talked hard all the time, all about Malta and what he has been doing ever since I last saw him. After lunch we - Harry, Eva and I - went to the National Portrait Gallery. The portraits were rather uninteresting I thought.

We walked back to Lancaster Gate, so we had a good deal of walking, but it was very nice. We went across the park, the leaves are coming down thick. Harry talked incessantly and was very amusing; I have never seen him in better spirits, and of course I was very happy. I dined with the Bishops, and afterwards played and sang; Harry loves music. It was a very happy day. Harry drove me home, and that was the first time we were alone all day; he is so kind and considerate and honest, it would be impossible for him to do anything mean or underhand. There is no one like him, and I shall never be able to marry him.

*Thursday 19 October* I had a rather disturbing letter from Mamma. Sybil seems to have been giving her trouble, and she wants me to go home so as to exert my influence over Sybil, but I don't like that prospect. I have difficulty enough with in managing my own affairs without interfering in other people's.

*Saturday 21 October* Harry Bishop came for me after lunch and we spent the whole afternoon together. There was a thick fog, and we did not quite know what to do; London was very disagreeable. We finally made up our minds to go to Richmond and walk about there, but the fog was so bad that we could not see a yard in front of us. We walked in the park not seeing anything, it was rather amusing, and I enjoyed being with Harry, he is so kind and nice and very amusing. He talked about hunting and polo; he is miserable at not having gone to the war, and it frets him so much being in London idle while so much is going on, that he has almost made up his mind to curtail his leave and go back to Malta. He is a keen soldier and it is hard for him not to see service. We stayed at Richmond until six o'clock, talking hard all the time.

The fog was so dense that we were a long time getting back to London. I don't think I enjoyed the day very much, it is very unwise seeing too much of him, it only unsettles one. Harry is everything I like in a man, he likes all the things I like and does all the things I admire, and above all he is a soldier.

*Sunday 22 October* The fog was rather worse today. I went up to Lancaster Gate for tea with great difficulty, it got into ones eyes and made them smart, and ones throat sore. I went to evening service with Harry at Christ Church, the church was full of fog, it softened all the outlines. The music was good, we waited till the very last and listened to the voluntary.

I was very happy. I liked sitting there quietly with Harry, and would have liked it to last for ever. Tip and Dolly and Billy Richardson dined, so we were a big and very jolly party at supper. I really think the Bishops are almost the nicest people I know. We all talked a great deal about the war. There was no music after dinner, for once I was not asked to sing. When the men came up I sat and talked to Harry about books. By the time I went home the fog was so bad that cabs were dangerous, so we had to walk part of the way. Harry came with me. It is so nice seeing so much of him, but it is unsettling and does me no good.

*Tuesday 24 October, Cromer, Norfolk, staying with Harry and Emily Eden* I had a very early start this morning and a long drive to Kings Cross, where I caught the train for Cromer, and spent the best part of the day getting there. I was met at the station by the shooting cart and Harry Eden's retrievers, who climbed up into the cart and were most demonstrative - dogs are darlings. The Edens live about four miles out of Cromer, the house is on the edge of the cliff.

I received a very kind welcome, and immediately went to lie down as I was awfully tired. Our party at dinner consisted of Emily and Harry, Mr Disney, and an elderly widower, who during the course of dinner told me I was magnetic.

*Thursday 26 October* Four men came to stay for the dance tonight, the squire of this place Mr Ketton, Mr Jolliffe and Mr Thompson, two officers quartered at Norwich, and a charming man in the $7^{\text{th}}$ Hussars, Mr Imbert Terry. We had a very gay afternoon. I played and sang a good deal.

I enjoyed the ball immensely; it was given by the bachelors of these parts and was very smart. I danced a great deal too much, but it was delightful, and I had the best dancers in the room and lots of compliments about my dancing. The last dance I divided between Mr Tuck and Mr Terry, giving them alternate rounds, which was rather fun. We went a party of eight men and three women only, I had enough attention to satisfy even my insatiable appetite and vanity. We all went and came back together in a big omnibus.

*Sunday 29 October* We were very quiet at dinner; just the house party. Mr Tuck has been my shadow all day; he is very kind and nice, it is a pity I don't like him. I had a long letter from dear Gac, and one from Harry asking when he could see me. I shall be back in town on Tuesday.

*Tuesday 31 October, London, staying with Mrs Macgregor and Maude* I left Cromer today, very sorry to say goodbye. Emily and her niece Minnie were so good to me and made me promise to come again next year, but I don't like to think of how long it may be before I find myself in England again. They came to see me off. Countess Spencer got into my carriage and talked all the way up to London. She offered me lunch first, and then we talked about the war; of course she takes the Liberal side and is down on it, her husband made a great speech against it last night. She is a charming woman, and we made great friends. The journey to town was a very long one.

Maude Macgregor met me at Kings Cross, and we drove home [to Earls Court] together. I am going to stay with them now. They were so kind and glad to see me; Mrs Magregor said she had been longing for me to come. She is looking very ill.

*Wednesday 1 November* I went to see Aunt Mary this morning; she is so deeply distressed about the war that she is going to Devonshire. It upsets her to hear the boys crying the news in the streets.

Harry Bishop came soon after lunch, and we went for a walk. We went to the park, and we sat there for a long time talking, it was very warm and the park looked very pretty with a soft bluish haze over it. We talked about all sorts of things, nothing very serious, we were in rather a happy frivolous mood. I admire and respect him more every time I see him. We went to tea with Gertrude Griffiths; she was looking charmingly pretty. Percy came in while we were there, and I had the pleasure of introducing my two best men friends to each other.

*Saturday 4 November* Today I was so tired that I got rather depressed. Mrs Macgregor and Maude are rather worried over some troubles of their own, and I have to keep cheerful for their sakes, but the prospect is not very bright: only ten more days of Harry (he sails on the 15"), and only five more weeks of England for me, and after that I know there will be all sorts of troubles and worries, and I shall have to take up responsibilities that are much too heavy for me, with no one to help me. My long happy holiday in England has made me awfully selfish: at one time I was never afraid of duty, but now I would lay everything aside to secure my own happiness.

*Sunday 5 November* Harry came to lunch, and I put on my newest and prettiest dress, pale mauve embroidered with silver. The rooms looked so pretty and the luncheon so good that I was quite happy, and Harry of course was charming, but rather shy I thought.

In the afternoon Harry and I went to service at the abbey; we had very good seats. The dear old abbey looked most beautiful. The music was glorious, and there was an excellent sermon from Canon Robinson. He made a very touching allusion to the war and the dead soldiers; the whole sermon was really about them, the text was 'And underneath are the everlasting arms'.

*Tuesday 7 November* I went to tea with Aunt Charlie who is in Sloane Street for a week or two on her way to Nice. She was very sweet, gave me a quantity of lace, and made me promise to come back to England very soon. She told me I had made friends in every direction, and that everyone liked me, which was a delightful thing to hear. I can't help noticing that wherever I go I get the most attention; at thirty-three I hold my own with young pretty girls. I am asked about more than anyone I know. I don't think it has made me conceited, but it amuses me sometimes, and of course I always feel it can't last.

*Wednesday 8 November* Just as I was dressing for dinner I had a letter from Harry written from the club, to tell me that he has to go to Malta on Saturday instead of next week, a dreadful blow, because now I know I may never see him again, and certainly not for many years. I am quite dazed. He was not to have gone until the 15$^{th}$, but the transport Dunera sails on Saturday, he must go in her, and his regiment is in the next division to be sent to the Cape.

*Thursday 9 November* I went to a delightful dinner party at the Griffiths given in my honour; the Lyons were there, the Messels and Harry. I was very late, the last to arrive, all dressed up in my prettiest dress, white silk. It was a very jolly party, we were all so congenial, and there was a great deal of laughing and talking. Harry sat next to me. We had a very nice dinner. Really a dinner party is a most charming function, the pretty table loaded with silver and flowers and pretty china, the women in their pretty clothes and men in their best tempers, make a perfect whole, only it passes so quickly. Harry drove me home and came in to see Mrs Macgregor, and stayed some little time.

*Friday 10 November* I dined at the Bishops, a *very* dull dinner party, there were twenty people and no one interesting among them. I sat next to Harry. He too was rather silent, he said he was tired, he had been very busy all day, and still had a great deal to do. He starts at 6.30 tomorrow morning, the Dunera sails from Southampton at 12.00. He is coming back to England next May and wants me to come too, but of course I can't possibly. He gave me a photograph of himself, not a very good one, and we said goodbye, and that episode in my life is closed. I feel a dreadful blank, but although I am lucky in little things, the big things that would make me happy don't come my way, and I must count my blessings, and above all not dream or think of what might have been.

*Saturday 18 November, South Kensington, staying at Aunt Mary's* I went to Bond Street with Maude and did some errands. We went to the War office, still no news. We saw them changing guard at St James's Palace, a very pretty sight, the red coats looked so bright on this very dull foggy day. But with all its fog and dinginess I love London dearly, and wish most earnestly it were my home, or at least I knew when I could come back to it again.

After lunch I said goodbye and left the Macgregors, very sorry to go, they have been so kind. I came to Aunt Mary's; she is away but I received a warm welcome from Tit. I shall stay here now until I sail, and shall be very busy getting ready to go.

*Monday 20 November* I had a letter from Jack Farnham this morning begging me not to go back to America.

Tit and I spent the usual quiet evening, she reading and I writing. I have so many letters of farewell to write now. As the time draws near I don't dread going to America so much, for I have an idea that I shall be able to come back to England very soon.

*Tuesday 28 November* Miss Hunneman, Muriel's old governess, came to see me; she is going out to America with me, it will be so nice having someone like her to look after me. Tit and I went to lunch with the Macgregors; they were very cheery and nice. I do enjoy seeing so much of them; they are going to Cairo in January. I went to the stores afterwards and did some shopping. I went to see Miss Mordey to say goodbye. Everyone seems nicer than ever now that I am leaving them. I went to say goodbye to Lady Shannon. She gave me a photograph of herself, it does not do her justice, she is so lovely. She wished me good luck and a quick return to England.

*Thursday 30 November* I had a letter from Mamma that made me rather miserable. They are going to leave the house in Staten Island, and are going to live near Newark. I do hate it so, almost the only compensation in going back to America was living in Staten Island. I like the people there better, but I can only hope that before long I shall be happy enough to come back to England.

*Friday 1 December* I sent off all my heavy luggage today to the docks, so now my packing is all off my mind, and I have only my farewells to think of. I went to lunch with the Bishops and had a long talk alone with Mrs Bishop, all about Harry. After lunch Eva and I went to see her aunt Miss Bishop, I went to say goodbye to her. She was very sweet, and said she hoped I would come back to England very soon. We went back to Lancaster Gate for tea, it was very cheerful, the girls were if possible sweeter than ever.

*Monday 4 December* I had a letter from Harry from Malta written in very low spirits; he is not well, and is fretting to death because he has not gone to the war.

I dined with the Bishops, a farewell dinner with my health drunk in champagne, and so many kind loving wishes that I nearly choked; the Bishops seem to have adopted me. After dinner they all came and sat round me, each trying to get as near as possible, it was so sweet of them, and they were all so bright that I had not time to realise it was my last evening with them. We sat in the drawing-room, and I sang all the songs I could remember. They all gave me lovely farewell presents; I shall feel cold and lost in America without all this love.

*Tuesday 5 December* I lunched with Miss Hanbury-Tracy; her cousin Mrs Hanbury-Tracy was there, also another cousin Lady Robert Bruce. We talked a great deal about the war, they have many relations out there.

After lunch we went to Agnew's gallery to see some beautiful old pictures, the most exquisite Gainsborough I have ever seen. There were about twenty, not enough to tire one: I like pictures in homeopathic doses.

I dined with the Griffiths and enjoyed it so much. Gertrude was so sweet, and asked me to come back and stay with her indefinitely; everyone has asked me to come back and stay. I had a long delightful talk with them, and then Percy brought me home.

*Wednesday 6 December* I lunched with Aunt Mary for the first time for this ten days past, and after lunch there was a steady stream of callers. Emily Lyon was the first, and everyone I knew seemed to come, the Macgregors, Alice, Dollie & Mabel, the Woolcombes, and countless others. I was in a whirl, and everyone of them made me promise to come back. I am rather dazed and tired, it is exhausting saying goodbye to so many people one cares for very much. If only I could be quite sure of coming back again soon I would not care so much, but it breaks my heart to think I may not see them again for years.

*Thursday 7 December, on board the SS Mariton* I was awake nearly all night, I could not sleep, so I got up very early and finished packing. I wrote a short letter to Harry and posted it myself before breakfast. Eva came to breakfast, and she went to the station with me. There was a thick fog so we could not see much, and I did want to see as much as I could of dear old London. Eva and I had a long talk: she told me that Harry had told her he could never ask any girl to marry him on account of his having no money - poor Harry, and poor me.

At Liverpool St Station we found Uncle Arthur waiting for me, and he looked after everything for me. The Macgregors, Griffiths, Lyons, Dollie and Edith Taylor were all there to see me off, and I was loaded with presents, but there was so much talking and excitement that I did not realise I was seeing them all for the last time. We had a special train to the docks where the Mariton was lying, Mrs Bishop and Eva came with me and saw me safe on board, also Uncle Arthur. He went away very soon, but the Bishops stayed with me for a long time, and when they left I broke down at last. They are so kind and good, and I felt so lonely without them.

The ship seems very comfortable. I have a very nice cabin and sit on the Captain's right hand at meals. Tonight all the excitement of saying goodbye is over and I feel miserable, it is like a dream. I cannot realise that once more I have left my beloved England, my own dear country; I dread going to America and the life there. It appals me to think of how I shall miss my friends, and all the love and kindness they lavished upon me. Miss Hunneman is very kind and a great comfort, but I am so unhappy. I long for Harry most of all, but I shall not see him again now I have left England.

*Friday 8 December* There has been some hitch or accident, and we were detained in the docks all day. I like Miss Hunneman very much, she is very kind and looks after me well. The ship is exceedingly comfortable. We sailed immediately after lunch and are now speeding towards Dover; I am sorry to say we shall pass it at night.

The passengers on this steamer do not seem to be very nice; we do not speak to any of them. The doctor made friends with me today, I rather like him.

*Saturday 16 December* It is a whole week since I wrote a line. The greater part of that time has been spent in bed, my cold got very bad, so bad that Miss Hunneman would not let me get up. The weather has been very cold and stormy, one day the machinery broke down and we had to stop. All the passengers are so disagreeable that we don't see more of them than we can help. The doctor is rather nice, and has looked after me very well.

Nothing of any interest has happened on board, even the storms we have had have not been sensational, only disagreeable and tedious. There are two parsons on board, which is always unlucky, and tonight the doctor told me a poor man is dying of pneumonia. It seems so extraordinary that I am not looking forward to the end of the voyage, to seeing Papa and all the others, but somehow I am not a bit. I am so full of regret at leaving England that I have no room for any other emotion.

*Monday 18 December* The poor man who was ill died last night of pneumonia. He was one of the crew, but was a gentleman, a university man, gone to the bad. He was most lovingly nursed, the doctor gave up his own cabin to him. He was buried at twelve o'clock. A bell tolled and all the crew gathered in the stern, the passengers were all on the saloon deck, and the engine slowed down. From the deckhouse six men came carrying the body wrapped in the Union Jack. It was laid on a plank jutting over the side, and then the service began.

The Captain read the service in the most intense stillness, there was no sound but an occasional cry from the seagulls and his voice. At the committal part of the service the plank was gently raised, and the body slipped off very quietly into the sea from under the flag and was gone. I suppose it sank at once. It was all most reverent and not very sad, though I noticed several of the crew wiping their eyes, and there was a sort of hush over everything all day. No one could have been buried with more reverence than this poor castaway, whose own friends had disowned him. He was only thirty.

Today for the first time I got a faint thrill of interest in going back to America, and began to think that perhaps I may be able to tolerate it, but it takes very little to send all my thoughts and heart back to England again.

*Wednesday 20 December, New Brighton, Staten Island* We lay at anchor off quarantine all last night and were up very early this morning. The medical inspector came aboard, and after his examination we proceeded with a clean bill of health. We were a long time getting up to our dock. New York looked very bright and clean. Mamma and Sybil came to meet me, both looking very well; I think they were glad to see me.

I got through the Custom House ordeal very well, but it was quite two hours before we left the dock. It seemed so strange being back again, like a dream, for my body is here, but all my thoughts are on the other side. Miss Hunneman was very much interested in all she saw; she has come to stay with us for a few days. Marie and her children are here. Henley has grown into a very handsome boy, and he is very sweet and affectionate; the other boy, Stuart, seems very cross and peevish, and is not as pretty as Henley. Maude has grown I am sure, she is a giantess, and she and dear Sybil are both very handsome, and so amusing that I have laughed ever since I came home. Papa is looking very well, and seemed more pleased than anyone to see me back. The house looks small after the big English houses; I went into every room to see how they looked.

Gertrude and Mrs Edsall came to see me. They were very glad to see me, but somehow I feel as if I did not care much for anyone here. Fitzroy came home very late, after I was in bed, and came into my room to see me. He has grown too, they are all big and tall except me, and they think I am smaller and slighter than ever.

*Friday 22 December* Staten Island looks more squalid and dull than ever, it seems to me a sort of agony to have to live here. I must try so hard not to let it make me miserable, but I feel tied up and shut away from the world. Apart from the girls and Papa and Mamma, I have absolutely no interests in this country, and will have to fall back upon myself. Mortie came this afternoon to spend Xmas; he is looking very well and was very nice to me, and was more interested in news from England than any of the others.

*Saturday 23 December* I am really settling down wonderfully, and look after things in the house as if I had never been away. I went for a walk with Miss Hunneman after lunch and confided my troubles to her. I dare not tell anyone else how much I hate this place; I don't want anyone to know I am unhappy. I went out with Maude too; I liked that, she is such a dear, so amusing, and so good, there is no one like her.

*Monday 25 December, Christmas Day* We were all up very early this morning and the hall was darkened and the Xmas tree lighted up before breakfast, which is an American custom. We all had a great many presents, and I distributed all those I brought from different people at home. Eva sent some lovely things. I had letters from Eva, Gladys and Sybil Bishop, and one from Lilla, all very kind but very sad on account of the war, which is casting a gloom all over England. We spent the morning in looking at each other's presents.

We had the usual Xmas dinner, and drank healths of absent friends and success to our soldiers in South Africa, but no one seems to care much about anything to do with England. I almost feel as if I were among Americans, Morton is completely Americanised, and Fitzroy becoming so, and I don't think any of them sympathises with me in my love of England.

*Thursday 28 December* I walked over to Arrochar to see the Willis's and found a whole crowd of children there, the Jeromes and Alexanders and Kate and Freddie, who have grown wonderfully and seem to be very nice children. Gordon was in and we had a short talk about England, he is very homesick still, poor Gordon, and he has so slight a chance of ever going there to live. I think he has aged a little since I last saw him, and Gertrude looks older too, but Mrs Edsall is just the same, kind and sweet as ever.

*Saturday 30 December* Sybil's fiancé, Mr Porter came in the evening; I don't think I like him. She treats him shockingly, makes fun of him to his face, and speaks of him most disrespectfully. She does not care for him, but has not the courage to break off the engagement.

## 1900

*Monday 1 January* M Porter dined with us. Sybil has broken off her engagement with him, and I am afraid he feels it very much, but she is very glad to be rid of him.

*Wednesday 3 January* After lunch I went to the post office, and in the presence of the postmaster and a Custom House officer opened a registered letter they had detained since Monday. It proved to be from Harry, with a turquoise brooch in it. The man examined it, and after a while said it was not dutiable as it was a present, and after signing a paper I was allowed to go off with my brooch and letter. The brooch is a very pretty one that Harry sent from Malta with a long letter full of grumbling. He is not going to the war, and his regiment is going into camp and he hates living under canvas; he says he is tired of soldiering, and writes in a very despondent vein.

*Tuesday 9 January, New York, staying with Grace Slocum* I went into town today to stay with Grace until tomorrow. She asked a lot of people to tea to meet me, all old friends, the Batleys, Howard Taylors, Nathalie and the Bells, it was delightful seeing them all again, and they were all so nice and said such kind things about my return.

Parke Bell dined with us. After dinner we went to the rink and saw a hockey match that I did not care much for, it was too rough and noisy, and the place was so brightly lighted it made my head ache. I hate noise and bright lights. After the hockey we went to Mr Bell's rooms and sat for a long time talking. I was delighted with what they said about England

and our war, they really do sympathise with us, and take almost as much interest in it as we do.

*Thursday 11 January, New Brighton* Today I lunched in New York with Mrs Wendell; she is Gertrude Griffiths' cousin and dearest friend. She lives in a very pretty house in 35ᵗʰ Street, and seems to be very nice, although I felt towards her as I do toward nearly all strangers, as if I never wanted to see them again. She had four girls there to lunch, all friends of Gertrude's asked to meet me. I did not like them; they all had such loud voices and talked rubbish.

*Friday 12 January* I was at home all day, and very glad to be quiet after the racket of the past few days. We had a great surprise, and rather a shock, on hearing that Reggie was married. Maria wrote and told us but gave no particulars, except that she had heard that the girl is very nice. Her name is Sophia Hartman. It seems so odd that Reggie never let us know. We are not going to take any notice until he writes and tells us himself.

*Saturday 13 January* My days are all so much alike that there is very little to write about. I am very happy so long as I am at home with the girls, and reading or working or practising, but I hate going out among the people here, and yet I long for society and feel very lonely. The only congenial person is Grace, and she is not much interested in things I care about.

*Monday 15 January* This morning while we were at breakfast Mr Porter, Sybil's fiancé, was announced. Sybil, who has broken off her engagement, refused to see him, and I had to receive him. It was most annoying; he is dreadfully upset at the way she has treated him, and she certainly has behaved shamefully. She has jilted him for no reason except that she is tired of him. He resents it very much, and talked to me for nearly an hour, walking up and down the room and gesticulating until I was frightened. It was rather mean of Sybil to place me in such an uncomfortable position. He provoked me a little, for I don't think people ought ever to grumble or complain about their troubles. He stayed for ages, I thought he would never go. Finally I made Sybil go into the drawing-room and see him. I don't know what she said to him for I fled to my room as soon as I was released. Sybil is utterly heartless and has no sense of honour. She engaged herself to this man and then calmly threw him over, and is enraged with him because he objects.

*Saturday 20 January* A month today since I landed, and I have quite shaken down into my place and am a little more cheerful, although I have always a vague sort of depression that is a form of homesickness. I feel as if I were wasting my time, and not making enough of each day. We have so few, and they pass so quickly, that it seems such ghastly waste not to make the most of each one.

*Sunday 21 January* I went to tea with Gertrude Willis. Minnie Walker was there, and she told me to my face that her sympathies were with the Boers, and she hoped they would win. I shall never like her again, to be told that today of all days, when we know that one of the most terrible fights of the campaign is in progress. In the papers this morning it said that a battle was beginning, and as I write probably hundreds of our men are dead or wounded, it is maddening, and to be among people like Minnie Walker who hope for our defeat is past endurance. It is things like that that make me so homesick.

*Friday 26 January* I went to town today and lunched with Grace. We drove afterwards and paid some calls; there was such a tremendous wind that I was afraid the men would be blown off the box or the carriage overturned. I went to the Manhattan and saw Mrs Edsall: she is getting on very well indeed, and told me all about her operation.

*Wednesday 31 January, New York, staying with Grace Slocum* Grace and I went out shopping this morning and to the Manhattan to see Mrs Edsall, who will soon be quite well. The great Dr Burney came in, he is rather a nice-looking man, and very amusing to talk to.

The Bells dined with us and we went to see a horrid play in which Elsie de Wolfe and Lord Yarmouth acted. It was adapted from the French, and was so vulgar that it made me feel hot all over, and I was sorry for the Bells because they hated it as much as I did. After the play we went back to the house and sat and talked for a long time, and the Bells as usual said all sorts of pretty things; they always make one feel pleased with oneself.

*Friday 9 February* I went for a long walk alone. I felt rather depressed; I get more homesick for England every day, and more restless and dissatisfied with the life here, and yet I feel I can't go away again and leave Papa and the girls. I miss them so when I am away from them, yet I am pining for England, and will never be happy away from it.

*Sunday 11 February* Frances Depue came to spend the night; she has altered, she looks ill. She had lots of Newark news, and spoke about Court Parker, and oddly enough the mention of his name made my heart beat a little faster. I would like to see him again, and wonder if I ever will.

*Tuesday 13 February, Newark, staying with Frances Depue* This was a very wet day, and in a drenching shower Frances and I started for Newark immediately after breakfast. The approach to Newark is not very cheerful at any time, today it was dreary beyond words. On reaching it I went straight to Mary Ogden's for lunch. She rushed to the door to greet me and gave me a very warm welcome.

*Friday 16 February* This was rather a nice day. I felt tremendously full of energy, and did everything well. I practised much better than usual and did lots of work, and went for a very long walk with Maude: everything in extremes.

*Saturday 17 February, New Brighton* All day long there was a dreadful gale and snowstorm; we went to the Bonnells to dinner in the worst of it. We had to go by train, and then had a long drive up a steep hill with the wind blowing so hard that the horses could hardly face it, and the snow coming down so hard that we couldn't see. We had to trust to luck to get to the house, the horses were exhausted and we nearly frozen. We were to have gone to a ball at the club, Sybil, Fitz and I with the Bonnells, but of course it was impossible. We telephoned to the club to find out who was there, and at eleven o'clock only ten people had arrived. We had a very jolly evening and spent the night with the Bonnells.

*Sunday 18 February* Every night before they go to bed the girls and Fitzroy come into my room and talk over things. Fitz is worried about his future, afraid he won't get on; they all sat on my bed in a row in front of me and discussed their plans. We are none of us to marry, but all live together. Sybil is to be a famous singer, Maude a great organist, and Fitz an eminent engineer. I am not to do anything as I am delicate, but they are to look after me, and that is how they have planned our lives.

*Wednesday 21 February, New York, staying with Mrs Pfizer* I went up to town to the Pfizers to stay overnight, and got there in time for dinner. Mr Wilmerding and Mr Emil Pfizer there. We all went to a big ball at the Waldorf, a *bal poudre*. Powdered hair is very unbecoming to me, and as I was rather tired and depressed I did not enjoy myself. There was no one I cared for, the men were all very stupid and rather common, the women were as usual beautifully dressed, and there was a wonderful display of jewels. There was an atmosphere of overpowering wealth and ostentation.

*Saturday 24 February, New Brighton* I went into New York with Mamma to do some shopping, and I noticed today that everyone one meets in the streets of New York looks either worried or sad, even the children have a sort of worn look on their faces. It must be the endless noise and confusion that causes it.

*Friday 2 March* Ladysmith has been relieved after a siege of 118 days. The papers say that the scene of rejoicing in London was without precedent. It is maddening to be out here away from it all.

*Saturday 3 March* I had a letter from Percy Griffiths to say that Gertrude's father is dead, and that she is coming out to America with her mother. I also heard from Tit, and her news is that poor Charles Eden is dead at last after months of suffering from cancer in the throat. Both letters were chatty and full of the war, and more cheerful in tone than they have been.

*Monday 12 March* I had a letter from Emily Lyon; she says Gertrude Griffiths is very delicate; I feel sorry for Percy. In the English papers this morning I saw that Charlie Veal was severely wounded at Paardberg and poor young Jack Hylton-Jolliffe killed. I was so rude to him at that ball at Cromer last October; I wish I had been nice to him now.

*Wednesday 14 March* I practised for a long time today. It really is all I have to do now and I must have something to throw myself into, but I often wonder to what end is all this hard work. And isn't it rather a waste of time to spend so many hours at the piano? I suppose it would be a greater waste of time to do nothing, besides being conducive to insanity.

*Saturday 24 March* I sent off some dessert doyleys to Emily Lyon as a birthday present, and practised and worked all day. It is all nonsense to say that a busy life is a happy one. I use up every minute of the day but I am not happy, and always feel unsatisfied and lonely. It is bad for me to become absorbed in my own pursuits, and yet it bores me unutterably to go about among the people here. I *cannot* be happy in America.

*Monday 26 March* Today was a typical day of my life, so I shall describe it. A long leisurely dressing, and down to breakfast at 8.30 with Sybil and Maude. Sybil as usual rather snappy, Maude as usual very sweet and cheerful. Then I hung about and waited for the postman, but there were no letters this morning, although the English mail is in. Then I read the paper, not much news, the war news very unimportant. The rest of the morning I practised hard, and played one piece alone for an hour (it must have been pleasant for the family). Then lunch, after which I did a little dressmaking and practised on the guitar; everyone was out, so I sat alone over the library fire with a book and the dogs. After tea I worked at some lace until dinner-time that I am making for Maude. Everyone came home for dinner. Then the evening papers, which were as dull as the morning ones, a little card playing, write my diary, and so to bed. Such are my days except for a long walk which I could not take today as the weather was so bad, snow again, and deep depression.

*Tuesday 27 March* I had a letter from Reggie's wife Sophie, the first she has written to any of us. It is a very nice letter, and I think she must be a nice woman.

*Thursday 5 April* I went up to town today to say goodbye to Miss Stephens who sails for England on Saturday, to be gone all the summer, lucky woman. It was a gloriously warm spring day, the trees were beginning to show green and Ted's grave is covered with crocuses. The spring is very late here, at home the primroses and daffodils have been in blossom for weeks.

*Tuesday 10 April* We got the sad news of the death of Morton's youngest child, Stewart, but no particulars. He was always very delicate. I am so sorry for Morton, for he was devoted to him.

*Thursday 12 April* A letter came from Morton with particulars of Stewart's death: he died of croup, very suddenly; Morton is heart-broken.

*Friday 13 April* I can't imagine why I am so unhappy. I wake in the night with horrible thoughts, and all day long everything seems miserable. I believe it must be this place does not agree with me, and I find it so dull after England. I feel so lonely, there is no one here I care to see or be friends with. I have horrible presentiments of coming misfortunes. Ever since I left England I have a feeling always with me that some great trouble was pending.

*Saturday 14 April* As we were sitting at dinner tonight a telegram came telling Mamma to go as soon as possible to Warren, as Morton and Marie are both ill with diphtheria. We are all terribly anxious, and I have never seen Papa more miserable.

*Sunday 15 April* Easter Sunday, and I did not go to church, but Fitz went twice. I was so pleased; I do like a boy who goes to church, and Fitz is so good and steady, but not a bit of a prig.

Mamma went off to Warren by the six o'clock train, Papa went with her as far as Philadelphia, so we are all alone tonight, and the house is so dreary and empty without them. We had no news from Warren, so we hope they are better.

*Tuesday 17 April* We heard that Morton and Marie are better.

*Wednesday 18 April* I went up to New York today for shopping. Papa came home, greatly to my relief. We always feel so unprotected while he is away.

*Saturday 21 April* Spring is really coming at last. The leaves are showing, and birds singing in the early morning, and I long more than ever to be in England, the primroses are out there now, and the woods at Waldershare will be yellow with daffodils, and thousands of birds singing. If only I could have a home of my own in the country in England, and stay there always.

*Monday 23 April* We had very bad news of Marie: her nurse does not think she will live.

*Wednesday 25 April* I suppose it is anxiety about Marie that makes us all so miserable, but it really does seem as if a cloud were hanging over us. I don't go anywhere or see many people and it is terrible.

*Saturday 28 April* Marie is so ill that there is very little hope.

*Sunday 29 April* I went over to tea with Gertrude, she was so nice that I felt all my old affection for her come back. When I got home I found a telegram to say that poor Marie died this morning. It is the most terrible crushing blow for Morton to lose his wife and his favourite child in two weeks.

*Tuesday 1 May* We had a very short letter from Mamma, she says Morton is distracted.

*Wednesday 2 May* Mamma came home today bringing Henley with her. He is so ill he cannot stand, a sick child is a very sad sight. He does not know his mother is dead, but he never mentions her and talks of Morton constantly. I think he must guess that something has happened to his mother. Mamma is very much shaken; she says the past fortnight has been terrible. I cannot realise what it must have done to Morton.

*Thursday 3 May* I was with Henley all day; he needs a lot of care but is mending very fast. I am his godmother so I feel he ought to be my special charge, but I am afraid I won't be allowed to have much to do with him. He is a dear little thing, and so pretty.

*Friday 4 May* Morton came today, he looks very ill. He talks incessantly of Marie and Stuart, sometimes as if they were still alive, it is heart-breaking to hear him. His one thought now is Henley, he never leaves him or allows anyone else to do anything for him.

*Tuesday 8 May* The garden is beginning to look lovely. This was the first really hot day we have had, and we could almost see the things growing. At night there was a thunderstorm that made me ill with terror.

*Wednesday 9 May* Henley is getting slowly better.

*Sunday 13 May* I went to service at Christ Church and sat with Sister Johnson. Mrs Edsall came to tea. Henley was out all day in the garden; he is getting on wonderfully well, thanks to Morton who never leaves him. It is a very good thing for Morton to have Henley to think of, as it keeps him from brooding.

*Monday 14 May* At home all day. It was intensely hot, the thermometer stood at 101. The garden is a blaze of blossom, chestnut trees, lilacs, and every sort of shrub and tree that can blossom is covered. The wisteria that climbs to the top of the tower is like a mauve curtain of blossom, it shades the balcony, and I sat under it all the afternoon and listened to the bees humming round it.

*Tuesday 15 May* I had a delightful letter from Muriel with an account of her coming of age on 16$^{th}$ April. They had a large house party, the Yeomanry had sports in the park, and there was a servants' ball. She had fifty-four presents, a lot of diamonds among them. She says if she wins any big stakes racing this season she will send the money to me to go back to England with.

*Thursday 17 May* Morton and Henley went away this morning. We were very sorry to part with them, but we hope that eventually Henley will live with us. Morton is going to Warren to arrange matters there, it will be a sad task for him.

Today is Harry's birthday; I think he is thirty-three, but I am not sure.

*Saturday 19 May* News has come of the relief of Mafeking, and Baden-Powell is the nation's hero. The war has been going on all these weary months, and I take as keen an interest as ever in it, but out here I have no one to talk it over with, at home they are mad with enthusiasm.

*Tuesday 22 May* There are the loveliest birds in the garden, crimson orioles, and a bright yellow bird, they sing beautifully in the early morning. I always get up at 6.00am now as it is the coolest, best part of the day.

*Tuesday 12 June* Absolutely nothing of interest occurs now, so it is no good writing my diary every day. I do the same things day after day.

*Thursday 14 June* I had a long letter from Harry that made me very unhappy. He writes in such utter depression, not going to the war has been such a disappointment that it seems to have quite changed him. He writes in a soured bitter way that hurts one, it seems such a cruel change in bright cheery Harry. He says he will not go back to England for years. I suppose when he does and I meet him again, we shall be middle-aged dull people who will have lost all interest in each other. Life *is* a muddle.

*Sunday 17 June* I dined with the Willis's; they go away tomorrow for the summer. Mrs Edsall gave me a lecture on the way I am shutting myself up, she says I will lose all my friends if I don't go about more, and I suppose she is right, but it is such a bore, and I don't care for the people here.

*Thursday 5 July* Last night was the most terrifying I can remember. At midnight a thunderstorm came up very suddenly, the lightning was incessant, and I was lying in bed trying not to notice it, when suddenly there came a deafening crash, and the house seemed full of red flames. I dashed out into the hall where I met all the others, we all thought the house was on fire, but the lightning had struck the oil tanks on the mainland about three-quarters of a mile away, and in an instant they were flaming. There are over 300 of them containing millions of gallons of oil. The fire raged all day, and tonight is worse than ever.

*Saturday 21 July* Nothing ever happens to write about. The weather has been intolerably hot, the thermometer has kept up in the nineties for days, it has been very damp, and there have been awful thunderstorms. I was in bed for two days with an attack of acute pain but am all well now.

I had a letter from Eva today to say she may be out here next month. I am glad in a way, but I have never quite trusted her since she tried to interfere between Harry and me.

*Sunday 5 August* I had a cablegram from Eva yesterday to say she was sailing on the Etruria, so she will be here next Saturday. It will be very nice seeing her again, and hearing all the latest news about everybody in London.

*Saturday 11 August* Eva came today. Mamma and Maude went to New York to meet the ship, and they all got down here at 10.30pm. Eva is looking much better than when I last saw her. She brought a dear dog with her, an Airedale, that Harry brought back from Malta last year. To be quite honest I am sorry Eva has come; I have never forgiven her for trying in a thousand ways to make mischief between Harry and me. I shall never trust her again, and having lost faith in her all other feeling for her has gone too. I have a horrid nature in that way. I never feel at my ease with her, and it makes me miserable.

*There are no entries in the diary between the last date above and the first one below. For the following two years Mabel's diary-keeping remains intermittent.*

*Sunday 23 September* I have got into a bad way of not writing in my diary, but there is so little to write about now; I am spending such a quiet life. Eva is still here, and will be here for some time. I don't like her any better, at times I hate her, and the odd thing is that I begin to think I hate Harry too because he is her brother and may be like her, but I don't think he really is.

*Sunday 28 October* My life is so quiet now that it is hardly worth while keeping a diary. All this summer and autumn I have done very little. I have practised and worked, but I have seen very few people. Now I am begin-ning to wake up again, and long for society. We are going to leave Staten

Island and go back to Newark. I am sorry for I love Staten Island, and I was unhappy in Newark. I suppose I shall see Court Parker again.

*Sunday 9 December* This is our last day in Staten Island. Tomorrow we go to Bloomfield, where I hope we may be as happy as we have been here. We all went to tea with Gertrude; she had invited some of my friends to meet us. Of course it was not like saying goodbye, as I shall often be down and see everyone again.

*Saturday 15 December, Bloomfield, near Newark* We have at last left dear old Staten Island, and we are here at Bloomfield, about two miles out of Newark. We have a very nice house, much larger than Hamilton Park, and in time we will be very comfortable. But it will never be as nice here as in Staten Island, the people here are horrid, it is depressing to go among them. On Wednesday we went to a tea at Mary Ogden's, and there we met all the old Newark people, looking just as dull and provincial as ever.

*Tuesday 25 December, Christmas Day* We spent rather a quiet Xmas. Henley enjoyed it, he hung his stockings in the big fireplace, and we filled them. He firmly believes in Santa Claus. Poor Morton kept up very well, but it must have been awfully sad for him, and he must have thought of last Xmas when he and Marie did the Xmas tree.

*Wednesday 26 December* Morton went away today and left Henley with us. I hope we will always have him; he is such a good child, and wonderfully clever. He speaks constantly of his mother and brother, and is always wishing they were with him, he won't go to bed quietly unless his mother's photograph is hanging over his bed.

*Tuesday 31 December* We all sat up to see the old year out and the new century begin, the century that they say is to be the most wonderful ever known. Its beginning sees us at war, and perhaps its end will see war gone for ever, a hideous memory only. At twelve o'clock the whistles all blew, bells rang, and guns were fired, and we all went out to listen, Mamma & Papa, Sybil, Maude, Fitzroy and me. Reggie and Morton were the absent ones.

### 1901
*Monday 21 January* The Queen is dead, and her death has caused a wide depression that is amazing. The sympathy shown in this country is most touching.

*Sunday 27 January* This morning I went to service at Trinity, Newark. The rector, Mr Osborne, preached one of the most powerful sermons I have ever heard; it was all about England, and our dear Queen. The pulpit was draped with the American and British flags, and at the close the organ played God Save the Queen.

Today I saw Court Parker again after all these years. He is as handsome as ever, but very grey. He sat in front of me in church. I don't think he saw me, and all the old feeling has come back with a rush, and I knew that he is the only one in the world for me. He has never married, so I have that consolation. I would have given anything to have spoken to him but I was too nervous, and hurried out of church and away. It was so strange to be in the same church with him again, like going back six years in my life.

*Friday 22 February* We have the news of Guilford's engagement to Violet Hargreave-Pawson. She is a very pretty sweet girl, a niece of Lord Harris's, but I am sorry Guilford is going to be married as Gac will have to leave Waldershare, and it will never be the same without her.

*Sunday 3 March* Morton came today. I think he is going to live with us altogether now, and it will be like old times. I did not go to church as Henley had a touch of croup and needed watching. I walked into Newark in the afternoon and spent an hour or two with Frances, and we had a long talk about Court Parker, and she said very nice kind things about him.

*Saturday 16 March* I went to see Mrs Wendell this morning. She told me That Gertrude Griffiths may come out to America this summer as Percy has to go to Russia on business. She is still very ill.

I went to a tea at Carnegie Hall, given by Mrs Bixby in honour of Sybil. There were a lot of people there from Staten Island as well as New York, and I rather enjoyed it.

*Saturday 23 March* I spent the whole day in New York. I went to see Miss Stephens; she has given me a bicycle, a most delightful present, I shall be able to scour the country now.

*Sunday 5 May* It is really dreadful the way I neglect my diary, and I have been doing a good deal worth recording lately. I went to morning service at Trinity, Newark this morning, and after service I saw dear old Mr Parker, and had a talk with him. He has aged very much, but his manner is as charming as ever.

*Monday 6 May* I heard today that Harry has gone to the war at last; he has gone with the Mounted Light Infantry, and is right at the front.

*Sunday 26 May* I have been spending ten days with Gertrude Willis at Staten Island. It was like one of the old visits, when I used to go so often and stay so long, but I don't think I enjoyed it much; I miss the girls and the dogs when I am away. It was delightful to come home yesterday, Papa was so cheery and the others so gay, and all four dogs jumped on me at once, and licked me and followed me all over the house. What darlings dogs are, I know they have souls.

*Sunday 2 June* This is Mabel's birthday, and this day twelve years ago I met Court Parker for the first time.

*Saturday 8 June* I went to lunch with the Wendells. Percy Griffiths was there, having arrived on the Majestic on Wednesday. Gertrude, who is in the Roosevelt Hospital, was operated upon on Thursday; it was terribly serious, but she is getting on splendidly and there is great relief.

It was such a pleasure seeing dear old Percy again, and he was so glad to see me. We had a charming little luncheon party, Percy and I, Mrs Tredick, and Mrs Wendell. After lunch Percy and I went for a little walk and talked over our old London friends; it was like old times being with him again.

*Sunday 9 June* Fitzroy and I went to service at Trinity. Court Parker was in church, and after service I spoke to him. He did not look in the least surprised to see me, but said it was a very long time since we had met, as it undoubtedly is: seven years at least. He has grown very grey and much older, but he has a kinder softer expression than he used to have. His face has a very sad expression; I was looking at him during the service, and was impressed by his melancholy look. His manner was disjointed and abrupt as it ever was, and I am as far from understanding it as ever; whether it is nervousness or conceit or boredness I never could make out. I am very glad to have spoken to him again.

*Thursday 11 July* I think I hate this dreadful country more every year. The vileness of the climate depresses me, the terrific heat that kills and prostrates so many, and cyclones that we have been having for a week or more, and then the cruel cold in winter, all these must have a bad effect on ones nervous system.

*Thursday 18 July* Today I went into New York to see Gertrude Griffiths at the Roosevelt Hospital. She has a very pretty room, and I was allowed to see her. She looks like death, so pale and pinched, but she is said to have made a very good recovery from a most dangerous operation.

*Friday 30 August* All this summer has been so quiet that there has been nothing to write here. I had a very sad letter from Muriel, leaving Waldershare has affected her very much. I heard from Aunt Flo who is still at Brockenhurst, and I had a most interesting letter from Harry written from a place called Christiana. The war is supposed to be nearly over, but there are guerrilla Boers to be caught and Harry is after them. He says it is very rough ugly work and he hates it. He says very few of his men get killed now, so I hope he is safe.

*Thursday 12 September* I heard from Gladys today, she tells me that Harry has been hurt in South Africa, his horse fell with him. I wrote to him today. I always feel a doubt in writing to him, for of course he is likely to be killed any day. As it takes a month for letters from here to reach Cape Town, and then perhaps a month longer for them to reach a flying column such as his, he might be dead for weeks before I knew anything about it. How I wish this horrible war were over, it is too cruel the way it drags on.

*Sunday 22 September* Our troops have had a serious reverse in South Africa. Harry's regiment has suffered worst, many officers being killed, and I have a feeling that he is among the number, but the papers here give no names, and I shall have to wait for news from home.

*Sunday 3 November* I wish I had not lost the habit of keeping my journal regularly, but lately I seem to have lost interest in it. Not very much has happened. I went into New York to say goodbye to Gertrude Griffiths, who sailed for England very much improved in health and looking very sweet. I promised to visit her next year at a new place in Hertfordshire they have taken, but I don't feel as if I would get to England next year.

## 1902

*Sunday 19 January* Since I last wrote in this book very little of any interest has happened. We had a very nice Xmas, all by ourselves, lots of presents and heaps of letters from England, also many invitations to go over there this summer, and I am *so* undecided about going. I had a very nice invitation from the bishop and Mrs Walsh to visit them at Canterbury, and one from Mary Eden, Lord Auckland's (5) daughter. I want to go to her, for that is a branch of the family I don't know much about.

I long to be back among all those dear people. I have so many friends over there and it seems sad not to see more of them. I really am beginning to feel more at home in America, but at times the feeling of loneliness is overpowering.

*Friday 24 January, New York, staying with Harry and Grace Slocum*
I went to New York today for the first time for weeks. I went to see Miss Stephens and had the usual home talk with her about Waldershare and Gac and the rest. I dined and slept at the Slocums. Grace is far from well, she is nervous and irritable. She goes to the doctor who asks her if there anything on her mind; she says 'no', but I don't believe her.

We went to the Bells after dinner, the Parkes were there, he is a Western millionaire. It was very pleasant. Gernie talked to me for a long time; when I talk to him I feel myself to be the most charming woman he knows. He is positively the most responsive man I ever met, he is an instrument from which one may draw any sounds one pleases, grave or gay, he understands and feels all ones moods instantly. No wonder Grace is making a fool of herself over him; Harry does not seem to see it. I watched them all night and wondered if a tragedy will ever come of it. It was very interesting. I felt as if I were a character in a novel, a minor character watching the plot unfold - although I was anything but minor tonight, for I wore a bright crimson silk dress with yards of train.

*Saturday 1 February, Staten Island, staying with Gordon and Gertrude Willis* I came down to Staten Island today to spend some time with the Willis's. It will be a very quiet visit as Gertrude is in mourning for her grandmother, Mrs Jerome. I am glad to be here, it is like another home. They are all very well, the children very sweet.

*Sunday 9 February* Gertrude and I spent a very quiet week. The weather has been too cold to go out much. I had a letter from Aunt Flora written from Arundel, where she was staying with the duke.

*Tuesday 11 February* I spent the day in New York, lunching with Nana Pfizer. She showed me lots of beautiful things. A dishonest butler stole most of her jewels last year, and she has a lot of new ones, diamond stars, a dragonfly, necklace etc and crowds of beautiful Paris dresses.

After lunch she took me to a reception at Miss Amy Baker's, where we met lots of professional singers, artists etc. Mlle Lucienne Breval was there, and stayed with us all the time. She has a lovely face with dark eyes that seem to glow. She was superbly dressed in white cloth and sable and her famous pearls. She is very amiable but rather stupid; she showed animation only once, when she saw a delicious cake on the tea table.

*Thursday 24 April, Bloomfield* This diary of mine is a farce nowadays, but I seem to have lost interest in it. I have been at home quietly for two months, very busy and very happy, but my quiet time is coming to an end for I have promised to spend the summer in New London with an aunt of Mrs Wright's, a Mrs Ashmore. I know her daughter Dora, they are connections of Emily Lyon's. I went down to Staten Island this morning to see Gertrude. Emily and Roquey Lyon are staying there. They have come back from England, and are going to live on the Island. It was delightful to see them again, both unaltered, as kind and cheery as ever.

In Newark this morning as I was passing through on my way to Staten Island, I met Court Parker and had a little talk with him, just a few utterly commonplace words, but enough to make me happy for the rest of the day. He was as nervous and abrupt as ever. I would give everything I have to know whether he cares for me. So many people who know him well have hinted as openly as they dared that he does, but it is impossible to believe, too much happiness for this life. And I don't believe I could endure very great happiness, it would turn my brain. Little things make me so wildly happy that I am afraid to think what a great thing like Court's devotion would do for me.

*Sunday 8 June* I have been leading a very quiet life lately, doing nothing but take walks and busy myself about the house and gardens, but now there is going to be a change, for on Wednesday I am going to New London to spend the summer with the Ashmores. It is good for me to go, for I get into a groove at home that I would be quite content to remain in for ever.

*Thursday 12 June, New London, staying with Mrs Ashmore* I went up to New London today to stay with the Ashmores. Miss Ashmore met me at the station with the bad news that her mother was so ill that my stay would have to be short. The poor old thing is paralysed and very ill. I did not see her at all, but dined very quietly with Miss Ashmore and walked down to the sea afterwards. It was too dark to see much.

*Friday 13 June* Mrs Ashmore is no better and I have decided to go home tomorrow. I went to see Mrs Rowland Keasby in the morning. She has a charming house near here; I had not seen her since we left Newark seven years ago. After lunch she took me for a drive and showed me New London. It is a very old-fashioned place, with beautiful old colonial houses that are probably full of good old-fashioned furniture and china. I had a nice long talk with her during our drive about the old days in Newark. She was always a friend of Court Parker's, and she told me very decidedly that he was a great admirer of mine, and had often spoken to her about me. It seems strange that I should not have known it at the time. What I want to be told now is that he admires me still. Even if I am never told that, it will be a comfort to know that he once liked me, and has never married anyone else.

*Saturday 14 June, Bloomfield* I left New London today, much to my regret; it is a place full of nice people and I know I would have enjoyed myself there. However I have had a glimpse of it, and I have seen Minna Keasby and heard that Court liked me once, so I don't consider the trip a failure. I was glad to get home again and be torn to pieces by the four dogs, who jumped all over me and whimpered with joy to see me again.

*Monday 7 July* Reggie and his wife and child have just left after paying us a little visit; it was the first time we had seen him for seven years. He has changed very much; he is very kind and gentle, but seems so weak and vacillating. Fortunately his wife seems to be quite the right sort of woman: she is most amiable and unselfish, not at all clever or a woman of the world; she is not pretty. The child Louise is eighteen months old, she walks and talks like a child much older, but she is spoilt. Reggie is simply infatuated with her, and he and Sophie talk of nothing but their wonderful child.

*Sunday 10 August* This seems to be such a long dull summer, and rather a disagreeable one, there has been so much rain. It seems a pity not to enjoy every day of summer for I do so hate the winter, but so far this summer has been rather a failure. Some days have been glorious, and the trees have been more beautiful than ever, but the flowers have failed on account of the cool weather. I shall atone for this secluded summer by a wild burst of gaiety. I heard from Gertrude Griffiths yesterday; she wants me to go over to England and spend the winter with her. It is a tempting invitation, but I think I shall spend this coming winter in America.

*Sunday 17 August* We got very sad news that dear Aunt Mary had fallen and hurt her head so badly that she may die at any time. Her death will leave a blank that can never be filled. I suppose as people grow older they learn to rely on themselves, but I have always had a comforting feeling that over in England there were four dear women who each loved me and petted me and took care of me. Peg is gone, and now Aunt Mary is going, and they were the kindest of the four. In time they will all go, and our parents too, and we in our turn will have to take care of and love the young coming on, and be (if we can) the same example that our beloved aunts were, but it makes me feel cold and lonely to think of it.

Aunt Mary was the sweetest and kindest woman I ever knew, and the best. She was like a saint, and at the same time so witty and cheerful that she was the best of company. She belonged to a past age, her manners were so grand that no one could have been rude to her. When she was a young girl it was said of her that she had the sweetest smile in Kent.

*Thursday 28 August* The news of Aunt Mary's death came today; she died on the 14th. She is buried at Ringmore church in Devonshire.

*Sunday 28 September* A great deal has happened lately. I went up to Stirling to stay with the Ogdens. Mary has a little country place of her own up there, it is very pretty. The visit depressed me. Mary is so young to have four big children: the eldest Lucy is terribly precocious, only fourteen, and she has long dresses, and young men who call on her as if she were grown up, and all that ages poor Mary. I am *most* thankful I did not marry at nineteen as many did. I long to marry now that I have had a long happy girlhood, but Mary's case is a warning against early marriages.

I was three days only at the Ogdens. When I came home Morton brought Henley to live with us, and is coming himself in a few weeks to make his home here. Henley is the dearest boy in the world, so good and wise, he spends all his time with me. He is very strong and sturdy.

*Monday 29 September, Staten Island, staying with Gordon and Gertrude Willis* I came down to Staten Island today to pay Gertrude a visit. May Busk heard I was coming and came to see me before I had been an hour in the house. Mrs Edsall is away, so there were just Gertrude and Gordon and myself at dinner.

*Tuesday 30 September,* Today Gertrude had to go to town, and I spent the morning with Emily Lyon. She has a house in Livingston, furnished with lovely old things they picked up in England.   We had a long talk about

England and all our friends there. Emily wants to go back; she hated it so at first, but like everyone else grew to love it.

*Friday 3 October* After lunch I went to see Emily (Gertrude went up to town, so I was free). I went to the cricket club with Emily, the club where we had so many good times in the old days. Now it is sadly changed, there were very few of the people we used to know. Emily and I found it rather dull and did not stay long.

Emily told me she was very fond of me, quite spontaneously, apropos of nothing in particular. I was delighted, for once she did not care much about me. People are all nice to me now, just as they were in England, when it seemed that everyone I met liked me and wanted to do something for me. Lately I have felt just the same spirit in the people here. I feel as if I had a power of attracting people, and at other times that power leaves me, and nobody cares for me and I am lonely and neglected.

Gertrude and Gordon have never been nicer to me than they are now, and today people I knew very slightly came up to me; one woman asked to be introduced, and Emily told me she was fond of me. Nina gave me some flowers, and altogether I feel popular and very happy.

*Sunday 5 October* It has rained almost incessantly for three weeks, and today it came down in such torrents it was impossible to go out until after tea, when it cleared up and I went for a walk alone along the beach. The air was very fresh and cool, and I walked along and listened to the waves, and watched the lighthouses along the Jersey shore and Sandy Hook light up as it grew dark. I do love the sea, and it never seems dreadful to me as it does to some people, to me it is always the road home to England, and the same old sea that I used to go to sleep by in dear old Dover long ago.

*Tuesday 7 October* I lunched and spent the afternoon with May Busk, and she told me all the news. She says that all the people here are quarrelling, she and Gertrude have had a fuss, and so have most of the others. It is all very childish, but Staten Island always was the most scandalous place that ever was, and now that people are beginning to find out that their dearest friends even do not spare them, there are sure to be rows.

*Thursday 9 October* We went out to the Country Club this afternoon, and made some calls. We dined with the Alexanders. The Lyons were there and Mrs Townsend, it was a very jolly party, Emily and Roquey very amusing. I sat on Mr Alexander's right, and he talked racing all the time; He is one of the governors of the Jockey Club. After dinner the men played billiards and we talked.

*Sunday 18 October, Bloomfield* I went for a long ride today. The country is looking beautiful, the trees just beginning to tint. I love autumn, and don't find it at all sad as some people do; it is a time of completion, everything done and well done, the harvests in and the year's work happily and beautifully ended.

*Friday 14 November, Bernardsville, staying with Mr and Mrs Pfizer* I went up to Bernardsville to stay over Sunday with the Pfizers. Mr Crowninshield and Jack Wilmerding are here, and others are coming tomorrow. I haven't been here for six years, and they have done a lot to the place. Nana has had a Japanese garden made, it adjoins a typical English garden, and covers about three acres. She has two Japanese gardeners always at work on it; it has a tea house, little winding paths, idols, lanterns, a cascade, and a pond with cranes and Japanese boats, three bridges and, of course, numberless rocks and all the Japanese plants, shrubs and cherry trees, also rickshaws to be pulled about in.

*Saturday 15 November* We were up very early this morning, and drove over to the kennels, about eight miles off from the house. There is a hunting box there with lots of accommodation, and a beautiful big room with a musicians gallery, and a hearth where they can burn logs twenty feet long. There was a big breakfast today for the farmers over whose country Mr Pfizer has hunted. The breakfast was laid in the big new stable, over two hundred farmers turned up with their wives, children, sweethearts etc. We had a party of our own of about forty, lots of people I knew among them. We also lunched in the stables, but not with the farmers, alone in the stud groom's quarters. We were very jolly, the jolliest being the Pfizers' parish priest, Father Ryan.

After lunch we pottered about and looked at the stables. He has about fifty horses here, hunters chiefly, he keeps his carriage horses and polo ponies at the home stables, and the racers in town. There was a short run before luncheon, but a small field. We did not follow but watched from the field. He has a very good pack and hunts them himself.

In the afternoon there were races, two for farmer's horses, and a very good steeplechase, all Mr Pfizer's horses, and his own friends up, Jacky Wilmerding, Carl Boyd etc. We watched it from the top of the brake, a very jolly party. We had a sweepstake; I drew Carnation, who simply romped home, Mr Nichols up. His wife was in the brake with us, pale with terror until it was all over. Jack Wilmerding came off three times, but came in second, a mass of mud and rage; he hates to be beaten.

After the steeplechase there was a gymkhana, by which time it was dark, so all the crowd went home, and our own party went back to the kennels, as they call the hunting box. We had tea and then danced, the noisiest, happiest crowd I have been with for ages. There were about forty all told, chiefly men, perhaps fifteen women.

We had a hunt dinner, most of the men in pink, lots of speeches, and so many funny things said that no one stopped laughing for a minute. I sat between two very nice men, Mr Shepherd and an Englishman, Mr Bowring. We were the only English, and they drank my health and said nice things, and he replied for me. After dinner the party thinned as many had to go back to New York. The cream of the lot remained, and we sang and had step-dancing and told stories until late. The men nearly all stayed at the kennels, and the rest of us drove back to Bernardsville, Mr Pfizer driving a four.

*Monday 17 November, Bloomfield* We had a very early start this morning, and all left together. The Pfizers are going to town for the week, also Mrs Duval and Miss Tobin. I did not fancy them much; they are Californian millionaires, and rather 'new'. I was sorry the party broke up. We were very jolly, and Bloomfield will be dull after the rackety times I have been having.

*Friday 28 November, New York, staying with Mr and Mrs Pfizer* Lula and I lunched alone at Sherry's, where I saw some few people I knew. It was the first time I had been in New York since the late summer, and it does not seem to have improved at all, it is all noise and dirt. We went for a short drive, and then to the Pfizers' house in 50" Street. We spent the afternoon very quietly.

There was a dinner of fourteen in honour of Mr Pfizer's sister, Mrs Duncan, who is sailing for Vienna next week. She is the most beautiful woman, and made quite a sensation. I did not enjoy the dinner at all. I sat between my partner and Mr Duncan, an Englishman, who talked politics with me as if I had been a man. I liked that part rather, as I love English politics, and I never hear them discussed nowadays.

Prince Hohenlowe took me in to dinner. He is the hero of a newspaper scandal, as the NY Herald has published a most dastardly report that he is out here to capture an American heiress, and has promised an agent a million dollars if he will secure one. He is a dreadfully dull ugly little man, short and fat. He could do nothing but eat, or rather gobble.

*Saturday 29 November, Bloomfield* Today quite made up for the dullness of yesterday. We all went out to the kennels by the midday train. At the Christopher Street station we met a lot of men who were going out to hunt, and people joined us at stations along the line. The meet was at Far Hills;

there was a very good field for this part of the world, twenty-seven in all. Lula and I did not see anything of the run, but drove straight to the kennels, where it was much warmer and cosier than following hounds on wheels. We sat in front of a big wood fire, and talked and had tea and rested until the men all came back. They were rather quiet today as there had been some rather bad falls, but no one was very badly hurt.

We dined at the kennels, twenty of us at two tables. I sat between two very nice men, Mr Tinker and Mr Shepard. We were a little bit depressed because Miss Tobin, who has ridden here for a month or more now, is going back to her home in California tomorrow. We have all grown to like her so much; she rides so splendidly that she has been a real ornament to the hunt.

*Friday 5 December* I had the dreadfully sad news that Mr Bishop died on 26ᵗʰ November, very suddenly. Sybil Bishop wrote just the base fact with no particulars. He was such a dear man, so kind and generous, and his death will make a terrible difference to them all. I am so glad Harry got home from the war in time to see his father again. He has been in London for over a month, but Darrell is in South Africa and Eva in Australia.

*Sunday 7 December* I went to service at Trinity in Newark in a blinding snowstorm. The church was nearly empty. I sat about two seats behind Court Parker, and watched him all through the service with the greatest interest. I have hardly ever seen him anywhere but in church; he is always associated with churches, hymns, sermons etc, it is a curious state of affairs. To put it very plainly I am in love with a man I have seen very little of, and whose character I can only judge of by stray glimpses. He may have all sorts of peculiarities and traits that would offend me dreadfully if I ever knew him better. Everyone says he is irritable and uncertain, but I feel I could overcome that.

He looks very grave and rather sad, and I have often seen him look villainously bad-tempered, but I know he is good, and very generous and sensitive. I believe he has the best character of any man I ever knew. He certainly attracts me more than anyone ever did. I believe most devoutly that we were made for each other, and if we don't come together in this life perhaps we will be able to explain things to each other in another existence. I think of him always, and sometime feel happy and hopeful, sometimes so despondent that everything seems utterly hopeless, and sometimes dully indifferent. It almost maddens me to think he once cared for me, and that I was such a blind fool as not to see it: to have had such a happiness as that within my reach and not to have taken it seems too cruel. This morning in church Court was the most restless, fidgety person in sight, changing his position every few minutes and staring about the church. He did not see me this morning and I saw too much of him, for I paid no attention to the service.

*Monday 22 December* I went to morning service at Trinity yesterday. Mr Wayne Parker was there, and after church he waited for me and his first words were, 'Why, how young you are'. The dear man, such a compliment as that makes me happy for a week. He had not seen me for quite seven years, and it is delightful that the first impression I gave him was one of youth. I am so terrified of growing old and losing my looks, it seems that my only chance of happiness lies in retaining them. If Court ever really cared for me it was all for my appearance, for what he knew of my character could never have attracted him, and if I am still as pretty as in those far off days, perhaps I may be able to win him back.

*Thursday 25 December, Christmas Day* Henley came into my room before seven this morning to find out what Santa Claus had brought him, and I put on my dressing gown, and went down to the dining-room with him. He had hung his stockings by the fireplace, and we arranged quantities of toys and presents that were too big to go in the stockings. He believes firmly in Santa Claus. All our presents were at our places on the breakfast table; we had great fun at breakfast-time untying them all. At night we had the usual family dinner party, and Henley was allowed to sit up and dine.

*Monday 29 December* I had a very nice letter from Guilford's wife Violet. She told me the latest news of Gac and Muriel, and said her baby was growing into such a nice child. He is six months old; fancy Guilford with a son of six months.

We went skating tonight on our pond; the ice was rough but as it was the first time I had ever skated, it did not matter much to me. I got on very well, and did not fall once.

### 1903
*Friday 2 January* I took Henley to Newark to play with Sherrard Depue's boys, he has three now. He has built a beautiful new house, quite a mansion, and they have just moved into it. Sherrard is rapidly growing rich, and becoming one of the first lawyers in New Jersey. I went to see Frances; she is still ill in bed and depressed and unhappy about herself.

*Monday 5 January* I had a letter from Harry written from London. He writes very sadly, he must feel his father's death deeply. He says the change at home is so great, his father was the centre and head of everything, and now a great deal will devolve on Harry, and he always hated responsibility. He is going to join his regiment at the Curragh..

*Friday 16 January, New York, staying with Harry and Grace Slocum* I went to New York today to spend a couple of days with Grace Slocum. She is in a new house in Thirty-eighth Street, a much larger one than their old house; it is very prettily arranged. Grace is looking ill, and her nerves seem to have gone to pieces.

Parke Bell dined with us, and was as always very attentive and charming. We played bridge after dinner, which bored me a little. I don't care for cards, and people nowadays care for nothing but bridge. Gernie Bell has gone to travel in Spain for six weeks, and I think Grace misses him very much. She came up to my room and talked while I brushed my hair; she is changed since I last saw her a year ago. I am afraid much of her worry is caused by her infatuation for Gernie Bell. It must be a ghastly thing to care for one man while one is married to another.

*Sunday 18 January* I spent the morning sitting over the library fire talking very intimately with Grace. She and Gertrude are on very bad terms. Poor Gertrude is quarrelling with, and offending, all her friends; everyone is down on her. If I had not had the extremist patience with her I would have quarrelled with her long ago, but would stand a great deal before I would quarrel with an old friend.

*Saturday 24 January, Bloomfield* I had a letter from Gac. She has been ill for six weeks, and she tells me that Aunt Charlie has softening of the brain. Her letter was most depressing. Of course I know that it is inevitable that all ones dear old relations and friends must die, but it leaves one with a dreadful lonely *old* feeling.

*Tuesday 3 February* Maude and I went to the play to see Mrs Langtry who is touring the United States with her own company. It was rather a sad performance: she never could act, and depended entirely on her beauty to draw; that has faded and she got a very cold reception. She is still pretty and very lady-like and graceful. She was gorgeously dressed. Her eyes are lovely, very blue and large, and her mouth expressive and well-shaped.

*Sunday 8 February* This was a long dull day spent in the house. The weather was so bad we could not go out, and I get so tired of everything, and thought a great deal too much about myself and my own affairs, such stale dull topics. I am not contented and yet I am afraid (or ought to be afraid) to wish for a change: granted prayers are sometimes such awful things. Many things that I have wished for very earnestly have been given to me, and have made me miserable. Years ago I remember longing to leave England, and go and see foreign countries. *That* prayer was granted, and I have hardly ever ceased to long to go back.

When Henley was a baby I wished so much that he could live with us, and we could bring him up, and now he is a poor little motherless waif, of whom I have the whole charge. The responsibility weighs me down, and frets and worries me, and with my best efforts I can never be half to him what his mother would have been had she lived. Other wishes have been granted, less important ones, and they have all been disappointing.

Sometimes I wonder if the most intense longing I have ever had, my wish to marry Court Parker, were to be vouchsafed me I would be satisfied. I expect so much from him, more than any man could ever give me, that I am sure to be disappointed. I would expect him to have inexhaustible sympathy and insight into my character, unfailing consideration, to be interested in me and all my moods beyond anyone else on earth, to be willing to listen to me whenever I wanted to talk about myself, and to receive the accumulated confidences and ideas and fancies of a woman who has never had an intimate friend to act as safety valve or refuse heap of worn out ideas. Poor Court; all that I expect from him. I wonder if I shall ever get it. I have my doubts.

*Wednesday 11 February, Livingston, Staten Island, staying with Gordon and Gertrude Willis* I went down to Staten Island to pay Gertrude a long visit. She is living in a new house; it is a very pretty house and near all the people we both know, so it will be much more amusing than it was at her old house at Arrochar.

*Sunday 15 February* We went to church this morning at St Mary's. It is horribly wicked and irreverent, but I never enter a church or go through the service with any other thought than Court Parker in my heart. For so many years I hardly ever saw him but in church that he is indissolubly bound up in my mind with the service; everything in it suggests him

After lunch I went for a walk with Nina Fowler; it was snowing hard so we did not go far. We went to tea with Emily Lyon. She had a lot of people, among them an Englishman, a Mr Fletcher Campbell, who has been in America for two weeks, and sails again tomorrow. He was exceedingly interesting, so much so that I did not say a word to anyone else, but sat apart on a sofa and listened to him. He was dreadfully shy at first, and then suddenly thawed, and after he had talked hard for an hour there was very little I did not know about him or that we had not discussed, including religion, a subject he spoke of with a reverence and appreciation that charmed me.

*Monday 16 February* I spent the afternoon with Emily, the first chance I have had of talking to her alone since she got back from England. She wants to go back; I think she finds life so much more difficult than in England, and she sees the vulgarity of society here and its ostentation.

We dined with Nellie Walker. The Busks were there and a man named Twining, a Canadian, who took me into dinner, and spent the whole evening after dinner talking to me. He heard me talk of a dance I think of going to, and asked if he could send me violets to wear at it. I thought that rather a marked attention for so short an acquaintance and declined as civilly as I could, but it was very amusing.

*Sunday 22 February, Bloomfield* It is horrid of me, but I simply hate being with the Willis's. For years I have been growing less fond of them, and have fought against it because I don't like the idea of changing towards old friends. Gordon I detest, he has grown into such a snob, and he is spoiling Gertrude. I always promise myself that each visit I make shall be the last, but when it comes to the point I cannot break with Gertrude. I have got into the habit of friendship with her, and although she is not the same, the memory of her past charm makes me sorry to give her up. All her friends are down on her, all say the same, that she is so difficult to get on with. I never quarrel with her, but I am never interested in her. Today I felt I must leave, so I made up some excuse and came home.

*Sunday 8 March* I went to service at Trinity this morning and afterwards I met Court Parker, and had a little talk with him. I felt my knees give way when I saw him, and I wanted to pass him by, but I made a tremendous effort to pull myself together, and I really think I was rather nice to him. He does look *so* old and grey, he is all grey together, hair, eyes, moustache, even his face looked grey today. He used to have a very bright smile that lightened up his face wonderfully, but even that seems to have faded a little. But I don't care how old or grey or faded he is, he is the only man I shall ever care for, and the few words I had with him today will make me happy for a week, especially as he really seemed as if he were a little glad to see me.

*Sunday 15 March* The last four days have been like an English summer, so warm and soft. The birds are beginning to sing and the grass looks green, it is heavenly. Each spring seems better than the last and absolutely novel, and I feel like spring myself, as if I were renewing my youth. I am out all day, roaming all over the country on my bicycle, perfectly happy.

*Tuesday 17 March* I lunched with the Wrights. I like going there, they always say nice things and make me feel pleased with myself. I went for a walk with Julia; she sang Court Parker's praise all the time, said how unselfish and generous he was, and how kind and attentive to his father, and then she asked me why I did not marry him, as if it were my fault that I don't. All these people seem to blame me, and it is very hard.

*Thursday 9 April* I had such a sad letter from Sybil Bishop telling me that they are utterly ruined, they have not even a home, all the girls are working for themselves, and poor Harry will be obliged to sell Mill Hill, the place he inherited from his father. It has been in his family for a long time and he loves every acre in it, and used to look forward to the time when he would leave the army and go and live there. It makes me miserable to think of my dear kind friends in such trouble.

*Sunday 26 April* I got three letters yesterday that unsettled me very much. One was from Maude Macgregor about her wedding, which is to occur in the autumn, and then she goes to India, perhaps for years. If I don't see her this summer it is hard to say when we will meet again. Another letter was from Muriel. She and Gac are going to spend the summer at Waldershare, and Muriel says that if I come over and stay with them it will be like old times again. The third letter was from Mrs Walsh, the wife of Papa's old friend at Oxford, the Bishop of Dover, and she asks me to visit her at Canterbury where I would meet the archbishop, and some of the best known people in England. These are three most tempting invitations to go back and be among my own people again, and I am distracted to know what to do.

I am so lonely here that I am morbid. I have never felt at home among the people here, and I am longing to be among friends again. If one does go out anywhere people never talk about anything that interests me much, at home in England I am thrown among people who are keen about politics and affairs outside their own circle; here everything is so narrow. All that keeps me in America is home, Papa and Henley, and perhaps the dear dogs, and I can't make up my mind if it is my duty to remain at home, or whether I owe it to myself to take a holiday and a rest by running over to England for a few months. I have an idea that I am indispensable at home, although Sybil and Maude assure me I am hardly missed.

I used to think I could be quite happy here in Bloomfield with my work and the garden, and Henley and the dogs and Papa, but it is not enough. I want life and people and events, clever men to talk to, such as I used to meet by the score in England. I want a place in the world, something to do. I don't want to be conspicuous or talked about, but I want the same chances that other women of our family have had of being in the lead; my ambitions are boundless, and I *know* I have the ability if only I had a chance - but here I am buried. Perhaps all this discontent is just restlessness, a sort of spring fever. I hope it is not wicked but I do long for action, for some chance of doing more than I can possibly do here in this lonely country.

*Thursday 7 May* I lunched with Dora Parker today, and was charmed with her. To think we have had a bowing acquaintance for about fourteen years, and today we had our first long talk. She talked a great deal about the Parkers, nothing but praise for Court, the praise that always hurts me, for it shows more and more clearly how much I have missed in him. I think it would be a relief to hear someone run him down. Dora Parker seems very happy, she says Chauncey is the best of husbands, but I think she must be an unusually good wife.

*Sunday 10 May* I wrote to Muriel and Gertrude Griffiths today and told them I would go over to England this summer. I have made up my mind to go, as far as I can make up my mind to do anything, but I never know. I may make a dozen different plans between now and July, which is the time I have promised to go. I am so unsettled, and perhaps the change will do me good, and give me something to think of. It is maddening to be so near Court Parker, to everlastingly have his name dinned into my ears, to meet him constantly, and yet never get any nearer. Parallel lines that never meet.

*Thursday 21 May, New York, staying with Harry and Grace Slocum* I went to New York today to spend the night with Grace Slocum. Parke Bell dined with us. I am always sorry to acknowledge that anyone is changed, but really he does not seem to be as nice as he was, perhaps I am not as nice to him, for he does not interest me as he used to. We played bridge after dinner, he was my partner and I played so badly that we lost a great deal. He was very kind about it, and did not curse me as I deserved. I loathe playing cards for money, bridge above all, it makes me so nervous.

I slept in Grace's room, and the night was so hot we could not sleep much. I never do sleep well in New York, the air is so flat and heavy, and the noise so great. I am spoiling myself by the life in Bloomfield, the quiet is so intense and the air so pure, that I pine for it when away. I spend all my days in the garden where all is serene and happy, and no unpleasant sights or sounds ever come, the result is I am growing hypersensitive, and when I go to Newark or New York am miserable at the things I see, overdriven tired-out horses, starving homeless dogs, and horrid cruel-looking bad people. They all seem to me to be to be a thousand times worse than they really are and the world, or at least the town part of the world, seems a dreadful place. It is a mistake to shield oneself so carefully from all that is unpleasant in life. I shrink from crowds and from people as a rule, and am only quite happy when I am sitting under the trees in the garden, far from towns and noise and people and horrors of all kinds.

*Tuesday 16 June* I have at last made up my mind to go to England, and today I went to the White Star SS office in New York, and after a lot of trouble got a passage on the Armenian sailing on the 30ᵗ. I feel I don't want to go at all, but it will do me good, and I have never been less needed at home than I am now.

*Sunday 28 June* I have been busy getting ready to go to England, and getting ready so unwillingly. I don't want to go at all; I feel as if dreadful things would happen in my absence. I hate leaving Papa and the dogs and the quiet home life that suits me exactly. However it is good for me to go away, I am getting to be a recluse, fitting into so comfortable a groove that I do not care to get out of it. I must rouse myself, and go out into the world, and see and do all I can while I have the chance to.

*Tuesday 30 June, on board the SS Armenian* Today I sailed for England on the White Star SS Armenian. She sailed very early at 10.00am, so we had to leave home at an unearthly hour; Papa, Mamma and Maude came to see me off. I hated saying goodbye to home, the cook was in tears, and all the dear dogs sat around in dejected attitudes. I am sure they knew I was going away.

I have a delightful stateroom on the upper deck opening on to the deck. It is very large and nicely furnished, and as fresh and airy as the deck itself. The passengers do not attract me very much, and I don't think I shall have much to do with them. The Captain and officers are very smart looking. The White Star regulations do not allow their officers to mix with passengers, or even speak to them. So far it has been very calm, but there are no less than seven parsons on board, so we shall of course have a bad passage.

*Wednesday 1 July* During the last four days I have had the worst headache of my life, it has been incessant, I have never left my deck chair except to go to bed. I tied a thick veil over my head, and pretended to be asleep if anyone approached me; I felt much too seedy to talk to anyone; I suppose it must be a form of seasickness. I have been dreadfully bored, which is a pity for one can have such a good time on board ship.

I was alone on deck, and the stewardess came to say a 'gentleman' wanted to call, and the Chief Officer, in spite of regulations, presented himself, such a nice man named Dyke. He said he saw me come aboard looking so brisk, and deplored the change the last few days had made. He thought I looked lonely, so asked the stewardess if he might talk to me. I don't quite like it, because an officer caught talking to a passenger is liable to dismissal; however he seems willing to take the risk. I had a talk with the Captain too; he is nice but not as polished as the Chief Officer.

*Monday 6 July* Today I was free from headache and managed to get about a little, and gave civil answers to the few passengers who ventured to address me. I spent a long time in the evening in the Captain's room (against regulations). He showed me some photographs, and showed me a sketch of a dog he had made, and of course when we got on the subject of dogs there was no end to our talk. It certainly makes the voyage more amusing when one has the officers to look after one, because they don't talk to any of the other passengers.

*Tuesday 7 July* One day is very like another on board ship. I get up rather late and have breakfast on deck. I settle down in a corner by the bridge and stay there all day. The Captain comes to see me constantly, and tells me interesting stories of his adventures. The few passengers I have met are very nice, and everyone has been more than kind. No one has been ill but myself, and that has given me a sort of notoriety. I believe it is one reason why the Captain spends so much time with me, and allows the officers to talk to me; they come and tell me all about the sailing of the ship, and yarns of all kinds. I am very happy, and enjoying myself now.

*Wednesday 8 July* The chief event of today was fog, slowing us down at intervals all through the day. I talked a great deal to Mr Dyke, the First Officer; he is so nice, very boyish and full of fun. I love being on board ship, and am sorry the voyage is nearly over.

*Friday 10 July* Last night was really a fearful night; the Captain said it was the worst he had ever experienced in the way of fog. He never left the bridge all night, and hardly at all during the day, for the fog did not lift until late in the afternoon, when we suddenly sailed out of it into bright sunshine. We took the pilot on board at 10.00pm, we land in Liverpool early tomorrow.

The Captain came and sat with me on deck for a long time in the evening, and I saw a lot of Mr Dyke. I am the only passenger that the officers have taken any notice of; I think it is because I have been so ill that they have broken the regulations.

*Saturday 11 July, London, staying with the Macgregors* We were up very early and the tender took us away from the ship before 9.00am. There were a great many goodbyes, and I really felt quite sad at leaving the Armenian. The stewardess went with me, and saw me through the custom house. It was a mere formality: they did not open any of my boxes. I spent the whole day in Liverpool with the stewardess. I wanted to see the town and could not wander about alone, so I asked her to go with me. She was exceedingly kind and took me everywhere; Liverpool is really a very handsome place.

We had a nice lunch, and in the afternoon went to the station where I took the train for London, the faithful stewardess staying with me to the last. We got to London very soon, and I got to the Macgregors in time for dinner. I am going to stay with them for a week, and am then going to Waldershare.

*Monday 13 July* I think I must be a little tired from all the excitement of the voyage and seeing London again, because today I feel a little bit flat.

I was rather upset by a letter and telegram I had from Mr Dyke, the First Officer of the Armenian. He has fallen in love with me, and sent a most imploring letter, but of course I cannot accept him, and I am so sorry about it. He is very nice and I shall try to keep him as a friend.

I went out with Maud and did some shopping, her trousseau takes up all her time now. The shops struck me as being extraordinarily cheap, and the people in them so polite and gentle that it was a pleasure to be served by them.

*Wednesday 15 July* This morning I went to see Lady Shannon. She was exactly the same, sitting in the same chair as when I last saw her. She was full of talk and gossip about everyone, everybody goes to see her from the King down. She is as handsome as ever, and as utterly reckless in her talk.

*Friday 17 July* I had a letter from Mr Dyke written on the Runic two hours before she sailed. He sailed for Australia yesterday, and will be back in December when he is coming to London to see me. Later in the morning I had a telegram that he sent off by the pilot when he left the ship. I hope Mr Dyke will get over his fancy for me during this long voyage, there will be nothing to remind him of me on the Runic. I am not to blame for his infatuation, as I have snubbed him in a way that has really hurt myself, for I hate to be unkind, and he was so nice that I can't bear to be unkind to him. I think it quite possible that he has the best and kindest character of any man who had ever cared for me, and perhaps I am a fool not to take him. Everyone on the ship spoke so well of him, from the Captain to the stewardess, and the passengers were all loud in their praises of him.

*Saturday 18 July, Waldershare Park, staying with Gac Guilford and Muriel North* I met Muriel North at Victoria, and went down to Waldershare with her. She really has altered, she looks older and is very fashionable and wears an eyeglass.

I felt rather dreamy and unreal all the way down. I always live in memories when I come to Waldershare. The park looks so lovely, the trees seemed bigger than ever, and the house grander and older. We got down very late, just in time for dinner. I had a long talk with Gac afterwards about family affairs; they don't seem to be very bright. Aunt Charlie is terribly altered, her mind failing fast, and Uncle Arthur may die any day. I begin to feel rather unhappy and depressed. I don't believe I shall enjoy this visit to England, so far I have not been very happy.

*Sunday 19 July* After tea Guilford and Violet came to see us; they live in a house in the park nearby. Guilford was so nice and gave me a very nice welcome, and Violet is charming. She has very gentle manners and she is very pretty. We all went up to the gardens together, those lovely gardens that seem more beautiful than ever. We walked back home with Violet and saw her baby. He is thirteen months, a huge boy, with the biggest hands I ever saw.

*Tuesday 21 July* We had a very busy morning. Muriel, Violet and I picked a quantity of flowers early in the morning to decorate the tables for an enormous luncheon that Guilford was giving to the tenants on the occasion of the annual cricket match. A big tent was put up on the cricket field in the park, and then the luncheon was laid. We filled large brass jardinieres with sweet peas and tall glass vases with crimson roses, and arranged them all down the tables. We worked very hard and made the tent into a fine banqueting hall.

We went to the field after lunch and watched the cricket match; it was rather mild cricket. We had the band of the Buffs from Dover and they played beautifully. They came in a big drag drawn by four horses and blew a bugle as they drove through the park. There were a great many people, all the tenants, their wives and children, and a great many of Gac's own friends. Lord Basing rode over from Shornecliff on a motor bicycle with a lady in a trailer.

Lady Harriet Ward came to stay for a few days; she is Guilford's and Muriel's great aunt. She was born and brought up here a great many years ago; she is very handsome and seems to be nice.

*Lady Harriet was a daughter of the 6ᵗʰ earl of Guilford; she was born at Waldershare in 1823.*

*Wednesday 22 July* Lady Harriet Ward is really charming, she is like a grande dame out of a book, so dignified and stately, but very sweet. She is the image of a Romney portrait in the hall. People in England seem to dress more than ever: Gac and Muriel come down to dinner even when we are alone in the most gorgeous gowns and covered with jewels, but everyone looks like a walking jeweller's shop. Lady Harriet is always covered with the loveliest things, even in the morning for breakfast. It is like the old Georgian days when people put their diamonds on when they got up and lived in them.

*Saturday 25 July* This was a long and most delightful day. I left Waldershare early and went to Canterbury and spent the whole morning wandering about the town, and revelling in the old churches and houses; it is an entrancing place. I lunched with Mrs Walsh and the bishop; they gave me such a kind welcome. My framed photograph is hanging in their drawing-room, and she told me it had been so much admired, such a nice compliment. Their house seemed more beautiful than ever, fancy what happiness to live in a beautiful old house that dates from the 14ᵗʰ century. The bishop is charming but he secretly awes me; I feel myself so brave when I talk to him, as if he were an ordinary man or a mere curate.

We went to afternoon service in the cathedral, it was profoundly impressive. We sat in the choir stalls, next to the choir, and in front of us were the boys from King's School, 240 of them, such manly, clean-looking English boys, who went through the service with the most reverent attention. The music was absolutely perfect. I went back to tea at the bishop's, we had it in the garden, the cathedral in front of us, ruins and flowers all round us, it was more beautiful than words can say.

*Sunday 26 July* It rained too hard to go to church; I wrote letters all the morning instead. I went to tea with Violet and Guilford. I like her so much, she is very sweet and so pretty; he adores her, and is so happy.

*Wednesday 29 July* This morning I was awakened at a very early hour by hearing guns fired in the park, and horses galloping and men shouting. I rushed to the window and saw the deer rushing past in a panic, and then guessed what was happening and did not look any longer. They were shooting the fawns, they increase so rapidly that Guilford is obliged to thin them out every year, so the tenants come and have a grand annual shoot. The deer are driven by men on horseback and then shot as they pass, forty fawns and a buck were killed this morning. I did not go in the park or even look out of the windows for fear of seeing them.

*Wednesday 30 July* I drove into Dover with Guilford and Violet this morning. Dover is very much changed, it has become a big bustling place with crowded streets instead of the dear old sleepy town I remember. I did a lot of shopping with Vi, and then walked to the Parade. Dover is supposed to be the port of the future, one of the big ocean liners called there last week, and they are to call regularly for the future.

*Friday 31 July* We went to a garden party at the Monins. There were a great many people there, Mrs Bampton from Dover among them; I knew her when I was a child. There was no one else I knew very well, but a lot of people I have met at various times. A garden party is rather a mild entertainment: we stood about on the lawns and talked; there was a band, and lots of tea and cake etc, a great many old ladies, a few girls and a *very* few men. We did not stay long but got back to cosy comfy Waldershare. We were so cold with standing about that we had whisky before we went up to dress for dinner.

*Saturday 1 August, Ticehurst, Sussex, staying with Uncle Arthur Eden*    I left Waldershare today. Vidie and Guilford came to say goodbye. I was so sorry to leave the dear old place; it feels so homelike there, and I love them all so much, but we shall meet again before long I hope.

I came to Ticehurst by way of Dover, where I had two hours walking about the old place. It is so changed that I have rather lost my old sentiment for it, but the sea is still the same, and the smell of the seaweed and fishing nets, and the sound of the waves breaking on the gravel. At 2.30pm I took the train for Wadhurst and arrived there very late and so tired and then had the seven mile drive to Uncle Arthur's. I got there just in time for dinner, and received the most loving greeting from them all.

*Sunday 2 August* I was still very tired all day. We went to morning and afternoon service. Chick and I went to tea with some people named Potts; they are nice, much nicer than their name.

*Wednesday 5 August* The life here is a typical country parsonage. Chick and Monk seem to be the centre of the village life, they are referred to for everything. They understand all about animals and plants; today a girl came with some plant she had found by the roadside for Chick to identify. She looked it up in a big book, and told the girl what it was, and she went off to make it into a lotion to bathe a sick child's arm. Everyone comes here, gentle and simple, and all get the kindest welcome; there is no difference shown, the vicarage doors stand open for all.

*Friday 7 August* This morning Mr Potts took Chick and me in his motor to Maidstone and back before lunch, a distance of fifty-six miles. The road all the way was beautiful, through old villages with lovely old churches that I longed to examine. At Maidstone we went all over the old church there, All Saints, it is very handsome and full of old monuments.

In the afternoon we went to a garden party, where we walked about on a lawn, and eat and drank a great deal. The only young men were curates, which seems typical of an English garden party in the country. I talked to Uncle Arthur's curate Mr Knox nearly all the time.

*Saturday 8 August* This was a very quiet day. I love the days here: we get up early, a cup of tea is brought to me at 7.00am with my letters, if there are any. I rest till 7.30 when my bath is brought in; there are no bathrooms in these old English houses. At 8.30 the bell rings, and we all meet in the dining-room, all the servants come in, and Uncle Arthur reads prayers. I kneel at a chair in front of the window, and look out on the lovely garden all the time. Then we pass the rest of the time in the ordinary country house way, riding, driving etc. A great many people come to call, and there is always a lot to do. I went for a bicycle ride this evening after tea, the roads round here are excellent.

*Sunday 9 August* Some people came to tea, a very nice man in the 4th Hussars named Bloomfield White among them. We walked round the garden and talked about all sorts of things, dogs and horses and sport. He plays polo, and said his ponies taught him the game, and he quoted my favourite poem, the Rubaiyat. He stopped to pick a flower, and that suggested the quotation.

How delightful these people are; everyone that I meet is clever and agreeable. English people seem so simple and kindly, they talk so easily on any topic. Every time I come back to England I am more impressed with the charm of the people. We go a great deal into the cottages to see the poor people, and they all have the same quiet exquisite manners, and classes and masses respect and love each other. People are polite to their servants, who are friendly and kind without the least familiarity. I have been in England over a month and have not once heard a rough word or unkind remark.

*Monday 10 August* Monk and I went to Tunbridge Wells today. We did a lot of shopping, and wandered over a good part of the town. It is very pretty and old-fashioned, and has a great air of prosperity. We went to tea with a Miss Hodgkinson, a cousin of Captain Steel's, he gave me a letter of introduction to her; she lives in a big house in Broadwater Down. She was very agreeable, and of course talked a great deal about her cousin. She was very cordial to me, as everyone is. I shall have to try and keep very cool over all the kindness and attention I am getting, and remember it is only because I am a visitor. I shall be very likely to lose my head, and think it is my own delightful self that makes people so good to me.

Mr Dykes' devotion to me rather unsettled me, and made me imagine myself irresistible, and since then everyone has been so overwhelmingly kind that I am getting utterly spoilt. However, when I go back to America I will have it all knocked out of me again.

*Friday 21 August, Bursledon, near Southampton, staying with Edith Perkins* (25) After lunch I went to Waterloo and took the train to Southampton, such a long journey for I missed the connecting train at St Denys, and had to wait an hour and a half for the next train. It was an express that did not stop at Bursledon, my station, but the station master telegraphed to have it stopped for me, which was very civil of him. I got to Edith's at nine o'clock thoroughly tired out, and went to bed after a dinner of a glass of port and a biscuit. I was too tired to eat anything more.

*Saturday 22 August* Things have rather changed since I was last here. Edith has married again, a man named Colonel Arthur Perkins. He is very good-looking, and as he was a Winchester boy he has very good manners. He is kind to Edith and makes her very happy, but it makes the place seem very different with a strange man about.

*Monday 24 August* After lunch I went with Edith to pay calls; the people who live round here seem to be all widows of admirals and generals. They live in comfortable houses with lovely gardens, they have dogs, and they are all rather fat, and look as if they eat and drank a great deal and took no exercise.

*A further two volumes of Mabel's diaries are planned. The next volume will include Mabel's life in the First World War. In particular it covers her time working in the censorship department of the War Office, which she found both satisfying and enjoyable.*

*The Diary of a Lifetime*

**Index of persons**
The numbers in bold refer to the numbers on the family trees (see pp 4 -7);
Mabel's parents are omitted;
Persons who are referred to only once or infrequently, and have no particular social or historical interest, are omitted;
Except as indicated, husbands and wives are entered under the same heading.

ISBN 142514477-2

9 781425 144777